First World War
and Army of Occupation
War Diary
France, Belgium and Germany

2 DIVISION
Headquarters, Branches and Services
General Staff
1 July 1918 - 31 July 1918

WO95/1300

The Naval & Military Press Ltd
www.nmarchive.com
Published in association with The National Archives

Published by

The Naval & Military Press Ltd

Unit 10 Ridgewood Industrial Park,
Uckfield, East Sussex,
TN22 5QE England
Tel: +44 (0) 1825 749494

www.naval-military-press.com

www.nmarchive.com

This diary has been reprinted in facsimile from the original. Any imperfections are inevitably reproduced and the quality may fall short of modern type and cartographic standards.

© Crown Copyright
Images reproduced by permission of The National Archives, London, England, 2015.

Contents

Document type	Place/Title	Date From	Date To
Heading	2nd Division General Staff July 1918 Aug		
Miscellaneous	War Diary July 1918 Original Diary		
War Diary	LA Bazeque V.27.7.7	01/07/1918	05/07/1918
War Diary	La Bazeque	06/07/1918	23/07/1918
War Diary	La Bazeque V.27.c.7.7.	24/07/1918	28/07/1918
War Diary	La Bazeque	29/07/1918	31/07/1918
Miscellaneous	War Diary July 1918 Intelligence Summaries		
Miscellaneous	2nd Division Tactical Summary No. 24 For 24 hours ending 8 Am 1/7/16	01/07/1918	01/07/1918
Miscellaneous	2nd Division Tactical Summary No. 25 For 24 hours ending 8 am 2/7/18	02/07/1918	02/07/1918
Miscellaneous	2nd Division Tactical Summary No. 26 For 24 hours ending 8 am 3/7/18	03/07/1918	03/07/1918
Miscellaneous	2nd Division Tactical Summary No. 27 For 24 hours ending 8 am 4/7/18	04/07/1918	04/07/1918
Miscellaneous	2nd Division Tactical Summary No. 28 For 24 hours ending 8 am 5/7/18	05/07/1918	05/07/1918
Miscellaneous	2nd Division Tactical Summary No. 39 For 24 hours ending 8 am 6/7/18	06/07/1918	06/07/1918
Miscellaneous	2nd Division Tactical Summary No. 40 For 24 hours ending 8 am 7/7/18	07/07/1918	07/07/1918
Miscellaneous	2nd Division Tactical Summary No. 41 For 24 hours ending 8 am 8/7/18	08/07/1918	08/07/1918
Miscellaneous	2nd Division Tactical Summary No. 42 For 24 hours ending 8 am 9/7/18	09/07/1918	09/07/1918
Miscellaneous	2nd Division Tactical Summary No. 43 For 24 hours ending 9 am 10/7/18	10/07/1918	10/07/1918
Miscellaneous	2nd Division Tactical Summary No. 44 For 24 hours ending 8 am 11/7/18	11/07/1918	11/07/1918
Miscellaneous	2nd Division Tactical Summary No. 45 For 24 hours ending 8 am 12/7/18	12/07/1918	12/07/1918
Miscellaneous	2nd Division Tactical Summary No. 46 For 24 hours ending 8 am 13/7/18	13/07/1918	13/07/1918
Miscellaneous	2nd Division Tactical Summary No. 47 For 24 hours ending 8 am 14/7/18	14/07/1918	14/07/1918
Miscellaneous	2nd Division Tactical Summary No. 48 For 24 hours ending 8 am 15/7/18	15/07/1918	15/07/1918
Miscellaneous	2nd Division Tactical Summary No. 49 For 24 hours ending 8 am 16/7/18	16/07/1918	16/07/1918
Miscellaneous	2nd Division Tactical Summary No. 50 For 24 hours ending 8 am 17/7/18	17/07/1918	17/07/1918
Miscellaneous	2nd Division Tactical Summary No. 51 For 24 hours ending 8 am 18/7/18	18/07/1918	18/07/1918
Miscellaneous	2nd Division Tactical Summary No. 52 For 24 hours ending 8 am 19/7/18	19/07/1918	19/07/1918
Miscellaneous	2nd Division Tactical Summary No. 53 For 24 hours ending 8 am 20/7/18	20/07/1918	20/07/1918
Miscellaneous	2nd Division Tactical Summary No. 54 For 24 hours ending 8 am 21/7/18	21/07/1918	21/07/1918

Miscellaneous	2nd Division Tactical Summary No. 55 For 24 hours ending 8 am 22/7/18	22/07/1918	22/07/1918
Miscellaneous	2nd Division Tactical Summary No. 56 For 24 hours ending 8 am 23/7/18	23/07/1918	23/07/1918
Miscellaneous	2nd Division Tactical Summary No. 57 For 24 hours ending 8 am 24/7/18	24/07/1918	24/07/1918
Miscellaneous	2nd Division Tactical Summary No. 58 For 24 hours ending 8 am 25/7/18	25/07/1918	25/07/1918
Miscellaneous	2nd Division Tactical Summary No. 59 For 24 hours ending 8 am 26/7/18	27/07/1918	27/07/1918
Miscellaneous	2nd Division Tactical Summary No. 60 For 24 hours ending 8 am 27/7/18	27/07/1918	27/07/1918
Miscellaneous	2nd Division Tactical Summary No. 61 For 24 hours ending 8 am 28/7/18	28/07/1918	28/07/1918
Miscellaneous	2nd Division Tactical Summary No. 62 For 24 hours ending 8 am 29/7/18	29/07/1918	29/07/1918
Miscellaneous	2nd Division Tactical Summary No. 63 For 24 hours ending 8 am 30/7/18	30/07/1918	30/07/1918
Miscellaneous	2nd Division Tactical Summary No. 64 For 24 hours ending am 31/7/18	31/07/1918	31/07/1918
Miscellaneous	Annexe to 2nd Division Tactical Summary No. 64		
Miscellaneous	Annexe No. 2 to 2nd Division Tactical Summary No. 64		
Miscellaneous	2nd Division Tactical Summary No. 65 For 24 hours ending 8 am 1/8/18	01/07/1918	01/07/1918
Heading	War Diary July 1918 Original Appendices		
Miscellaneous	2nd Division Dispositions And Movement Report No. 18		
Miscellaneous	2nd Division-Casualty Return For June 1918	03/07/1918	03/07/1918
Miscellaneous	2nd Division Strength Return Made Up To 12 Noon Saturday 6th July 1918		
Miscellaneous	Explanation of Increase And Decrease.		
Miscellaneous	Explanation Of Column "B"		
Miscellaneous	2nd Division Strength Return Made Up To 12 Noon Saturday 13th July 1918		
Miscellaneous	Explanation of Increase And Decrease.		
Miscellaneous	Explanation Of Column "B"		
Miscellaneous	2nd Division Deposition And Movement Report No. 29	21/07/1918	21/07/1918
Operation(al) Order(s)	2nd Division Order No. 344	18/07/1918	18/07/1918
Miscellaneous	Headquarters 154th Brigade. American E.F. June 6th 1918		
Miscellaneous	Strength Return Made Up To 12 Noon Saturday 27th July 1918		
Miscellaneous	Explanation of Increase And Decrease.		
Miscellaneous	Explanation Of Column "B"		
Miscellaneous	Strength Return Of 319th Regiment American E.F.		
Miscellaneous	2nd Division-Casualty Return For July 1918		
Miscellaneous	2nd Division No. G.S.	30/07/1918	30/07/1918
Miscellaneous	2nd Div No. G.S. 12/25/1	02/07/1918	02/07/1918
Miscellaneous	Narrative Of Raid Night By 1st Royal Berks 22nd/23rd July 1918		
Miscellaneous	Head Quarters 99th. Infantry Brigade.	24/07/1918	24/07/1918
Diagram etc	Area Raided Dugont TM. Ammunition Post		
Miscellaneous	Raid Commander Report.	24/07/1918	24/07/1918
Miscellaneous	Raid by 1st. Royal Berkshire Regiment.	24/07/1918	24/07/1918
Miscellaneous	1st. Royal Berkshire Regt.	03/07/1918	03/07/1918

Miscellaneous	2nd. Division 1st Royal Berks. Regt. Right Group R.F.A. Sherer's Group R.G.A.	03/07/1918	03/07/1918
Operation(al) Order(s)	99th Infantry Brigade Order No. 244	19/07/1918	19/07/1918
Diagram etc	Raid Map		
Diagram etc	99 to Inf. Bde. (order No. 244)		
Diagram etc	99 to Inf. Bde. (order No. 244) Machin Gun Standing Barrage		
Miscellaneous	To all recipients of 99th Infantry Brigade Order No. 244	21/07/1918	21/07/1918
Operation(al) Order(s)	To all recipients of 99th Infantry Brigade Order No. 244	21/07/1918	21/07/1918
Operation(al) Order(s)	Order No. 184 by Lieut. Colonel D.W. Powell.	22/07/1918	22/07/1918
Miscellaneous	1st. Royal Berks. Regt.	07/07/1918	07/07/1918
Miscellaneous	2nd Division No. G.S. 12/33	03/07/1918	03/07/1918
Miscellaneous	2nd Division General Staff G.S. 6/15 6.7.18		
Miscellaneous	A Form. Messages And Signals.		
Diagram etc	Maps		
Miscellaneous	99th. Infantry Brigade No. B.M. (S) 377	05/07/1918	05/07/1918
Diagram etc	Raid Map		
Map	Intelligence Map Reference		
Diagram etc	Raid Map		
Diagram etc	Maps		
Miscellaneous	2nd Division No. G.S. 13/46/1	06/07/1918	06/07/1918
Miscellaneous	99th Infantry Brigade No. B.M. (S) 379	05/07/1918	05/07/1918
Miscellaneous	99th Infantry Brigade No. B.M. (S) 378	05/07/1918	05/07/1918
Miscellaneous	2nd Div. Inf. Brigade.	07/07/1918	07/07/1918
Miscellaneous	2nd Division No. G.S. 13/46/3	08/07/1918	08/07/1918
Miscellaneous	99th Inf. Bde. No. B.M.S. 377/1	09/07/1918	09/07/1918
Miscellaneous	99th Infantry Brigade No. B.M. (S) 393	09/07/1918	09/07/1918
Miscellaneous	O.C. A.B.C.D. Cos. 5th. 6th 99th. Inf. Bdes. 37th. M.G. Battalion. 2nd Division "G".	09/07/1918	09/07/1918
Miscellaneous	2nd Division No. G.S. 13/48/1	10/07/1918	10/07/1918
Miscellaneous	2nd Division No. G.S. 13/46/6	10/07/1918	10/07/1918
Miscellaneous	99th Inf. Bde. No. B.M.S. 377/1	09/07/1918	09/07/1918
Miscellaneous	2nd Div Right Corps (for In Battalion)	09/07/1918	09/07/1918
Miscellaneous	2nd/Div G.S. 13/46/10	11/07/1918	11/07/1918
Miscellaneous	A Form Messages And Signals.		
Miscellaneous	R.A. 2nd Divn. BM/33/4	11/07/1918	11/07/1918
Miscellaneous	C Form Messages And Signals.		
Miscellaneous	2nd. Division "G". C.R.E. C.M.G.O.	12/07/1918	12/07/1918
Miscellaneous	2nd Division. No. G.S. 13/46/8	11/07/1918	11/07/1918
Miscellaneous	2nd. Division. "G".	14/07/1918	14/07/1918
Miscellaneous	2nd Division No. G.S. 13/46/11	14/07/1918	14/07/1918
Miscellaneous	2nd. Division "G".	14/07/1918	14/07/1918
Miscellaneous	5th Inf. Bde. No. G.S. 740/94/1	14/07/1918	14/07/1918
Miscellaneous	5th Inf. Bde. No. G.S. 740/94	15/07/1918	15/07/1918
Miscellaneous	General Staff, Third Army G. 12/295 28/7/18	27/07/1918	27/07/1918
Miscellaneous	99th. Infantry Brigade No. B.M. (S) 445	25/07/1918	25/07/1918
Miscellaneous	2nd. Division	16/07/1918	16/07/1918
Miscellaneous	2nd Div G.S. 6/16	16/07/1918	16/07/1918
Map	Maps		
Miscellaneous	2nd Division No. C.S. 12/40	17/07/1918	17/07/1918
Diagram etc	Ref. Ayette Sheet Scale 1.20000		
Miscellaneous	A Form Messages And Signals.		
Miscellaneous	2nd Divisional Artillery	17/07/1918	17/07/1918
Miscellaneous	2nd Division Medical Arrangements For Minor Operations Of 99th Infantry Brigade	18/07/1918	18/07/1918
Operation(al) Order(s)	2nd Division Order No. 344	18/07/1918	18/07/1918

Type	Description	Date 1	Date 2
Diagram etc	Maps		
Miscellaneous	Amm. Col.	18/07/1918	18/07/1918
Miscellaneous	Issued With Operation Order No 42 March Table 19th Infantry Brigade.	18/07/1915	18/07/1915
Miscellaneous	2nd Division.	18/07/1918	18/07/1918
Miscellaneous	2nd Div No. G.S. 13/46/13	16/07/1918	16/07/1918
Miscellaneous	2nd. Division "G". C.R.E. 2nd Division. C.M.G.O.	19/07/1918	19/07/1918
Miscellaneous	Third Army	19/07/1918	19/07/1918
Operation(al) Order(s)	99th Infantry Brigade Order No. 244	19/07/1918	19/07/1918
Miscellaneous	To all recipients of 99th Infantry Brigade Order No. 244	19/07/1918	19/07/1918
Diagram etc	Raid Map		
Diagram etc	99th Inf. Bde. (Order No. 244)		
Diagram etc	Maps		
Map	Maps		
Miscellaneous	A Form. Messages And Signals.		
Map	Maps		
Operation(al) Order(s)	VI Corps Order No. 340	20/07/1918	20/07/1918
Miscellaneous	Table "A".-To Accompany VI Corps Order No. 340		
Miscellaneous	5th Inf. Bde. 6th Inf. Bde. 99th Inf. Bde.	20/07/1918	20/07/1918
Miscellaneous	C Form Messages And Signals.		
Miscellaneous	A.B.D. Cos. No. 2 Bn. M.G.C. 99th Infantry Brigade. 6th Infantry Brigade. 5th Infantry Brigade. 2nd Division "G".	20/07/1918	20/07/1918
Miscellaneous	2nd Division General Staff		
Miscellaneous	5th Inf. Brigade. 6th Inf. Brigade. 99th Inf. Brigade.	21/07/1918	21/07/1918
Miscellaneous	Guards Division. 2nd Division 160th Inf. Bde. A.E.F. C.E. VI Corps. S.M.T.O. VI Corps.	21/07/1918	21/07/1918
Miscellaneous	To all recipients of 99th. Infantry Brigade Order No. 244	21/07/1918	21/07/1918
Miscellaneous	Q. 117 War Passed To 99th Brigade On 20th		
Miscellaneous	Amendment No. 1 To VI Corps Heavy Artillery Operation Order No. 117 Of 19th July, 1918	21/07/1918	21/07/1918
Miscellaneous	Reference para. 7 of O.O. No. 117 of 19/7/18 Unless Otherwise Notifeid Zero Will Be 12.30 On Night 22nd/23rd July.	22/07/1918	22/07/1918
Miscellaneous	99th Inf Brigade	21/07/1918	21/07/1918
Miscellaneous	2nd Division No. G.S. 13/46/22	21/07/1918	21/07/1918
Miscellaneous	2nd Div. G.		
Operation(al) Order(s)	Fight Group Operation Order No. 20	19/07/1918	19/07/1918
Diagram etc	Use With Artmery Maps		
Miscellaneous	To all recipients of 99th Infantry Brigade Order No. 244	21/07/1918	21/07/1918
Miscellaneous	Guards Division. 2nd Division. 160 Inf. Bde. AEF.		
Miscellaneous	Headquarters 319th Infantry, American Expeditionary Forces 23rd July 1918		
Miscellaneous	2nd Division. No. G.S. 13/46/25	23/07/1918	23/07/1918
Miscellaneous	5th Inf. Brigade. 6th Inf. Brigade. 99th Inf. Brigade.	23/07/1918	23/07/1918
Miscellaneous	Headquarters, 2nd Division 'G'.	23/07/1918	23/07/1918
Miscellaneous	2nd Division.	24/07/1918	24/07/1918
Diagram etc	Maps		
Miscellaneous	Headquarters 2nd Division. 'G'.	24/07/1918	24/07/1918
Miscellaneous	99th Inf. Brigade.	25/07/1918	25/07/1918
Miscellaneous	A Form Messages And Signals.		
Miscellaneous	6th Infantry Brigade.	23/07/1918	23/07/1918
Miscellaneous	G.S.O. I. 2nd Division.	28/07/1918	28/07/1918
Operation(al) Order(s)	2nd. Battalion, Machine Gun Corps, Order No. 22	25/07/1918	25/07/1918
Miscellaneous	No. 2 M.G. Battalion.	25/07/1918	25/07/1918

Type	Description	Date 1	Date 2
Miscellaneous	2nd Division No. C.S. 13/52/2	25/07/1918	25/07/1918
Miscellaneous	2nd Div No. G.S. 13/52/3	26/07/1918	26/07/1918
Miscellaneous	2nd Division No. G.S. 13/52/4	26/07/1918	26/07/1918
Miscellaneous	2nd Division No. G.S. 13/55	26/07/1918	26/07/1918
Miscellaneous	319th Regt. 5th Inf. Brigade. 6th Inf. Brigade. 99th Inf. Brigade. "Q" 2nd Division A.D.M.S. 2nd Div. Gas Officer A.P.M.	26/07/1918	26/07/1918
Miscellaneous	Composition Of Battalion Headquarters.		
Miscellaneous	2nd. Division. "G". C.R.E. 2nd. Division. C.M.G.O. VI Corps.	23/07/1918	23/07/1918
Operation(al) Order(s)	6th Infantry Brigade Order No. 375	27/07/1918	27/07/1918
Miscellaneous	O.C. A.B.D. Co. O.C. 1st. Bn. "The Kings"' Regt. 5th Infantry Brigade. 6th Infantry Brigade. 99th Infantry Brigade. 2nd Division. "G".	27/07/1918	27/07/1918
Miscellaneous	319th Regt A.E.F. 2nd M.Gun Battn	27/07/1918	27/07/1918
Miscellaneous	A Form. Messages And Signals.		
Map	Identification Trace for use with Artillery Maps.		
Map	Maps		
Miscellaneous	2nd Div No. G.S. 13/54	28/07/1918	28/07/1918
Miscellaneous	2nd Division No. G.S. 13/54	23/07/1918	23/07/1918
Miscellaneous	2nd Division.	28/07/1918	28/07/1918
Operation(al) Order(s)	VI Corps Counter Battery. Operation Order No. 2 July 1918	28/07/1918	28/07/1918
Miscellaneous	5th Inf. Bde. 6th Inf. Bde. 99th Inf. Bde. 319th Regt. A.E.F. (3)	28/07/1918	28/07/1918
Miscellaneous	No. 2 M.G. Battn.	28/07/1918	28/07/1918
Miscellaneous	2nd Division.	27/07/1918	27/07/1918
Miscellaneous	2nd Division "G".	27/07/1918	27/07/1918
Miscellaneous	160th Inf. Bde. A.E.F. 319th Regt. A.E.F. 315 M.G. Battn. A.E.F. 319th M.G. Coy. A.E.F. No. 2 M.G. Battalion	28/07/1918	28/07/1918
Miscellaneous	Guards Division 2nd Division. 160th Infantry Brigade A.E.F. S.M.T.O. VI Corps.	27/07/1918	27/07/1918
Miscellaneous	5th Inf Brigade	29/07/1918	29/07/1918
Miscellaneous	5th Infantry Brigade.	28/07/1918	28/07/1918
Miscellaneous	2nd. Division. No. G.S. 13/52/8	29/07/1918	29/07/1918
Miscellaneous	VI Corps. Guards Division. 37th Division.	29/07/1918	29/07/1918
Miscellaneous	6th Inf. Bde.	29/07/1918	29/07/1918
Miscellaneous	G.O.C. 6th Infantry Brigade.	24/07/1918	24/07/1918
Miscellaneous	2nd Division No. G.S. 13/47/6	18/07/1918	18/07/1918
Miscellaneous	G.O.C. 2nd Division.	15/07/1918	15/07/1918
Miscellaneous	Headquarters 6th Infantry Brigade.	15/07/1918	15/07/1918
Miscellaneous	Headquarters 2nd Division 'G'.	16/07/1918	16/07/1918
Miscellaneous	G.O.C. 76th Inf. Bde.	16/07/1918	16/07/1918
Map	Maps		
Miscellaneous	G.O.C. 2nd Division.	15/07/1918	15/07/1918
Miscellaneous	2nd Div G.S. 13/47/2	12/07/1918	12/07/1918
Miscellaneous	All Recipients Of 14th Brigade R.H.A. C. No. 326/1	13/07/1918	13/07/1918
Miscellaneous	2nd Division No. G.S. 13/47	12/07/1918	12/07/1918
Miscellaneous	Messages And Signals.		
Miscellaneous	To all recipients of 6th Brigade Order No. 375	29/07/1918	29/07/1918
Operation(al) Order(s)	6th Infantry Brigade Order No. 375	27/07/1918	27/07/1918
Miscellaneous	Guards Division. 2nd Division. 160th Inf. Bde. A.E.F. S.M.T.O. VI Corps.	29/07/1918	29/07/1918
Miscellaneous	6th Inf. Bde. 319th Regt. A.E.F. (2 Copies)	29/07/1918	29/07/1918

Miscellaneous	Guards Division. 2nd Division. 160 Infantry Brigade A.E.F.	30/07/1918	30/07/1918
Miscellaneous	319th Regiment A.E.F. 5th Inf. Brigade. 6th Inf. Brigade. 99th Inf. Brigade.	30/07/1918	30/07/1918
Miscellaneous	Relief Orders	31/07/1915	31/07/1915
Miscellaneous	Relief Order By 19th Infantry Brigade.	31/07/1915	31/07/1915
Miscellaneous	5th Inf. Brigade. 6th Inf. Brigade. 99th. Brigade.	31/07/1918	31/07/1918
Miscellaneous		31/07/1918	31/07/1918
Miscellaneous	2nd Division.	31/07/1918	31/07/1918
Miscellaneous	List Of Contents.		
Miscellaneous	Defence Scheme Right Division VI Corps.		
Miscellaneous	Defence Scheme Right Division VI Corps.	04/07/1918	04/07/1918
Miscellaneous	2nd Division Defence Scheme.		
Miscellaneous	2nd Division Scheme		
Miscellaneous	2nd Division Defence Scheme Appendix "A" Heavy Artillery.		
Miscellaneous	2nd Division Defence Scheme-Aeroplane Calls.		
Miscellaneous	2nd Division Defence Scheme		
Miscellaneous	2nd Division Defence Scheme Appendix 'C'		
Miscellaneous	2nd Division Defence Scheme Appendix 'D'		
Miscellaneous	2nd Division Defence Scheme Appendix E		
Miscellaneous	2nd Division Defence Scheme Appendix F		
Miscellaneous	2nd Division Defence Scheme Appendix G		
Diagram etc	Diagram Of Communication Right Division		
Diagram etc	Diagram Of Visual Communication Right Division		
Diagram etc	Diagram Of Wireless & Power Buzzer Amplifier Communication Right Division.		
Diagram etc	Diagram Communications Right Division Buried Cable System		
Miscellaneous	Appendix "H"		
Miscellaneous	5th Inf. Bde. 6th Inf. Bde. 99th. Inf. Bde. C.R.A C.R.E.		
Miscellaneous	List Of Contents		
Miscellaneous	Defence Scheme Right Division VI Corps.		
Miscellaneous	Defence Scheme Right Division VI Corps.	04/07/1918	04/07/1918
Miscellaneous	Appendix A		
Miscellaneous	Amendments To 2nd Division Defence Scheme Appendix "A"	14/08/1918	14/08/1918
Miscellaneous	2nd Division Defence Scheme.		
Miscellaneous	2nd Division Defence Scheme Appendix "A" Mutual Support.		
Miscellaneous	2nd Division Defence Scheme Appendix "A" Heavy Artillery.		
Miscellaneous	2nd Division Defence Scheme-Aeroplane Calls.		
Miscellaneous	2nd Division Defence Scheme Appendix B		
Miscellaneous	2nd Division Defence Scheme. Appendix 'C'		
Miscellaneous	2nd Division Defence Scheme. Appendix D		
Miscellaneous	2nd Division Defence Scheme. Appendix E		
Miscellaneous	2nd Division Defence Scheme. Appendix F		
Miscellaneous	2nd Division Defence Scheme. Appendix G		
Diagram etc	Diagram Of Communications Right Division		
Diagram etc	Diagram Of Visual Communications Right Division		
Diagram etc	Diagram Of Wireless & Power Buzzer Amplifier Communication Right Division		
Map	D Communications Right Division Buried Cable System		
Miscellaneous	Appendix "H" Administrative Arrangements		

Map	Machine Gun Positions		
Map	Track Map		
Miscellaneous	Map D		
Miscellaneous	2nd Division Trench Strength 10th Sept. 1918		
Map	Map Showing Disposition Of Troops		
Miscellaneous	5th Inf. Bde. No. G.S. 740/97	16/07/1918	16/07/1918
Miscellaneous	Defence Scheme Left Brigade. Right Division. VI Corps.	16/07/1918	16/07/1918
Miscellaneous	Appendix "A" "S.C.S."		
Miscellaneous	Orders In The Event Of Shelling By Yellow Cross Gas		
Miscellaneous	Administrative Instructions Issued In Connection With 5th Infantry Brigade Defence Scheme Dated 16th July 1918		
Map	Maps		
Miscellaneous	Appendix "D" 5th Brigade Defence Scheme.		
Diagram etc	Appendix II 5th Bde. Defence Scheme.		
Diagram etc	Appendix D III 5th Bde. Defence Scheme.		
Miscellaneous	Appendix "B" Lewis Gun Positions-Purple Front Life.		
Map	Map A		
Map	Map B		
Heading	B.E.F. France & Flanders. 2 Division. H.Q. General Staff. 1918 July.		

2ND DIVISION

GENERAL STAFF

JULY 1918.

Aug

2ND DIVISION

(6339) Wt. W160/M3016 1,500,000 10/17 McA & W Ltd (E 1898) Forms W3091.   Army Form W.3091.

Cover for Documents.

Nature of Enclosures.

War Diary.

July, 1918.

Original Diary

Notes, or Letters written.

Army Form C. 2118.

WAR DIARY
or
INTELLIGENCE SUMMARY.

(Erase heading not required.)

Instructions regarding War Diaries and Intelligence Summaries are contained in F. S. Regs., Part II. and the Staff Manual respectively. Title pages will be prepared in manuscript.

Ref. Sheets 51c 51d 1/40000

JULY, 1918

Place	Date	Hour	Summary of Events and Information	Remarks and references to Appendices
LA BAZEQUE V.27&7.7.	July 1st		The disposition of the 2nd Division on this date was as follows:- The Division was the Right Division of the VI Corps and holding the AYETTE Sector from F.23.a.1.6.(57.d.N.E.) to S.27.a.0.1.(51.b.S.W.). The 99th Brigade on the right - the 6th Brigade in the centre and the 5th Brigade on the left.	Appen.1
			The 37th Division (V) Corps) on the Right Flank - The 32nd Division on the Left Flank. Location Statement of 2nd Division attached. Weather fine and warm. Situation unchanged. Special Counter Battery shoot by our Artillery during night.30th June - July 1st between 10 and 11 p.m. Patrols report no particular activity by the enemy beyond the usual improvement of trenches and a little wiring. 2nd Division casualty returns for June attached.	Appen.2
	July 2nd		Weather fine. Enemy artillery normal. Our artillery active with harrassing fire on roads and tracks and selected targets. 1st Battn,King's Regt.(6th Brigade)endeavoured to secure an identification by means of a Fighting patrol but were unsuccessful.	
	July 3rd		Fine. Situation unchanged.	
	July 4th		Weather fine. Situation unchanged. Artillery activity normal on both sides. A patrol of the 2nd H.L.I.visited the enemy post at S.26.d.7.2.and was driven off by M.G.Fire. The patrol leader was wounded. One German was shot but no identification was secured.	
	July 5th		Weather fine. Situation unchanged. We carried out harrassing fire and bursts of fire on selected targets. Active patrolling was continued. The enemy were alert and no information of value was obtained	

Army Form C. 2118.

WAR DIARY
or
INTELLIGENCE SUMMARY.

(Erase heading not required.)

July, 1918. No. 2.

Instructions regarding War Diaries and Intelligence Summaries are contained in F. S. Regs., Part II. and the Staff Manual respectively. Title pages will be prepared in manuscript.

Place	Date	Hour	Summary of Events and Information	Remarks and references to Appendices
LA BAZEQUE	July 6th		Fine. Situation unchanged. Enemy artillery activity below normal. Our artillery and T.Ms active. 100 round 6" Hows. fired on huts North of ABLAINZEVILLE. Our patrols were active along the whole front. The enemy outpost line was at all points found to be occupied and a certain amount of patrolling is being done by him. 2nd Division Strength Return issued. The Guards Division took over Command from the 32nd Div. on our left flank at 10 p.m.	App.3.
	July 7th		Weather fine. Situation normal. Usual artillery activity. Patrols reported nothing unusual.	
	July 8th		Weather fine. Situation unchanged. Enemy fired a few Yellow Cross Gas shells in the COJEUL VALLEY. Our 6" Trench mortars active on new enemy work. Artillery and M.Gs harassed enemy approaches. Active patrolling was carried out. Nothing special reported.	
	July 9th		Heavy shower in the afternoon. Situation unchanged. Our 6" Trench Mortars active on enemy work. Artillery fired 300 rounds on Posts and wire E.of AYETTE. Our patrols were active.	
	July 10th		Some rain during the day. Situation unchanged. Our artillery was active on enemy wire and posts, also on T.M. emplacements in F.23 . A party of 1 N.C.O. and 4 men of the 2nd Ox. and Bucks L.I. out covering a wiring party was attacked by a German Patrol of 8. In hand to hand fighting 2 Germans were shot and one made prisoner - the remainder retired. Prisoners belonged to 452nd I.R.234th Div.(Normal)	
	July 11th		Heavy rain during the afternoon and night.	

Army Form C.—

WAR DIARY
or
INTELLIGENCE SUMMARY.
(Erase heading not required.)

July, 1918.   No. 3

Instructions regarding War Diaries and Intelligence
Summaries are contained in F. S. Regs., Part II.
and the Staff Manual respectively. Title pages
will be prepared in manuscript.

Place	Date	Hour	Summary of Events and Information	Remarks and references to Appendices
LA BAZEQUE	July 12th		Fair - rain in the afternoon.	
	July 13th		Wet with fine intervals. 2nd Division Strength Return issued.	App. 4
	July 14th		Fair. Heavy showers during the evening.	
	July 15th		Fair. Some rain. 9 Prisoners captured by 1st Bn. Kings Regt. in successful raid E. of AYETTE during night 14/15th. About 9 of the enemy were killed in hand to hand fighting - our casualties were a few men slightly wounded - prisoners belonged to 453rd I.R., 234th Division.	
	July 16th		Heavy rain during early morning - otherwise fine. Very hot during greater part of the day. A daylight patrol of the 1st K.R.R.C.occupied enemy post W. of AYETTE - ABLAINZEVILLE road without opposition. Our Field Artillery active carrying out harassing fire on enemy's forward areas.	
	July 17th		Heavy showers in early morning, otherwise fine. Usual harassing fire concentrations by our artillery. Situation unchanged.	
	July 18th		Fine with few showers. Concentration of about 2000 Gas Shells, cheifly Yellow Cross, put down on DOUMY area and area to the East of it at 5 a.m, causing about 30 casualties to our troops. Situation unchanged.	

Army Form C. 2118.

WAR DIARY
or
INTELLIGENCE SUMMARY. July, 1918. No. 4.

(Erase heading not required.)

Place	Date	Hour	Summary of Events and Information	Remarks and references to Appendices
LA BAZEQUE	July 19th		Increase in hostile artillery and aircraft activity. Our artillery was constantly active harassing the enemy's forward system. Movement in enemy's lines above normal. Fine day. Few showers. Situation unchanged.	
	July 20th		Fine. Hostile artillery active harassing our front & support lines during the night. Situation unchanged.	
	July 21st		Fine. COJEUL VALLEY heavily shelled at 5.20 a.m. - ADINFER, DOUCHY and the COJEUL VALLEY were continually harassed during the night. Our Artillery active on frequented areas and dead ground during the day. The usual harassing fire and concentrations were carried out on enemy communications, etc., during the night.	App. 6.
	July 22nd		Fine. Our artillery carried out usual harassing fire on enemy's forward system. Hostile artillery active during the morning on DOUCHY - QUESNOY FARM - ADINFER WOOD and COJEUL VALLEY.	
	July 23rd		Heavy rain throughout the day. At 12.30 am 2 companies of the 1st R. Berks Regt., 99th Inf. Bde. raided enemy positions N. of ABLAINZEVILLE - 5 prisoners of the 10th Bav. I.R.,5th Bav. Mgn.Res.Div. and 1 M.G. were captured About 50 of the enemy were killed by the infantry and several believed to have been killed by our artillery barrage which was very effective. As a result of identifications secured the 5th Bav. Divn. was discovered to be holding the line opposite the right half of this Divisional Front. This Division was previously believed to be in local reserve. Our casualties totalled 1 Off. and 50 3 O.Rs killed and 30 O.Rs wounded, most of the wounded being only slight cases. Enemy retaliation was slight. Hostile Artillery activity normal. Our artillery carried out usual harassing fire.	App. 7 6 am

Army Form C.21

WAR DIARY
or
INTELLIGENCE SUMMARY

No. 5.

(Erase heading not required.)

Instructions regarding War Diaries and Intelligence Summaries are contained in F.S. Regs., Part II. and the Staff Manual respectively. Title pages will be prepared in manuscript.

Place	Date	Hour	Summary of Events and Information	Remarks and references to Appendices
LA BAZEQUE V.27.c.7.7.	July 24th		Fine Situation remains unchanged. Our Field Artillery was active during the day and the enemy's artillery was fairly active on our forward areas. 131 rounds were fired by our 6"T.Ms.and 21 light bombs were fired by enemy Minenwerfer. Patrols reported nothing of particular interest. Movement was normal. Enemy reconnaissance aircraft are reported more active and in larger numbers. 8 machines seen appeared to be of a new type with narrow wings.	
"	25th		Showery with fine intervals. Our artillery displayed usual activity. Hostile artillery activity below normal. Considerable dog traffic observed in forward areas. Germans appear to be using messenger dogs to a large extent on this front probably owing to difficulties in maintaining wires and to danger of movement which is continually sniped by our Field Arty,. Situation unchanged.	
"	26th		Heavy showers. Our artillery normally active. Hostile artillery activity below normal. Situation unchanged.	
"	27th		Heavy showers. Usual artillery activity on both sides. More movement than usual observed in enemy lines, this probably being due to the bad condition of the enemy's trenches.caused by recent rains. Situation unchanged.	
"	28th		Fine day. Enemy attempted to rush one of our posts N.of AYETTE held by 2nd Bn.Highland Light Infantry at 2.25 a.m. this morning. This attempt was repulsed and the German officer in charge of the party was killed and his body brought into our lines. Identification showed he belonged to 451 I.R. 234th Divn. Normal artillery activity on both sides. Our Trench Mortars were active and obtained several direct hits on enemy trenches.	App.8.

Army Form C. 2118

WAR DIARY
INTELLIGENCE SUMMARY

(Erase heading not required.)

No. 6

Instructions regarding War Diaries and Intelligence Summaries are contained in F.S. Regs., Part II. and the Staff Manual respectively. Title pages will be prepared in manuscript.

Place	Date	Hour	Summary of Events and Information	Remarks and references to Appendices
LA BAZEQUE	July 29th		Fine. Normal artillery activity on both sides. At 10.40 p.m. the 1st Bn. Kings Regt., 6th Inf. Bde. raided enemy outpost line E. of AYETTE - this raid was highly successful, 6 prisoners of the 2nd Bn.453rd I.R. 234th Divn. were captured and several casualties inflicted on the enemy - our casualties were;- Killed 1 Officer and 2 O.R. Wounded 7 O.Rs.	
	" 30th		Fine. Situation unchanged. Normal artillery activity on both sides. Our patrols report enemy patrols seen N. of AYETTE, these were fired on by L.Gs and dispersed. Very little movement seen in enemy lines owing to bad visibility.	
	" 31st		Fine. Slight increase in hostile artillery activity. Our artillery normally active carrying out harassing fire on enemy forward system, communications etc. Enemy patrols were fired on and dispersed E. of AYETTE.	
			Casualty Return for July	App. 9

(6339) Wt. W160/M3016 1,500,000 10/17 McA & W Ltd (E 1898) Forms W3091.   Army Form W.3091.

Cover for Documents.

Nature of Enclosures.

War Diary

July, 1918

Intelligence Summaries

Notes, or Letters written.

2nd Division Tactical Summary No. 24.
For 24 hours ending 8 am 1/7/16.

Not to be taken forward of Bn. H.Q. in the line.

1. OPERATIONS.

General. Situation is unchanged.

Artillery. Ours. Generally active during the period. Hows. 60-pdrs and 18-pdrs engaged targets on various parts of the enemy front, including COURCELLES and ABLAINZEVILLE.
Hostile. Less active than usual.

Trench Mortars. Ours. About 32 3" rounds were fired at low flying E.A. and 43 rounds at suspected hostile M.G. positions.
Hostile. Quiet. 6 light T.Ms. were fired at our line about F.22.b.8.5.

Machine Guns. Ours. Fired about 5000 rounds at various parts of the enemy's line, including the crest in A.8.a and tracks in neighbourhood and sunken road in A.3.b and A.3.d.
Hostile. Fired bursts at intervals during the night. Otherwise inactive.

Aircraft. Ours. Active. At about 10.40 am 1 Raiding E.A. which had been flying low over our lines was engaged by three of our scouts and brought down in flames E. of LOGEAST WOOD. An observation balloon was also forced to descend.
Hostile. Very active over our forward areas.

Patrols. The Right Battn. Right Bde. sent out a small listening patrol only. The Left Battn. sent out 3 patrols.
The first. 1 N.C.O. and 2 riflemen left F.17.a.3.5 at 10.45 pm returning to same place at 12.5 am. They heard the enemy working at F.17.a.7.4 and a large working party at about F.17.d.3.1. An enemy patrol or covering party was seen at about F.17.c.45.30. Artificial bird calls were heard. (NOTE. This method of signalling was also reported by a patrol of the Brigade on our right on night 28/29th June in F.29.a. It is now to the Sector and may indicate a relief.
The second. 2/Lt.R.J.ANDERSON, Sgt. MOORE and 3 O.Rs. left No.24 post (F.11.c.9.2) at 10.45 pm returning to same place at 1.10 am. They approached the enemy posts at about F.11.d.10.00, but extreme caution had to be observed as they were on a forward slope and the moon was very bright. No wire was encountered. A M.G. fired from F.11.d.20.00.
The third. Consisting of 2/Lt.R.J.ANDERSON and Sgts. HOLLINGS-WORTH and MOORE left No.25 post (F.11.c.85.65) at 2.30 am returning at 3.20 am. They got into snipers post at F.11.d.15.12. Here they found a number of slit trenches - not connected with corrugated iron shelters and cubby holes. These had all been blown in and a body was found half buried and decomposed. 4 dozen bombs were found in the posts and other material. Sgt.MOORE proceeded further to about F.11.d.22.00 where a dead horse and a dead German lay. Only plain concertina wire was found. It was daylight when the patrol returned.

2/Lt.TOMKINS and 8 O.Rs. of the Centre Brigade left our lines at 1.15 am and searched the ground from F.11.d.4.8 to F.11.d.8.5. No trace of the enemy was seen.
2/Lt.SWEENEY and 19 O.Rs. left our trenches at F.5.d.9.5 and thoroughly explored ground in F.6.c. Nothing was seen or heard of the enemy beyond a solitary sniper who fired as the patrol was returning shortly before daybreak.

P.T.O.

2/Lt. KIRKALDY and 10 O.Rs. of Centre Bde. left our lines at F.11.b.85.80 and made straight for F.12.a.4.2. When about 150 yds. from this point a Boche was heard to shout, and as the patrol slowly approached, about 50 of the enemy were seen digging and carrying. Our party crawled forward about 20 yds. further, but, not being strong enough to fight, decided to return with information. The Boche ceased work as day was breaking, moved S. along top of trench towards the AYETTE-COURCELLES Road, and then disappeared. The patrol re-entered our trenches at F.5.d.9.1.

An N.C.Os. patrol of the Left Bn. Left Bde. in A.2.a reports digging heard at about A.2.a.8.5. Patrol was out between 1.30 am and 2.30 am.

2/Lt. MATHIE and 9 O.Rs. of the same Battn. left L.4 post at 11.30 pm and proceeded along track to point A.2.a.5.6. An enemy patrol was thought to be seen and our patrol advanced in that direction., but the enemy patrol was lost. There was some rifle fire from about point A.2.a.9.4. Patrol returned to point of departure at 1.30 am.

Lt. STANESBY and 1 N.C.O. of the same Battn. left L.8 post at midnight to ascertain if M.G. post at S.26.c.8.2 is occupied. Patrol advanced to a shell hole within 30 yds. of enemy post. Nothing was heard or seen for half an hour. The patrol exposed themselves in bright moonlight but were not fired on. Patrol returned to our line at 12.50 am.

A N.C.Os. patrol out 30 yards in front of our wire between L.8 and L.10 post reports shouting in German outpost line opposite No.9 post. Patrol was out between 1.15 am and 2.10 am.

2. INTELLIGENCE.

Movement. 52 men were observed in the area A.20.b, c & d. Movement apparently centering on the mound at A.20.d.2.9. Our field artillery dealt with movement amongst the huts in F.17 and F.23 effectively, the first shell falling right amongst the enemy party.

Movement was also observed about the sunken road in A.20.b and in the following areas - B.30.c, A.20.d, tracks from MORY TO VRAUCOURT.

Transport & Trains. 5.40 pm 1 G.S. wagon going along cross country track from MORY in direction of VRAUCOURT. 5.45 pm 1 as above and 1 going N. on ECOUST-BAPAUME Road. 6 pm 1 proceeding towards MORY on track from VRAUCOURT. 6.20 pm 1 on same track but going in opposite direction. Also on road A.22.c.1.3 going Northwards.

Work. Digging has been observed on enemy front line at F.11.d.30.10 and the concertina wire at this point has been increased.
Patrols report considerable work in progress on shell hole system at F.12.a.4.2.

General. A fire was caused by our gunfire at 116° grid from F.10.c.05.50. At 12.20 am a gun fired 4 rounds, bearing on flash 101° grid from F.10.c.5.5.

Captain.
for Lieut. Colonel,
General Staff, 2nd Division.

1/7/18.

2nd Division Tactical Summary No. 25
For 24 hours ending 8 am 2/7/18.

Not to be taken forward of Battn. H.Q. in the line.

1. OPERATIONS.

General. Situation unchanged.

Artillery. Ours. Roads, tracks, hostile batteries and dumps were subjected to intense bursts from 10 to 11 pm, and from 3 to 4 am. Otherwise normal.
Hostile. Quiet to normal. Amongst the points which were subjected to intermittent shelling were COJEUL VALLEY, LE QUESNOY FARM and DOUCHY. Retaliation to our counter-battery work was slight.

Trench Mortars. Ours. Fairly active. A hostile M.G. at A.2.b.7.5 was silenced.
Hostile. Generally quiet, but becoming more active (L.T.Ms.) on left of Right Sector front in the neighbourhood of PEMBERTON BILLING and MAUD ALLAN trenches.

Machine Guns. Ours. About 1000 rounds were fired at E.A.
Hostile. Active against our aircraft. An enemy M.G. was seen in action at S.27.c.8.7.

Aircraft. Increasingly active on both sides. An explosion was caused by our bombing machines about A.16.d.8.3 followed by a large cloud of smoke lasting about 30 minutes.

Patrols. 2/Lt. R.J. ANDERSON, Sgts. HOLLINGSWORTH and MOORE and 6 O.Rs. were out from 11 pm to 1.10 am leaving and returning to 23a post (F.17.a.90.95) with the object of investigating new work and what appeared to be a machine gun visible through the periscope at this post. They moved S.S.E. through 2 belts of wire (1 plain and 1 barbed concertina) to F.17.b.1.8 thence East to their objective at F.17.b.3.8. The work was found to be a snipers post, which was clean and in good condition, with a shelter for 2, and steps out to a track leading back. A luminous sighted rifle, a cigar box, some bottles and a postcard were found in the post. The "M.G." turned out to be a bottle.

2/Lt. LANG, another officer and 4 O.Rs. of the Left Bn. Left Bde. left L.6 post at 12.10 am and proceeded S.E. whence they listened for ¾ hour. Digging, wiring and shouting were heard and three Germans were seen to leave the outpost line and disappear in the valley. A small light was seen and a wagon was heard about 400 yards away. Patrol returned to our lines at 2.10 am. About 3.15 am a M.G. was seen firing tracer bullets.

2/Lt. KIRKALDY and 23 O.Rs. of the Centre Bde. left our lines at F.11.b.85.75 and proceeded towards F.12.a.4.2 for the purpose of securing an identification. One man was slightly wounded by shrapnel at this period, and returned to our trenches. The party was deployed into line at a previously chosen position, about 80 yards in front of enemy shell hole system, with Lewis Guns on flanks, when two bombs exploded just on the left. A shout was heard & three men were seen to disappear over the ridge. The patrol kept very still and waited for our artillery and trench mortars to put down the pre-arranged barrage. When fire was opened two shells fell behind the party but no one was injured. Upon the signal being given our patrol moved quickly towards the objective, but was held up about 30 yds. ahead by an entanglement of the double concertina type with strands in front. Two more bombs exploded near by at this point and the leader came to the conclusion that it was impossible to get through. He therefore brought back the party and re-entered our lines at F.5.d.95.15.

P.T.O.

2. INTELLIGENCE.

Movement. Two men were seen to enter road at A.21.a.6.2. 32 men were seen in area A.20.b, c & d at 4.40 am. A party of 12 to 15 was seen moving about in A.21.d.

Trains & Transport. Transport can be plainly heard behind the enemy line at night.

Work. New wire has been located in front of SHELL HOLE SYSTEM at F.12.a.4.2; it runs in a series of Vs. New wire also at F.6.c. 55.25. At 8.50 pm 12 men were seen digging in the open at A.21.d. At 4.20 am 4 men were seen digging in rear of the mound at A.20.d.2.9.

Balloons. A hostile balloon was up from 4 to 5.30 am and 7.30 to 7.50 am. True bearing from F.12.a.7.9 gave 130°.

Lights. During counter-battery work by our artillery at 10.30 pm a red light was sent up from approx. F.29.d.9.4. Several rockets which burst into two orange lights were sent up from F.12.c. No apparent response in either case.

Smoke. At 1.55 am dense clouds of smoke rose from approx. A.16.b. True bearing of 109° 30' from F.2.b.8.8. Probably dump fired by our heavies, which were active at the time.

Captain.
for Lieut. Colonel,
General Staff, 2nd Division.

2/7/18.

2nd Division Tactical Summary No. 26
For 24 hours ending 8 am 3/7/18.

Not to be taken forward of Bn. H.Q. in the line.

1. OPERATIONS.

General. There is no change in the situation. The Division on our left captured 7 prisoners and inflicted many casualties in a raid during the night.

Artillery. Ours. A short concentration of intense fire was put down on suspected T.M. at A.3.a.5.3 at 7 pm. Three batteries of Left Group fired in support of raid by the Division on our left at 11 am. Otherwise, normal harassing fire.
Hostile. Exceptionally quiet.

Trench Mortars. Ours. Fired 64 rounds on S.O.S. lines at F.6.c.55.35, suspected M.G. at F.12.a.48.80, S.O.S. lines at F.6.c.50.35, Minnie at F.23.a.8.7, camp huts in F.17.c & 23.a, datum point F.17.c.7.4 and road at F.17.c.90.90.
Hostile. More active than usual. At 3.25 pm 10 rounds from Medium T.M. were fired on our front line in F.17.a, probably from emplacement at A.13.a.6.3. At 3.30 pm T.Ms. from ABLAINZEVILLE fired on front line in F.22.d. At 9.15 pm about 40 rounds were fired on trenches and communications in AYETTE.

Machine Guns. Ours. Active against aircraft. Fired 4000 rounds on the AERODROME A.7.d.7.1, the shell hold system at A.8.a.1.7 and road junction at A.3.d.8.9.
Hostile. Active at night sweeping our forward areas and against aircraft.

Aircraft. Ours. Actively patrolled forward areas at intervals throughout the day.
Hostile. On the whole less active than during the previous period. Active over our left forward area during the morning - a few machines flying low were heavily engaged by M.G.s. and T.Ms. and later by A.A. guns.

Patrols. A listening patrol of the Right Bn. Left Bde. out in front of R.4 post between midnight and 12.40 am reports enemy heard working on the road due S. of post.
2/Lt. COLBORNE and 5 O.Rs. of the Right Bn. Right Bde. left our lines at F.17.c.25.60 at 10.45 pm and returned to F.16.d.80.50 at 1.10 am.
It found wire at F.17.c.6.4 consisting of 1 low belt of concertina running back to sunken road at F.17.c.80.40 forming a 'Y'
The old posts at F.17.c.4.4 - 2.2 and 3.1 were found unoccupied. There are no shell holes in No Man's Land more than 70 yards from our line. Voices could be heard at about F.17.c.8.5 and a large working party was removing corrugated iron from the huts in F.17.c & d and F.23.a.
Wiring could be heard in progress North East of ABLAINZEVILLE.

2. INTELLIGENCE.

Movement. Between 6 and 8 am a great deal of individual movement was seen from sunken road in A.20.b to sunken road in A.21.a. About 20 men went along road in B.29.d and B.30.c.
A total of 67 men were seen in area A.20.b, c & d, the majority going to and from the mound A.20.d.2.9.

P.T.O.

- 2 -

<u>Trains & Transport.</u> Usual transport movement. At 12.30 pm smoke from an engine was seen on a bearing of 115° grid from X.21.c.9.9.
    At 5.55 am a light engine was observed in B.17.c and another in B.21.d at 7.15 am.

<u>Balloons.</u> Hostile observation balloon ascended at 4.15 am and remained up until 5.15 am - grid bearing of 108° from F.2.b.8.8.

<u>General.</u> Guns were observed firing on grid bearing of 112° from O.P. at F.10.c.05.50 as follows:-
        5.40 pm   3 rounds.
        8.40 - 8.50 pm 14 rounds.
An enemy box periscope was seen at about F.17.a.65.30 at 6 pm.

	<u>Barometers</u>	<u>Thermometer.</u>	
		Min.	Max.
July 2nd 10 am	29'-57"	52	76
July 3rd 10 am	29'-80"	53	74

                                        Captain.
                                for Lieut. Colonel,
3/7/18.   General Staff, 2nd Division.

2nd Division Tactical Summary No.27.
For 24 hours ending 8 am 4/7/18.

Not to be taken forward of Bn. H.Q. in the line.

1. OPERATIONS.

The situation remains unchanged.

Artillery. Our artillery continued to harass the enemy throughout the period under review. Hostile tracks and roads were engaged by field guns and 4.5" Hows, and good results were obtained from shoots on the T.Ms. in the vicinity of ABLAINZEVILLE, on the O.P. at A.14.a.7.2 and on the trenches in A.8.a.
Light concentrations were fired by our 18-pdrs. on A.8.c.20.85 and A.8.c.36.98.
The 60-pdrs. and 6" Hows. were active at intervals against COURCELLES and the ABLAINZEVILLE- LOGEAST WOOD road, also against hostile O.Ps., dumps, H.Qs. and new work.
Hostile Artillery carried out light harassing fire only and the principal areas affected were the ADINFER-RANSART Road, LE QUESNOY FARM, DOUCHY, and HAMEAU FARM. The calibres mostly used were 77 mm and 4.2s.; very few 5.9s. are reported.

Trench Mortars.
Our 6" Newtons fired 20 rounds against the enemy new work at F.23.a.8.7 and F.17.d.1.4. The 3" Stokes were active against selected targets firing about 150 rounds principally opposite the Left Bde. front.
Hostile T.Ms. were active against the Right Bde. front, firing occasionally on to the AYETTE - BUCQUOY Road in F.16.d.

Machine Guns.
Harassing fire was carried out at intervals during the night, about 5000 rounds being fired against the hostile trenches in A.8.a and A.2.d, and into ABLAINZEVILLE.
2000 rounds were fired at hostile aircraft. The enemy's machine guns were normally active at intervals during the night.

Aircraft.
Our machines were active.
A hostile aeroplane was over our forward area in the early morning and again between 7 am and 8 am. In each case the machines were engaged by A.A. and M.G. fire..

Patrols.
Two officers patrols of the Left Bde. report digging in progress in A.1.d.
2/Lt. BEVAN and 30 O.Rs. reconnoitred the shell hole positions at A.2.a.8.5 and found them unoccupied and unwired.
2/Lt. COCKBURN and 4 O.Rs. on patrol report wiring in progress at F.12.a.50.75 approx. The wire at this point appears thick and high and extends N. for a distance of about 200 yards.
2/Lt. ANDERSON and 14 O.Rs. went out and visited the enemy positions in F.11.d in search of an identification. The post at F.11.d.2.0 was found unoccupied and the trenches and shell holes in the vicinity were searched but no sign of the enemy was found.

2. INTELLIGENCE.

Movement.
The usual individual movement is reported on the roads and tracks W. of COURCELLES.
The trench in A.8.a was seen to be occupied and movement was seen about the bank A.14.central.

P.T.O.

- 2 -

A few small parties were seen on the road in B.30.c going in the direction of MORY.

7.50 am - 2 parties of 6 men were observed on the road going from ST LEDGER to ERVILLERS.

Transport.

Between 5 am and 6.30 am transport was seen on the ECOUST - BAPAUME Road going both ways.

The tracks in B.30.b going to MORY was seen in use by wagons at 6 am.

At 11.15 am 2 limbers were seen going South on the road at B.23.a.15.20.

Trains.

During the day 4 trains were seen on the normal gauge railway between VAULX - VRAUCOURT and FREMICOURT going South and 1 going N.

The light railway in B.23 was in use - 3 trains were seen going East and 1 West.

Posts.

Sentries were seen at A.8.a.6.4, A.8.a.7.5, A.8.d.5.1, F.12.c.6.4 and A.3.a.65.25.

Work.

New work is visible on the main trench line at A.8.a.55.30 and at A.13.d.5.3.

Lights.

During the gas projection on our right last night the enemy we sent up numerous Red and Green flares.

Fires.

A fire was observed burning in COURCELLES between 1.45 am and 5 am this morning.

	Barometer	Temperature.	
		Max.	Min.
July 3rd	29.80	74	53
July 4th	29.85	62	49

2/Lieut,
for Lieut. Colonel,
General Staff, 2nd Division.

4/7/18.

2nd Division Tactical Summary No. 28.

For 24 hours ending 8 am 5/7/18.

Not to be taken forward of Bn. H.Q. in the line.

1. OPERATIONS.

The situation remains unchanged.

Artillery. Our artillery continued to harass the enemy in his forward and back areas. At 12 noon the field guns and 4.5" Hows. shelled enemy new work and dugouts in F.8.a, and 300 rounds were fired by our 18-pdrs. on enemy wire in F.12.a.

During the night the usual harassing fire was carried out on roads and tracks, and enemy centres of activity.

The 6" Hows. were active against the Sunken road in A.20.d & b, the banks in A.20.d and A.14.central and the new trench A.15.a.05.85 to A.14.b.8.9. The 60-pdrs. shelled the hostile roads, tracks, light railways and hutments opposite the Divisional front.

Hostile artillery was slightly more active than usual. At 4.45pm about 150 rounds of 5.9s. fell in the vicinity of ADINFER and between 4.15 pm and 6 pm about 200 4.2s. fell in the area around F.2.d.8.2 in the COJEUL VALLEY.

Other targets for hostile artillery were the area just N. of BILLY'S BANK, LE QUESNOY FARM and AYETTE.

Trench Mortars. Our 6" Newtons fired about 35 rounds on suspected T.M. positions at F.23.a.8.7, (N. of ABLAINZEVILLE) and F.18.a.30.50 and the surrounding areas, in retaliation for hostile activity.

The 3" Stokes fired 153 rounds on selected targets in the enemy forward area.

Hostile Minenwerfer were occasionally active on the Right and Centre Brigade fronts. The points receiving attention were principally F.18.d.6.2 and F.5.d.5.6.

Machine Guns. Our machine guns harassed the enemy approaches to his forward areas during the night.

The Western exits of MOYENNEVILLE, the shell hole positions in A.8.a and new work in the enemy lines were dealt with, 7500 rounds being fired. 750 rounds were fired at hostile aircraft.

Hostile machine guns fired occasional bursts during the night.

Aircraft. Hostile machines were over our lines at 7.30 am, 1.30 pm and 6.45 pm, the latter machine had a RED Fuselage, a white tail with a black cross.

Our machines were active at intervals patrolling our forward areas.

Patrols. A fighting patrol of the Left Bde. consisting of 14 O.Rs. under 2/Lt.BLAIR went out towards the hostile post at S.26.d.7.2. When about 150 yds. out the officer, 1 N.C.O. and 1 man went forward to reconnoitre and came under heavy M.G. fire from approx. S.26.d.9.3 and the officer was wounded. A German who exposed himself was shot and seen to fall. The patrol returned to our lines and the post was engaged with 3" Stokes, Lewis Guns sweeping the ground around it.

Later a patrol of 1 N.C.O. and 2 men visited the post and found it badly damaged, also the wire in front of it, but there were no signs of the enemy.

2/Lt.W.L.DUNSTALL and 2 O.Rs. when out on patrol in A.1.b heard work in progress at A.1.b.9.8.

P.T.O.

2/Lt. RICKETTS and 3 O.Rs. located a hostile post at approx. F.11.d.35.20 and reported a T.M. active from F.18.a.35.90 (Previously suspected).

2/Lt. T.G.J. BINNIE and 4 O.Rs. patrolling in F.17.a reported a large party digging East of the road at F.17.a.7.5. The patrol found some insulated wires running from the enemy's line and disappearing into the ground in the direction of our trenches, these were cut about by the patrol about 80 yards from our line.

2. INTELLIGENCE.

Movement. Hostile movement was normal yesterday. Individual movement was reported in the usual areas. Between 4.30 am and 7 am a few parties of men varying from 3 to 6 in number were seen going towards the enemy rear on the tracks in A.14.d and A.20.a & c.

At 8.35 am 6 parties carrying stretchers were seen going in the direction of COURCELLES from A.20.c. Movement was seen at A.3.c.6.2 and in the trenches in A.8.a & c.

Timber was seen being carried along the trench at A.2.d.85.70.

Transport. 2 G.S. wagons were seen on the ACHIET LE GRAND-COURCELLES Rd

Work. New earth is reported visible at A.3.c.2.7, A.3.c.6.4 and A.7.d.2.4. Wiring is in progress at F.12.c.1.7 and F.12.a.4.2; work also appears to have been done in the trench at these points.

Posts. A snipers post is suspected at A.3.c.6.2, (movement has been reported about this point), A.7.b.25.75 and A.7.b.35.50.

General. During our shelling yesterday afternoon, some of the enemy were reported to have crawled away from the post at F.12.a.4.2.

At 7.45 pm a large explosion took place just E. of COURCELLES; columns of smoke were seen to rise.

	Barometer.	Max. Temp.	Min. Temp.
July 4th	29.85	62	49
July 5th	29.80	68	48

July 6th   Sun rises 3.46 am.
           Sun sets 7.59 pm.

C.C. Timms
2/Lieut.
for Lieut. Colonel,
General Staff, 2nd Division.

5/7/18.

* The usual transport movement was seen on the ECOUST-BAPAUME Rd. At 9.10 am a motor ambulance was seen on the COURCELLES-ABLAINZEVILLE Road going towards COURCELLES.

2nd Division Tactical Summary No. 139
For 24 hours ending 8 am 6/7/18.

Not to be taken forward of Bn. H.Q. in the line.

1. OPERATIONS.

The situation remains unchanged.

Artillery. Our artillery carried out registration and harassed the enemy's centres of activity at intervals throughout the period.

Light concentrations were fired by our 18-pdrs. and 4.5" Hows. on to the T.M. emplacements in ABLAINZEVELLE in retaliation for enemy activity.

At 2.30 am a burst of fire was fired on A.7.d.40.25 to A.7.d.52.22 and at 2.45 am on F.12.b.81.25 to A.7.d.15.25. Harassing fire on roads and tracks was kept up during the night.

The 60-pdrs. were active against hostile roads, tracks and light railways on the Divisional front.

6" Hows. fired on enemy dug-outs, H.Qs., new work and trenches.

Hostile artillery was normally active. A concentration of 4.2s. was fired into X.21.d, otherwise the hostile fire was scattered, harassing the forward areas at intervals, and the principal targets were AYETTE, DOUCHY, COJEUL VALLEY and ADINFER VILLAGE.

Trench Mortars. Our T.Ms. were active, the 3" Stokes fired 50 rounds on to enemy work at A.2.d.6.5 and between 10.40 pm and 11.30 pm, 60 rounds on the enemy trench and suspected post from F.12.a.4.2 to F.12.a.40.35.

87 rounds were fired on the huts in F.17.c & d, and the road at F.17.a.80.25.

The 6" Newtons were active against the road at F.6.c.4.3, the enemy post at F.12.a.4.2, the bank at A.2.c.4.2 and enemy work in F.18.a. 96 rounds were fired.

Hostile minenwerfer were rather more active on the Right Bde. front where M.T.Ms. and L.T.Ms. fell at intervals throughout the day damaging our front line from F.23.a.1.6 to F.16.d.8.4.

Machine Guns. Our M.Gs. fired 8000 rounds as harassing fire on the following targets:- New work around F.23.b.0.6, F.17.d.0.6, A.8.a.2.0 and A.8.c.3.3, the trenches and shell holes in S.27.c.

Hostile machine guns fired occasional bursts at night, principally between the hours of 2 am and 4 am.

Patrols. 2/Lt.WALLIS and 4 O.Rs. left our lines at F.11.b.60.10 and proceeded in a S.E. direction until fired on by a M.G. from F.11.d. 45.30.

The wire in front of this post appears to have been thickened. Nothing else of importance was seen by the patrol.

2/Lt.FORD and 5 O.Rs. left our line at A.5.d.9.2 and proceeded along the AYETTE-MOYENNEVILLE Road for about 200 yds. Nothing was seen of the enemy. The enemy wire in the vicinity of the road appears to be in good condition.

One officer and 8 O.Rs. of the Right Bde. went out for the purpose of ascertaining the nature of the work in progress in the huts at F.17.d.2.4. They were, however, held up by heavy M.G. fire and could get no information.

Aircraft. There was a slight increase in hostile activity yesterday.

From 8 am to 9 am an E.A. flew over our lines until driven off by A.A. and M.G. fire.

At 10.15 am, 5 E.A. crossed our lines and were heavily engaged and driven back.

At noon 6 E.A. were over our forward area.

Our machines were active, patrolling our forward areas at intervals.

P.T.O.

2. INTELLIGENCE.

Movement. Movement throughout the day was normal and no large parties were seen.

3 men were seen carrying timber at A.3.a.7.2.

At 6.15 am 3 mounted men were observed going N. along the road at A.22.c.1.3.

At 8.55 am 2 men were seen standing on the parapet of the trench at A.14.c.15.25.

Individual movement was seen along the road in A.5.c & d, in A.20.b and in A.14.c.

Transport. The usual transport was seen on the ECOUST-BAPAUME Road, and a few wagons were seen on the COURCELLES-ACHIET LE GRAND Road. The ST LEGER-MORY Road in B.10.d was also occasionally in use for wagons.

2 4-horsed wagons were seen on the CROISELLES-VRAUCOURT Road

Trains. At 8.15 am a light engine was seen in B.22.b where it was stationary for 25 minutes afterwards moving towards MORY.

At 8.57 am 2 trains went from MORY to ECOUST.

Work. New work is in progress at A.2.c.25.75 and digging was seen at A.27.b.35.85.

Wire is visible from A.2.a.9.4 to A.2.b.20.35.

The enemy post at A.3.a.7.2 has been deepened and at A.2.c.2.2 a loophole is now visible with about 30 yds. of concertina wire in front of it.

Posts. A sniper was active from F.11.d.50.35 until silenced by rifle grenades.

Batteries. The following grid bearings taken from F.2.b.8.5 on guns thought to be firing from A.22.d - 119° 15' and 119° 5'.

Grid bearings on active guns taken from X.27.d.65.75 were 131°25' (each time this gun fired 2 men were seen observing from A.20.b.55.40), 132° (4.2") and 124° 30' (5.9").

	Barometer.	Max. temp.	Min temp.
July 5th	29.80	68	48
July 6th	29.65	68	54

July 7th	Sun rises 3.48 am	Moon rises 2.48 am.
	Sun sets 7.58 pm	Moon sets 7.16 pm

2/Lieut.
for Lieut. Colonel,
General Staff, 2nd Division.

6/7/18.

2nd Division Tactical Summary No.40.
For 24 hours ending 8 am 7/7/18.

Not to be taken forward of Battn. H.Q. in the line.

1. OPERATIONS.

The situation is unchanged.

Artillery.   Our field artillery carried out normal registration and calibration and fired at all observed movement within range.   T.Ms. in ABLAINZEVILLE were engaged at noon and 7 pm by 4.5" Hows and new work in F.18.a and F.17.d was fired on by field guns and Hows.   Known centres of activity and dead ground were harassed with odd bursts during the day and night.

Enemy artillery was very quiet.   There was slight shelling of the forward area of the Left Bde. and of ADINFER WOOD, AYETTE, DOUCHY, F.14.d & 20.b.

Trench Mortars.   Our 6" Newtons fired 187 rounds during the period on the following targets:-   Road running through F.6.c and A.1.c, the enemy front line in A.8.a, the withy bed in A.2.c, the M.G. emplacement at A.7.a.90.95 and the hutments in F.17.d and F.23.b.   Good results were obtained.   3" Stokes fired 43 rounds at E.A., 28 rounds on the enemy trench in A.2.d scoring several direct hits.   16 rounds on the suspected T.M. at A.3.a.55.25 and 35 rounds on the enemy lines in F.17. (Total T.M. bombs fired 309).

Hostile minenwerfer were inactive except on the extreme right. A few L.T.Ms. were active against the road in F.16.d and on our front in F.11.c on two occasions during the day.

Machine Guns.   Our Vickers guns fired 4,500 rounds on the enemy's front system in S.27.c.central and on new work in F.23.b and F.17.d. 1850 rounds were fired on low flying enemy aircraft.

Enemy M.G. activity was normal.

Aircraft.   Our aeroplanes were particularly active throughout the day. Several enemy machines are reported to have been seen but none were flying low.   3 which crossed our lines during the morning between 7 and 9 am were driven off by A.A. fire.

Patrols.   Lt.OXENDEN M.C. M.G.Battn., Lieut.BLYTH and 6 O.Rs. went out to reconnoitre the enemy's front system about S.27.c.central and on finding it to be   occupied returned with the information.   An M.G. laid by day thereupon opened fire on this area and harassed it until the morning

2/Lt.LAUGHTON and 4 O.Rs. reconnoitred each side of the AYETTE-MOYENNEVILLE Rd. for a distance of 450 yds. from our line.   An enemy rifle was discovered near the two tall trees at F.6.c.4.3 but the post was unoccupied.   All the cubby holes in the bank were searched but found empty.   At a point about 300 yds. S.E. from the two trees the patrol came upon what was apparently a vacated M.G. position from which a small but well worn footpath led away with a broken plain wire lying alongside.   The party returned to our lines without seeing or hearing anything of the enemy.

2/Lt.H.J.SMITH and 12 O.Rs. went out at 12 midnight from F.17.c.1.5. No sign of the enemy was seen in F.17.a or c. until 2.15 am when a large enemy patrol of about 40 men was observed moving South.   Fire was opened on the hostile party which took cover in the sunken road.

Reconnaissance patrols were also carried out under Lieut.COLVILL and 2/Lts.FOX, KIRKPATRICK and CATCHPOLE.   Voices were heard from the sunken road in front of the point F.6.c.7.6 and sounds of work were heard in the sunken road by a patrol in A.1.a.   A patrol in A.2.a between 11.15 pm and 12.15 am reports no sign of movement in the sunken road during its tour.

An enemy working party of about 20 was also seen to come from the direction of the AERODROME at 11.15 pm.   It picked up tools near a bush and disappeared.

P.T.O.

- 2 -

2. INTELLIGENCE.

Movement. Individual movement seen in the forward areas was normal. At 9.15 pm 5 pair-horse wagons went North along the road at A.22.c.1.5. At 5.25 am 1 wagon full of men went South and another at 5.50 am. At the same time a 4-horsed wagon with two led horses went South at the same point with 4 men seated on top of what appeared to be a load of grass and 2 walking behind.

Enemy Defences. Ground observers report work in progress at the AERODROME and digging at A.20.c.9.5.
A new belt of concertina is visible at F.6.c.7.2.

Lights & Signals. Between 1.30 am and 2.15 am while enemy artillery was firing on the front of the Left Brigade, the enemy infantry sent up a large number of red lights, both single and double. These were apparently a lengthen range signal as many of the rounds were falling short of our line.
An enemy lamp was signalling at 10.30 pm from a direction 5° left of COURCELLES Church from X.21.c.9.9.

Enemy Artillery. Batteries were observed in action at the following grid bearings from F.10.c.05.55 - 112° (yellowish brown smoke), 96° and 116°.

Meteorological.

	Barometer.	Max.Temp.	Min.Temp.
July 6th	29.65	68	54
July 7th	29.70	70	48
July 8th	Sun rises 3.47 am.		Sun sets 7.58 pm.
	Moon rises 3.55 am		Moon sets 7.53 pm.

7/7/18.

Lieut.
for Lieut.
General Staff, 2N

2nd Division Tactical Summary No.41.
For 24 hours ending 8 am 8/7/18.

Not to be taken forward of Battn. H.Q. in the line.

1. OPERATIONS.

The situation remains unchanged.

Artillery. Throughout the day our artillery continued to harass the enemy's forward areas. Registration and calibration was carried out as usual. 4.5" Hows. engaged AW.7 at 4.0 pm and fired 100 rounds on T.Ms. in ABLAINZEVILLE., in retaliation for activity on our right front.

During the night gas shell was fired on A.9.b and A.10.a and three concentrations put down on selected points in AERODROME TRENCH and A.1.d. Trenches and known centres of activity and new work were continually harassed.

Hostile artillery was quiet on our front line except for a slight concentration on our trenches in F.23.a between 12.30 and 1.15 am. Harassing fire on our forward area increased. A few rounds were fired on MONCHY AU BOIS between 10 pm and midnight, and POMMIER was engaged by long range guns. About 20 Yellow Cross gas shells were fired on F.20.b and F.16.c between 2 and 3 am.

Trench Mortars. Our 6" Newtons fired 44 rounds during the period on :- Road and trench junction in A.3.a.35.25, new work in A.2.c, and the AYETTE-ABLAINZEVILLE Rd. in F.17.a. 6" Stokes engaged low flying E.A. and hostile posts East of AYETTE.

Hostile T.Ms. were inactive except on our right. Our retaliation by 6" Newtons and 4.5" Hows. was rapid and effective.

Machine Guns. 3500 rounds were fired on new work in F.13.d and F.18.c and the hutments North of ABLAINZEVILLE. 750 rounds were fired at E.A.
The enemy's M.Gs. showed normal activity.

Aircraft. Fairly active. 2 E.As. were attacked by 3 of our Scouts – one E.A. was reported crashed and the other driven down under control.

Patrols. 2/Lt.STEADMAN and 2 O.Rs. patrolled in A.1.b from 1.15 to 2.30 am. Sounds of digging and wiring were heard in the sunken road in A.1.b.

2/Lt.SAWERS and 4 O.Rs. reconnoitred the bank at A.2.a.9.3 when a light was fired and M.G. fire opened on the patrol from A.2.a.8.2 approx. 1 man was wounded. M.G. and Granatenwerfer fired on the patrol which withdrew bringing the wounded man with them.

2/Lt.PEARSON and 6 O.Rs. were out between 11.15 pm and midnight. None of the enemy were encountered.

2/Lt.LOUGHTON and 4 O.Rs. reconnoitred the AYETTE-MOYENNEVILLE Rd. as far as the TWO TREES. Nothing was seen or heard of the enemy.

4 officers and 16 O.Rs. went out to gain access to the enemy's outpost line before he took up his position for the night.

Thick wire was encountered at F.12.a.2.8 and movement was seen at F.12.a.4.2. One party established themselves with a Lewis Gun inside the enemy's wire near this point and another approached the post at F.12.a.4.2 This was found strongly held and is apparently held by day as well as by night.

2/Lt.SMITH and 12 O.Rs. left F.17.c.1.8 at midnight to secure identifications from hostile patrols. None of the enemy were encountered and no movement observed. Patrol returned to our lines at 2.15 am.

1 Sgt. and 20 O.Rs. left our lines at 10.30 pm to ambush a hostile working party that had been observed the night before assembling at the bush in F.17.b. No enemy were seen. Patrol returned at 12.15 am.

P.T.O.

2. INTELLIGENCE.

Movement. Individual movement was normal throughout the period.
A good deal of individual movement was seen W. & N.W. of COURCELLES between 6 and 9 am. This was engaged. The trench at A.21.d.60.35 was seen to be occupied.

Enemy Defences. Wire appears to have been strengthened between A.8.a.35.20 and A.8.c.25.10. Work was in progress in the trench at F.11.d.4.2.
A M.G. was located at A.2.c.8.2.

Lights & Signals. The usual "flaming onions" were put up on the approach of our night bombing machines. Three hostile searchlights were active.

Fires & Explosions. At 9.15 pm an explosion was caused in COURCELLES. The subsequent fire lasted two minutes. At 6.15 pm a small dump blew up West of MOYENNEVILLE at grid bearing of 113° from E.15.d.35.20.

Enemy Artillery. A 5.9" H.V. gun was seen firing at 5.20 pm and 5.38 pm at a grid bearing of 119° from F.2.b.8.8.
AY.16 was active between 3.15 and 3.30 pm.

Meteorological.

	Batometer.	Max.Temp.	Min.Temp.
July 7th	29.70	70	48
July 8th	29.35	83	53

July 9th	Sun rises 3.48 am	Sun sets 7.57 pm.
	Moon rises 5.6 am	Moon sets 8.23 pm.

8/7/18.

Lieut.
for Lieut. Colonel,
General Staff, 2nd Division.

2nd Division Tactical Summary No.42.
For 24 hours ending 8 am 9/7/18.

Not to be taken forward of Bn. H.Q. in the line.

1. OPERATIONS.

The situation is unchanged.

Artillery. Our artillery engaged hostile movement, new work and centres of activity during the day. The hostile T.Ms. in ABLAINZEVILLE received retaliatory fire from 4.5" Hows. three times during the day.

At 5.30 pm a practice barrage of H.E. and smoke was successfully carried out by the Left Group on the area W. and N.W. of MOYENNEVILLE. 170 rounds were expended by 18-pdrs. in cutting wire in F.18.a.

Between 9 pm and 1 am the enemy's shell hole & trench system in A.1.d, A.7 and A.8 were kept under constant fire.

Hostile artillery was normal. A few Yellow Cross gas shells fell in the COJEUL VALLEY between 9 pm and 10 pm. The retaliation to our practice barrage lasted 15 minutes and was mainly directed against the Sector on our left.

Our front line in F.16.d and F.22.b was lightly shelled during the morning, and the valley in F.20.b and F.15.c received attention at midnight. The area N.E. of MONCHY AU BOIS was harassed from 7 to 7.30 pm.

Trench Mortars. 134 rounds were fired with good results by our 6" Newtons on the following targets:- F.12.a.20.13, new work in F.12.c and F.17.a, the withy bank in A.7.a, the road in F.6.c, wire in F.12.c and A.1.c and AERODROME TRENCH in A.8.a. 3" Stokes fired 34 rounds on A.3.a.50.25 and the hutments North of ABLAINZEVILLE. 7 rounds were fired at E.A.

Enemy L.T.Ms. were active against our front line South of AYETTE at intervals during the day.

Machine Guns. Our M.Gs. fired 5500 rounds on enemy work and shell holes and 500 rounds direct fire on A.1.d.2.5. During the operation a hostile M.G. was engaged at A.7.b.central (approx.) and is thought to have been put out of action.

Hostile M.Gs. normal.

Aircraft. 4 hostile machines patrolled the area North of COURCELLES at 7.30 am. At 8.20 1 machine crossed our lines over A.2 but was driven by A.A. and M.G. fire. 2 machines patrolled our lines at 9.20 am and at 9.45 am. One was observed over AYETTE.

Patrols. 2/Lt.HART and 2 O.Rs. went out at 12.30 am and proceeded to A.2.a.3.1. No sounds of the enemy were heard. Patrol returned at 1.10 am.

Sgt.HOLDEN and 2 O.Rs. reconnoitred A.1.a. None of the enemy were seen or heard.

2/Lt.BENNETT and 4 O.Rs. left our lines at F.5.b.8.1 to examine the road running East from that point. Patrol proceeded East for 300x and then turned South reaching the AYETTE - MOYENNEVILLE Road near the TWO TREES (F.6.c.4.3). Patrol waited here for a few minutes and then returned to our trenches having seen and heard nothing of the enemy.

One Sgt. and 9 O.Rs. left our lines at 10.30 pm and returned at 11.30 pm. The enemy were heard moving corrugated iron sheets in F.17.d and Very lights were fired from F.11.d.4.2. All shell holes investigated by the patrol were found to contain stick grenades.

P.T.O.

- 2 -

2/Lt.MURRAY and 4 O.Rs. were out from 10.30 pm to 12 midnight. Patrol passed through the enemy wire and across the road 25 yards North of post at F.17.a.7.4. This post appeared to be strongly held with a M.G. A working party was heard in F.17.d.

2/Lt.STOKES and 8 O.Rs. patrolled F.17.c from 12 midnight to 2 am. The post at F.17.c.7.4 was found unoccupied. Patrol worked South to unoccupied post at F.17.c.4.2 approx. and were fired on by M.G. from F.17.c.8.2.

2. INTELLIGENCE.

Movement. The usual individual movement N. and N.W. of COURCELLES was observed. At 6.50 am 2 parties each of 10 men moved from A.14.c.7.5 to the trench at A.14.c.5.2; they were accompanied by stretcher bearers. The trench at A.21.d.60.55 was again seen to be occupied and men were seen shaking blankets at this point.

At 9.15 pm 2 parties of 5 men each went N.E. along the COURCELLES - LOGEAST WOOD Road in A.20.c. At 5.20 pm about 50 men were seen on the track in B.30.b going towards MORY.

Transport. 6 2-horsed wagons went North on road in A.22.c.1.3 at 8.5pm. At 5.27 am 4 men were seen loading a wagon with grass at A.21.d.9.6. The wagon then proceeded North and a few minutes later was seen moving South, loaded with grass.

Enemy Defences. Work has been done on the trench at F.11.d.4.3

Fires & Explosions. An explosion took place at 10 pm - location uncertain. At 10.30 pm a fire was observed West of MOYENNEVILLE.

Enemy Artillery. At 6.15 pm the puff of a gun shelling S.26.a & b. was observed on a true bearing of 102° 30' from X.27.d.65.75.

Meteorological.

	Barometer.	Max.Temp.	Min Temp.
July 8th	29.35	83	53
July 9th	29.25	78	55
July 10th	Sun rises 3.49 am	Sun sets 7.56 pm	
	Moon rises 6.17 am	Moon sets 8.47.	

................Lieut.
for Lieut. Colonel,
General Staff, 2nd Division.

9/7/18.

2nd Division Tactical Summary No.43
For 24 hours ending 8 am 10/7/18.

Not to be taken forward of Battn. H.Q. in the line.

1. OPERATIONS.

There is no change in the situation.

Artillery. The usual harassing fire was continued. 18-pdrs. fired 300 rounds on enemy posts East of AYETTE and 300 rounds on enemy wire in the same locality. 4.5" Hows. engaged AY.15 and AY.11 intermittently during the day and retaliated on enemy T.Ms.

At night AERODROME TRENCH in A.8 and shell holes in A.7 were brought under fire.

Centre Group carried out a practice S.O.S..

Hostile artillery was normal except on our extreme right where the AYETTE-BUCQUOY Road received incessant attention from 5.9s. and 4.2s.

ADINFER was shelled between 7 and 8 pm and MONCHY AU BOIS was again engaged.

Trench Mortars. 6" Newtons fired 200 rounds on F.23.a.3.7 and new work in F.18.a.

The enemy T.Ms. were less active than usual.

Machine Guns. 7500 rounds were fired by our M.Gs. on new work and the enemy's shell hole system in A.8.a. 700 rounds were fired at E.A.

Hostile M.Gs. normal.

Aircraft. Hostile activity normal. Ground observers report one of our machines was apparently brought down near COURCELLES. A hostile K.B. was shot down by 2 of our machines at 8.30 am.

Patrols. Cpl.FOGGO and 2 O.Rs. patrolled A.1.b from 2 to 2.40 am. Shouting was heard from A.2.central as well as metallic noises as of moving a T.M. or M.G. from A.1.d.

2/Lt.MARTIN and 4 O.Rs. left F.11.b.5.1 at midnight. Patrol proceeded S.E. for about 200x. A Very light was fired from F.12.c.2.8 (approx.) and movement was observed on road at F.12.a.20.05. Patrol then continued S.E. and halted at F.11.d.3.4. A Very light was fired from F.11.d.5.3. Patrol entered our lines at 1.15 am.

2/Lt.BECKWITH and 4 O.Rs. left F.5.d.85.20, reached the TWO TREES (F.6.c.4.3). Wiring had been reported near F.12.a.48.30 - the officer and 1 O.R. went forward to F.6.c.3.0 where they waited about 25 minutes. Nothing was seen or heard of the enemy. Patrol then proceeded along AYETTE-MOYENNEVILLE Road for about 200x and then turned N.W. and re-entered our lines at F.5.b.80.15. No signs of the enemy were observed.

2/Lt.SANDERS and 9 O.Rs. were out from 11.30 pm to 1.15 am. F.17.d was reconnoitred and F.23.a.6.9 (approx.) reached. No enemy were encountered.

2. INTELLIGENCE.

Movement. A decrease in individual movement is reported. No large parties were observed.

Transport. At 4.15 am 8 wagons were seen on the track in A.27.b proceeding towards the COURCELLES-ACHIET LE GRAND Road.

Trains. At 9 am and again at 6.15 pm a train was observed on the normal gauge in I.7 going North.

Between 6.30 and 7.15 pm 4 trains were seen on the same line all going South. An engine with 10 trucks was seen going South on the light railway in I.7 at 8.30 pm.

P.T.O.

Enemy Defences. The wire at F.6.c.5.4 has been improved. A new trench about 30 yards long is reported at A.14.b.3.1. The post at F.17.a.7.4 has been worked on. Men working on AERODROME TRENCH in A.8 were engaged.

Observation Posts. The O.P. A.9.b.2.7 is reported to be still in use.

Headquarters. Smoke was seen rising from H.Q. at A.16.b.50.15.

General. At 3.15 pm a black dog left A.8.d.1.2 and was seen to go over the ridge towards COURCELLES. It returned an hour later.

Enemy Artillery. A H.V. gun was observed firing on T.B. of 124° 30' from X.27.d.65.75.

Meteorological.

	Barometer.	Max.Temp.	Min.Temp.
July 9th	29.25	78	55
July 10th	29.28	64	54

July 11th	Sun rises 3.50 am	Sun sets 7.56 pm.
	Moon rises 7.26 am	Moon sets 9.7 pm.

10/7/18.

............Lieut.
for Lieut. Colonel,
General Staff, 2nd Division.

2nd Division Tactical Summary No.44.
For 24 hours ending 8 am 11/7/18.

Not to be taken forward of Bn. H.Q. in the line.

1. OPERATIONS.

The situation is unchanged. At 11.30 pm a party of 1 N.C.O. and 4 men of the Left Battn. Left Bde. which was out to cover one of our wiring parties was attacked by a German patrol strength estimated at 8. In the hand to hand fight which ensued 2 Germans were shot and one made prisoner. The remainder retired. 2 of our men were wounded including the N.C.O. who afterwards died. The prisoner taken belongs to the 452nd I.R. 234th Division (normal).

Artillery. Our field artillery carried out the usual harassing fire on enemy centres of movement and on dead ground within range. New work in F.18.a & c. was also engaged. At 8 am 200 rounds 18-pdr. were fired on the wire in F.18.a and F.6.c with satisfactory results and at 5 pm a further 100 rounds were fired on these points. S.O.S. tests were carried out at 10.20 pm and 2.40 am by the Centre Group. At 10.30 am a heavy concentration was fired on F.23.b & d and F.24 and at 3 pm this was repeated by the Artillery of the Division on our right, heavy and siege artillery co-operating. Between 3 and 4 pm 4 .5" Hows. carried out a destructive shoot of 150 rounds on T.Ms. about F.23.d.6.8. Several hits were obtained on the emplacements.

Enemy artillery continued to be very quiet. There was some slight shelling of the COJEUL VALLEY, North end of ADINFER WOOD in X.21.c, MONCHY, DOUCHY, LE QUESNOY FARM and AYETTE.

Trench Mortars. Our 6" mortars fired 79 rounds on the enemy trench in F.17.a & c. Direct hits were scored and camouflage & timber were thrown up at F.17.c.72.82. 8 rounds were fired on enemy T.Ms. at F.17.c.5.1. 3" mortars fired 30 rounds on the huts and the road in F.17.a & c, and a few rounds at enemy aircraft.

Enemy minenwerfer were completely inactive except on the front of the Right Bn. Right Bde. where a light trench mortar was active in bursts from F.23.d.55.70. It is reported that after the last round of each burst 3 Germans carried the gun from the emplacement and got into the trench at F.23.d.7.7.

Machine Guns. Our M.Gs. fired 7500 rounds on the enemy positions and work in A.3.a, F.23.b to F.17.d and between A.13.d and F.18.c.
Enemy M.G. activity was normal.

Aircraft. Air activity was slightly less than on the previous day especially so in the case of the enemy. One enemy artillery machine made several attempts to cross our line in the early morning but was eventually driven off by our A.A. and Scouts. Our aeroplanes were active as usual in reconnaissance, artillery and photographic work.

Patrols. 2/Lt.DOIG and 8 O.Rs. of the Right Battn. Left Bde. went out at 12.5 am to a point near the sunken road in F.6.c. No movement was seen on the road but voices were heard on the South side. Transport could be heard apparently on the MOYENNEVILLE-ABLAINZEVILLE Rd. and a working party in the neighbourhood of F.6.c.3.3.

2/Lt.WILLIAMS and 3 O.Rs. of the same Battn. were out between 11.40 pm and 1.25 am. The movements of the party were hampered all the time by a hostile M.G. active about A.2.central. When the patrol was at A.1.b.6.0 about 1 am, 4 Germans without equipment were seen running back to their lines. An M.G. was active at approx. A.1.d.95.80 and as many as 7 or 8 M.Gs. fired intermittently from position about 200 yds. South of the sunken road.

P.T.O.

2. INTELLIGENCE.

Movement. Movement in the forward areas was normal, and in the usual places. In the back areas there was a considerable increase in the amount of transport observed especially on the roads in B.30.b. During the afternoon there was considerable activity on all the railways about BAPAUME and this activity continued early this morning. Visibility was very good except during rain storms.

Enemy Work. New work is reported in A.20.b & d. and A.14.a. Digging was seen at A.13.d.5.7 and in the enemy trench in A.15.c. Work was also observed in progress at A.13.d.4.7 and at A.20.d.1.9. The trenches at F.11.d.5.3 and 3.1 have been repaired.

Posts. The post at F.12.c.2.8 was seen to be occupied yesterday. The post in the vicinity of F.6.c.4.3 was occupied at 10.30 pm. Very lights were seen to go up from this point. An O.P. is suspected at A.20.c.60.05. Very lights are also reported by a patrol at F.12.c.3.8.

234th Division. Each of the Regts. of the 234th Regt. has apparently a storm Company which is used as a training Coy. while the Division is in the line. All 3 storm Coys. appear to be located at either CANTIN or BLECOURT.

There will probably be an inter-Battn. relief in the Sector of the 452nd Inf. Regt. on the night of 14th, but it appears that the enemy postpones his reliefs if he has any reason to believe that we are aware of the date. The harassing fire of our artillery has had considerable moral and material effect on the troops of this Regt. (see attached translation of extracts from prisoner's diary).

It is probable that the 452nd Regt. adheres to the usual arrangement of one Battn. in the front line, one in support and one in rear. The second Battn. is at present in line, the first in support and the third in rest. The support Battn. appears to be located in the railway embankment and the trenches on either side of the railway South of MOYENNEVILLE. Of the Battn. in line it is probable that only three Coys. are actually in the front line and one is in close support in or about the outskirts of MOYENNEVILLE.

The 7th Coy. 452nd I.R. has a strength of about 108 all ranks with 6 L.M.Gs.

The field kitchens of 2nd battn. 452nd I.R. come up to a point about 20 minutes walk from the front line, probably along one of the roads in A.11.c East of THE HALTE.

Meteorological.

	Barometer.	Max.Temp.	Min.Temp.
July 10th	29.28	64	54
July 11th	29.35	72	47

July 12th   Sun rises 4.51 am   Sun sets 8.55 pm
            Moon rises 9.35 am   Moon sets 10.26 pm.
            (All Summer Time).

J. Macgwan,
Lieut.
for Lieut. Colonel,
General Staff, 2nd Division.

11/7/18.

2nd Division Tactical Summary No.45
For 24 hours ending 8 am 12/7/18.

Not to be taken forward of Bn. H.Q. in the line.

1. OPERATIONS.

The situation is unchanged. Enemy artillery was slightly more active during the period than of late and more movement of individuals than usual was reported in the forward areas during the day. Our artillery dealt with all seen within range.

Artillery. Harassing fire was carried out by siege, heavy and field artillery during the night and day on known centres of movement and enemy activity. Special attention was paid to shell holes in F.23 and A.12.d. Hows. fired on T.M. emplacements in ABLAINZEVILLE and new work in A.7.d. Between 9 and 10 3 N.F. calls were taken up and answered and an S.O.S. test was fired by the Right Group at 10.20 pm. During the morning 200 rounds were fired by 18-pdrs. on the wire in F.12.a and 350 rounds were fired on AERODROME TRENCH in A.7.d, A.8.c and A.7.a during the night.

Hostile artillery was more active than usual although shelling was not particularly heavy. ADINFER, the COJEUL VALLEY in X.24.c and X.29.b, DOUCHY, AYETTE, CARUSO COPSE and LE QUESNOY FARM all received attention from calibres up to 5.9. The area South of DOUCHY was shelled intermittently throughout the day with field and heavy Hows. and the front line of the Right Battn. Right Bde. was heavily shelled between 10.15 and 10.50 am. Between 10.45 pm and 11 pm some gas shells (chlorine) fell between DOUCHY and AYETTE and in the COJEUL VALLEY in X.29. High wind and rain soon dispersed the gas.

Trench Mortars. Our 6" mortars fired 135 rounds on the following targets:-
Camp in F.17.d and F.23.b.
Suspected T.M. in F.23.a.
New work in F.18.a and F.17.central (several hits obtained on supposed M.G. emplacement.
Trench A.12.b.85.65 to A.12.b.80.50 and wire A.12.b.55.55 to A.12.b. 55.75. (concertina wire scattered but no definite gap made).
Hostile Trench mortars were only active on the extreme right of the Divnl. front. 45 light T.M. and Granatenwerfer bombs are reported in all.

Machine Guns. Our Vickers guns fired 7500 rounds on targets as under:-
4000 rounds on enemy work etc. at A.8.a.0.0.
2500 rounds on new enemy work F.17.d.0.6 to F.23.b.0.6.
1000 rounds on A.13.d.4.8 to F.18.c.6.0.
Enemy M.G. fire was normal.

Aircraft. Air activity was normal. Several R.E.A. attempted to cross our lines in the early morning yesterday and again at about 4.30 pm. All were driven off by our A.A. and M.G. fire. At 4.10 am this morning an E.A. flew low (reported 600 ft.) over ESSARTS, E.11.b and the MONCHY-BIENVILLERS Road. It was heavily engaged by our M.G. and L.G. fire but succeeded in recrossing the lines.

Patrols. Cpl. FOWLER and 3 O.Rs. patrolled No Man's Land in A.1.a between 2 am and 3 am. An enemy patrol of 4 was seen to approach our wire but suddenly made off to the enemy line. Sounds of stakes being driven into the ground were heard.

A patrol under Lieut. WALLACE which went out at 10.40 pm and listened at A.2.a.0.2 till 12.15 am reports Very lights fired from the sunken road about A.1.d.3.6.

2/Lt. BARNES and 4 O.Rs. report concertina wire at A.2.a.8.6 and movement on the other side of it. On advancing a Very light was fired & 6 Germans could be plainly seen. The patrol returned and had a L.G. directed on the post. At 1 am the patrol went out again and found no sign of the enemy in that neighbourhood.

P.T.O.

2/Lt. O.L. BRIDGES and 4 O.Rs. went out at 12.5 am from F.11.d.20.75. At about F.11.d.5.5, some enemy equipment was found and sounds were heard from the enemy outpost line.

2/Lt. J.J. EVANS and 9 O.Rs. went out from F.11.b.9.7 on an offensive patrol. The enemy outpost line at F.12.a.45.85 was found to be unoccupied. Patrols proceeded South for about 70 yards when one of the enemy was seen walking towards the post. He was fired on and believed to have been killed. On going forward to search him for an identification the patrol was bombed with Mills bombs from the post probably at F.12.a.5.8. 2/Lt. EVANS and 1 O.R. were wounded. The strength of the enemy in this post was estimated to be 12 to 14. The patrol returned to our lines at 3.15 am.

No signs of the enemy were discovered by a patrol under 2/Lt. G. NORRIS which reconnoitred the area round F.6.c.5.4.

A listening patrol in F.17.a between 11.45 pm and 2.20 am saw and heard nothing of the enemy.

2. INTELLIGENCE.

Movement. Yesterday individual movement in the forward area was greater than it has been for the past week. In the early morning small parties of men in twos and threes were seen on the COURCELLES - ABLAINZEVILLE Rd. and on the tracks in A.20.b. After 9 am only a few individuals were observed in A.20.b.

Abnormal movement was seen in the trenches in A.10.a & c. and dealt with by our artillery during the day. Between 5 and 5.30 am this morning continual individual movement was seen in A.14.c.

2 men were seen observing our lines from about F.18.a.70.25.

3 stretcher cases and a party of 6 of whom 2 had bandaged heads were seen in A.20 during the day.

At 2.40 pm there was considerable movement at A.27.b.9.4.

Transport. There was considerable train movement yesterday morning up to 10 am on the normal gauge and light railway North of BAPAUME. No special tendency of the traffic was noticed.

Individual horse and motor transport on the ECOUST-BAPAUME Road showed a slight tendency Southwards. No convoys were observed.

At 4.55 am this morning 3 wagons with about 20 men loading grass were seen at A.21.d.9.6 and at 5.55 am a 4-horse wagon with 10 men was seen at the same place. Cars (probably ambulances) are reported in A.11. and 6 2-horse wagons were seen this morning passing A.22.c.1.3. At 5.20 am horse transport was seen on the ABLAINZEVILLE-COURCELLES road.

Posts. Sentries were seen at A.15.a.4.2 and F.18.a.7.2.

Machine Guns. Bursts were fired this morning at 4 am from F.11.d.4.3. The gun at A.1.d.5.6 fired short bursts during the night.

Work. Work was seen in progress on the trenches in A.9.b and at A.21.a.5.3. Digging is reported at F.6.c.5.3. The dumping of iron was heard on the road about F.17.c.8.7 during the night. Early this morning several men who appeared bigger than usual were seen working at A.13.c.4.8.

Lights & Signals. At 9.30 pm a large number of double reds from about MOYENNEVILLE, also one double green from in rear of MOYENNEVILLE.

12 midnight to 1 am about 20 double whites at intervals from behind COURCELLES.

2.10 am one double white from the same place.

Twin green lights were seen all along the line behind ABLAINZEVILLE during the night. No apparent result was observed in connection with any of these.

General. Independent observers of the Right Bde. comment on the large stature of some of the enemy seen opposite their front.

Meteorological.

	Barometer.	Max.Temp.	Min.Temp.
July 12th	29.85	68	52

July 13th Sun rises 4.52 am, sets 8.54 pm. (Summer
Moon rises 10.40 am, sets 10.44 pm. (Time.

Lieut.
for Lieut. Colonel G.S.

12/7/18.

2nd Division Tactical Summary No.46.
For 24 hours ending 8 am 13/7/18.

Not to be taken forward of Bn. H.Q. in the line.

1. OPERATIONS.

The situation is unchanged. The day and night passed very quietly.

Artillery. Our field artillery carried out harassing fire during the day and night on the enemy's forward system, roads tracks, centres of movement and deadground. Movement in COURCELLES ABBEY in A.20.d and in the trench in A.8.a was engaged. 70 rounds were fired by an 18-pdr battery on the M.G. post at F.17.a.98.50. 2 direct hits were obtained and camouflage and a shovel were thrown up into the air. At 5 pm 65 18-pdr shell were fired on A.7.d.65.45 from which point smoke was observed to rise. A direct hit removed some camouflage and timber, exposing what looked like a trench tank gun (confirmation required). Field Hows. engaged hostile battery AW.9 with balloon observation at 7 pm. One explosion and 2 fires were caused.

Enemy artillery activity showed a decrease. Only desultory harassing of our forward system, battery areas and tracks is reported and no registration was noticed. COJEUL VALLEY, AYETTE and DOUCHY received most attention. Between 11 pm and midnight about 20 4.2s. and 5.9s. were fired on F.9 and 10.

Trench Mortars. Our 6" mortars fired 140 rounds with satisfactory results on the following targets:-
  Camp in F.17.c and d.
  Work and suspected T.M.Es. in F.18.a.
  Test S.O.S.
  M.G. emplacement at F.17.a.95.35.
  Road and trench junction A.3.a.49.30.
  Timber on road in A.2.b.2.1.
  New work (probably loopholes) on parapet at A.2.d.0.0 - 12 hits were obtained on this work and on the shell hole trench at A.2.c.9.3.
  No enemy minenwerfer activity is reported.

Machine Guns. Our Vickers guns fired 9500 rounds on the following targets:-
  2000 rounds on enemy work around F.23.d.40.65.
  1000 rounds on enemy work F.18.a.35.70 to F.18.a.35.45.
  1000 rounds on ABLAINZEVILLE cross roads F.23.d.41.65.
  4500 rounds on enemy work and trench from A.8.a.0.0 to A.8.c.3.0.
  1000 rounds direct fire on track running North West through A.2.central.
  Enemy M.G. fire was normal.

Aircraft. There was normal air activity yesterday between showers. This morning between 4 and 5 am E.A. were very active over the Divnl. forward area. One machine flew low over ADINFER.

Patrols. 2/Lt.DOIG and 7 O.Rs. report that a Very light was fired from F.6.c.9.4 during their tour about midnight.

2/Lt.ROBERTON and 3 O.Rs. saw 7 Germans walking round the North side of the sunken road about 1.45 am by the light of a parachute flare dropped by one of our aeroplanes. The Germans disappeared at once into the sunken road in A.1.d.

2/Lt.G.W.COLSAR and 30 O.Rs. patrolled F.17.a from midnight to 3 am. The enemy post at F.17.a.5.0 was unoccupied and the trench from F.17.a.8.5 to F.17.a.8.0 was also empty. The M.G. post at F.17.a.80.15 was occupied apparently by about 4 men and an M.G. The wire here has been slightly strengthened but is not a formidable obstacle.

Patrols led by N.C.Os. of the Left Battn. Right Bde. saw no sign of the enemy in No Man's Land opposite our front. Enemy work in the vicinity of F.17.a.7.5 was examined but only shovels were found.

P.T.O.

2. INTELLIGENCE.

Movement. Normal movement was observed in the forward areas yesterday. One party of about 25 was seen at 9 pm going towards COURCELLES in loose dress from about A.20.b. This morning there was considerable movement of men and transport on the COURCELLES-ABLAINZEVILLE Road. Our artillery took action and stretcher parties were afterwards seen in this area. The trenches at A.9.c.85.60, A.14.c.80.65 and A.8.c.35.50 were seen to be occupied.

At 2.25 pm 2 Germans carrying sticks inspected the new trench and spoil which is visible at about A.1.c.1.9. They were fired on but re-appeared at 2.45 pm.

Small dark blue flags about 3 ft. high and 9 inches squares are visible in A.7.b., one apparently being in a shell hole.

Trains and Transport. Horse and motor transport seen in back areas was normal. No convoys were observed. Train movement continues to be considerable but no special tendency of the traffic is reported.

Fires & Explosions. A small explosion was seen in ABLAINZEVILLE during our bombardment this morning - probably S.A.A. in the Cemetery.

A high amount of smoke followed by loud explosions appeared during our shelling at 7 am on a grid bearing of 187° from A.1.b.2.8.

Machine Guns. The enemy M.G. at F.17.a.80.15 and F.11.d.4.3 were active occasionally last night. Guns are reported active at A.2.c.5.2

Posts. Sentries were seen at A.9.a.5.3 and F.18.c.9.2. Flashes of a periscope and movement were observed during the afternoon at A.2.d.6.5. At 5.30 pm our artillery drove 2 men from their post at A.2.c.3.3.

Enemy Work. 2 men were seen working at the cross roads in F.14.a. Digging is reported at A.14.a.5.2. New work is visible at A.13.b.7.4

Enemy Artillery. Infantry observers report a 4.2 battery firing on DOUCHY on a true bearing of 130° from F.2.b.8.8. Another on a T.B. of 135° firing on X.28.a - probably AY.1. This battery was active from 6.20 to 6.30 am and again from 7.5 am to 7.15 am.

Enemy Dispositions. Information obtained to-day tends to show that the 234th Divn. has only 2 Regts. in line. It is believed that the 453rd Regt. is still in back areas. The Order of Battle opposite the Divnl. front is very obscure and appears to be N. to S. 452nd I.R. (with Right Boundary about S.20.central), 451st I.R. with Left Bdry. about A.4.d) From here Southwards it is not known what troops are in line. Two Regts. of the 111th Divn. have been identified South of BUCQUOY. The German Divn. holding the line between BUCQUOY and AYETTE has therefore yet to be identified.

Meteorological.	Barometer.	Max. Temp.	Min. Temp.
July 13th	29.45	71	49

July 13th Sun rises 4.53 am Sun sets 8.83 pm.
Moon rises 11.44 am Moon sets 11.2 pm.
(All Summer Time).

J. McGowan,
Lieut.
for Lieut. Colonel,
General Staff, 2nd Division.

13/7/18.

2nd Division Tactical Summary No.47
For 24 hours ending 8 am 14/7/18.

Not to be taken forward of Bn. H.Q. in the line.

1. OPERATIONS.

There is no change in the situation.

Artillery. Our field and heavy artillery carried out a normal programme of harassing fire on enemy's forward system, centres of activity and routes of approach during the 24 hours. In addition registration and calibration were carried out. Field Hows. fired 60 rounds gas at 11 pm on a hostile 77 mm battery (AY.13) which was shelling F.1 and 2. No more was heard from this battery during the night. Registration on F.13.b.8.2 was also carried out by 4.5s. by balloon observation.

Hostile artillery activity was still slight but showed an increase on the previous day. Our front line and supports in S.26.c & d and F.5.b, X.29.c and X.27.d were shelled by field artillery. AYETTE, DOUCHY and ADINFER WOOD were shelled with 77 mms and 4.2s. Some 5.9s. were reported in the forward system of the Right Battn. Right Bde. during the morning and F.16.b and F.10.d were slightly shelled during the evening - the enemy apparently searching for our 6" mortars.

Trench Mortars. Our 6" mortars fired 55 rounds on the following targets:-
 M.G. nest at F.17.c.95.95 and points F.17.b.2.6 and F.17.b.5.5.
 Suspected M.G. at F.17.b.0.7.)
 Sunken road in F.12.c.) Registration.
 Work on road at F.12.c.95.95.) Satisfactory results were obtained
 New trench in A.7.b.10.50) and a small fire caused.

3" mortars fired 20 rounds on the Right of the Divnl. front in retaliation for enemy fire.

Enemy minenwerfer were more active yesterday. 31 medium bombs are reported from ABLAINZEVILLE on the front of the Right Battn. Right Brigade. Three granatenwerfer bombs fell about F.11.d.2.8. There was no enemy T.M. activity on the left.

Machine Guns. Our M.Gs. fired 6000 rounds on targets as below:-
 4000 rounds on road S.W. of MOYENNEVILLE.
 1000 rounds on enemy work in F.18.a.35.70 to F.18.a.35.52.
 1000 rounds on enemy work in F.23.d.40.65.
 Enemy M.G. fire was normal.

Aircraft. Hostile air activity was normal. At 7.30 pm 1 E.A. flew over DOUCHY and AYETTE at about 2000 feet. It had a red body with white tail and a plain black cross. At 9.25 pm 1 E.A. flew low over ESSARTS and HANNESCAMPS. An enemy bombing plane dropped 4 bombs between 11 pm and midnight in the area BIENVILLERS - BERLES AU BOIS - MONCHY. At 4.30 am this morning 3 E.A. low over our front line were driven off with L.G. and rifle fire.

Patrols. Patrols of the Left Bde. report voices heard South of the sunken road and transport on the AYETTE-COURCELLES Road (probably), at 2 am. Talking was heard and concertina wire was seen at about A.1.d.1.6. Very lights were fired at intervals from the enemy outpost line between 1.40 am and 2.45 am. Very lights were fired and the sounds of moving corrugated iron came from the outpost line (note - the enemy uses corrugated iron with which to construct cubby holes and shelters in his outpost line. See Summary of 11th inst).

2/Lt.N.C.GURNEY and 2 O.Rs. went out from F.23.a.1.8 at 10.45 pm and worked across to F.17.c.7.3. The enemy wire at this point consists of 2 or 3 thin belts. The patrol followed it South to F.23.a.7.7 where single concertina wire only was found. All enemy trenches and posts visited were unoccupied and no enemy were seen or heard. The patrol returned to our lines at 12.30 am.

Other patrols of the Right Bde. report considerable shouting and noise in F.18.a and a working party of 25 to 30 Germans in the enemy posts in F.17.a & b. between 1 and 3 am. A small slit in good repair and showing signs of recent occupation was found at about F.17.a.75.70.

P.T.O.

2. INTELLIGENCE.

Movement. Normal movement was seen on tracks and roads in the forward area and a normal amount of transport is reported on the roads under observation in back areas.

At 7 am a party was seen moving along the communication trench at A.8.b.8.5 and was engaged by our artillery. Between 7 and 8 am individual movement was considerable on the road between A.14.a.0.0 and A.13.d.5.3. The trench at A.9.c.80.75, A.8.d.90.92, A.27.b.2.8 and A.20.b.7.5 was seen to be occupied.

Visibility was good in the early morning but after 6.30 am was only fair.

Posts. A periscope is visible at A.2.d.10.15. A man fired a rifle at our aircraft from A.8.d.4.2. A post is suspected at A.13.b.95.30.

Machine Guns. A M.G. at F.11.d.4.3 was again active last night.

Enemy work. Work continues at A.13.a.7.4. New earth and a slit in the parapet of AERODROME TRENCH is visible at A.8.a.9.7. Men were seen working at A.7.d.5.2 and A.19.b.80.35.

An O.P. or M.G. emplacement apparently of concrete is visible at A.20.d.2.8.

O.Ps. An O.P. is suspected in a mound on the road at about A.15.c.2.1. A slit can be seen at the top of the mound.

A man was observed looking over the trench at A.9.b.25.70 for 3 hours yesterday morning.

Fires & Explosions. At 4 pm and again at 6.40 pm fires were caused among the huts in F.17 and F.23. S.A.A. could be heard exploding.

Meteorological.

	Barometer.	Max.Temp.	Min.Temp.
July 14th	29.40	68	50

July 15th   Sun rises 4.54 am   Sun sets 8.53 pm.
Moon rises 12.50 pm Moon sets 11.21 pm.
(All Summer Times).

J.D. Macewan.
Lieut.
for Lieut. Colonel,
General Staff, 2nd Division.

14/7/18.

2nd Division Tactical Summary No.48.
For 24 hours ending 8 am 15/7/18.

Not to be taken forward of Battn. H.Q. in the line.

1. OPERATIONS.

At 11.30 pm we raided the enemy outpost line astride the AYETTE-COURCELLES Road under cover of a T.M. and artillery barrage. 9 prisoners of the 9th and 10th Coys. 453rd I.R. were captured. Our casualties were 8 slightly wounded. Except for this enterprise the day and night passed without event.

Artillery. Harassing fire was continued on enemy approaches, centres of activity, communications etc. Field guns and 4.5" Hows. engaged targets in A.14.c, A.20.a & b, A.13.b & d, A.15.a & c, A.7.d, COURCELLES and ABLAINZEVELLE; Movement in A.20.b was sniped by 18-pdrs.; the MOYENNEVILLE area received particular attention owing to a suspected local relief in that sector.

Heavy artillery fired on enemy back areas and on targets in A.16.b and d, A.15.b and A.9.d. At 11.30 pm batteries co-operated in the raid referred to above, counter-battery work being particularly successful.

Hostile artillery was quiet during the day and chiefly confined to harassing fire on our forward areas. About 200 rounds of all calibres fell in the area F.11.c, F.17.a, F.16.a, b & d, QUESNOY FARM and Ridge were searched at intervals throughout the day with 77 mm^s fired in short bursts of from 6 to 10 shells; the COJEUL VALLEY, ADINFER WOOD, Sugar Factory and ROTTON RAVINE were shelled occasionally with 4.2s. and 5.9s. Hostile retaliation for our raid was slight. A few gas shells fell in DOUCHY and ADINFER WOOD.

Trench Mortars. Our 6" Newtons and 3" Stokes mortars co-operated with the artillery in support of the raid - 754 rounds being fired by the latter.

Hostile T.M. activity was very slight; a few M.T.Ms. were reported on our extreme right posts and about 15 L.T.Ms. fell in S.25.c.

Machine Guns. Our M.Gs. fired 7000 rounds on the following targets:-
4000 rounds on enemy work in A.8.a.0.0 to A.8.c.3.0 and on trench in A.8.c.
2000 rounds on enemy work in F.23.d.40.65.
1000 rounds on enemy work from F.18.a.35.70 - F.18.a.35.52.
Enemy M.Gs. displayed normal activity.

Aircraft. Hostile air activity was normal. 4 E.As. were patrolling their lines between 6 am and 9.30 am; one of these crossed our line at 6.45 am at 8000 feet but was not engaged.

Between 6 am and 8 am 5 E.As. approached our lines; one flew low over S.26 but disappeared on the approach of our machines. Three enemy observation balloons were in position at 82°, 103°, and 115° grid bearing from F.10.c.05.55 from 9 am to 11.15 am.

Patrols.
Capt.L.P.WALSH, Lieut.MacLURE and 2 O.Rs. left our lines at F.23.a.05.95 at 1 am. A line of plain and barbed wire was found at F.17.c.8.4. Patrol proceeded South, passed through a gap in the wire and reached a point 5 yds. from road at F.17.c.80.35. One of the enemy was seen to cross the road to an isolated hut about 25 yards away and sounds of digging or a bucket dropped were heard. A Very light was sent up from about F.17.c.80.25. No signs of a post were found. Patrol returned at 3 am.

Patrols of the Left Bde. report voices heard in F.6.c,central and sounds of transport on the AYETTE-COURCELLES Road. Very lights were fired from about A.1.d.05.40. Concertina wire in front of the sunken road in A.1.d was found to be very thin.

P.T.O.

- 2 -

A single shot was fired at one of our patrols by a post at about A.2.c.05.85.

A M.G. opened fire on a patrol of the 2nd H.L.I. from about A.1.d.05.40.

Another M.G. and Very lights were fired from the direction of the bank at A.2.a.9.3.

Numerous Very lights were fired from AERODROME TRENCH.

2. INTELLIGENCE.

Movement. Between 4 pm and 9 pm there was much movement about A.14.a.9.0 where a red cross flag and a dugout has previously been reported.

Movement in the sunken road in A.20.b about midday was dealt with by our M.Gs. and men were seen to run back. Between 7.30 and 8 am a number of coils of wire were being carried from the sunken road in A.20.b to trenches in A.14.c.

At 11.30 am yesterday a party of 30 Germans entered the sunken road at F.17.d.2.5 re-appeared at F.17.c.8.4 and were immediately lost to view. There was no time to inform the artillery.

An increase of movement due East of COURCELLES is reported. There is an R.E. dump between COURCELLES and the railway embankment at about A.16.c.8.5 (air photographs should be consulted).

Transport. Between 9 and 10 am several horse wagons were seen in the neighbourhood of MORY COPSE. Trains are reported in MORY at 8.15 am and 2 pm.

At 4.5 pm a column of about 50 lorries was seen going East of the BIHUCOURT-SAPIGNIES Road in H.7.a & b.

5 pair-horse wagons were seen moving North at 8.55 pm at A.22.c.1.3. Transport is constantly reported as passing this point at dusk and at dawn.

Posts. An L.M.G. is reported active from F.12.a.4.2. The post already reported at A.7.d.25.45 is again reported occupied. Also the post at F.6.c.4.3.

The shell hole system in A.7.b is reported occupied by day. Men are reported to have carried rations to this spot from AERODROME TRENCH.

The enemy outpost line in front of AYETTE is held by day and by night. Double sentries are mounted by night and single sentries by day. The look out by day is reported to be very slack and all sentries except the sentry on duty sleep in cubby holes and corrugated iron shelters in the system during the hours of daylight. There are no officers in the outpost line but there is a platoon commander - a Sergt. Major-in a post just South of the area raided last night. There is also an M.G. post in his vicinity.

The orders of the garrison of this part of the outpost line are to keep a sharp look out to the front, and in case of a heavy attack by us to retire fighting to the main line (AERODROME TRENCH)

No work beyond the improvement of cubby holes and shelters is being done in the outpost line.

Enemy dispositions. It appears that the 453rd Inf. Regt. holds the front shown on Div. map No.N/18 of 13/6/18 as held by the 90th F.R. i.e. from about F.11.b.9.9 to F.23.a.7.9. It appears that all four Coys. are in line (of the Battn. holding the front system). Each Coy. is disposed in depth - probably 1 platoon in outpost line, 1 platoon in intermediate shell hole line and 1 platoon in AERODROME TRENCH.

The support Bn. is in the railway embankment in A.22.b & d. The resting Bn. is in huts just West of MORY.

The 9th & 10th Coys. of 453 I.R. have 5 L.M.Gs. each - 2 of each Coy. being in the outpost line.

The AYETTE-COURCELLES Rd. is the boundary between the 9th & 10th Coy

P.T.O.

- 3 -

Reliefs. The 3rd Battn. 453rd I.R. relieved a Battn. of the 7th Bav. R.I.R. in the front system on the night 12th/13th. Normally an inter-Battn. relief is due on the night 18/19th in the sector held by the 453rd I.R. but tours of duty are rarely regular and relief nights are never known beforehand to the men in the front line. This is due to the risk of capture of some of the garrison of the outpost line and the consequent increase in our harassing fire in the area over which the relief takes places.

Area crashes are more feared than single rounds fired continuously.

Trench Accommodation. There are good dugouts in AERODROME TRENCH in A.13 and in the railway embankment. Some of these are still under construction. In the outpost line there is nothing better than corrugated iron shelters and cubby holes.

Lights & Signals. The enemy barrage did not come down after our raid last night until a large white stationary light was sent up followed by a steady red light. Left Bde. observers report the following lights during the raid:-

For the first 10 minutes ordinary Very lights.

For the next 10 minutes about 30 orange lights and occasional single greens and single reds. At 11.50 pm a rocket was fired bursting into a number of different colours - red, green, orange and blue.

Lieut.
for Lieut. Colonel,
General Staff, 2nd Division.

15/7/18.

2nd Division Tactical Summary No.49
For 24 hours ending 8 am 16/7/18.

Not to be taken forward of Bn. H.Q. in the line.

1. OPERATIONS.

A daylight patrol of the Right Bn. Right Bde. occupied the enemy posts West of the AYETTE-ABLAINZEVILLE Rd. in F.17.a yesterday. These new posts were not molested during the night and are still held by us. There is nothing else of importance to report.

Artillery. Our field artillery harassed the enemy's forward areas throughout the 24 hours. Between 8 and 8.20 pm field guns and Hows. fired a Chinese barrage on enemy's positions opposite the Left Bde.. Another concentration was fired on the same area at 10 pm.
 Enemy artillery activity slightly increased during the period under review and the following areas received most attention:-
X.15, X.21, X.22 and S.26. The retaliation for our bombardment at 8 pm was directed almost entirely on the front of the Left Bn. Left Bde. It began when our barrage ceased, lasted about 10 minutes, and fell between the front line and the AYETTE - BOIRY Road. 4.2s. predominated. AYETTE received a few 5.9s. during the day. The Eastern edge of ADINFER WOOD and the road in F.3.d were also shelled, the latter heavily between 10 and 11.30 pm.

Trench Mortars. Our 6" mortars fired 52 rounds in support of the patrol which occupied the enemy's posts in F.17.a, on the road at A.1.d.4.6 and the wire at F.6.c.5.1. Several hits were obtained on the road. 2 cubby holes were destroyed at a point where a M.G. is reported active and concertina wire was thrown up at F.6.c.5.1. 3" Stokes mortars fired 20 rounds in registration and retaliation on the right of the Divisional front.
 At 11.30 pm about 12 L.T.M. bombs were fired on A.2.a from about A.2.c.4.1. Pieces found shew these to have been Stokes shells (Stokes shells have been found by patrols in unoccupied enemy posts opposite the Left Bde. front.) Elsewhere enemy Minenwerfer were inactive.

Machine Guns. Our Vickers guns fired 7100 rounds on targets as under:-
 3000 rounds on the trench junction A.8.c.35.70 and shell holes about A.8.a.9.7.
 750 rounds on track A.2.central to A.2.d.3.8.
 1600 rounds on enemy work F.18.a.4.7 to F.18.a.4.5.
 2000 rounds on cross roads F.23.d.4.7.
 Enemy M.G. fire was normal.

2. PATROLS.

Lieuts. LANG, ALLISON, GUNTHER and FULTON patrolled the front opposite the Left Bde. during the night. The following information was brought back:-
 Very lights fired from F.6.c.45.35 and A.2.c.3.8.
 Talking heard in post at approx. A.2.a.90.25.
 Post located at A.2.a.75.20.
 Sounds of digging and wiring from S.26.d.80.15.
 M.G. active at about S.26.d.9.2.
 A patrol of the Centre Bde. under 2/Lt. R.W.AKERS reports an M.G. active at approx. F.11.d.2.3.
 Night patrols of the Right Bde. under 2/Lts. F.W.COSSAR and A.MACLEAN report as follows:-
 Enemy working party heard at F.17.c.9.2.
 Enemy shell hole post East of road at F.17.a.85.40 found unoccupied.
 Very lights fired from F.17.b.05.55 which is also apparently occupied by a sniper.

3. INTELLIGENCE.

Movement. Movement seen in forward areas was normal. Working parties in A.8.a and A.9.a were dispersed by our field guns.
 During our bombardment of the enemy lines opposite the Left Bde. Germans were seen manning AERODROME TRENCH.

P.T.O.

The following trenches were seen to be occupied yesterday -
A.15.c.20.25, A.15.b.2.4, A.21.d.60.35, A.15.c and F.18.a.
At 8.55 pm 15 Germans passed down COURCELLES ALLEY towards AYETTE and a party of 8 (unarmed) crossed the sunken road in F.17.d.2.5 to the road at F.17.c.7.1.

Trains & Transport. Normal train and transport movement was observed in back areas under observation.   At 5.30 am a 4-horse wagon with 2 men in it moved South past the point A.22.c.1.3.

Enemy Defences.
(a) Wire and work.
Work is reported to be in progress at A.14.a.42.67. Fresh white chalk is visible at A.15.c.37.10 (apparently a dugout) New earth is visible at A.14.c.0.6.

(b) Posts.
A sentry was seen at A.13.b.8.1. Very lights were fired from F.12.a.47.68.

(c) Machine Guns.
An M.G. is suspected at A.2.c.4.5.   A.A. M.Gs. at A.8.d.5.7 and A.9.a.90.25 were silenced by the aeroplane on which they were firing diving on them and retaliating. L.M.Gs. are also reported active at F.12.a.4.2 and F.11.d.2.3.

(d) O.Ps.
An O.P. is suspected at A.7.d.4.2 at which point the flash of a telescope was observed and where there is a mound on the parapet.

(e) Headquarters.
Smoke was seen to rise from a small chimney at A.8.d.8.6 which is probably a Coy. H.Q. Confirmation is required.

Hostile Aircraft. Several enemy machines patrolled yesterday between COURCELLES and AYETTE at a considerable height. No E.A. crossed our lines and no low flying machines are reported.

Lights & Signals. At 8.10 pm during our bombardment of the enemy lines opposite the Left Bde. one red light was fired from COURCELLES. At 8.15 pm an enemy balloon behind LOGEAST WOOD dropped a green light.

Fires & Explosions. About 8.15 pm a large dump went up S.E. of MOYENNEVILLE. A large flash was seen but no explosion was heard. Dense volumes of smoke were seen rising and continued till midnight.

Miscellaneous. A notice board can be seen at about A.14.a.5.6. During the afternoon a red cross flag was seen flying at the AERODROME at A.13.a.5.8.

Lieut.
for Lieut. Colonel,
General Staff, 2nd Division.
16/7/18.

2nd Division Tactical Summary No.50.
For 24 hours ending 8 am 17/7/18.

Not to be taken forward of Battn. H.Q. in the line.

1. OPERATIONS.

There is no change in the situation.

Artillery. During the morning our 18-pdrs engaged the AERODROME and co-operated with field Hows in a concentration on the Cemetery in ABLAINZEVILLE. Harassing fire was carried out as usual on all the enemy's forward positions, tracks and roads. Zero and S.O.S. lines were checked and all movement observed engaged. During the night, frequented tracks and roads were engaged at intervals and between 2 & 3 am advanced field guns fired on the enemy front line in answer to a request from the Infantry.

Hostile artillery activity was normal and was chiefly harassing fire of our battery positions. One of our positions in X.25.c received about 50 rounds at 11 am. There was a slight increase in activity against the Centre Bde. front. The AYETTE-BUCQUOY Road, X.21.d, W.30.d and F.2.d were the chief shelled areas. Early in the afternoon an aeroplane registered with 5.9s. on the well and trenches near QUESNOY FM.

Trench Mortars. Our 6" mortars fired 74 rounds on the following targets-
  Loopholes in the parapet at A.2.a.9.9 - excellent shooting, one loophole completely destroyed and several good hits scored on the trench.
  Suspected T.M.E. at A.2.c.2.3.
  Bank in F.18.a.
  Huts in F.23.a.
  Enemy minenwerfer were inactive during the period.

Machine Guns. Our Vickers guns fired 6000 rounds on the following targets:-
  3000 rounds on enemy shell hole positions in A.8.a.
  1000 rounds on enemy work in F.18.a.
  1000 rounds on ABLAINZEVILLE cross roads.
  1000 rounds on huts in F.23.a.
  Enemy M.Gs. were active during the day against our aircraft and were more active than usual during the night on the front of the Right Bde.

2. PATROLS.

Lieut. McLEAN and 7 O.Rs. went out at 11 pm and lay for an hour in on the North side of the AYETTE - MOYENNEVILLE Rd. at about F.6.c.35.35. No movement was seen. The patrol went East along the road for about 200 yds. and eventually returned to our lines at 1.15 am having seen nothing of the enemy except a Very light fired from A.8.a.

Lieut. SMITH and 6 O.Rs. went out at 1 am to a point about A.1.d.40.98 Talking, digging and wiring were heard at A.1.d.10.55 and single rifle shots came from the same direction. The patrol returned at 2 am.

2/Lt. LANE and 7 O.Rs. report digging in the enemy outpost line in S.26.d between 1.5 am and 2.25 am.

2/Lieut. MACLURE and 10 O.Rs. went out from F.17.c.1.0 at 12.50 am. to ascertain if the bank running S.W. from F.17.d.1.5 was held by the enemy. The patrol was unable to get through the enemy wire and returned at 3.20 am.

2/Lt. PERKINS and 11 O.Rs. left our line at F.17.a.3.4 at 11.45 pm. and on approaching the fork road at F.17.c.9.9 were fired on by a M.G. and bombed. Casualties were suffered and the patrol withdrew returning to our lines at 1.10 am.

A patrol of the Left Bn. Right Bde. reports no sign of the enemy on the road from F.17.a.7.5 to 90.98.

P.T.O.

3. INTELLIGENCE.

Movement. Visibility was good until 6 am. After the rain storm which lasted from 6 am till 8 am the air cleared and visibility was very good until dusk. Rear areas faded quickly after 8.15 pm.

A large party, 300 to 400 strong was seen marching South along the road in A.5.b (time not reported). Except for this movement on foot in back areas was normal.

At 9.25 pm about 30 men were seen walking alongside the C.T. between A.9.b and A.8.b. They were dispersed by our artillery. This C.T. was observed in use throughout the day.

DOROTHY TRENCH, MILK WORK and AERODROME TRENCH were all seen to be occupied. A man stood up out of the trench for a few minutes near the M.G. post at A.13.d.2.3. Movement in forward areas was otherwise normal.

At 6.30 pm a party of about 60 men and a man mounted on a white horse were seen manoeuvring at I.14.d. They disappeared at 6.45 pm.

Trains & Transport. Road and railway movement observed in back areas appeared to be normal.

Individual wagons are constantly reported in the early hours of the morning in A.21.d. These are usually loaded with hay. One was engaged this morning by our artillery at 4.50am

Enemy Defences.
(a) Posts. A sentry was seen at A.13.d.9.6. A post is reported at F.17.d.5.5 where a periscope is visible.
(b) H.Q. and dugouts. Movement has been observed around a suspected dugout at A.I.d.60.35 (DOROTHY TRENCH)

Lights & Signals. At 5 am about 40 Very lights were fired simultaneously from and behind AERODROME TRENCH. A few more followed during the next 5 minutes. The meaning was not apparent but several short bursts of 77 mm^8 are reported to have followed. At 4.45 am double green lights have been put up without apparent result.

Fires & Explosions. There was a series of small explosions in ABLAINZEVILLE at 8.30 pm and later a fire which burned throughout the night.

Dumps. What appears to be a small camouflaged dump of material is reported by ground observers at A.7.b.9.4.

Hostile aircraft. Enemy aircraft were rather more active than usual yesterday forenoon. Several crossed our lines flying high evidently on back area reconnaissance work. Several R.E.A. which attempted to cross our lines at medium height were driven off by A.A. and M.G. fire. One machine was brought down by two of ours S.W. of MOYENNEVILLE at 11.50 am. The E.A. twice turned turtle and the pilot together with 2 or 3 other small objects fell out before the machine crashed. At 5.20 pm one of our machines fired an enemy balloon near GOMMECOURT and returned safely to our lines.

General. A large plank or notice board is visible fixed to a tall tree in COURCELLES on a grid bearing of 103° from F.10.c.05.55

Jo McGowan
Lieut.
for Lieut. Colonel,
General Staff, 2nd Division.

17/7/18.

2nd Division Tactical Summary No.51
For 24 hours ending 8 am 18/7/18.

Not to be taken forward of Bn. H.Q. in the line.

1. OPERATIONS.

This morning at 5.5 am, the enemy bombarded the COJEUL VALLEY, DOUCHY and AYETTE with Yellow cross gas shell. The bombardment lasted till 7 am and about 1000 rounds were fired. 3 batteries carried out the bombardment; one 77 mm battery fired from the direction of COURCELLES on the front line and AYETTE, another engaged DOUCHY from LOGEAST WOOD, and a 4.2 battery firing from COURCELLES engaged DOUCHY and the Valley. The bombardment was intense up to 5.45 am when the batteries appeared to rest in turn. Fire slackened about 6.30 am and ceased at 7. Between 7.40 and 7.55 am a further 60 rounds were fired on F.10.a.
Apart from the above the day and night passed quietly.

Artillery. Our field artillery carried out the usual harassing fire of enemy forward system and communications. The dump at A.20.a.30.35, H.Q. at A.14.b.90.15 and COURCELLES ALLEY received special attention. Forward 18-pdrs. engaged all movement seen and obtained direct hits on the suspected O.P. at A.20.c.95.90. 25 rounds were fired by a 4.5" battery on the hostile battery AW.7. Normal harassing fire was carried out during the night.
Except for the gas bombardment this morning, enemy artillery activity was normal. 77 mm^s harassed X.22.c & d, X.21.a & c, X.27.b and X.28.c. The S.E. corner of ADINFERWOOD, QUESNOY FARM and the COJEUL VALLEY in F.1.c & d and E.12.a also received attention from 77 mm^s and 4.2s. QUESNOY FARM received some 5.9s.

Trench Mortars. Our 6" mortars fired 147 rounds during the day on the following targets:-
Suspected T.M.E. at A.2.c.2.3.
Trench at A.3.a.35.15.
O.P. and loopholes at A.8.a.95.95.
Post with tin roof at F.12.a.35.35.
M.G.E. at F.11.d.40.15.
Cross roads F.17.c.9.9.
Sunken road F.17.c.2.5.
New work in F.18.a.
3" Stokes fired 31 rounds on the enemy outpost line in A.2.b and in registration of targets opposite the Right Bde..
6 heavy minenwerfer bombs (3 being air-bursts) were fired on the extreme left of the Divnl. front in S.28.b. No other enemy T.M. activity is reported.

Machine Guns. Our Vickers guns fired 6000 rounds on the following targets:-
2000 rounds on enemy work F.23.d.4.7.
1000 rounds on enemy work F.18.a.4.7 to 4.5.
3000 rounds on enemy shell hole positions in A.8.a and C.T. running E. & W. through A.8.b.
Enemy M.G. activity was normal.

2. PATROLS.

Patrols of the Left Bde. report hearing voices in the sunken road between 12.45 am and 2.10 am.
2/Lt. BELLERSON and 6 O.Rs. went out from F.5.d.85.30. After listening at F.6.c.3.4 the patrol turned North and found a disused trench at F.6.c.3.5. The only signs of the enemy were Very lights and M.G. fire coming from about F.6.c.50.35.
2/Lt. WOOLLEY M.C. and 4 O.Rs. went out to F.11.d.70.55 encountering no enemy wire. An M.G. is reported active at F.11.d.4.3.

P.T.O.

Patrols (contd.)

2/Lt. BUXTON and 15 O.Rs. occupied a position at about F.17.c.7.9 from 10.30 pm to 3.30 am. A few of the enemy were seen but they showed no signs of attacking our new forward positions in F.17.a.

2/Lt.G.W.S.MACLURE and 9 O.Rs. went out from F.23.a.05.35 at 11.15 pm, got through the enemy wire at F.17.c.7.4 and reconnoitred the corner of the bank at F.17.c.8.4. There were no signs of an enemy post here. The isolated hut and the 4 old gun pits West of the sunken road were also unoccupied. The approach of daylight prevented the patrol reaching the fork roads at F.17.c.9.9. 2 Germans were seen at 200 yds. distance on the track running along the bank but they disappeared immediately. The wire along the West of the road was concertina only.

2/Lt.F.WRIGHT and 5 O.Rs. reconnoitred the enemy shell hole positions near F.17.a.9.4 at 1.30 am. 3 rifle shots were fired and 4 hand grenades thrown at the patrol from a point further South.

3. INTELLIGENCE.

Movement. Visibility was good for forward areas from dawn till 9 am, poor until 3 pm and good till 8.15 pm. Rear areas were only visible for short periods

Less individual movement than usual is reported, probably on account of periods of poor visibility. Individuals and small parties were seen in the usual places, and traffic observed in clear intervals in back areas was normal.

Wagons loading up with hay in the early morning in A.21.c & d are again reported. Our artillery caused one to move on suddenly this morning in A.21.c.

Enemy Defences.
(a) Wire and work. New earth is reported at A.8.d.6.2 and A.13.b.1.8.
(b) Posts. The flash of a telescope was seen at A.7.d.4.4 at 12.15 pm. An M.G. is reported active from the road at about F.17.d.1.8. and others are reported at F.12.a.3.8 (unlikely) and F.11.d.4.3 (probable). See under patrols.

Trench Mortars. Centre Bde. suspect a T.M. active against the front of the Right Bde. from F.12.c.90.55.

Fires & Explosions. At 1.15 am our artillery exploded a dump in A.3.d.

Hostile aircraft. Enemy aircraft activity was normal during the early part of the day. At 5.30 pm 3 enemy machines crossed our line flying at a height of 2000-3000 feet. One was turned back by our A.A. & M.G. fire; the other two flew over the trenches South of ADINFER WOOD and ESSARTS. Another enemy machine crossed our lines at 7 pm but was driven off by our Scouts.

Meteorological.

July 19th   Sun rises 4.59 am   Sun sets 8.49 pm.
            Moon rises 5.10 pm Moon sets 1 am.
            (All Summer Times).

18/7/18.

Lieut.
for Lieut. Colonel,
General Staff, 2nd Division.

2nd Division Tactical Summary No.52
For 24 hours ending 8 am 19/7/18.

Not to be taken forward of Battn. H.Q. in the line.

1. OPERATIONS.

During the period under review hostile artillery has shown increased activity particularly during the night. Enemy aircraft were also increasedly active over the front of the Left Bde. yesterday and this morning. Otherwise the situation is unchanged.

Artillery. Yesterday the enemy's forward system was continually harassed. Between 12 noon and 7 pm 200 rounds 18-pdr were fired in bursts on A.8.c & d and A.14.a. The O.P. at A.14.a.72.85 was engaged and three direct hits obtained. Support was given to the raiding party of the Divn. on our right and to one of our own patrols. 4.5" Hows. engaged several hostile batteries and retaliated for the enemy shelling of CARUSO COPSE. The usual harassing fire was carried out during the night on tracks, trenches, H.Qs. and communications.

The enemy artillery was more active than usual during the day and kept up lively harassing fire during the night. From 8.30 pm till dawn activity was considerably above normal. 6 77-mm, 1 10.5cm and 1 15-cm How. batteries kept up an almost continuous fire on AYETTE, DOUCHY, COJEUL VALLEY, ROTTON RAVINE, the JEWEL VALLEY and the S.W. edge of ADINFER WOOD. A few Yellow Cross gas shells are reported in the COJEUL VALLEY. Fire was heaviest between 3 and 4 am. CALVERLY COPSE and CARUSO COPSE were persistently shelled during the night and early this morning a few rounds of shrapnel were fired in the vicinity of the MONCHY-BIENVILLERS Road.

Trench Mortars. Our 6" mortars fired 55 rounds during the day on the following targets:-
Posts at F.12.a.55.30 and 50.70.
M.G. at F.12.c.95.60.
Suspected T.M. at F.12.c.9.6. and sunken road at F.12.c.4.9.
Our 3" Stokes fired 17 rounds on AERODROME TRENCH in A.2.d obtaining 2 direct hits.
15 rounds were also fired on the enemy M.G. at F.11.d.30.15.
Enemy minenwerfer were only active on the extreme right where our three Southernmost posts were bombed from ABLAINZEVILLE CEMETERY.

Machine Guns. Our Vickers guns fired 6000 rounds on the following targets:-
3000 rounds on new C.T. in A.8.a & b, AERODROME TRENCH in A.8.c & a.
3000 rounds on enemy work about F.18.a.98.17 and F.23.d.4.7.
Enemy M.G. activity normal.

2. PATROLS.

Patrols of the Left Bde. under Lieuts. GILES and PRING and 2/Lt. FOX report -
(a) Voices heard in the sunken road between 11.40 pm and 1 am.
(b) Rifle pits at A.2.a.8.6 have apparently been recently used
(c) Patrol in S.26.d was fired on when 100 yds. out from our line.
2/Lt.RICKETTS and 7 O.Rs. Centre Bde. took up a position in shell holes just West of the enemy's outpost line at F.6.c.40.15. 2 of the enemy were seen about 30 yards left of the patrol but they disappeared before the patrol could reach them. A working party about 20 strong was seen at F.12.a.5.9 (approx.)
Nothing was seen or heard of the enemy by 2 patrols of the Centre Bde. which reconnoitred the ground about F.6.c.5.9 and F.11.d.5.5.
2/Lt.DEWHURST and 12 O.Rs. lay out from 10.45 pm to 3.30 am at F.17.c.7.9 but observed no traces of the enemy.

P.T.O.

3. INTELLIGENCE.

Movement. Movement in the forward area was about normal yesterday, but it is reported that individual movement in the forward area practically ceased after 8.30 pm. The tracks and roads in A.14 and A.20 were as usual the most frequented areas.

At 5.15 am 50 men were seen in A.21.c marching towards COURCELLES. A further party seen in A.20.a at 5.30 am was dealt with by our artillery.

Centres of movement are reported at A.21.d.60.35, the trenches in A.15.c and the ruin in A.15.c.

A party of 12 came West over the ridge at A.20.b.7.4 at 7 am. At 5 am a party of 6 went East over this ridge. The Right Battn. Right Bde. report having seen a party of 70 Germans on the ridge S.W. of COURCELLES at 8.30 pm.

In back areas the movement observed was considerable but perhaps not above normal considering the good visibility.

At 2.20 pm a party of 70-80 men left the ECOUST-BAPAUME Road at B.30.b.2.3 and went along the track towards MORY.

Between 2.30 and 4 pm about 2 Coys. of men were seen drilling in I.14.d.

At 3.35 pm a party of about 30 men marched towards VRAUCOURT on the track in B.30.c & d.

Constant movement of individuals and small parties was also observed in these areas.

Trains & Transport. Several horse wagons are again reported in the early morning in A.21. At 5.30 am and again at 8.30 pm individual horse traffic was seen on the road in A.22.c.

Right Bde. report that at 6.8 am a large number of men were being conveyed Southwards on what appeared to be a light railway (?) in A.22.c. This train was again seen going North at 7.20 am.

The usual traffic of lorries and horse transport was observed on the ECOUST-BAPAUME Road. 20 G.S. wagons went South along this road between 5.30 pm and 6 pm.

Enemy Defences.
(a) Wire & Work. Work observed at A.7.b.5.3 and in COURCELLES ALLEY was fired on by our 18-pdrs. At 4.25 am 5 men were seen at work on the mound at A.20.d.2.9 and the O.P. at A.20.c.95.90. These also were dealt with by the artillery.
(b) Posts & M.Gs. Right Bde. reports a M.G. active at F.11.d.40.15.
(c) O.Ps. Men were seen observing our lines from A.14.b.30.85 (at this point there is a small piece of trench, one of many in the vicinity. Air photographs show that some of these are occupied).

An O.P. is also suspected at A.14.a.65.15 where a loophole is visible and into which a man was seen to go.

Fires & Explosions. At 9.35 pm a dump in A.14.d was set on fire during a concentration burst by our heavy artillery.

Lights & Signals. An enemy signalling lamp was active about A.3.a last night sending towards MOYENNEVILLE.

Helio flashes were seen coming from the rear of ST LEGER on a T.B. of 92° from F.2.b.8.8.

At 2 am the sending up of one red, 2 white, 1 green and a double green caused the enemy artillery to open fire. At 2.37 am a double red and a single red resulted in renewed artillery activity. In some quarters it is held that the double red light is the enemy's lengthen range signal.

Enemy Aircraft. No cases of low flying E.A. are reported but enemy machines were active yesterday at a considerable height especially over the front of the Left Bde. Several enemy bombing machines crossed our lines during the night.

General.
(a) At 3.15 pm 2 pigeons flew over ABLAINZEVILLE from COURCELLES. At 4.45 pm 7 pigeons crossed our lines from the direction of COURCELLES (this afternoon 19th a German pigeon was captured in POMMIER with a code message dated 18/7/18).

Meteorological. Sun rises 5 am, sets 8.45 pm.
Moon rises 6.8 pm, sets 1.25 am

19/7/18.

Lieut.
for Lieut. Colonel, G.S.

2nd Division Tactical Summary No.53.
For 24 hours ending 8 am 20/7/18.

Not to be taken forward of Battn. H.Q. in the line.

1. OPERATIONS.

The enemy artillery was again very active during the night. Some Yellow Cross gas shell were mixed with H.E. and scattered about DOUCHY and JEWEL VALLEY. Activity was normal during the day and there were no infantry operations.

Artillery. Our field artillery harassed the enemy's forward system and communications as usual paying particular attention to A.2.c & d, A.8.b & c, H.Qs. at A.15.a.2.9 and A.9.b.60.35, AERODROME TRENCH and tracks in A.8.b. At 3.50 am a concentration was fired in retaliation for the enemy's shelling of our front line and DOUCHY. This was repeated at 4 am. Counter-battery work was carried by out by 4.5" Hows. 1 pit being hit direct. An explosion and fire were caused. Harassing fire was continued throughout the night.

Enemy artillery activity was normal during the day. Our front line, the COJEUL VALLEY and QUESNOY FARM being the chief targets. At 9.30 pm hostile batteries became extremely active and kept up a continuous fire until 4.30 am. AYETTE, DOUCHY, ADINFER WOOD, X.27.d, COJEUL VALLEY and ROTTON RAVINE were the principal targets. Between 3 and 3.30 am a heavy bombardment of calibres up to 15 cm. was placed on AYETTE and along our front system to S.25.d. This was repeated between 3.35 am and 3.55 am on the front of the left Bde. Between 6 and 8 am 4.2s. were active on the S.E. corner of ADINFER WOOD. Yellow Cross gas shell were mixed with H.E. and fell in DOUCHY and the JEWEL VALLEY between 10 and 11 pm. Fire was most intense between 10 pm and midnight and 3 and 4 am.

Trench Mortars. Our 6" mortars fired 62 rounds yesterday on the following targets:-
New work in F.18.a.
Suspected T.M. at A.2.c.4.5.
Track and trench junction at A.8.a.9.9.
Loophole recently appeared in parapet at A.8.a.89.88. / 3" Stokes fired 183 rounds as under:-
18 on front line in A.2.d.
20 on sunken road in A.1.d.
115 on wiring parties in S.27.d and S.26.d.
6 rounds on the AYETTE-MOYENNEVILLE Road.
24 rounds in registration and on low flying E.A.

Machine Guns. Our Vickers guns fired 6250 rounds on the following targets:-
3000 rounds on C.T. in A.8.a and enemy outpost line in F.12.a.
750 rounds direct fire on area round A.2.c.8.0.
1000 rounds on enemy work in F.23.b.
1000 rounds on enemy work F.18.a.78.18 to F.24.a.53.82.
500 rounds on E.A.
Enemy M.G. activity was normal.

2. PATROLS.

2/Lieuts. HART and FOX with 8 O.Rs. fired Very lights into the sunken road from various points in A.2.a with the object of decoying a hostile patrol into an attempt to outflank them while another of our parties lay in wait for the enemy. The enemy only replied with Very lights from A.2.b.

Lieut. PRING and 3 O.Rs. reported enemy wiring parties busy at about S.27.c.3.4 at 10 pm. On the return of the patrol these parties were engaged by our Stokes mortars. 4 further wiring parties located by the same patrol at midnight in S.26.d were also dispersed by Stokes mortars.

Sgt. STEVENS and 1 O.R. report the wire at F.6.c.9.5 to be thin.

P.T.O.

Patrols (contd.).

2/Lieut. WOOLLEY M.C. and 1 O.R. went out to reconnoitre new work observed at F.11.d.55.35. 2 of the enemy were seen walking on top of the trench and much talking was heard in the enemy's lines at this point. Sounds of work were also heard in the trench. The patrol was fired on both going and coming and on its return to our lines L.G. and artillery fire was directed on the enemy working party.

No signs of an enemy post were found by a patrol which investigated the fork roads at F.17.c.9.9.

3. INTELLIGENCE.

Movement. Ground observers report that the movement in forward areas yesterday was less than usual though individuals were still seen in the usual frequented areas. One party of 8 was seen at A13.b.5.2.

No parties of more than 20 were observed in back areas under observation. 20 horsemen were seen riding about in I.14.d at 6.10 pm. They rode away South at 6.15 pm. At 3.55 pm a party of about 20 men marched North along the ECOUST-BAPAUME Rd. in B.30.

Trains & Transport. One pair horse wagon was seen on the road at A.22.c.1.3 but no other transport was observed in the forward area.

Train and transport movement in back areas under observation was normal. Only a few trains were observed and no large convoys of H. or M.T. are reported.

Enemy Defences. Patrols report assiduous wiring in S.26 and S.27, also work on the outpost line in F.11.d. New work is suspected at F.12.c.60.65. The right Bde. report the enemy to be deepening his trenches between A.13.d.4.7 and 2.8. Work is also reported at A.13.b. 5.2 and at A.14.b.7.1. At the latter point an M.G. emplacement is suspected under construction.

Working parties at A.14.c.2.3 and A.20.b.7.4 were dealt with by our artillery.

O.Ps. A man was seen to enter the suspected O.P. at A.14.a.65.10. This spot was shelled yesterday.

Lights & Signals. It is again reported that 2 red lights is the enemy's longthen range signal.

At 4.30 pm helio flashes were seen on a T.B. of 92° from F.2.b.8.8.

Fires & Explosions. At 6.45 pm a large column of smoke was observed behind ABLAINZEVILLE. At 5.50 pm an ammunition dump was blown up on a grid bearing of 116° from X.27.d.75.35.

Enemy Aircraft. Hostile machines reconnoitred our front at 8.30 pm last night and were active this morning early, several flying high over areas West of ADINFER WOOD. No low flying E.A. are reported.

General. The enemy's increased artillery activity by night is considered to be of a counter-preparatory nature and to be due to nervousness.

The abnormal movement reported early yesterday morning South of COURCELLES may have been due to -
(i) An inter-battalion relief in the Sector of the 463rd Inf. Regt. A relief was due on the night 18/19th in this Sector.
(ii) The reserve Battn. or Support Bn. may have come up to the main line in anticipation of an attack by us.

No such abnormal movement is reported in this Sector this morning.

Meteorological.	Barometer.	Max.Temp.	Min.Temp.
July 20th	29.37	81	57
July 21st	Sun rises 5.1 am	Sun sets 8.46 pm.	
	Moon rises 6.59 pm	Moon sets 2.18 am.	
	(All Summer Time).		

20/7/18.

J. McIlvain
Lieut.
for Lieut. Colonel, G.S.

2nd Division Tactical Summary No. 54.
For 24 hours ending 8 am 21/7/18.

Not to be taken forward of Battn. H.Q. in the line.

1. OPERATIONS.

The situation is unchanged. The enemy's artillery harassed our front and support lines persistently during the night but the volumn of fire was much less than on the preceding two nights. The front of the Left Bde. received most attention.

Artillery. Our field artillery was normally active during the day in harassing fire and in sniping enemy movement observed in the forward area. During the morning 4.5s. fired 100 rounds on A.3.c and A.8 and in the afternoon 200 rounds 18-pdr were fired on A.8.b, A.2.d, A.3.c and A.14.a. A concentration of 232 rounds 18-pdr and 204 rounds 4.5 was fired on AERODROME TRENCH in A.8.a and A.2.d at 2.27 am in retaliation for the enemy's shelling of our front system.

Hostile artillery activity was normal during the day. Harassing fire was again considerable throughout the night but less so than on the two preceding nights. AYETTE, DOUCHY, and the forward system generally were shelled at intervals with 4.2s. and 77 mm? At 1.50 am a half-hour bombardment of our lines in S.26 and the COJEUL VALLEY by field and heavy Hows. was begun. Our retaliation caused fire to slacken. At 3.20 am, S.26.a and the COJEUL VALLEY were again heavily shelled for 20 minutes. Of the 5.9s. used half were instantaneous and half delayed action.

During the day ADINFER WOOD and Village, LE QUESNOY FARM and F.3.b received some attention from 5.9 batteries.

Trench Mortars. Our 6" mortars fired 89 rounds yesterday on the following targets:-
M.G. at F.11.d.30.15.
Trench and road junction at A.3.a.35.25.
M.G. at A.1.d.6.5. and track at A.1.d.4.2.
  Our 3" mortars fired 48 rounds on enemy wiring parties in S.26.d.
  Enemy minenwerfer were only slightly active. 6 medium bombs are reported in our wire in F.17 about 2 am.

Machine Guns. Our Vickers guns fired 6750 rounds on targets as under:-
1000 rounds on enemy work between F.23.b.75.15 and F.23.b.90.35.
1000 rounds on enemy work from S.18.a.78.18 to F.24.a.55.82.
4000 rounds on C.T. and shell hole positions in A.8.
750 rounds on E.A.
  Enemy M.G. fire was normal.

2. PATROLS.

Patrols of the Left Bde. in A.1.b and A.2.a report all quiet and no sign of the enemy.
  2/Lt. FORREST and 6 O.Rs. located 2 enemy wiring parties and a covering party in S.26.d. and had the Light Trench Mortars turned on to the parties on their return, the wire having been previously registered. No sign of the enemy was discovered about F.3.c.40.25.
  2/Lt.O.L.BRIDGES and 4 O.Rs. discovered an enemy working party at about F.11.d.50.25 but on trying to work round to the South of the party the patrol came under M.G. fire, probably from the known enemy post S.W. of the location of the working party.
  2/Lt.F.B.WELLS and 1 N.C.O. saw 10 men cross the AYETTE-ABLAINZEVILLE Rd. at about F.17.a.8.1 at 1.15 am. There was no sign of movement at the fork roads at F.17.c.9.9.

3. INTELLIGENCE.

Movement. Visibility was fair yesterday for rear areas and good for forward areas throughout the day. After the thunderstorm the air was exceptionally clear.
  Yesterday individual movement in the forward area was considerable, centring on the tracks in A.20 and in AERODROME TRENCH. This morning

P.T.O.

up to 10 am, observers of the Right and Left Bdes. report numerous individuals and small parties exposing themselves in A.8, 9, 14 and 20. 4 parties of 6, 9, 4 and 10 respectively were seen in A.20 between 4.30 and 6 am. Parties larger than 4 are very unusual in this area. Observers also report that the enemy seen this morning wandered about aimlessly as if they were new to the country.

Foot traffic in back areas under observation was normal; no large parties were seen.

Trains & Transport. Wagons are again reported on the road in A.22.c at dusk and at dawn. At 5.30 am a wagon was seen going S.E. on the track in A.20.b.

Normal H. and M.T. traffic is reported in back areas. Train movement was also normal as far as could be seen.

Enemy Defences.
(a) Wire & Work. New work is reported in progress on enemy's outpost line between F.12.a.45.70 and F.6.c.45.10.

A patrol heard stakes being driven into the ground about F.17.d.2.4.

New work is reported at A.20.b.7.4.

(b) Posts & M.Gs. A sniper's post is reported at A.13.b.2.2 from which point shots were fired in the direction of AYETTE. A sentry was seen at A.14.b.2.1.

An M.G. is reported active at about F.17.b.1.6 (previously reported as an enemy post). 5 men were seen to leave a suspected post near this point and move off towards ABLAINZEVILLE. 20 minutes later 5 men came from ABLAINZEVILLE and moved towards the Post – evidently a relief.

At 11.45 am smoke was seen rising from about A.9.a.4.5.

Enemy Aircraft. Hostile aeroplanes were more active than usual over our forward areas yesterday morning between 7 and 11 am. At 10.25 am 3 R.E.A. flew over our lines fairly low but were driven off by our A.A. & M.G. fire assisted by 5 of our Scouts.

A small balloon was carried in the direction of RANSART from in rear of ABLAINZEVILLE at 3.25 pm.

5 enemy observation balloons were observed aloft between 5 and 7.15 am yesterday. 1 was anchored at 11.20 am at B.29.c.6.7 but was taken behind the ridge after being made fast.

General. At 6 pm a large black dog was seen running from A.8.b.4.3 to A.9.a.9.1 where it was lost to view.

Meteorological.

	Barometer.	Max.Temp.	Min.Temp.
July 21st	29.45	77	56

July 22nd Sun rises 5.2 am Sun sets 8.45 pm.
Moon rises 7.45 pm Moon sets 3.22 am.
(All Summer Time).

21/7/18.

Lieut.
for Lieut. Colonel,
General Staff, 2nd Division.

2nd Division Tactical Summary No.55
For 24 hours ending 8 am 22/7/18.

<u>Not to be taken forward of Battn. H.Q. in the line.</u>

1. OPERATIONS.

The enemy continued lively harassing fire last night chiefly on ADINFER, DOUCHY, the COJEUL VALLEY and F.3.c & d. Heavy concentrations were put down on the Left Bde. front at intervals from midnight till dawn. About 600 rounds are estimated to have been fired by field artillery. Between 5 and 6 am, up to 1000 rounds Yellow and Green Cross gas shell were fired on X.16.c & d, and X.22.b & d. There is nothing else of importance to report.

<u>Artillery.</u> Our forward field artillery was active throughout the day firing on frequented areas and dead ground. At 2.30 am our field artillery fired over 550 rounds on AERODROME TRENCH in retaliation for enemy fire. Tracks and trenches were also vigorously harassed during the night.

The enemy artillery was quiet during the day but from 10 pm onwards showed considerable activity. Between 10 and 10.30 pm, 5.9" Hows. were active on back areas. Concentrations were fired on the front of the Left Bde. at 2.10 am, 2.50 am and 3.20 am, each of 5 to 10 minutes duration. AYETTE, ADINFER WOOD, CARUSO COPSE and the JEWEL VALLEY, also received short bursts.

<u>Trench Mortars.</u> Our 6" mortars fired 118 rounds yesterday as under:-
T.M.E. at F.12.c.90.55 and F.18.a.
Trench and post at F.11.d.55.35.
Enemy front line in A.8.a & b., A.2.b, A.3.a.
M.G. night position at A.1.d.1.0.
Our Stokes mortars fired a few rounds on the enemy post at F.12 c.4.9 and carried out registration.
Very slight enemy minenwerfer activity is reported, 4 rounds falling in our wire about F.17.c.0.4 at 7 pm.

<u>Machine Guns.</u> Our Vickers guns fired 6000 rounds as below:-
3000 rounds on track and trench junction at A.8.a.8.6.
1000 rounds on enemy outpost line about F.12.a.4.4.
1000 rounds on enemy work in F.23.b.
1000 rounds on enemy work in A.15.d.
Enemy M.G. fire was normal.

2. PATROLS.

Patrols of the Left Bde. report all quiet and no sign of the enemy. Consolidated shell holes found at A.2.a.7.6 were unoccupied and unwired.
2/Lt.T.C.LAWRENCE and 4 O.Rs. report Very lights and an M.G. fired from F.12.c.3.9.
2/Lt.S.CULE and 5 O.Rs. report an enemy M.G. active from F.12.c. 2.8 and work in progress at F.12.c.05.60.
(M.G. reported by latter two patrols is probably at F.12.c.15.78 which is a known post. Until recently there was no active M.G. in this post but it is possible that the M.G. previously located a little South of this point has now been moved closer to the road.)
2/Lt.L.S.MILCH and 7 O.Rs. saw an enemy wiring party about 20 strong at approx. F.6.c.40.62.
No signs of enemy occupation or activity were seen at F.17.c.9.9 between 11 pm and 11.45 pm.

P.T.O.

2. INTELLIGENCE.

Movement. The amount of movement observed yesterday and this morning in the forward area was about normal but observers report that the enemy attitude to our harassing fire has undergone a change. Fewer men are seen at the double and most individuals observed proceed in a leisurely fashion. Movement is also reported in COURCELLES village which is a new feature.

At 9.30 pm 2 men with rifles appeared at F.17.b.7.3 and disappeared at F.17.b.1.6 (suspected post). At the same time 20 men appeared at F.17.b.7.5 and approached the road opposite BLIZZARD POST (F.17.a.7.4) The garrison of this post prepared to fire on the party which, however, suddenly turned left and disappeared into a dip moving in the direction of ABLAINZEVILLE. All the men wore overcoats.

At 8.45 am a party of 12 men including 3 supposed officers each carrying shiny map case was seen moving about in A.9.c. They were engaged by our artillery.

During a shoot on the suspected O.P. at A.15.c.90.55 (in COURCELLES) a party of 10-12 was driven out of the Copse near this point. It doubled East over the ridge.

Foot traffic in back areas was normal.

Trains & Transport. At 7.25 am a 2-horse ambulance flying a red-cross flag went North on the road at A.22.c.1.3, returning South at 7.45. At the same time a pair-horse wagon went North at the same point. No other transport movement was observed in the forward area.

Train, horse and mechanical traffic in back areas under observation appeared to be normal yesterday.

Enemy Defences.
 (a) Wire & Work. A patrol reports an enemy wiring party last night at F.6.c.40.62.
  A belt of wire was put out last night between F.18.c.75.30 and A.13.d.2.8. New wire is also visible in front of COURCELLES trench.
  14 men were observed at work on the trench in A.9.a at 6.40 am.
 (b) Batteries. A 15-cm H.V. gun was active between 4.10 and 4.25 am on our back areas on a T.B. of 119° 5' from F.2.b.8.8. Time between flash and report 19 seconds.
 (c) O.Ps. Movement was observed at the following suspected O.Ps:- A.20.b.25.05, A.15.c.3.1 and A.14.a.65.10. RIDGE WORK was seen to be occupied.
 (d) Dump. Coils of concertina wire can be seen at A.14.b.7.2 running very thickly East to West for about 20 yds.

Lights & Signals. At 12.30 am a red and green light was fired from F.18.a without apparent result.

Between 3.30 and 4 am enemy guns opened fire when a light was fired from F.11.d.30.15 and ceased when a second light was put up.

The usual chain lights were fired when our aeroplanes were crossing the front line during the night.

Enemy Aircraft. Conditions were unfavourable yesterday and few enemy aircraft were seen. One flew low over COURCELLES at 2 pm but made no attempt to cross No Man's Land. During the night bombing machines of both sides were active. This morning there was slight activity of R.E.A., one machine patrolling our line between F.27.? and A.2.a at 4.40 am. At 4.45 am 3 machines patrolled our line between F.17 & F.23. At 5.30 am a machine believed to be British was brought down in the enemy's lines.

Meteorological.	Barometer.	Max.Temp.	Min.Temp.
July 22nd	29.45	54.74	52

July 23rd Sun rises 5.4 am, sets 8.44 pm.
Moon rises 8.16 pm, sets 4.34 am.
(All Summer Time).

22/7/18.

Lieut.
for Lieut. Colonel, G.S.

2nd Division Tactical Summary No.56.
For 24 hours ending 8 am 23/7/18.

Not to be taken forward of Battn. H.Q. in the line.

1. OPERATIONS.

At 12.30 am we raided the enemy positions in F.17.c & d and F.23 a & b. under cover of a barrage laid down by artillery, T.Ms. and M.Gs. The Division on our left co-operated by an artillery demonstration at 12.20 am. All the objectives were reached, 5 prisoners and 1 M.G. being captured. Many casualties were inflicted on the enemy both by the raiding party and by our artillery. 10-15 of the enemy bolted from the strong point at F.18.c.0.2 on the approach of the raiders. Some of them were killed and the rest driven into our barrage. The dugout was bombed. The raiding party returned with light casualties.
There is nothing else of importance to report.

Artillery. Our field artillery carried out the usual harassing fire on the enemy's forward system during the forenoon. Direct hits were obtained on the M.G.E. at F.18.a.9.2. Between 2 pm and 4 pm field Hows. and forward 18-pdrs co-operated with the heavy artillery in the bombardment of LOGEAST WOOD. Field Hows. fired 200 rounds with balloon observation on A.21.b.55.50. Between 12.30 and 1.30 am all batteries fired the barrage programme arranged in support of the raid of the Right Battn. Right Bde. At 4.35 am 400 rounds 4.5 and 18-pdr were fired on AERODROME TRENCH in retaliation for enemy shelling of AYETTE.
Enemy artillery was active yesterday morning with How. fire on DOUCHY, LE QUESNOY FARM, ADINFER WOOD and the COJEUL VALLEY. Shelling was less in these areas during the afternoon. During the evening there was some harassing fire in F.15.c and 14.d. The barrage laid down in reply to our raid was severe on the BUCQUOY-AYETTE Road, CALVERLY COPSE, CARUSO COPSE and the JEWEL VALLEY. Much of it came down on the front of the Left Bde. of the Division on our right. Some Blue Cross and Lachrymatory gas shells were fired on our support positions especially near CALVERLY COPSE.

Trench Mortars. Our 6" mortars fired 434 rounds on the following targets:-
New work at F.12.c.95.55. Good hits observed on sunken road.
Front line in A.2.d. At least 10 direct hits on trench.
Front line in A.3.a and trench in F.11.d. Direct hits observed.
F.18.a.0.4 & F.18.a.3.5. 284 rounds in support of raid.
Our 3" mortars were also active. 85 rounds were fired on enemy posts opposite AYETTE during the raid. 1764 rounds were fired by the L.T.M. battery of the Right Bde. in support of the raid.
Slight enemy minenwerfer activity is reported on the extreme right where 6 light bombs were fired on F.17.c at 10.30 am.

Machine Guns. Our Vickers guns fired 60,000 rounds to cover the raiding party and in addition 4000 rounds harassing fire as under:-
2000 rounds on track junction A.4.b.4.7 and C.T. in A.8.b.
1000 rounds on enemy work in F.23.b.
1000 rounds on enemy work in A.13.d.
A few enemy M.Gs. opened fire during our raid but most of them appear to have been neutralised by our barrage. Harassing fire was normal.

2. PATROLS.

2/Lt.H.VAIZEY and 3 O.Rs. report an M.G. active at F.12.a.45.80 (previously reported as an occupied post.
During the progress of the raid a party from the Left Bn. Right Bde occupied the fork roads at F.17.a.9.9.

P.T.O.

3. INTELLIGENCE.

Movement. Movement observed in the forward area was normal and in the usual places. Foot traffic in rear areas was also normal. 2 parties of about 30 mounted men each were seen going towards BAPAUME on the ECOUST Road at 10.50 am. At 11.30 am 2 parties, one of 6 and another of 12, were seen on the MORY-ST LEGER Road at B.8.b.

Trains & Transport. This morning an abnormal amount of horse transport was seen going in both directions on the road at A.22.c.1.3. Between 5 and 6 am 19 H.T. and 2 mounted men were seen to pass this point. Most of the traffic was Southwards.

In rear areas train and transport movement appeared to be normal.

Enemy Defences.
(a) **Wire & Work.** Ground observers report work in progress in enemy trench at A.14.c and a party of 6 was seen working at F.23.b.3.3.

The enemy is busily engaged in the construction of dugouts in AERODROME TRENCH and by far the greater part of his activities is centered on this work. The hitherto unexplained loop of 'work' visible on recent air photographs in F.24.a is probably ill-camouflaged chalk spoil from the dugouts under construction in this trench.

(b) **Posts & M.Gs.** A white flag apparently used for signalling was seen at F.18.c.7.3. At this point a sentry has been previously reported. A sentry was seen at A.2.d.9.9.

A post is suspected at F.17.a.9.1 from which point a number of bombs were thrown at the patrol of the Left Battn. Right Bde. which occupied the fork roads during the raid. Judging by the number of bombs, this post is strongly held.

The enemy holds posts along the road in F.17.c and F.23.a by night only. These posts vary in position and are 50 to 100 metres apart. Before dawn the garrisons withdraw to the Eastern road and remain in a dugout until dark again. One sentry is posted by day on the Eastern road, none on the Western. One or two L.M.Gs. are pushed forward to the Western road at night.

There are 2 heavy M.Gs. at F.18.c.0.2.

(c) **T.Ms.** A L.T.M. is reported firing from F.23.b.6.0. Air photos show work resembling a twin T.M.E. just off the road at this point.

(d) **Headquarters.** The Commdr. of the Coy. holding the front in F.17 & 23 lives in AERODROME TRENCH in A.13.d or F.18.c. The H.Q. of the Battn. of the 10th Bav. R.I.R. in line is in either DOROTHY TRENCH or the bank at A.27.a.0.4.

(e) **Dugouts.** There are 3 good dugouts in the trench immediately N. of ABLAINZEVILLE CEMETERY and another in the main AYETTE-ABLAINZEVILLE Road somewhere about F.17.d.1.0. The latter is occupied by day (see under Posts & M.Gs.).

(f) **Batteries.** Hostile batteries were observed on T.Bs. of 132° 20', 127°, 140° and 87° 30' from X.27.d.65.75.

Fires & Explosions. Ground observers report at 1.40 pm, 2.30 pm and 4.36 pm dense clouds of smoke on a T.B. of 132° 40' from X.27.d.65.75 (probably BAPAUME). At 4.5 pm clouds of smoke were seen on a T.B. of 147° 35' from the same O.P.

Enemy Aircraft. Hostile 'planes were more active than usual during the period. At 5.30 pm a machine flew low over our lines and disappeared in a Northerly direction. At 6 pm 7 E.A. flew over AYETTE. At 6.15 pm 2 E.A. reconnoitred the battery positions in F.20 and between 8.30 and 9.30 pm 8 machines flew low over F.8.

Lights & Signals. From observation of the enemy's light signals fired during our raid last night, it would appear that the enemy S.O.S. is a succession of green lights and annihilating fire 2 orange lights.

A great profusion of single and double green and red lights was sent up during the raid not only on the front of attack but for some distance on either flank. Most of them were fired from

P.T.O.

behind the front line.

Enemy Dispositions. Last night's raid afforded an important Identification. Apparently the front from North of ABLAINZEVILLE to about BUCQUOY is held by the 5th Bav. Res. Div. with 2 Regts. in line. The boundary between the 234th Div. and the 5th Bv. Res. Div. is apparently about F.17.central.

The order of battle North to South appears to be:-
  453rd I.R. (234th Divn.)
  10th Bav. R.I.R. } 5th Bav. Res. Div.
  7th   "
  An unknown Div. (probably 111th)

The 12th Bav. R.I.R. was relieved by the 7th Bav. R.I.R. which had previously been relieved by the 453rd I.R. and is now in rest either at RUMAUCOURT or in the FAVREUIL-SAPIGNIES Area.

The 10th Bav. R.I.R. has one Battn. in line with 3 Coys. in and about AERODROME TRENCH and 1 Coy. in the outpost line. Another Battn. is in close support in the area A.15, 20 & 21 and a third Battn. in the railway embankment about A.28 and G.4.

Reliefs are uncertain and irregular and it is impossible to ascertain the exact date on which an inter-battalion or regimental relief takes place. It is considered likely, however, that the 12th Bav. R.I.R. will shortly relieve the 10th Bav. R.I.R.

Enemy Intelligence. Our raid last night was expected. The Coy. Commdr. of the 4th Coy. 10th Bav. R.I.R. told an N.C.O. some days ago that a coup de main might be expected any day or night either about BUCQUOY or ABLAINZEVILLE. This information was understood to have emanated from Regtl. H.Q. Last night the whole Divn. from the support in instant readiness and it is reported that 2 Coys. from the support Battn. reinforced the garrison of AERODROME TRENCH and ABLAINZEVILLE in anticipation of an attack by us.

Prisoners taken have no idea how this information was obtained. They know of no listening set in action in their sector.

Miscellaneous.
(a) There is nothing whatever stored in the huts in F.17 & 23.
(b) The 4th Coy. 10th Bav. R.I.R. are not aware that we occupy the posts in F.17.a (these posts were however shelled by the enemy arty. last night).
(c) Food conditions in Divisions not engaged in active operations appear to be very bad and the men complain that they do not get enough to compete with the conditions of trench life.
(d) As far as can be ascertained there are no indications of an enemy offensive on this front.
(e) The morale of the 10th Bav. R.I.R. is not high but is better than that of the 453rd I.R. Bavarians are usually good fighters.

Meteorological.

	Barometer.	Max.Temp.	Min.Temp.
July 22nd	29.05	79	57
July 23th	Sun rises 5.5 am, sets 8.43 pm. Moon rises 8.45 pm, sets 5.52 am. (All Summer Times).		

Lieut.
for Lieut. Colonel,
General Staff, 2nd Division.

23/7/18.

2nd Division Tactical Summary No. 57.
For 24 hours ending 8 am 24/7/18.

Not to be taken forward of Battn. H.Q. in the line.

1. OPERATIONS.

The situation is unchanged. Hostile artillery fire by night has decreased to normal again but there was some activity between 1.30 and 2.30 am last night on the right of our front due to the enterprise carried out by the Division on our right.

Artillery. Our field artillery harassed frequented areas and communications in the forward area throughout the 24 hours, paying special attention to AERODROME TRENCH and the new wire in F.18.c and A.13.d. At 1.45 am the active guns of the Right and Centre Groups fired a crash on ABLAINZEVILLE in conjunction with the raid by the Division on our right.

Hostile artillery activity was normal though considerable at intervals. The Purple Line in X.27, ADINFER, DOUCHY and AYETTE were the chief targets. The COJEUL VALLEY and our front system received some attention. During the operation by the Division on our right, a barrage was put down on the BUCQUOY - AYETTE Road and CALVERLY COPSE for half an hour.

Trench Mortars. Our 6" mortars fired 10 rounds on the enemy front line in A.2.b, silencing an enemy M.G.. 3" Stokes fired a few rounds on the enemy M.G. at F.12.c.2.8.

Except on the right, enemy minenwerfer were quiet. During the day and night a few bombs were fired on FLARE TRENCH and 12 were fired at F.17.c.1.5.

Machine Guns. Our Vickers guns fired 3750 rounds on targets as under:-
1000 rounds on enemy work in A.13.d.
2000 rounds on enemy trench in A.2.a.
750 rounds on enemy trench in F.12.a.

A Vickers gun, in conjunction with 4 Lewis Guns, engaged a large enemy party seen South of the AYETTE - MOYENNEVILLE Road.

Enemy M.G. fire was normal. The guns in the sunken road in A.1.d were active in retaliation for our getting on to the large party mentioned above.

2. PATROLS.

A reconnaissance patrol under Lt. G.W.STANESBY found a dead German at about S.26.d.65.30. Papers found on him identified the 452nd I.R. (normal). This German was probably one of the enemy killed in the patrol encounter on the night of 10/11th July.

2/Lt. L.C.NORRINGTON and 2 O.Rs. report new work at F.12.a.45.70 but no movement or sign of activity was visible at this point.

Other patrols which were out on the fronts of the Centre and Left Bdes. report all quiet and no sign of the enemy in No Man's Land.

3. INTELLIGENCE.

Movement. Observers of the Right Bde. report movement in the forward area above normal this morning. Between 4 and 6 am 50 men all in full marching order and wearing steel helmets passed singly at long intervals from COURCELLES to about A.20.b.5.9. Steel helmets are unusual; most of the Germans seen in this area hitherto wore soft caps. About 8 pm 10 men were seen going West in F.S.M.O. along COURCELLES ALLEY.

Apart from the increase reported in individual traffic South of COURCELLES, movement in the forward area was normal and in the usual places.

P.T.O.

Trains & Transport.   Between 7.25 and 7.55 pm 5 trains of 7 - 8 wagons each were seen coming West on the line between VRAUCOURT and L'ABBAYE.   4 wagons of 1 train appeared to be loaded with long planks.   No other abnormal movement on the railways under observation was observed.

Horse and motor transport observed in back areas appeared to be normal.

Enemy Defences.
(a) Wire & Work.   New stakes have been erected and coils of wire are visible at A.3.a.4.3.   Ground observers report new work in F.11.d.5.0.   2 men were seen repairing the parapet at F.17.d.2.3 and driven away by L.G. fire.   3 men were seen throwing earth out of the trench at A.20.b.85.80 and moving timber (5.45 am).   Timber can be seen on the side of the trench at A.13.d.0.9 - probably dugout under construction.
(b) Posts. & M.G.   A sentry was seen at A.3.a.25.00.   The M.G. at F.12.c.3.9 is again reported active.

Lights & Signals.   At 9 pm 6 white Very lights were sent up from COURCELLES at 5 second intervals without apparent result.   A green light was fired in the same place at 1.50 am but no result was observed.   During our crash on ABLAINZEVILLE this morning a green light was fired from the village followed by a double red.

Enemy Aircraft.   There was no air activity yesterday.   This morning at 5 am one machine crossed our line and flew West over ADINFER WOOD. At 5.45 am 5 E.A. patrolled our lines over AYETTE.   They were driven off by M.G. and L.G. fire.

Miscellaneous.
(a) At 6 am 2 pigeons crossed No Man's Land flying in the direction of COURCELLES.
(b) A large red cross flag is visible among the trees at H.1.d. - BEHAGNIES.
(c) 2 very tall wireless masts are visible on a T.B. of 123° 30' from X.21.a.4.5.

Meteorological.

	Barometer.	Max.Temp.	Min.Temp.
July 24th	29.35	68	54

July 25th   Sun rises 5.6 am, sun sets 8.42 pm
            Moon rises 9.11 pm, moon sets 7.12 am.
            (All Summer Time)

J.D. Macgowan.
Lieut.
for Lieut. Colonel,
General Staff, 2nd Division.

24/7/18.

2nd Division Tactical Summary No.56
For 24 hours ending 8 am 25/7/18.

Not to be taken forward of Battn. H.Q. in the line.

1. OPERATIONS.

The situation is unchanged.

Artillery. Our field artillery was active during the day and night harassing the enemy's positions and routes of approach. Movement in A.14 and A.20 was engaged, 50 rounds were fired by field Hows. on T.MEs. in ABLAINZEVILLE with good results, 40 rounds were fired on the M.G. at A.3.c.9.7 and 25 rounds on the enemy battery AW.9. A suspected camouflaged gunpit in A.7.d and the suspected dump of ammunition at F.17.d. 05.00 were also engaged.

Enemy artillery was fairly active during the day on our forward areas with harassing fire. At 10.30 pm AYETTE was shelled by field artillery with a mixture of gas and H.E. Most of the enemy fire was directed on the front of the Centre Bde. and on the vicinity of our forward field gun positions in X.28.a which received about 100 rounds 4.2. Our front line in F.6 and A.1, AERODROME SWITCH, OSTRICH SUPPORT, DOUCHY, ADINFER WOOD ' in X.27.c, LITTLE FARM and BADEN AVENUE also received some attention.

Trench Mortars. Our 6" mortars fired 131 rounds on the following targets:-
Trenches and new work at F.12.c.6.4 and F.11.d.6.5.
Suspected ammunition dump and dugout in F.17.d - good bursts observed.
Enemy front line at A.2.b.9.1. Effective retaliation for enemy
  M.G. fire from this direction.
Points on the enemy front line in A.2.d and A.3.a. A good percentage
  of hits were obtained on the trench and an A.A. M.G. silenced.
  A direct hit was obtained on the fire bay from which the gun was
  active and a dark mass, believed to be a Boche, was blown out of
  the trench.
    Our 3" Stokes fired 20 rounds on enemy wire in A.1, 20 rounds on
a working party in A.2.b (5 direct hits on trench) and a few rounds on
a suspected M.G. position in F.12.a.
    21 light bombs were fired by enemy minenwerfer yesterday morning
and evening on the front of the Right Battn. Right Bde. No other
activity is reported on the Divisional front.

Machine Guns. Our Vickers guns fired 6500 rounds on the following targets:-
  4000 rounds on the trench and track in A.7.d.
  1000 rounds on new enemy work and traffic in F.23.b.
  1000 rounds on enemy work in F.17.c and F.24.a.
   500 rounds at enemy aircraft.
  Enemy M.G. activity was normal.

2. PATROLS.

Lt. STANESBY and 5 O.Rs. patrolled in F.26.d from 12.20 am to 1.20 am. About S.26.d.95.40 where there are a number of dead Germans, two deserted snipers posts were found, one with a canvas cover. 15 yards South of this an artificial shell hole has been dug to a depth of 6½ foot and the spoil removed. The patrol was fired on from about S.26.d 99.31.

Sgt. TALLETT and 3 O.Rs. report seeing 3 Germans in the outpost line, one in F.S.M.O. On the approach of our patrol, the Germans made off.

2/Lt.A.EASTON and 4 O.Rs. report an enemy party of about 10 at F.12.a.5.5 which was, however, lost to view before an L.G. could be brought to bear.

P.T.O.

3. INTELLIGENCE.

Movement. Movement in the forward area was normal during the period. Parties of 4 to 6 men wearing grey overcoats and without rifles were seen going East at intervals along the C.T. in A.8.b and A.9. Our field Hows. caused casualties among these parties. The usual movement of individuals was seen in the area between COURCELLES and A.20.c.

At 4.25 pm about 30 men carrying timber disappeared in a sunken part of the road in A.4.c.

At 9.10 pm 2 parties of 10 each (only 1 man in F.S.M.O.) came West over the ridge at A.20.b.7.4.

Foot traffic in back areas under observation appeared to be normal.

Trains & Transport. At 10.35 am 2 columns of 6 limbers each went North on the ECOUST-BAPAUME Road. At 12 noon one column of 12 6-horse limbers went South on the same road (the same convoy returning?)

Early this morning an increase of traffic was noticeable on this road. Between 7.25 and 7.50 am 40 vehicles were seen going in both directions with a slight tendency Northwards.

Train movement observed appeared to be normal.

Enemy Defences.
(a) Wire & Work. Work was seen in progress in A.10.c, at A.9.c.4.4 and at A.15.c.10.15. Ground observers report new work on the short length of trench at F.12.c.6.5. Fresh earth is visible at A.14.c. 15.40. Camouflage seen at about A.7.d.65.40 was shelled by our field guns. Camouflage at F.23.d.3.9 and F.23.d.20.65 – Suspected as work on T.M. emplacement – is being dealt with by the artillery.

The enemy appears to be strengthening AERODROME TRENCH. Much movement is seen in it and all information received recently tends to confirm the impression that his main activities are devoted to making this trench into a strong line of resistance.

(b) Posts & M.Gs. An M.G. emplacement is suspected at A.13.a.3.8. This point was fired on yesterday. An M.G. is reported active at A.2.c.9.7. The post at F.12.a.4.2 still appears to be occupied. An M.G. is reported active from about F.17.d.5.3.

(c) T.Ms. A T.M. located active from F.23.d.3.8 was dealt with by our artillery.

(d) O.Ps. Movement was again observed about the O.Ps. already reported. Another is suspected (or possibly a M.G.E.) at A.15.c.1.2 where a square sandbag mound with a loophole in the centre can be seen.

(e) Batteries. Bearings were taken on active guns from X.27.d.65.75 as follows:- 124° 40' true – H.V. gun firing in direction of BEAUMETZ 127° 20' true – large calibre H.V. gun firing at 6 pm.

Fires & Explosions. Dense columns of black smoke rose from a fire burning in BAPAUME from 4.15 to 6.45 pm.

The following dumps were observed from X.27.d.65.75 to be exploded by our artillery:-

7.40 pm – true bearing 106°   7.50 pm – true bearing 113°
8.10 pm – true bearing 103½°.

Enemy Aircraft. No low flying E.A. are reported but R.E.A. are reported more active on the whole and in larger formations. At 7 pm 8 R.E.A. were engaged over their own lines by our machines and forced to retire. At 3 am this morning 6 machines were over F.16. The 3 machines seen yesterday appear to be of a new type with narrow planes. The iron cross on the wings was hard to distinguish.

Meteorological.	Barometer.	Max.Temp.	Min.Temp.
July 25th	29.50	76	55

July 26th Sun rises 5.6 am, sun sets 8.42 pm
Moon rises 9.11 pm, moon sets 7.12 am.
(All Summer Times).

Lieut.
for Lieut.Colonel, G.S.

25/7/18.

War Diary

2nd Division Tactical Summary No.59.
For 24 hours ending 0 am 26/7/18.

Not to be taken forward of Battn. H.Q. in the line.

1. OPERATIONS.

The situation is unchanged.

Artillery. Our field artillery was active as usual during the day & night harassing the enemy's positions and communications in the forward area. Forward 18-pdrs. were particularly active sniping movement. Shoots were carried out on the camouflaged pit at A.7.d.60.45 and on the O.P. at A.20.c.9.9.

Hostile artillery was not particularly active. One concentration of field artillery was put down for 10 minutes on our lines in F.20.c & d. and a 5 minutes bombardment with about 6 batteries was directed on our front system about AYETTE. DOUCHY and F.3.c received intermittent attention. The COJEUL VALLEY and F.10.b & d also received a few rounds.

Trench Mortars. Our 6" mortars fired 158 rounds on the following targets:-
Enemy outpost line in F.11.d - good bursts observed in the trench near parties of the enemy; none, however, were induced to bolt.
M.G. emplacement in F.12.a & c and A.7.d.
Enemy front line in A.8.a - retaliation.
Road in A.2.a and front line in A.8.a and A.2.a - sandbags and trench boards thrown up at different points.
3" mortars fired 50 rounds on enemy wiring parties in S.26.d and S.27.c and on the front line in A.3.a.
4 L.T.M. bombs are reported about F.23.a.1.5. No other enemy minenwerfer activity took place.

Machine Guns. Our M.Gs. fired 2750 rounds on targets as under:-
750 rounds direct fire on the enemy outpost line in F.12.a.
1000 rounds on enemy positions and new work at F.23.b.95.30
1000 rounds on enemy work from F.18.c.78.17 to F.24.a.53.82.
Enemy M.G. activity was normal.

2. PATROLS.

2/Lt.A.K.McLEAN, Capt. JONES and 7 O.Rs. located enemy wiring parties about S.27.c.4.4 between 12.15 am and 1.45 am.
Reconnaissance patrols sent out by the Right Bde. had nothing of importance to report.

3. INTELLIGENCE.

Movement. Movement observed in the forward area was normal. Most of the enemy seen in the forward area moved at the double. The report that the enemy attitude in this respect had undergone a change some days ago was probably due to the arrival in line of a Battn. of 453rd I.R. which has not been in this Sector recently and had not learnt to dread our harassing fire.

Observers report considerable dog traffic in the forward area. At 7.35 am and again at 12 noon a large dog was seen at A.14.b.00.35. At 7 am and again at 8.30 am a man was seen leading a dog at the AERODROME. Shortly after 6 am a man came West along the AYETTE-COURCELLES Road followed by a black dog. A dog is often seen running to and fro along COURCELLES ALLEY and AERODROME TRENCH. (In view of the difficulty of maintaining wires and the danger of movement in the open the Germans probably make great use of messenger dogs in this Sector).

P.T.O.

Trains & Transport. Train and H. and M.T. traffic appeared to be normal in back areas under observation.. No convoys were seen on the ECOUST-BAPAUME Rd. and the traffic of individual vehicles on this road had a slight tendency Northwards.

Enemy Defences.
(a) Wire & Work. The Right Bde. reports that a new trench can be seen running S.E. over the ridge at A.8.d.75.10. Work has been done on the trench at F.23.d.35.65.
(b) Posts & M.Gs. Sentries are reported at A.3.a.10.05 and A.2.d.6.5 (both previously reported). Two men were seen at a suspected post at A.3.d.0.2. An A.A. M.G. is reported active from the trench at A.7.d.9.6.
(c) O.Ps. Movement was seen about the O.P. at A.9.b.20.65. Whilst the enemy artillery was shelling our lines in S.26 the flashes of glasses were observed at several points in AERODROME TRENCH.
(d) Batteries. The following grid bearings were taken from F.2.b.8.8:- 9.5 am H.V. gun at 118° 30'
          10.15 am battery active at 113° in approx. A.15.o.
          7.35 pm A.A. gun active at 109° - very close to the
            ECOUST-BAPAUME Road.
    Observers at X.27.d.65.75 report the following bearings:-
        4.2 battery at 132° 50' - 133° 15' true.
        5.9 battery at 127° 25' true.
        A.A. battery of 4 guns at 109° 10' (apparently behind
          bank in C.25.d).
(e) Dugouts. The entrance to a dugout can be seen at about F.23.b.8.1.

Fires & Explosions. A dump was seen on fire E. of COURCELLES at 11.50 pm. A large flash was seen to come from the camouflage at A.7.d.65.40 during a shoot by our artillery.

Enemy Aircraft. Hostile machines were active this morning about 5.30 am but all attempts by low flying E.A. to cross our lines were repulsed by A.A. and M.G. fire.

Miscellaneous. What appear to be sheets of tarpaulin can be seen on each side of trench at A.9.b.10.05.
    S.26.d.9.3 appears to be a permanent night M.G. position.

Meteorological.
                    July 27th Sun rises 5.9 am, sun sets 8.39 pm.
                            Moon rises 9.56 pm, moon sets 9.54 am.
                                (All Summer Times).

27/7/18.
                                            Lieut.
                                  for Lieut. Colonel,
                                General Staff, 2nd Division.

2nd Division Tactical Summary No.60
For 24 hours ending 8 am 27/7/18.

Not to be taken forward of Battn. H.Q. in the line.

1. OPERATIONS.

The situation is unchanged.

Artillery. Our field artillery engaged movement observed in the forward area, suspected O.Ps in A.20, work and camouflage at F.23.b.35.85 and the suspected gunpit at A.7.d.65.40. During the 24 hours, harassing fire was kept up on frequented areas and routes, special attention being paid to suspected H.Q. at A.9.b.55.28, the railway at A.9.a.70.35, trenches in A.8 & A.9, and occupied positions in A.7.b, 14.c & d, and F.17 & 18.

Enemy artillery activity was below normal. Our forward system, DOUCHY, ADINFER WOOD and BILLY'S BANK received a few rounds and at 1 am a few rounds of 77 mm gas shell were fired on X.19.a & b.

Trench Mortars. Our 6" mortars fired 105 rounds on the following targets:-
AERODROME TRENCH in A.8.a and A.2.d - heavy timber thrown up at spots where mining was suspected (A.2.d.2.2).
Trench and road junction A.3.a.40.25 - 10 direct hits on trench.
Suspected T.M. dump and sunken road in F.17.d - direct hits on road.
Work and trenches in F.12.c. - Many direct hits observed.
Our 3" mortars fired 121 rounds on the enemy outpost line in S.27.d, the enemy trench in A.2.d and an M.G. at S.26.d.9.3. 8 rounds were also fired at E.A.

No enemy T.M. activity is reported.

Machine Guns. Our Vickers guns fired 6000 rounds on the following targets:-
3000 rounds on track and trench in A.7.d.
1000 rounds on tracks in F.23.b.
1000 rounds on enemy work in F.23.b.85.30.
1000 rounds on enemy work in A.13.d.

Our Lewis Guns engaged an enemy party in A.3.b at 5 am. One man fell and the remainder made for cover.

Enemy M.Gs. were quiet during the night.

2. PATROLS.

A patrol of the Left Bde. reports the consolidated shell holes at A.2.a.7.6 to be unoccupied. The noise of picks was heard in the sunken road.

Lieut.R.PERCY and 2 O.Rs. passed through two belts of enemy wire about F.11.d.central. The outer was concertina and the inner a belt of thick roughly made entanglements. After passing a third belt, the party took up a position in shell holes from which movement was seen about 30 yards to the left. Shortly afterwards a voice from the enemy post in front called out in a foreign accent "Get off". Our party remained quiet. A party was then seen working round the left of our patrol and a voice from the post in front again called out "Go on, get off". No shots were fired at the patrol but one Very light was sent up. The post in question appears to be located at about F.12.c.05.60.

Patrols of the Right Bde. report the following positions unoccupied by the enemy:- Gun pits at F.17.c.8.5, sunken road from BLIZZARD POST to F.23.a.6.7, sniper's posts at F.17.b.10.85 and 35.75, posts at F.17.a.9.5 and F.17.b.1.6.

P.T.O.

3. INTELLIGENCE.

Movement. Considerable individual movement in both directions was observed on the track alongside COURCELLES ALLEY in A.14.c - probably due to the bad condition of this C.T. after the rain. Otherwise movement in the forward area was normal.

At 8 am a party of 20 was seen going East in COURCELLES ALLEY.

At 5.30 am a large working party was seen at the new trench at A.8.d.8.1 (a known occupied position), and was engaged by our artillery. At 6 am 4 men left the trench and ran East. At 6.12 am 11 followed suit and at 6.20 am 8 more were bolted.

Visibility was too poor to admit observation of individual movement in rear areas.

Trains & Transport. Throughout the day considerable evidence of movement on the light railways East and S.E. of MORY was observed but visibility was too poor for observation of the direction of traffic and the nature of the load. A considerable amount of the traffic observed appeared to be on the railway in I.7 and the tendency is reported to have been Southwards.

No abnormal M. or H.T. traffic is reported.

Enemy Defences.
(a) Wire & Work. The enemy wire at about F.11.d.5.4 is reported to consist of one thin line of new concertina about 40 yds. from the outpost line with a second thick rough belt about 25 yds out. There appears to be also a semi-circular belt in front of the posts, strong but not far enough out to prevent the post being bombed.

A large party was observed at 5.30 am working on what is reported to be a new trench at A.8.d.8.1 (see under movement). At this point there already exists a short piece of trench which is known to be occupied.

New work can be seen at A.20.a.0.8 and A.14.c.1.1.
(b) Posts & M.Gs. Work is reported on a post at A.14.a.1.2. Posts are also reported at F.11.d.50.35, F.12.c.05.60 and F.11.d.35.15 all previously approximately located. An M.G. was reported to be firing last night from a position about F.17.b.3.8.

Fires & Explosions. At 9.30 pm a dump burst into flames and died down quickly East of COURCELLES.

Enemy Aircraft. Two 2-seaters patrolled the enemy's lines at 6.15am. No other activity is reported. 2 of our machines dropped bombs on AERODROME TRENCH at 6.25 pm.

Miscellaneous. About 8 pm a pigeon flew across the lines from ADINFER WOOD direction to beyond MOYENNEVILLE.

Meteorological.	Barometer.	Max.Temp.	Min.Temp.
July 27th	29.20	73	52
July 28th	Sun rises 5.10 am, sun sets 8.32 pm. Moon rises 10.20 pm, moon sets 11.15 am. (All Summer Times).		

Lieut.
for Lieut. Colonel,
General Staff, 2nd Division.

27/7/18.

2nd Division Tactical Summary No.61.
For 24 hours ending 8 am 28/7/18.

Not to be taken forward of Battn. H.Q. in the line.

1. OPERATIONS.

At 2.25 am this morning an enemy party attempted to raid our front line in S.26.d. The hostile party entered our trench about S.26.d.9.2 and had taken one man and an L.G. prisoner when our counter-attack from both flanks drove him off, recaptured our man and the Lewis Gun and resulted in the death of a German officer who was apparently leading the raiders. Further casualties were inflicted on the party as it withdrew through our wire. Except for this the situation is unchanged and the day and night passed without incident.

Artillery. Our field artillery carried out the usual harassing fire throughout the day on enemy works and trenches. Tracks received special attention during the night. Movement and working parties were engaged with good effect during the day by forward 18-pdrs. Between 10.30 and 11.30 pm 300 rounds were fired on A.2.c & d, A.8.a & b and A.7.b and between 11.30 pm and 4 am a further 300 on A.3.a, A.2.d and A.8.b.

Hostile artillery activity was slight. ADINFER WOOD, X.27, F.3 & 4 were harassed and between 12.30 pm and 2.30 pm 3 guns carried out a shoot on the Purple Line in F.3 firing about 100 rounds. At 4.50 pm and again at 6.5 pm field and heavy Hows. put down a light barrage on our line on the front of the Left Bde. firing in all about 320 rounds. VALLEY WOOD, the COJEUL VALLEY, the DOUCHY - ESSARTS Road, CARUSO COPSE and QUESNOY FARM were shelled at intervals and a few (Blue Cross ?) gas shell were fired about F.15.a.3.0.

Trench Mortars. Our 6" mortars fired 75 rounds on the enemy positions in F.17, F.18.a, A.8.a and A.3.a. Good results were observed. 3" mortars fired 50 rounds on the enemy line in A.2.b & a and in retaliation for the enemy attempted raid. 22 rounds were also fired at the enemy M.G. at F.11.d.3.5. This gun was silenced.

A few light bombs fell near the road at F.16.d.7.4 but no other hostile minenwerfer activity is reported.

Machine Guns.. Our Vickers guns fired 5000 rounds on tracks in A.7.d, F.23.b and A.13.d. Lewis Guns fired intermittent bursts and were used effectively against the enemy during his attempted raid this morning.

The enemy raid was apparently supported by a L.M.G. pushed forward from the sunken road. No other special activity is reported.

2. PATROLS.

A patrol of the Left. Bn. Left Bde. was out during the enemy raid reconnoitring the ground in S.26.d.

Capt. BEESLEY and 5 O.Rs. report the enemy post at F.12.a.4.2 occupied. 6 men in all were seen in the vicinity.

2/Lt.A.J.KIRKCALDY and 3 O.Rs. report no sign of the enemy anywhere near the TWO TREES at F.8.c.4.3. The wire running along the North side of the road at this point is in good condition and is an obstacle. An M.G. was active from about A.7.b.3.7.

2/Lt.J.C.WALKER and 3 O.Rs. were fired on at close range by an M.G. in the known post at F.12.a.45.80. There appears to be no wire West of a point 40 yds. East of F.12.a.35.85.

Patrols of the Right Battn. Right Bde. covered the whole of No.Man's Land in F.17.c and F.23.a without finding any trace of the enemy.

P.T.O.

3. INTELLIGENCE.

Movement. More movement than usual of individuals and small parties was observed yesterday especially in the morning in the area between AERODROME TRENCH and COURCELLES and South of this. Apparently COURCELLES ALLEY and AERODROME TRENCH are in very bad condition after the heavy rain and traffic consequently diverted to the tracks. Our artillery was active throughout the day on targets offered in this vicinity.

Considerable individual movement is reported for the first time about the Cemetery in ABLAINZEVILLE.

A.9.a.5.2 was a centre of messenger dog traffic.

Trains & Transport. Train & transport traffic observed in rear areas appeared to be normal. Bad visibility prevented detailed observation.

Enemy Defences.
(a) Wire & Work. The enemy wire at A.12.a.35.30 consists of a double row of large concertina, one plain and one barbed. This row of double concertina is continuous and in good condition as far as the COURCELLES Road.

Work was reported in progress at F.12.a.45.95.

New earth - apparently a new C.T. under construction - is reported to be visible at A.8.d.3.1. Work is also reported at A.14.a.1.9 and A.14.c.10.95.

(b) Posts & M.Gs. An M.G. is reported active from A.7.b.0.8.
(c) Artillery. A H.V. gun was firing on a true bearing of 124° 20' from X.27.d.65.75. A 4-gun field How. battery was firing at the Sugar Factory on a true bearing of 87° 40' from the same point.

Lights & Signals. At 2.25 pm a white light was sent up from behind COURCELLES. At 3.37 pm a green light and at 3.41 pm a double green were seen but no result was observed. Just before dawn a white light breaking into two was fired opposite the centre of the Right Bde. front without apparent result.

Enemy Aircraft. No E.A. were seen yesterday. Several reconnoitring machines were seen at 6000 feet early this morning. During the night about 40 bombs were dropped in the BIENVILLERS-POMMIER area.

Enemy Dispositions. The officer killed this morning in S.26.c belongs to the 451st I.R. (normal). Indications go to show that there will be a Battn. relief in this Sector on the night 28/29th or following night. The 3rd Battn. is at present in line.

The raid last night had apparently the sole object of securing an identification. It is possible that the enemy suspects or expects a relief to have taken place in the ABLAINZEVILLE - MOYENNEVILLE Sector and if this is the case it is highly probable that he will repeat his effort to get an identification on this part of the front.

Meteorological.	Barometer.	Max.Temp.	Min.Temp.
July 28th	29.60	66	57

July 29th Sun rises 5.12 am, sun sets 8.36 pm.
Moon rises 10.46 pm, moon sets 12.36 pm. /
(All Summer Times).   (following day)

Lieut.
for Lieut. Colonel,
General Staff, 2nd Division.

28/7/18.

2nd Division Tactical Summary No.62
For 24 hours ending 8 am 29/7/18.

Not to be taken forward of Battn. H.Q. in the line.

1. OPERATIONS.

The situation is unchanged.

Artillery. Our field artillery fired as usual on the enemy's forward trench system, outposts and communication trenches. Several O.Ps. and emplacements were also engaged. Harassing fire was carried out during the night, special attention being directed to tracks and trenches in the area of the 451st I.R. in view of a possible relief in that Sector.

Hostile artillery activity was slight. The COJEUL VALLEY, ADINFER, AYETTE, DOUCHY and QUESNOY FARM received a few rounds and field guns fired occasional rounds on our forward system. Night firing was slight.

Trench Mortars. Our 6" mortars fired 147 rounds on the following targets:-
  AERODROME TRENCH in A.8.a - enemy M.G. silenced.
  Road in A.1 - timber thrown up.
  Loophole in trench at A.8.a.95.95 - good bursts on trench.
  New work and the bank at F.18.a.6.6 - 6 direct hits obtained on
    trench. 6 Germans driven out of trench after 5th direct hit.
3" mortars fired 89 rounds on suspected work at A.2.d.6.5, on the outpost line in A.2.a & b in registration and on low flying E.A..

No enemy minenwerfer activity is reported.

Machine Guns. Our Vickers guns fired 5,000 rounds on enemy work between F.18.c.78.17 and F.24.a.53.82 and on the recently dug trench and tracks in A.8.b.

Enemy M.G. fire was normal.

2. PATROLS.

2/Lt.A.K.MACLEAN, 1 officer and 2 N.C.Os. made a daylight reconnaissance of the enemy outpost line in A.2.b. No movement was seen. The enemy wire is continuous from A.2.b.6.8 into S.27.c with one gap at about S.26.d.7.1.

2/Lt. MOLD, 1 officer and 7 O.Rs. report the enemy wire in F.17.c to be very poor. M.Gs. were active from about F.17.c.8.6, and from the outskirts of ABLAINZEVILLE. Very lights were sent up from about F.23.a.70.75.

Lieut.T.G.J.BINNIE, 1 officer and 11 O.Rs. left our lines at 10.30 pm and proceeded to the enemy post at F.17.a.85.43. This was unoccupied and was found to be a trench 40 yds. long in bad condition with 2 shelters and a stock of 100 egg bombs, 100 stick bombs and a number of Very lights. What appeared to be wiring was in progress in the valley between F.17.b.0.0 and F.12.c.0.0. An enemy post at about F.17.b.05.65 (previously reported F.17.b.1.6 - which was, however, reported unoccupied by a patrol two night's ago) was on the alert and a man was seen to run from it. At F.17.b.05.85 where a small sniper's post sited for firing in a Northerly direction, was found. The patrol was challenged, and bombs were thrown from about F.17.b.1.6. M.Gs. were active at F.17.b.15.95 and F.17.a.9.0.

3. INTELLIGENCE.

Movement. Movement in the forward area was normal. One large party of 24 was seen marching South on the COURCELLES - ACHIET LE GRAND Rd. at U.15 pm. At 6.20 am 3 parties were seen to leave the post at F.12.a.4.2 and go East over the ridge. These parties were of 6, 10 and 20 men respectively.

P.T.O.

At 7.30 pm a party of 25 was seen on the road in A.22.c. The track along COURCELLES ALLEY was again considerably used and the usual movement in the area A.14, 20 & 21 is reported.

Trains & Transport. Normal train, H. and M.T. traffic in rear areas is reported. Visibility was poor for back areas.

Enemy Defences.
(a) Wire & Work. Work observed yesterday evening on a dugout at F.18.a.3.3 was broken up by our 8" mortars. Fresh earth - possibly spoil from a dugout - is visible at F.24.a.2.3. New trench work can be seen at A.14.c.3.5 running N.E. towards RIDGE WORK. Telephone wires were seen to be repaired at this latter point.
The new trench reported by the Right Bde. in A.8.d is extending West down the slope.
(b) Posts & M.Gs. The M.G. in the post at F.12.a.4.2 was active against our aircraft yesterday.

Lights & Signals. At 3.45 am one green and at 3.55 pm two green lights were fired opposite the Right Bde. without apparent result.
Between midnight and 1 am a small beam of light was seen at F.17.d.1.3 for about 20 minutes.
At 6.15 pm 2 pigeons were seen to fly from the N.E. corner of ABLAINZEVILLE near the COURCELLES Road.

Enemy Aircraft. E.A. activity was very slight. Between 6.30 am and 7.15 am 2 E.E.A. flew over our lines but were driven off by A.A. and L.G. fire. 3 others were seen well behind the enemy's lines.

Meteorological.	Barometer.	Max.Temp.	Min.Temp.
July 29th	29.7	67	55

July 30th Sun rises 5.13 am, sun sets 8.35 pm.
Moon rises 11.18 pm, moon sets 1.55 pm.
(All Summer Times)

29/7/18.

Lieut.
for Lieut. Colonel,
General Staff, 2nd Division.

2nd Division Tactical Summary No.63.
For 24 hours ending 8 am 30/7/18.

Not to be taken forward of Battn./H.Q. in the line.

1. OPERATIONS.

At 10.40 pm we raided the enemy's outpost line East of AYETTE. 6 prisoners of the 2nd Battn. 453rd I.R. were captured and many casualties were inflicted on the enemy. In one post alone, 6 Germans were counted, killed by our T.M. fire which opened at Zero and which is reported to have been very effective. Field artillery, M.Gs. and Heavy Artillery also co-operated in covering the raid. The enemy artillery retaliation fell mostly on the front of the Right Bde. and was chiefly from two 5.9 batteries.

Artillery. Our field artillery carried out the usual harassing fire on enemy works, communications and movement during the day. A well timed barrage was put down in support of the raid by the Centre Bde. at 10.40 pm.
Hostile artillery was normally active during the day. HAMEAU FARM, ADINFER WOOD, VALLEY WOOD, DOUCHY and the AYETTE-BUCQUOY Road received some attention at intervals. The retaliation for the raid fell behind STORK SUPPORT, in AYETTE, along the AYETTE-BUCQUOY Road, on CARUSO and CALVERLY COPSES and the N.E. end of JEWEL VALLEY. Fire lasted for about half an hour but was only heavy at one period.

Trench Mortars. Our 6" and 3" mortars co-operated with the raiding party of the Centre Bde. and good results are reported. In addition 68 rounds were fired by the 6" mortars on various targets in the enemy outpost line and in AERODROME TRENCH.
No enemy minenwerfer activity is reported.

Machine Guns. Our Vickers guns fired 40,000 rounds in conjunction with the raid and in addition 4,000 rounds on tracks and trenches in A.7.d.
Enemy M.Gs. were only more than usually active during the attack on their outpost line. The road running through the COJEUL VALLEY, JEWEL VALLEY and the AYETTE-BUCQUOY Road were swept.

2. PATROLS.

2/Lt.GUNTHER M.C. and 3 O.Rs. report voices and movement at A.1.d.10.55 and 3 Germans seen in a post at approx. A.1.d.60.65.
Patrols of the Centre Bde. under Capt.BEESLEY, Lieuts.G.V. HARRISON and R.PERCY and 2/Lts. H.L.KIRKCALDY, W.ELLIS and J.T.WALKER reconnoitred the enemy's positions in F.12.a and F.6.c on the nights 27/28th and 28/29th July obtaining a detailed information and thorough acquaintance with the ground preliminary to the attack on these posts last night.
On the night 28/29th 2 enemy were seen at F.6.c.40.15. Otherwise no signs of enemy activity were observed about the AYETTE-MOYENNEVILLE Road in F.6.c.
Patrols of the Right Bde. report noises of hammering at about F.17.d.1.4. No sign of the enemy was seen by a patrol which reconnoitred the enemy wire from F.23.a.7.6 to F.17.b.8.3.

3. INTELLIGENCE.

Movement. Visibility was very poor and very little movement was observed. Such as was seen was in the usual places and did not appear to be abnormal. Observation of rear areas was impossible.

P.T.O.

2nd Division Tactical Summary No.64
For 24 hours ending 8 am 31/7/18.

Not to be taken forward of Battn. H.Q. in the line.

1. OPERATIONS.

The situation is unchanged.

Artillery. Our field artillery harassed enemy's forward system as usual during the day and night. Observation was prevented by poor visibility during the morning, but later in the day movement was engaged with good effect. A direct hit was obtained on the O.P. at A.20.c.95.90 by a 4.5 How. battery. At 1.15 am all active guns and Hows. fired a crash and barrage in support of a raid by the Divn. on our right.

Enemy artillery was not particularly active. There was some harassing fire at intervals during the day and night on the usual targets in our forward area. The retaliation for the raid by the Divn. on our right was fairly heavy, the AYETTE-BUCQUOY Road and CALVERLY COPSE coming in for most of the shelling.

Trench Mortars. Our 6" mortars fired 54 rounds on the enemy camouflaged post at F.17.b.00.55. Much damage was done.
3" mortars fired on an enemy M.G. and on movement in the enemy outpost line in A.1.c.
No enemy minenwerfer activity is reported except on the front of the Right Battn. Right Bde. during the enemy retaliation for the raid on our right.

Machine Guns. Our Vickers guns fired 8000 rounds on tracks and trenches in A.7.d, the huts in F.23.b and enemy work in A.13.d and F.23.b.
There was increased activity of enemy M.Gs. on the COJEUL VALLEY during the night; elsewhere fire was normal except during the raid.

2. PATROLS.

2/Lt.HART and 3 O.Rs. reached the track at A.1.d.1.6 and listened for 10 minutes without hearing or seeing any sign of the enemy except transport in the distance.
2/Lt.FILLINGHAM and 10 O.Rs. left our lines at 10 pm and after going out about 100 yds. saw an enemy party lying in extended formation about 30 yards from our wire. In rear of this party about 20 of the enemy were seen moving North. The patrol returned to our line, brought out a Lewis Gun and fired on the enemy. At 12.30 am there was no sign of the enemy party.
(It is possible that the party seen in F.11.d was a patrol sent out under Battn. orders from AERODROME TRENCH. It has been ascertained that much of the movement recently seen in front of AYETTE is due to large patrols coming down to this area during the night. So far, however, they have not shown much enterprise).

3. INTELLIGENCE.

Movement. Visibility was very poor yesterday and observation of rear areas was impossible. In the forward area slight movement of individuals was observed in the usual places when it was possible to see the enemy's lines.

Lights & Signals. During the operation on our right last night, the enemy sent up several double green lights. These were followed by single green, single reds and double reds. 2 greens appears to be the S.O.S. signal South of ABLAINZEVILLE as well as East of AYETTE.

O.P. The flash of glasses was seen at 12.15 pm at A.13.a.8.1. At this point a sentry has previously been reported.

P.T.O.

Enemy Aircraft. One enemy machine was seen patrolling the enemy's lines at 10 am. No others were seen.

Fires & Explosions. A small explosion was observed at 3.20 pm in A.27.b. A large cloud of white smoke was afterwards seen to rise.

Enemy Patrols. As well as the patrol which is reported by our patrol of the Centre Bde. in F.11.c, one of our posts in S.26.d reports that at 12.30 am a strong enemy patrol in front of our post at S.26.d.1.2 was dispersed by L.G. fire.

Enemy's patrol activity shows a marked increase and the appearance of these two patrols tends to confirm the evidence already to hand that he wishes to secure an identification in the Sector between MOYENNEVILLE and ABLAINZEVILLE.

Meteorological.

August 1st   Sun rises 5.16 am, sets 8.32 pm
             Moon rises 12.43 am, sets 4.22 pm.
             (All Summer Times).

31/7/18.

Lieut.
for Lieut. Colonel,
General Staff, 2nd Division.

Annexe to 2nd Division Tactical Summary No.64.

Notes on Photos taken 30/7/18.

12 LB 6088 & 6089.

What look like tool or material dumps are at A.14.a.40.45 and A.14.c.83.23 (near Battn. H.Q.) There are signs of considerable activity about the bank running through A.20.a & 14.c & d.
Work on the points of resistance manned by the support Battn. in A.14.b is also apparent.

12 LB 6101, 6102 & 8093.

These photos show the enemy work about the strong point in F.18.a.

12 LB 6090.

No Man's Land and the enemy and our outpost line in A.2.b & S.26.d.

12 LB 6087.

COURCELLES ALLEY is very wet. Water is visible at several points notably A.13.d.80.63 and 55.75. F.18.c.85.05 is a centre of activity - possibly a ration rendezvous or tool dump. Some parts of AERODROME TRENCH in F.18.c and A.13.d appear to be wet.

12 LB 6103, 6105 & 6106.

These photos show very clearly the individual enemy outposts in F.12 & F.11.d. Work has been done on the short piece of trench about F.12.c.central. The effect of our T.M. fire in F.11.d is visible.
There is a series of organized shell holes running E. of North behind the enemy outpost line in F.12.a & F.6.c. The outpost line proper does not appear to be occupied N. of F.12.a.45.80 as no tracks are visible N. of this point. The shell holes appear to be patrolled and visited from the N.E. and are probably the left flank posts of 451 I.R. They are too far forward to be the "intermediate line" posts of 453 I.R.

12 LB 6095 & 6096.

The withy beds at A.2.c.70.25 - 10.20 are occupied - probably by an "intermediate" group. A short length of trench is visible at A.2.c.5.2. The slits in the sunken road in A.1.d & A.2.c shew nothing new.

12 LB 6091, 6084, 6097, 6104, 6099, 6092 & 6086.

A new C.T. has been dug from about A.8.d.05.60 to AERODROME TRENCH about A.8.c.35.55. Two circular M.G. emplacements at A.7.d.95.60 approx. have been connected by a C.T. to the trench spur running from AERODROME TRENCH to the AYETTE-COURCELLES Road. Numerous dug-out entrances are visible all along AERODROME TRENCH in A.2, 8 & 14. Work has been done on the short C.Ts. and slits E. of AERODROME TRENCH in A.8.b and A.2.d.

Annexe No.2 to 2nd Division Tactical Summary No.64.

Extracts from correspondence captured on the night 29/30th July,
East of AYETTE.

(a) 28/6/17 5 am "Direct hit on a party of labour men - 9 dead and 21 wounded".

(b) Letter written by a N.C.O. 29/7/17 - "It's miserable about the offensive going wrong. The whole thing was betrayed of course. We are between ARRAS and ALBERT. Nothing doing here. The English are pretty lively and from their recent air activity we thought there'd be an attack. But that doesn't appear to be so. He's thinking we're turning over something in our minds which is also not the case.....The whole Corps that we belong to is to be relieved one of these days"

(c) Platoon Commander's letter written 29/7/18 before AYETTE. "We're to be relieved to-night. Last night I got a chit from Regtl. H.Q. telling me to reconnoitre and report on the wire in front of our position. I set to at once, had a look and then drew a sketch with particulars in writing on the other side and sent it off to Regtl. H.Q. I'm curious to know if the Regtl. Commander is satisfied with it for it's not much. I hope to-night goes off quietly and our relief comes up to time for from 1 - 4 am is always a very quiet time. We're going back 30 mins. march or so and will be in good deep dug-outs. So let them shoot as much as they like .....We will be 6 days in COURCELLES and on the night 4/5th we go to MORY. There I'll see what I can do about going on leave. If we go into the line again I shan't have to go in the outpost line but will sit in a good dug-out."

2nd Division Tactical Summary No.65
For 24 hours ending 8 am 1/8/18.

Not to be taken forward of Battn. H.Q. in the line.

1. OPERATIONS.

The situation is unchanged.

Artillery. During the day and night our field artillery harassed the vicinity of A.3.a.4.0, A.8.a, A.9.a, AERODROME TRENCH, COURCELLES ALLEY, the H.Q. at A.8.d.80.55 and the area about A.8.c and A.7.d. Hows. fired on the M.G. post at A.7.d.2.5 and on the trench junction at A.13.d.5.7. 60 rounds 4.5 were also fired on enemy posts and trenches in F.11.d and F.17.a. At 9.30 pm and 10.25 pm AERODROME TRENCH was bombarded with gas, particular attention being paid to trench junctions and dug-outs.

Enemy artillery fire showed a slight increase on the activity of the past few days. AERODROME SWITCH, OSTRICH SUPPORT, the COJEUL VALLEY in X.29, AYETTE, DOUCHY, ADINFER and STORK SUPPORT were shelled desultorily at intervals. Between 4 and 5 pm BADEN AVENUE was carefully registered with aeroplane observation and then heavily bombarded by 5.9s. The JEWEL VALLEY also received some attention.

Trench Mortars. Our 6" mortars fired 91 rounds on enemy work in F.18.a and A.7.d. Several direct hits were obtained at points where movement had been observed. 61 rounds were fired by the 3" mortars on enemy work in F.11.d, on low flying E.A. and in registration.

No enemy minenwerfer activity is reported.

Machine Guns. Our Vickers guns fired 9,000 rounds on the following targets:-
3000 rounds along AERODROME TRENCH and track in A.8.c.
500 rounds direct fire on enemy outpost line running S. through F.6.e.
2000 rounds on enemy work in F.25.b.
2000 rounds on enemy work in A.13.d.
1500 rounds on the enemy line F.23.b.75.15 to F.23.b.90.35.

Enemy M.G. activity was less than usual on the front of the right Brigade - normal elsewhere.

2. PATROLS.

Lieut. BARTLETT and 7 O.Rs. were fired on at a range of 20 yds. from an advanced enemy post at about S.27.a.15.60.

2/Lieut. J. FILLINGHAM with 1 platoon took up a position in an old trench at about F.11.d.4.7 about 10.30 pm and lay in wait for hostile parties. No signs of enemy activity were seen and the patrol returned to our lines. About 12.30 am 2/Lieut. FILLINGHAM returned to the same position with 2 O.Rs.. After a little while several of the enemy were seen crawling towards the party which withdrew to our lines. The enemy bombed the old trench at F.11.d.4.7 and advanced towards our wire. They were met with rifle grenades and 2 L.Gs. and dispersed with shouts.

Capt. J. WEST with 1 officer and 2 O.Rs. left our lines at 7.30 am under cover of the mist and made straight for the enemy trench at F.11.d.50.25. Very little wire was encountered and this consisted mostly of concertina all trodden down. The party was on the point of entering the German trench when a German appeared round the traverse, fired his rifle and bolted. The party gave chase but could not catch him and fearing to encounter a strong party our patrol withdrew and returned to our lines.

P.T.O.

Patrols (contd.).

2/Lt.G.R.WOOLLEY and 2 O.Rs. went out under cover of the mist at 6.45 am as far as the enemy slits at F.11.d.40.45. The wire in front of this length of trench was weak being mostly plain concertina. The trench was entered and found unoccupied at this point and the patrol returned to our lines without having seen or heard any signs of enemy activity.

2/Lt.F.J.SANDERS with 1 officer and 12 O.Rs. came across a large enemy working party in the AYETTE-ABLAINZEVILLE Road between F.17.c.95.95 and F.17.d.1.5. On the approach of our patrol a bird-call signal was heard and all sound and movement ceased. There was no sign of the enemy at F.17.c.95.95. A belt of barbed wire mixed with concertina runs from F.17.a.9.1 N.E. for about 100 yds. It is knee-high.

Lieut. R.J.ROBINSON and 4 O.Rs. report the enemy post at F.17.b.1.6 occupied last night. Work was heard both in this post and some distance behind it.

2/Lt.R.BOYLE and 3 O.Rs. lay out at about F.17.b.3.9 for some time and report everything very quiet and no sign of enemy activity.

3. INTELLIGENCE.

Movement. Only the usual individual movement and that in the usual places was observed yesterday. Transport in rear areas under observation appeared to be less than usual.

Enemy Defences.
(d) Wire & Work. New work is reported at A.8.a.6.5. Part of it has been camouflaged. New earth is visible at A.12.a.5.8. Two parties of 8 and 6 were seen digging at MILK WERK A.20.b.8.7 and fired on by our artillery.

The O.P. in the mound at A.20.d.2.9 has altered considerably in appearance during the last few days. 3 loopholes facing S.W., W. & N.W. can now be seen and a white flag on a sign-board is visible at the S. end of the MOUND.

2 rows of white poles can be seen running E. & W. in A.21.d on a grid bearing of 118° from F.10.c.05.65.

A sign-board can be seen on the bank of the road at A.14.a.10.15.

There appears to be a dressing station in the N.E. corner of COURCELLES. A Red Cross flag is visible at about A.15.b.7.7.

Lights & Signals. At 3.55 am one red followed by two green lights went up in the direction of MOYENNEVILLE without apparent result. Between 12 and 1 am twin red lights were sent up opposite the Right Bde.

Hostile Aircraft. Between 3.30 and 6.45 pm the area COURCELLES-BUCQUOY was patrolled by 2 reliefs of 2 R.E.A. each. At 5.55 pm one machine was over QUESNOY FARM. These appeared to have been observing for the 5.9 shooting on BADEN AVENUE and were engaged by our Scouts. At 7 pm one E.A. appeared to be hit and to land behind COURCELLES.

Single machines were seen opposite and over the Centre Bde. front during the morning, all flying high. No E.A. activity is reported by the Left Bde.

Meteorological.	Barometer.	Max.Temp.	Min.Temp.
July 31st	29.60	72	56
August 1st	29.45	78	56

August 2nd Sun rises 5.17 am, sun sets 8.30 pm.
Moon rises 1 am, moon sets 5.23 pm.
(All Summer Times).

1/7/18.

Lieut.
for Lieut. Colonel,
General Staff, 2nd Division.

(6339) Wt. W160/M3016 1,500,000 10/17 McA & W Ltd (E1898) Forms W3091. Army Form W.3091.

Cover for Documents.

Nature of Enclosures.

War Diary

July 1918

Original Appendices

Notes, or Letters written.

2nd DIVISION DISPOSITION AND MOVEMENT REPORT No 18

Shewing position of Units at 12 Noon 30th June 1918

Ref. BUCQUOY
1/40000

Serial No.	Unit	Headquarters		Transport
1.	2nd Division H.Q.	V.27.c.7.7		
2.	2nd Signal Co R.E.	V.27.c.7.7.		
3.	205 Empl. Co	HUMBERCAMP		
4.	2nd Div Recept.Camp	LUCHEUX	(Billet 34)	
5.	A.P.M.	V.27.c.7.7		
6.	S.C.F.(C of E)	V.27.c.7.7		
7.	S.C.F.(Non C of E)	POMMIER		
8.	D.A.D.O.S.	LA BELLE VUE		
9.	D.A.D.V.S.	V.27.c.7.7		
10.	Salvage Officer	HUMBERCAMP	(V.29.a.4.2	
11.	Div Gas Officer	HUMBERCAMP		
12.	Claims Officer	HUMBERCAMP		
13.	Burials Officer	HUMBERCAMP		
14.	French Mission	LA BELLE VUE		
15.	Rhd Disburs.Offr	SAULTY		
16.	O/c Coffee Bars	HUMBERCAMP		
17.	S.A.A. Section	GAUDIEMPRE	(D.1.d)	Entrance D.2.c.0.8
18.	No 2 M.T.Co.	BARLY		
19.	No 3 Mob Vety Secn	HUMBERCAMP	(V.22.b)	
20.	Main Salvage Dump	V.29.c.5.2		
21.	Divnl Baths	HUMBERCAMP, MONCHY & GAUDIEMPRE		
22.	Divnl Laundry	HUMBERCAMP		
23.	Reinforce. R'hd	MONDICOURT		
24.	Supply R'hd	SAULTY		
25.	Field Cashier	NOYELLE VION		
26.	5th Inf Brig.	W.23.c.1.8	LEFT	
27.	24th R.Fusiliers	X.19.c.8.2	Reserve	W.28.a.0.8
28.	2nd High L.I.	X.27.b.2.6	Left	W.25.a.1.9
29.	2nd Oxf & Bucks L.I.	X.27.b.9.5	Right	W.25.b.3.2
30.	5th T.M.Batty	X.21.d.3.8		W.25.a
31.	6th Inf Brig	E.4.a.6.3	CENTRE	V.30.b.8.4
32.	1st King's Reg.	F.1.c.0.0	Support =	V.30.b.8.4
33.	17th R.Fusiliers	F.9.a.8.4	Front %	V.30.b.8.4
34.	2nd S.Staff. Reg	E.5.d.2.3	Reserve *	V.30.b.8.4
35.	6th T.M.Batty	E.4.b.2.0		
36.	99th Inf Brig.	E.4.c.2.4	RIGHT	D.15.b.7.2
37.	1st R.Berks Reg	F.20.b.6.8	Right	D.10.c.5.4
38.	23rd R.Fusiliers	E.5.d.4.3	Reserve	D.15.c.9.8
39.	1st K.R.R.C.	F.9.b.6.1	Left	D.9.d.8.1
40.	99th T.M.Batty	E.5.b.2.6		
41.	C.R.A. 2nd Div	V.27.c.7.7		
42.	36th Bde R.F.A.	E.5.d.25.30 Right Group		ST AMAND
43.	41st Bde R.F.A.	ST AMAND		W.28.a.5.7
44.	14th Bde R.H.A.	W.24.b.25.65 Centre		W.24.a.2.7
45.	34th Bde A.F.A.	W.18.a.5.0 Left		W.18.a.5.0
46	75th Bde R.F.A.	X.13.a.1.5		GAUDIEMPRE
47.	D.T.M.O.	V.27.c.7.7		W.21.d.25.95
48.	2nd D.A.C.	GAUDIEMPRE		GAUDIEMPRE
49.	14th Bde B.A.C. (Advanced Sn)	GAUDIEMPRE W.28.b.2.8		GAUDIEMPRE W.28.b.2.8
50.	34th Bde B.A.C.	GAUDIEMPRE		GAUDIEMPRE
51.	75th Bde B.A.C.	GAUDIEMPRE		GAUDIEMPRE

* Front % Reserve = Support onnight 30/1st.July.

-2-

Serial No	Unit	Headquarters	Transport
52.	C.R.E.	V.27.c.7.7	
53.	5th Fd Co R.E.	E.5.c.3.2	W.19.d.97.95
54.	228 -do-	W.23.c.5.4	POMMIER
55.	483 -do-	E.12.c.15.43	POMMIER
56.	10/D.C.L.I. (Pioneers)	E.4.c.2.7	V.23.c.0.3
57.	No 2 M.Gun Bn	W.26d.8.3	HUMBERCAMP
58	2nd Div Train	V.21.b.5.5	
59.	No 1 Coy	LA BAZEQUE FARM	
60.	No 2 Coy	V.21.b.7.8	
61.	No 3 Coy	V.15.d.7.3	
62.	No 4 Coy	V.15.d.8.5	
63.	A.D.M.S.	V.27.c.7.7	
64.	5th Fd Ambce	BERLES AU BOIS	W.15.c.3.0
65.	6th Fd Ambce	WARLINCOURT	
66.	100th Fd Ambce	W.13.d.5.7	W.13.c.5.9

G. Diary (2)

2nd DIVISION - CASUALTY RETURN FOR June 1918.

UNIT	KILLED O.	KILLED O.R.	WOUNDED O.	WOUNDED O.R.	MISSING O.	MISSING O.R.	INJURED O.	INJURED O.R.	Names of Officers and Remarks
H.Qrs. 2nd Divn.									Attached units
5th Inf. Bde.									14th Army Bde R.F.A.
A. 24th R. Fus.			3	11					Wounded O.R. 2
B. 2/Oxf.& Bucks.LI		1	1	15		3			Injured O.R. 1
C. 2nd High. L.I.		1		9					34th Army Bde R.F.A.
5th T.M. Bty.									Wounded O.R. 1
6th Inf. Bde.									74th Bde R.F.A. Guards Divn
D. 17th R. Fus.	1	8	2	17					Wounded Officer 1 O.R. 1
E. 1st King's R.		6		10					
F. 2nd S.Staffs.R.		9		27					75th Bde R.F.A. Guards Divn
6th T.M. Bty.				2			1	4	Wounded O.R. 3
99th Inf. Bde.									31st D.A.C.
G. 23rd R. Fus.		8	1	23			1	1	Wounded O.R. 1
H. 1/R.Berks.R.	4	9	3	22				1	165 Bde R.F.A. 31st Division
K. 1st K.R.R.C.		1	9	114				3	Wounded O.R. 2
99th T.M. Bty.									170th Bde R.F.A. 31st Division
P. 10th D.C.L.I.		1		3					
X. No.2 M.G.Bn.		3	2	28					Wounded O.R. 4
R.A., 2nd Divn.									178th Bde R.F.A. 40th Division
36th Bde.									
41st Bde.				2					
2nd D.A.C.								1	Wounded O.R. 3
X/2 T.M.Bty.									
Y/2 T.M.Bty.									181st Bde R.F.A. 40th Division
R.E., 2nd Divn.									
5th Field Co.		1		1					Wounded O.R. 7
226th Fd. Co.									
483rd Fd. Co.				3					
2nd Signal Co.									
205 Employment Co				1					
Totals.	5	51	18	288		3	2	10	

3/7/1918.

G.H. Birkett, Major,
D.A.A.G., 2nd Division.

"B"

(3)

2nd DIVISION.

STRENGTH RETURN MADE UP TO 12 NOON SATURDAY 6th July 1918.

UNIT.	(i.) Fighting strength for previous week, complied in accordance with A.Gs. instructions.		(ii.) Increase during week, due to drafts, etc., taken on strength of unit.		(iii.) Totals from (i.) and (ii.)		(iv.) Decrease during week—casualties, etc., deducted from strength of unit.		"A" Strength, excluding Attached.		"B" Not present with the Unit and not at the disposal of C/O. included in column A.		"A" minus "B" Available Fighting Strength including Personnel Battalion Transport and Quartermaster's Stores.		REMARKS. (Brief notes regarding (ii.), (iv.) and "B", etc.)
	Officers.	O.R.	Officers.	O.R.	Officers.	O.R.	Officers.	O.R.	Officers.	O.R.	Officers.	O.R.	Officers.	O.R.	
5th INFANTRY BRIGADE.															
24th Royal Fusiliers.	33	823	4	3	39	826	2	11	37	815	9	161	28	654	
2nd Oxf. & Bucks L.I.	37	1003	1	11	38	1014	—	16	38	998	11	259	27	739	
2nd Highland L.I.	41	906	1	2	42	908	—	14	42	894	11	216	31	678	
Total Brigade.	115	2732	6	16	119	2748	2	41	117	2707	31	636	86	2071	
6th INFANTRY BRIGADE.															
17th Royal Fusiliers.	38	867	—	31	38	898	1	62	37	836	13	187	24	649	
1st King's Regiment.	40	893	2	53	42	946	3	49	39	897	21	172	18	725	
2nd S.Staffs Regt.	38	873	1	38	39	911	—	57	39	854	19	164	20	690	
Total Brigade.	116	2633	3	122	119	2755	4	168	115	2587	53	523	62	2064	
99th INFANTRY BRIGADE.															
23rd Royal Fusiliers.	36	862	2	5	38	867	3	24	35	843	11	163	24	680	
1st Royal Berks Regt.	34	995	2	16	36	1011	2	63	34	948	14	171	20	777	
1st K.R.Rifle Corps.	36	914	3	13	39	927	—	31	39	896	12	241	27	655	
Total Brigade.	106	2771	7	34	113	2805	5	118	108	2687	37	595	71	2092	
Pioneer Battalion.															
10th D.C.L.I.	36	907	—	7	36	914	—	28	36	886	9	181	27	705	
TOTAL DIVISION.	371	9043	16	179	387	9222	11	355	376	8867	130	1935	246	6932	
No.2 Bn. M.G.Corps.	37	869	2	22	39	891	2	51	37	840	2	58	35	782	
TOTALS															

(Sgd.) C.E.Pereira
Major General,
Commanding 2nd Division.

EXPLANATION OF INCREASE AND DECREASE.

UNIT.	INCREASE.	DECREASE.	AUTHORITY.
5th INFANTRY BRIGADE.			
24th Royal Fusiliers.	4 Officers (names will be notified later) 5 O.R. from hospital.	2/Lieut.L.J.DAY, evacuated to England sick. 2/Lieut.F.W.PARTRIDGE wounded 4-7-18. 9 O.R. evacuated sick. 1 " commission. 1 " trans. to R.Es.	D.A.G.,List No.1173 dated 27/6/18.
2nd Oxf. & Bucks L.I.	1 Officer (name will be notified later) 11 O.R. reinforcements.	1 O.R. commission. 14 " trans. to 20th Bn.M.G.Corps. 1 " evacuated sick.	
2nd Highland L.I.	Lieut. R.M.SMITH joined 28-6-18. 1 O.R. trans. from 16th Lan.Fus. 1 " from hospital.	4 O.R. battle casualties. 1 " trans. to 2nd Signal Coy.R.E. 9 " evacuated sick.	
6th INFANTRY BRIGADE.			
17th Royal Fusiliers.	3 O.R. reinforcements. 28 " from hospital.	Major S.J.M.HOLE, M.C. to Senior Officers' Course, ALDERSHOT. 1 O.R. wounded. 59 " evacuated sick. 2 " miscellaneous.	A.G's No.5146 dated 27/6/18.
1st King's Regiment.	2/Lieut. P.SWERNEY) Lieut. & Q.M. J.R.WHITE) joined 28-6-18. 29 O.R. from hospital. 24 " reinforcements.	Lieut. R.T.SYMONDS, M.G. to England for R.A.F. 2-7-18. Lt. & Q.M.A.J.BENNETT trans. to 7th Bn. West Indies Regt. 2/Lieut.G.P.WRIGHT killed 2-7-18. 40 O.R. evacuated sick. 2 " commissions. 6 " wounded. 1 " miscellaneous.	A.G's No.2154/275(o) dated 26/6/18. A.G's No.AG/2158/2750(O) dated 23/6/18.
2nd S.Staffs Regt.	R.Q.M.S. A.HELLERSON promoted to commissioned rank 2nd Lt.29-6-18. 56 O.R. reinforcements. 2 " from hospital.	51 O.R. evacuated sick. 1 " transfer. 1 " commissioned. 4 " miscellaneous.	
99th INFANTRY BRIGADE.			
23rd Royal Fusiliers.	2/Lieut. T.J.SANDERS)joined Divl. " E.W.SIMPKINS)Reception Camp 2-7-18. 5 O.R. reinforcements.	A/Capt. J.P.COULL, wounded (gas) 30-6-18. A/Capt. R.SIZEN taken on Estab. Third Army Infantry School. 2/Lieut. C.R.TERRELL, wounded (gas) 30-6-18. 2 O.R. wounded. 3 " commissions. 19 " evacuated sick.	Third Army No.G-/33/85 dated 14/6/18.

P.T.O.

EXPLANATION OF INCREASE AND DECREASE (Continued)

UNIT.	INCREASE.	DECREASE.	AUTHORITY.
99th INFANTRY BRIGADE (Continued) 1st Royal Berks.Regt.	Capt. E.M.ALLFREY, DSO., joined 17-6-18. 2/Lieut. K.B.CATCHPOLE, joined Divl. Reception Camp 4-7-18. 16 O.R. from hospital.	2/Lieut. P.MURRAY wounded 29-6-18. 2/Lieut. L.BOURA evacuated to England sick 25-6-18. 1 O.R. killed. 6 " wounded. 53 " evacuated sick. 1 " commission. 1 " to Base Depot.	D.A.G.'s List No.1176 dated 30/6/18.
1st K.R.Rifle Corps.	Bt.Lt.Col. C.A.HOWARD joined 1/7/18. Lieut. G.A.BURNETT joined 30-6-18. 2/Lieut. P.C.SOMERVILLE joined 30-6-18. 5 O.R. reinforcements. 8 " from hospital.	9 O.R. wounded (gas). 2 " wounded. 1 " to Base Depot. 1 " commission. 17 " evacuated sick. 1 " miscellaneous.	A.G's No.A.G./2158/3264 (O) dated 1/7/18. A.G's No.A.G./2158/3489 (O) dated 10/6/18.
10th D.C.L.I.(Pioneers).	3 O.R. reinforcements. 4 " from hospital.	28 O.R. evacuated sick.	
No.2 Bn. M.G.Corps.	Lieut. P.GRATTEN. " G.A.W.HEATH. 2 O.R. from hospital. 20 " reinforcements.	Lieut. E.M.GROSE to H.Q.Fourth Army for duty, as a "P.B. Officer. 2/Lieut. H.S.HUDSON evacuated sick. 8 O.R. casualties. 26 " evacuated sick. 17 " to Base Depot.	A.G's No.A.G.13/577(M).

EXPLANATION OF COLUMN "B".

(a) On leave and at Army Rest Camp.
(b) Sick in Divisional Area.
(c) Courses.
(d) Officers admitted to hospital sick and not reported as invalided to England.
(e) Extra regimentally employed and not at disposal of the C.O.
(f) At Divisional Reception Camp.

UNIT.		Off.	O.R.
5th INFANTRY BRIGADE.			
24th Royal Fusiliers.	(a)	1	13
	(b)	-	3
	(c)	-	25
	(d)	3	-
	(e)	3	53
	(f)	2	67
		9	161
2nd Oxf. & Bucks L.I.	(a)	1	17
	(b)	-	58
	(c)	3	18
	(d)	3	-
	(e)	1	42
	(f)	3	124
		11	259
2nd Highland L.I.	(a)	3	12
	(b)	-	14
	(c)	5	19
	(d)	1	-
	(e)	1	38
	(f)	1	133
		11	216
6th INFANTRY BRIGADE.			
17th Royal Fusiliers.	(a)	-	7
	(b)	-	22
	(c)	6	39
	(d)	4	-
	(e)	3	45
	(f)	-	74
		13	187
1st King's Regiment.	(a)	3	15
	(b)	-	19
	(c)	4	31
	(d)	8	-
	(e)	1	29
	(f)	5	78
		21	172
2nd S.Staffs Regt.	(a)	2	7
	(b)	-	2
	(c)	5	35
	(d)	8	-
	(e)	3	41
	(f)	1	79
		19	164
99th INFANTRY BRIGADE.			
23rd Royal Fusiliers.	(a)	-	11
	(b)	-	35
	(c)	5	15
	(d)	1	-
	(e)	2	41
	(f)	3	83
		11	185

P.T.

29th INFANTRY BRIGADE (Cont'd)		Off.	O.R.
1st Royal Berks Regt.	(a)	2	11
	(b)	-	23
	(c)	6	18
	(d)	3	-
	(e)	1	43
	(f)	2	76
		14	171
1st K.R.Rifle Corps.	(a)	1	12
	(b)	-	31
	(c)	5	20
	(d)	3	-
	(e)	1	35
	(f)	2	143
		12	241
10th D.C.L.I. (Pioneers)	(a)	1	6
	(b)	-	84
	(c)	2	32
	(d)	4	-
	(e)	1	16
	(f)	1	43
		9	181
No.2 Bn. M.G.Corps.	(a)	1	7
	(b)	1	12
	(c)	-	14
	(d)	-	-
	(e)	-	1
	(f)	-	24
		2	58

G. Diary

"B."

2nd DIVISION.

STRENGTH RETURN MADE UP TO 12 NOON SATURDAY 13th JULY, 1918.

UNIT.	(i.) Fighting strength for previous week, compiled in accordance with A.Gs. instructions.		(ii.) Increase during week, due to drafts, etc., taken on strength of unit.		(iii.) Totals from (i.) and (ii.)		(iv.) Decrease during week—casualties, etc., deducted from strength of unit.		"A" Strength, excluding Attached.		"B" Not present with the Unit and not at the disposal of C.O. included in column "A".		"A" minus "B" Available Fighting Strength including Personnel of Battalion Transport and Quartermaster's Stores.		REMARKS. (Brief notes regarding (ii.), (iv.) and "B", etc.)
	Officers.	O.R.	Officers.	O.R.	Officers.	O.R.	Officers.	O.R.	Officers.	O.R.	Officers.	O.R.	Officers.	O.R.	
5th INFANTRY BRIGADE.															
24th Royal Fusiliers.	*34	815	4	41	38	856	1	10	37	846	11	198	26	648	* 3 Officers added to last week's Return as Reinforcements were Officers returning from Hospital and consequently were still on strength of Battn.
2nd Oxf.& Bucks L.I.	#37	998	1	3	38	1001	1	22	37	979	11	241	26	738	
2nd Highland L.I.	42	894	—	31	42	925	1	13	41	912	7	201	34	711	
Total Brigade.	113	2707	5	75	118	2782	3	45	115	2737	29	640	86	2097	
6th INFANTRY BRIGADE.															
17th Royal Fusiliers.	37	836	4	20	41	856	5	23	36	833	12	169	24	664	# 1 Officer added to last week's Return deducted for reasons as stated above.
1st King's Regiment.	39	897	3	97	42	994	1	39	41	955	19	198	22	757	
2nd S.Staffs Regt.	39	854	4	62	43	916	—	19	43	897	19	159	24	738	
Total Brigade.	115	2587	11	179	126	2766	6	81	120	2685	50	526	70	2159	
99th INFANTRY BRIGADE.															
23rd Royal Fusiliers	35	843	3	10	38	853	—	42	38	811	12	220	26	591	
1st Royal Berks Regt.	34	948	2	34	36	982	1	85	35	897	14	190	21	707	
1st K.R.Rifle Corps.	39	896	3	29	42	925	1	19	41	906	16	229	25	677	
Total Brigade.	108	2687	8	73	116	2760	2	146	114	2614	42	639	72	1975	
Pioneer Battalion.															
10th D.C.L.I.	36	886	—	10	36	896	1	52	35	844	11	158	24	686	
TOTAL DIVISION.	372	8867	24	337	396	9204	12	324	384	8880	132	1963	252	6917	
No.2 Bn. M.G.Corps.	37	840	7	41	44	881	2	12	42	869	3	44	39	825	

TOTALS

(Sgd) C. E. Pereira,
Major General,
Commanding 2nd Division.

EXPLANATION OF INCREASE AND DECREASE.

UNIT.	INCREASE.	DECREASE.	AUTHORITY.

5th INFANTRY BRIGADE.

24th Royal Fusiliers.

INCREASE:
- Capt. G.G. NELSON.
- Lieut. GRIFFITHS.
- Lieut. T.L. STOCKER
- 1 Officer - name will be notified later.
- 56 O.R. reinforcements.
- 5 " casuals.

DECREASE:
- 2/Lieut. A.KIRKPATRICK wounded 7-7-18.
- 2 O.R. killed
- 2 " wounded (1 since died)
- 5 " evacuated sick.
- 2 " trans. to R.E.
- 1 " commission.

2nd Oxf. & Bucks L.I.

INCREASE:
- Lieut. L.W. GILES, M.C., joined 10-7-18.
- 3 O.R. reinforcements.

DECREASE:
- Capt. G.H. FULLER killed 10-7-18.
- 1 O.R. killed.
- 11 " wounded
- 10 " evacuated sick.

2nd Highland L.I.

INCREASE:
- 30 O.R. reinforcements.
- 1 " from hospital.

DECREASE:
- 2/Lieut. W.A. BLAIR wounded 5-7-18.
- 1 O.R. battle casualty.
- 11 " evacuated sick.
- 1 " commission.

6th INFANTRY BRIGADE.

17th Royal Fusiliers.

INCREASE:
- Capt. D.G. GIBSON.
- 2/Lieut. F.S. WATERS.
- " W.S. WAY.
- 1 Officer - name will be notified later.
- 4 O.R. from hospital.
- 15 " reinforcements.
- 1 " miscellaneous.

DECREASE:
- Capt. F.S. BEAUFORD to England sick 4-7-18.
- 2/Lieut. J.L. WHITE to England sick 23-6-18.
- 2/Lieut. W.F. WILLIAMS to England sick 5-7-18.
- 2/Lieut. A.H. WOODCOCK posted to 8th T.M. Battery 21-6-18.
- 2/Lieut. J.J. EVANS wounded 12-7-18.
- 18 O.R. evacuated sick.
- 6 " wounded.
- 1 " miscellaneous.

D.A.G., List No.1185 dated 2-7-18.
D.A.G., List No.1182 dated 6-7-18.
D.A.G., List No.1184 dated 5-7-18.
A.G's No.AG.109/284(o) dated 5-7-18.

1st King's Regiment.

INCREASE:
- Lieut. W.J.A. PRATT
- " W. HARRADINE } joined 3-7-18.
- " G.W. HARRISON
- 45 O.R. reinforcements.
- 38 " do.
- 15 " from hospital.

DECREASE:
- 2/Lieut. S.G. COCKBURN to England for trans. to R.A.F.
- 5 O.R. wounded.
- 33 " evacuated sick.
- 3 " miscellaneous.

A.G's No.AG.2154/283(o) dated 2-7-18.

2nd S.Staffs Regt.

INCREASE:
- Lt.(A/Capt.) G. DUTTON } joined
- Lieut. C.R. WORMLEY, MC } 10-7-18.
- " E.R. SHAKESPEAR
- 1 Officer - name will be notified later.
- 58 O.R. reinforcements.
- 4 " miscellaneous.

DECREASE:
- 16 O.R. evacuated sick.
- 2 " commissions.
- 1 " transfer.

P.T.O.

EXPLANATION OF INCREASE AND DECREASE (Continued)

UNIT.	INCREASE.	DECREASE.	AUTHORITY.
99th INFANTRY BRIGADE.			
23rd Royal Fusiliers.	Capt. W.B.CLUFF,M.G. joined 11-7-18. 2/Lieut. F.WRIGHT " 10-7-18. " A.W.SMITH " 10-7-18.	7 O.R. wounded (gas). 5 " wounded. 1 " commission. 29 " evacuated sick.	
1st Royal Berks Regt.	10 O.R. from hospital. 2/Lieut. H.GATLING joined 9-7-18. " G. BYSH " 10-7-18. 34 O.R. from hospital.	Lieut. R.E.POWELL to England 7-7-18. 34 O.R. evacuated sick. 1 " wounded.	A.G's No.AG.2153/2883(O).
1st K.R.Rifle Corps.	2/Lieut. R.BOYLE joined 12-7-18. 2 Officers - names will be notified later. 20 O.R. reinforcements. 9 " from hospital.	Lieut. & Q.M. F.PEACOCK to Base (Pool). 1 O.R. commission. 2 " wounded. 1 " trans. to 99th T.M.Bty. 15 " evacuated sick.	A.G's No.AG/2153/1995(O). dated 5-7-18.
10th D.C.L.I.(Pioneers)	10 O.R. from hospital.	Lieut. E.WILLS to England to join R.A.F. 11-7-18. 51 O.R. evacuated sick. 1 " to hospital in England.	A.G's No.AG/2154/283(O) dated 6-7-18.
No.2 Bn. M.G.Corps.	Lt.(A/Capt.) A.O.ROBINSON,M.G. rejoined from Base. Lieut. A.K.O.FULLBROOK-LEGGATT rejoined from 99th Bn. M.G.C. Lieut. E.S. RAWSON. 2/Lieut. G.W.HAYWARD. " S.G. MARSH. " F.W. ORTON. " R.A. PICKUP. 39 O.R. reinforcements. 2 " from hospital.	Hon.Lt. & Q.M. R.D.BURGESS,M.G. evacuated to Base sick. Lieut. A.A. HAYES, evacuated to Base sick. 3 O.R. casualties. 8 " evacuated sick. 1 " to Base underage.	

EXPLANATION OF COLUMN "B".

(a) On leave and at Army Rest Camp.
(b) Sick in Divisional Area.
(c) Courses.
(d) Officers admitted to hospital sick and not reported as invalided to England.
(e) Extra regimentally employed and not at disposal of the C.O.
(f) At Divisional Reception Camp.

UNIT.		Off.	O.R.
5th INFANTRY BRIGADE.			
24th Royal Fusiliers.	(a)	2	15
	(b)	-	11
	(c)	-	25
	(d)	2	-
	(e)	3	51
	(f)	4	98
		11	198
2nd Oxf. & Bucks L.I.	(a)	3	11
	(b)	-	43
	(c)	3	15
	(d)	2	-
	(e)	1	42
	(f)	2	130
		11	241
2nd Highland L.I.	(a)	-	17
	(b)	-	11
	(c)	4	19
	(d)	1	-
	(e)	1	38
	(f)	1	116
		7	201
6th INFANTRY BRIGADE.			
17th Royal Fusiliers.	(a)	1	12
	(b)	-	11
	(c)	7	39
	(d)	-	-
	(e)	1	41
	(f)	3	66
		12	169
1st King's Regiment.	(a)	4	19
	(b)	-	7
	(c)	5	33
	(d)	6	-
	(e)	*1	27
	(f)	3	112
		19	198

*Includes 1 Officer at Base as Evidence for F.G.C.M.

		Off.	O.R.
2nd S.Staffs Regt.	(a)	2	8
	(b)	-	3
	(c)	5	32
	(d)	9	-
	(e)	2	40
	(f)	1	76
		19	159
99th INFANTRY BRIGADE.			
23rd Royal Fusiliers.	(a)	-	17
	(b)	-	61
	(c)	6	16
	(d)	1	-
	(e)	2	41
	(f)	3	85
		12	220

99th INFANTRY BRIGADE (Cont'd)		Off.	O.R.
1st Royal Berks Regt.	(a)	1	15
	(b)	-	7
	(c)	6	17
	(d)	4	-
	(e)	1	46
	(f)	2	105
		14	190
1st K.R.Rifle Corps.	(a)	4	13
	(b)	-	35
	(c)	5	12
	(d)	2	-
	(e)	1	30
	(f)	4	139
		16	229
10th D.C.L.I.(Pioneers)	(a)	1	7
	(b)	-	30
	(c)	3	33
	(d)	5	-
	(e)	1	14
	(f)	1	74
		11	158
No.2 Bn. M.G.Corps.	(a)	1	8
	(b)	1	24
	(c)	1	12
		3	44

Appdx. 6 Diary

2nd DIVISION.

DISPOSITION AND MOVEMENT REPORT No. 29. SECRET.

Shewing Positions of Units at 12 noon 21st July, 1918.

Reference BUCQUOY 1/40,000.

Unit No.	UNIT.	Headquarters.		Transport.
1.	2nd Division H.Q.	V.27.c.7.7.		
2.	2nd Signal Coy. R.E.	V.27.c.7.7.		
3.	205th Emplt. Coy.	HUMBERCAMP		
4.	2nd Divn. Reception Camp.	LUCHEUX (Billet 34)		
5.	A.P.M.	V.27.c.7.7.		
6.	S.C.F. (C.of E.)	V.27.c.7.7.		
7.	S.C.F. (Non C.of E.)	POMMIER		
8.	D.A.D.O.S.	LA BELLE VUE		
9.	D.A.D.V.S.	V.27.c.7.7.		
10.	Salvage Officer	HUMBERCAMP V.29.a.4.2.		
11.	Gas Officer	HUMBERCAMP		
12.	Claims Officer	HUMBERCAMP		
13.	Burials Officer	HUMBERCAMP		
14.	French Mission	LA BELLE VUE		
15.	R'hd. Disburs. Offr.	SAULTY		
16.	O/c Coffee Bars	HUMBERCAMP		
17.	S.A.A. Section	GAUDIEMPRE D.1.d.		
18.	No.2 M.T. Coy.	BARLY		Entrance D.2.c.0.8.
19.	No.3 Mobile Vet. Sec	HUMBERCAMP V.29.a.3.5.		
20.	Main Salvage Dump	V.29.c.5.2.		
21.	Divisional Baths	HUMBERCAMP, MONCHY & GAUDIEMPRE		
22.	Divisional Laundry	HUMBERCAMP		
23.	Reinforce. R'hd.	MONDICOURT		
24.	Supply R'hd.	SAULTY		
25.	Field Cashier	NOYELLE VION		

26.	5th Inf. Brigade	W.23.c.1.8.		
27.	24th R. Fusiliers	X.24.c.2.0.	LEFT.	W.19.c.0.6.
28.	2nd High. L.I.	X.19.c.8.2.	Left.	W.25.a.1.9.
29.	2nd Oxf. & Bucks L.I.	X.27.b.9.5.	Reserve	W.25.b.3.2.
30.	5th T.M. Batty.	X.21.d.3.8.	Right	W.25.a.

31.	6th Inf. Brigade.	E.4.a.6.3.		
32.	1st King's Regt.	F.1.c.0.0.	CENTRE.	V.30.b.8.4.
33.	17th R. Fusiliers	F.9.a.8.4.	Support	V.30.b.8.4.
34.	2nd South Staffs.	E.5.d.2.5.	Front	V.30.b.8.4.
35.	6th T.M. Batty.	E. .b.2.0.	Reserve	V.30.b.8.4.

36.	99th Inf. Brigade.	E.4.a.2.4.		
37.	1st R. Berks.	F.16.c.6.3.	RIGHT	D.15.b.7.2.
38.	23rd R. Fusiliers	F.9.b.6.1.	Right	D.10.c.5.4.
39.	1st K.R. Rif. C.	E.5.d.4.1.	Left	D.15.c.9.8.
40.	99th T.M. Batty.	E.5.b.2.6.	Reserve	D.9.d.8.1.

41. C.R.A. ....

- 2 -

Unit No.	UNIT.	Headquarters.		Transport.
41.	C.R.A. 2nd Division.	V.27.c.7.7.		
42.	36th Bde. R.F.A.	E.4.c.25.30.	Right Gp.	ST AMAND
43.	41st Bde. R.F.A.	E.5.c.85.75.	Centre Gp.	D.9.c.9.2. (Rear) E.2.c.3.6. (Adv.)
44.	14th Army Bde. R.H.A.	W.24.b.25.65.	Left Gp.	W.24.a.2.7.
45.	34th Army Bde. R.F.A.	W.18.a.5.0.	Left Gp.	W.18.a.5.0.
46.	76th Army Bde. R.F.A.	W.13.b.9.9.	Mob. Res.	W.13.b.9.9.
47.	D.T.M.O.	V.27.c.7.7.		
48.	X/2 & Y/2 T.M. Batts.	F.2.c.9.3.		
49.	2nd D.A.C.	GAUDIEMPRE		POMMIER
50.	14th Army Bde. R.H.A. Ammn. Col.	D.1.d.8.5.		GAUDIEMPRE D.1.d.8.5.
51.	34th Army Bde. R.F.A. Ammn. Col.	GAUDIEMPRE		GAUDIEMPRE
52.	76th Army Bde. R.F.A. Ammn. Col.	GAUDIEMPRE		GAUDIEMPRE
53.	C.R.E. 2nd Division.	V.27.c.7.7.		
54.	5th Field Coy. R.E.	E.5.c.3.2.		
55.	226th Field Coy. R.E.	W.23.c.5.4.		W.19.d.97.9.
56.	483rd Field Coy. R.E.	E.12.c.15.43.		POMMIER POMMIER
57.	10th D.C.L.I. (Pioneers)	E.4.c.2.7. (Adv.) POMMIER (Rear)		V.27.c.0.3.
58.	2nd M.G. Battn.	W.26.d.8.3. F.13.d.9.9. Right E.11.b.5.7. Centre X.28.a.65.35. Left E.5.a.6.9. Reserve		HUMBERCAMP
59.	2nd Divl. Train.	V.21.b.5.5.		
60.	No. 1 Company	LA BAZEQUE FARM		With D.A.
61.	No. 2 Company	V.21.b.7.8.		
62.	No. 3 Company	V.15.d.7.3.		
63.	No. 4 Company	V.15.d.8.5.		
64.	A.D.M.S.	V.27.c.7.7.		
65.	5th Field Ambulance	BERLES AU BOIS (W.15.c.2.0.)		W.15.c.3.0.
66.	6th Field Ambulance	WARLINCOURT		C.6.a.2.8.
67.	100th Field Ambulance	W.13.d.5.7.		W.13.c.5.9.

CHANGES NIGHT 21st/22nd July. * to reserve
≠ to Left front.

21st July, 1918.

B.N. Harrison

Captain,
for Lieut.-Colonel,
General Staff, 2nd Division.

S E C R E T.

SECRET   War Diary Appendix 5

Copy No 15

2nd Division Order No.344.

18th July, 1918.

1. A raid will be carried out by 2 Coys. of 1st Royal Berks Regt. 99th Brigade on the night of July 22nd/23rd.

2. The objectives are as follows:-

   First Objective.- The huts in F.17.c & d and F.23.a & b (vide attached map 'X'). no map

   Second Objective - Enemy's trench about F.18.d.0.4 (marked 'B' on map).

3. The artillery action will be as follows:-

   (a) Right Group. (reinforced by Batteries from 37th Div. Artillery, Centre and Left Groups 2nd Div. Artillery).

   (i) At zero will put down a creeping barrage in front of the first objective, moving forward to a point covering the first objective.

   (ii) On the right flank, will cover the block of buildings marked 'C' on map, special attention being paid to the small works immediately North of F.23.central.

   (iii) Left flank - will cover the enemy trench line West of road running from F.17.a.7.0 Northwards to F.17.a.6.5.

   (iv) A standing barrage will be put on to the second objective from zero until the raid approaches.

   (v) When the move forward to the second objective takes place, a creeping barrage will move forward through the second objective and will remain on approximately, the line of the German main trench running from the corner of ABLAINZEVILLE CEMETERY to about A.13.d.5.7 thence to about F.18.a.3.6.

   (vi) Protective barrages will be arranged to protect the raid when at the second objective.

   Detailed arrangements for the above will be made by G.O.C. 99th Brigade with O.C. Right Group.
   The Right Group Guards Div. Artillery is arranging to bombard the enemy's trenches at zero – 10 opposite MOYENNEVILLE.

   (b) Heavy Artillery.

   (i) A bombardment is being carried out by Heavy Artillery IV Corps from Zero of the Northern part of the village of ABLAINZEVILLE and enemy main line from the corner of ABLAINZEVILLE CEMETERY up to grid line F.18.d.7.0.

   (ii) The enemy main trench from the grid line F.18.d.7.0 to trench junction about A.13.d.5.7 thence along the trench running N.W. to the strong point about F.18.a.3.6 is being bombarded by Heavy Arty. VI Corps from Zero.

   (iii) Counter battery work is being carried out by the H.A. of both IV and VI Corps under a programme being drawn up by C.B.S.O. of IV and VI Corps

   Details of Heavy Artillery action are being arranged by VI Corps H.A. in conjunction with C.B.S.O.

P.T.O.

- 2 -

(c) 6" Newton Mortars.

The D.T.M.O. 2nd Division will engage with 2 mortars the enemy work West of the strong point in the grid line between F.18.a and F.17.b. He will also arrange with the D.T.M.O. of 37th Division to engage the enemy's main line at the Cemetery about F.23.d.8.9 during the whole operation.

4. 99th T.M.Battery, 3" Stokes, will put down a continuous barrage from the corner of ABLAINZEVILLE F.23.c.4.7 along the Northern edge of the village up to the road to about F.23.central.

5. The 2nd M.G.Battn. will arrange -

(a) A machine gun barrage along the Northern edge of ABLAINZEVILLE.

(b) A machine gun barrage to cover the left flank from about F.18.a.2.4 to about A.13.b.0.0.

6. Watches will be synchronised by 2nd Division Signals as follows:-

(a) A watch will be sent to 99th Brigade H.Q. at 6 pm on 22nd July.

(b) Watches will be synchronised with VI Corps H.A. under arrangements to be issued later, and with the Right Group Guards Division Artillery.

7. Zero hour will be notified later.

8. Acknowledge.

E.R.Clayton

Lieut. Colonel,
General Staff, 2nd Division.

Issued at 12.30 pm to -

Copy No. 1 to 5th Inf. Bde.
2   6th Inf. Bde.
3   99th Inf. Bde.
4   No.2 M.G.Battn.
5   C.R.A.
6   2nd Signal Coy.
7   37th Division.
8   Guards Division.
9   VI Corps.
10   Shoner's Group H.A.
11   VI Corps H.A.
12   IV Corps H.A.
13-17 G.S.Records.

SECRET.   Copy No 16

2nd Division Order No.344.

19th July, 1918.

1.   A raid will be carried out by 2 Coys. of 1st Royal Berks Regt. 99th Brigade on the night of July 22nd/23rd.

2.   The objectives are as follows:-

First Objective.- The huts in F.17.c & d and F.23.a & b (vide attached map 'X').

Second Objective - Enemy's trench about F.18.d.0.4 (marked 'B' on map).

3.   The artillery action will be as follows:-

(a)   Right Group. (reinforced by Batteries from 37th Div. Artillery Centre and Left Groups 2nd Div. Artillery).

   (i)   At zero will put down a creeping barrage in front of the first objective, moving forward to a point covering the first objective.

   (ii)   On the right flank, will cover the block of buildings marked 'C' on map, special attention being paid to the small works immediately North of F.23.central.

   (iii)   Left flank - will cover the enemy trench line West of road running from F.17.a.7.0 Northwards to F.17.a.6.5.

   (iv)   A standing barrage will be put on to the second objective from zero until the raid approaches.

   (v)   When the move forward to the second objective takes place, a creeping barrage will move forward through the second objective and will remain on approximately, the line of the German main trench running from the corner of ABLAINZEVILLE CEMETERY to about A.13.d.5.7 thence to about F.18.a.3.6.

   (vi)   Protective barrages will be arranged to protect the raid when at the second objective.

   Detailed arrangements for the above will be made by G.O.C. 99th Brigade with O.C. Right Group.
   The Right Group Guards Div. Artillery is arranging to bombard the enemy's trenches at zero - 10 opposite MOYENNEVILLE.

(b)   Heavy Artillery.

   (i)   A bombardment is being carried out by Heavy Artillery IV Corps from Zero of the Northern part of the village of ABLAINZEVILLE and enemy main line from the corner of ABLAINZEVILLE CEMETERY up to grid line F.18.d.7.0.

   (ii)   The enemy main trench from the grid line F.18.d.7.0 to trench junction about A.13.d.5.7 thence along the trench running N.W. to the strong point about F.18.a.3.6 is being bombarded/Heavy Arty. VI Corps from Zero.   by

   (iii)   Counter battery work is being carried out by the H.A. of both IV and VI Corps under a programme being drawn up by C.B.S.O. of IV and VI Corps

   Details of Heavy Artillery action are being arranged by VI Corps H.A. in conjunction with C.B.S.O.

                                                                P.T.O.

- 2 -

    (c)   <u>6" Newton Mortars.</u>

        The D.T.M.O. 2nd Division will engage with 2 mortars the enemy work West of the strong point in the grid line between F.18.a and F.17.b. He will also arrange with the D.T.M.O. of 37th Division to engage the enemy's main line at the Cemetery about F.23.d.8.9 during the whole operation.

4.   99th T.M.Battery, 3" Stokes, will put down a continuous barrage from the corner of ABLAINZEVILLE F.23.c.4.7 along the Northern edge of the village up to the road to about F.23.central.

5.   The 2nd M.G.Battn. will arrange -

    (a)   A machine gun barrage along the Northern edge of ABLAINZEVILLE.

    (b)   A machine gun barrage to cover the left flank from about F.18.a.2.4 to about A.13.b.0.0.

6.   Watches will be synchronised by 2nd Division Signals as follows:-

    (a)   A watch will be sent to 99th Brigade H.Q. at 6 pm on 22nd July.

    (b)   Watches will be synchronised with VI Corps H.A. under arrangements to be issued later, and with the Right Group Guards Division Artillery.

7.   Zero hour will be notified later.

8.   Acknowledge.

                                               E.R.Clayton

                                            Lieut. Colonel,
Issued at 12.30 pm to -   General Staff, 2nd Division.

    Copy No.1 to 5th Inf. Bde.
         2   6th Inf. Bde.
         3   99th Inf. Bde.
         4   No.2 M.G.Battn.
         5   C.R.A.
         6   2nd Signal Coy.
         7   37th Division.
         8   Guards Division.
         9   VI Corps.
        10   Shores's Group H.A.
        11   VI Corps H.A.
        12   IV Corps H.A.
      13-17   G.S.Records.

(1)

Headquarters 154th Brigade.
American E.F., June 8th 1918.

Lieutenant-General Sir Aylmer Haldane,
Commanding 6th Corps British Army.

My Dear General:

On our departure from this area for other duty, I desire to express to you, the members of your Staff, and through you, to the Officers and men of the 2nd Division British Army, our great appreciation of the services which have been rendered in advancing our instruction. Not only have your Officers and men been indefatigable in their efforts to aid us, but by their unvarying courtesy and the tact which they have displayed in the performance of their duties, there has resulted the most cordial relations and a feeling of camarderie between the two services. We leave with regret and with the hopes that we may some day be even more closely associated in the work which the future has in store for us.

With the kindest personal regards, I am,

Very sincerely yours,

(sgd.) Evan M. Johnson.
Brigadier-General, N.A.
Commanding Brigade.

(2)

2nd Division No. G.S.1594/28.

5th Inf. Bde.
6th Inf. Bde.
99th Inf. Bde.
2nd M.G. Battn.

For your information.

The above is a copy of a letter received by the Corps Commander

8/6/18

Lieut-Colonel.
General Staff – 2nd Division.

(1)

Headquarters 154th Brigade.
American E.F., June 6th 1918.

Lieutenant-General Sir Aylmer Haldane,
Commanding 6th Corps British Army.

My Dear General:

On our departure from this area for other duty, I desire to express to you, the members of your Staff, and through you, to the Officers and men of the 2nd Division British Army, our great appreciation of the services which have been rendered in advancing our instruction. Not only have your Officers and men been indefatigable in their efforts to aid us, but by their unvarying courtesy and the tact which they have displayed in the performance of their duties, there has resulted the most cordial relations and a feeling of camarderie between the two services. We leave with regret and with the hopes that we may some day be even more closely associated in the work which the future has in store for us.

With the kindest personal regards, I am,

Very sincerely yours,

(sgd.) Evan M. Johnson.
Brigadier-General, N.A.
Commanding Brigade.

(2)

2nd Division No. G.S.1594/28.

5th Inf. Bde.
6th Inf. Bde.
99th Inf. Bde.
2nd M.G. Battn.

For your information.

9/6/18

Lieut-Colonel.
General Staff – 2nd Division.

"G" Diary
Appendix 8
Appendix "B"

2nd DIVISION.

STRENGTH RETURN MADE UP TO 12 NOON SATURDAY 27th July 1918.

UNIT.	(i.) Fighting strength for previous week, compiled in accordance with A.Gs. instructions.		(ii.) Increase during week, due to drafts, etc., taken on strength of unit.		(iii.) Totals from (i.) and (ii.)		(iv.) Decrease during week—casualties, etc., deducted from strength of unit.		"A" Strength, excluding Attached.		"B" Not present with the Unit and not at the disposal of C.O. included in column "A".		"A" minus "B" Available Fighting Strength including Personnel of Battalion Transport and Quartermaster's Stores.		REMARKS. (Brief notes regarding (ii.), (iv.) and "B", etc.)
	Officers.	O.R.	Officers.	O.R.	Officers.	O.R.	Officers.	O.R.	Officers.	O.R.	Officers.	O.R.	Officers.	O.R.	
5th INFANTRY BRIGADE.															
24th Royal Fusiliers.	39	886	—	44	39	930	1	23	38	907	11	165	27	742	*1 Officer shown on last week's Return was returning from hospital and was consequently still on the strength of his Battalion.
2nd Oxf. & Bucks L.I.	40	934	3	3	43	937	—	7	43	930	10	200	33	730	
2nd Highland L.I.	40	953	—	50	40	1003	—	14	40	989	2	254	31	735	
Total Brigade.	119	2773	3	97	122	2870	1	44	121	2826	23	619	91	2209	
6th INFANTRY BRIGADE.															
17th Royal Fusiliers.	39	865	2	75	41	940	—	31	41	909	10	176	31	733	
1st King's Regiment.	*37	944	4	7	41	951	—	8	41	943	17	182	24	761	
2nd S.Staffs Regt.	#40	971	1	74	41	1045	2	53	39	992	11	199	28	793	#2 officers shown on last week's Return deducted for reasons as stated above.
Total Brigade.	116	2780	7	156	123	2936	2	92	121	2844	38	557	83	2287	
99th INFANTRY BRIGADE.															
23rd Royal Fusiliers.	38	842	1	74	39	916	—	24	39	892	12	164	27	728	
1st Royal Berks Regt.	33	899	6	16	39	915	2	55	37	860	15	152	24	708	
1st K.R.Rifle Corps.	47	866	1	32	48	898	—	34	48	864	12	200	36	664	
Total Brigade.	118	2607	8	122	126	2729	2	113	124	2616	44	516	80	2100	
Pioneer Battalion.															
10th D.C.L.I.	36	856	1	17	37	873	1	27	36	846	9	132	27	714	
TOTAL DIVISION.	389	9016	19	392	408	9408	6	276	402	9132	121	1822	281	7310	
No.2 Bn. M.G.Corps.	45	873	—	47	45	920	1	31	44	889	2	39	42	850	
TOTALS ...															

(Sgd.) C. E. Pereira,
Major General,
Commanding 2nd Division.

EXPLANATION OF INCREASE AND DECREASE.

UNIT.	INCREASE.	DECREASE.
5th INFANTRY BRIGADE.		
24th Royal Fusiliers.	43 O.R. reinforcements. 1 " from hospital.	1 Officer wounded 23/7/18. 1 O.R. killed. 11 " wounded. 10 " evacuated sick. 1 " commission.
2nd Oxf. & Bucks L.I.	5 Officers reinforcements. 5 O.R. reinforcements.	5 O.R. killed. 2 " wounded. 2 " evacuated sick.
2nd Highland L.I.	46 O.R. reinforcements. 4 " from hospital.	4 O.R. battle casualties. 10 " evacuated sick.
6th INFANTRY BRIGADE.		
17th Royal Fusiliers.	2 Officers posted. 68 O.R. reinforcements. 10 " from hospital.	1 O.R. killed. 12 " wounded. 18 " evacuated sick.
1st King's Regt.	4 Officers reinforcements. 6 O.R. reinforcements. 1 " from hospital.	1 O.R. wounded. 5 " evacuated sick. 2 " miscellaneous.
2nd S.Staffs Regt.	1 Officer reinforcement. 74 O.R. reinforcements.	1 Officer to England sick. 1 do. wounded (gas), 19-7-18. 41 O.R. wounded. 10 " evacuated sick. 2 " miscellaneous.
99th INFANTRY BRIGADE.		
23rd Royal Fusiliers.	1 Officer reinforcement. 74 O.R. reinforcements.	2 O.R. killed. 10 " wounded. 10 " evacuated sick. 2 " commissions.
1st Royal Berks Regt.	6 Officers reinforcements. 16 O.R. reinforcements.	1 Officer killed 23/7/18 1 do. wounded 23/7/18 5 O.R. killed. 38 " wounded. 15 " evacuated sick. 2 " commissions. 1 " trans. to T.M.Bty. 1 " trans. to M.G.Corps.
1st K.R.Rifle Corps.	1 Officer reinforcement. 32 O.R. reinforcements.	27 O.R. evacuated sick. 1 " killed. 5 " wounded. 1 " transferred.
10th D.C.L.I.(Pioneers)	1 Officer reinforcement. 7 O.R. reinforcements. 10 " from hospital.	1 Officer posted to 1st Bn.D.C.L.I. 24-7-18. 2 O.R. wounded. 23 " evacuated sick.
No.2 Bn. M.G.Corps.	38 O.R. reinforcements. 9 " from hospital.	1 Officer killed 20/7/18. 6 O.R. casualties. 3 " commissions. 20 " evacuated sick.

NOTE. Complete Nominal Roll of Officers will be forwarded later.

EXPLANATION OF COLUMN "B".

(a) On leave and at Army Rest Camp.
(b) Sick in Divisional Area.
(c) Courses.
(d) Officers admitted to hospital sick and not reported as invalided to England.
(e) Extra regimentally employed and not at disposal of the C.O.
(f) At Divisional Reception Camp.

UNIT.		Off.	O.R.
5th INFANTRY BRIGADE.			
24th Royal Fusiliers.	(a)	3	15
	(b)	-	16
	(c)	-	21
	(d)	1	-
	(e)	3	60
	(f)	4	61
		11	163
2nd Oxf. & Bucks L.I.	(a)	2	17
	(b)	-	10
	(c)	4	17
	(d)	1	-
	(e)	1	40
	(f)	2	116
		10	200
2nd Highland L.I.	(a)	1	19
	(b)	-	11
	(c)	2	17
	(d)	3	-
	(e)	2	39
	(f)	1	168
		9	254
6th INFANTRY BRIGADE.			
17th Royal Fusiliers.	(a)	1	13
	(b)	-	14
	(c)	4	41
	(d)	-	-
	(e)	1	40
	(f)	4	68
		10	176
1st King's Regt.	(a)	1	20
	(b)	-	4
	(c)	4	32
	(d)	4	-
	(e)	2	28
	(f)	6	98
		17	182
2nd S.Staffs Regt.	(a)	1	18
	(b)	-	5
	(c)	4	34
	(d)	1	-
	(e)	3	42
	(f)	2	100
		11	199
99th INFANTRY BRIGADE.			
23rd Royal Fusiliers.	(a)	2	19
	(b)	-	6
	(c)	5	14
	(d)	2	-
	(e)	2	43
	(f)	1	82
		12	164

P.T.O.

99th INFANTRY BRIGADE (Cont'd)

		Off.	O.R.
1st Royal Berks Regt.	(a)	2	15
	(b)	—	10
	(c)	4	17
	(d)	5	—
	(e)	1	41
	(f)	1	69
		13	152
1st K.R.Rifle Corps.	(a)	4	26
	(b)	—	35
	(c)	3	9
	(d)	2	—
	(e)	*7	31
	(f)	3	99
		19	200
10th D.C.L.I. (Pioneers)	(a)	1	12
	(b)	—	35
	(c)	3	16
	(d)	3	—
	(e)	1	13
	(f)	1	56
		9	132
No.2 Bn. M.G.Corps.	(a)	1	15
	(b)	—	17
	(c)	1	5
	(d)	—	—
	(e)	—	2
	(f)	—	—
		2	39

* Not yet joined.

STRENGTH RETURN OF 319th REGIMENT, AMERICAN E.F.

	"A" Strength		"B" Details away from Units - on Courses, sick &c.		"A" minus "B"	
	OFF.	O.R.	OFF.	O.R.	OFF.	O.R.
First Battalion.	22	944	4	12	18	932
Second Battalion.	16	943	4	12	12	931
Third Battalion.	21	950	4	61	17	889
Hd.Qrs.Company.	6	307	3	43	3	264
Supply Company.	4	155	—	1	4	154
Machine Gun Coy.	6	166	1	1	5	165
Medical Detachment.	10	51	1	1	9	50
Ordnance do.	—	6	—	—	—	6
Field & Staff.	10	—	—	—	10	—
Chaplains.	2	—	—	—	2	—
Attached.	20	—	2	—	18	—
Unassigned.	13	—	2	—	11	—
	130	3522	21	131	109	3391

Appdx. 9   "G" Diary.

2nd DIVISION — CASUALTY RETURN FOR July 1918.

UNIT	KILLED O.	KILLED O.R.	WOUNDED O.	WOUNDED O.R.	MISSING O.	MISSING O.R.	INJURED O.	INJURED O.R.	Names of Officers and Remarks
H.Qrs. 2nd Divn.									Attached units
5th Inf. Bde.									34th Army Bde RFA
A. 24th R. Fus.	–	2	3	13					wounded OR 3.
B. 2/Oxf.& Bucks.LI	1	6	–	16					14th Army Bde RHA
C. 2nd High. L.I.	–	4	1	12					wounded OR 3.
5th T.M. Bty.									
6th Inf. Bde.									1/Bn 319 Infy Regt
D. 17th R. Fus.	–	1	1	20					A.E.F. killed OR 1
E. 1st King's R.	2	1	1	35		1			wounded Officers 1
F. 2nd S.Staffs.R.	–	3	3	41					OR 6.
6th T.M. Bty.	–	1	–	4					
99th Inf. Bde.									
G. 23rd R. Fus.	–	4	2	25				1	
H. 1/R.Berks.R.	1	4	1	38					
K. 1st K.R.R.C.	–	2	–	22		1		4	
99th T.M. Bty.	–	–	–	4					
P. 10th D.C.L.I.	–	–	1	6				1	
X. No.2 M.G.Bn.	1	1	1	10					
R.A., 2nd Divn.									
36th Bde.	–	–	–	4				8	
41st Bde.	–	3	–	4				2	
2nd D.A.C.	–	–	–	3			1		
X/2 T.M.Bty.	–	–	–	1					
Y/2 T.M.Bty.	–	–	–	1					
R.E., 2nd Divn.									
5th Field Co.	–	–	–	1					
226th Fd. Co.	–	–	–	2					
483rd Fd. Co.	–	–	–	–				1	
2nd Signal Co.									
5th F. Ambulance				3					
Totals.	5	32	14	264	–	2	1	17	

31/7/1918.

G.H. Birkett, Major,
D.A.A.G., 2nd Division.

99th Inf.Brigade.

2nd Division No.G.S.

Herewith remarks of the Army Commander on the raid recently carried out by the 1st Royal Berks Regiment.

This paper can be retained.

30th July, 1918.

E R Clayton
Lieut-Colonel,
General Staff, 2nd Division.

2nd Div No G.S.12/25/1

C.R.E.

Reference 2nd Division G.S.12/25 dated 24-6-18:
Please delete F.13.c.5.2. and substitute F.14.a.8.0.

2-7-18

Lieut Colonel
General Staff 2nd Division.

NARRATIVE OF RAID
BY 1ST ROYAL BERKS.
NIGHT 22ND/23RD JULY. 1918.

Appendix 'A'

Headquarters
99th. Infantry Brigade.

1st. Royal Berks. Regt. No. R.R.72

Report of Raid carried out by 1st. Royal Berks. Regt.

Officer Commanding, Raiding Party - Captain V.G. STOKES, M.C.

A raid was carried out by 200 men from B and D Companies 1st. Royal Berkshire Regt. on night of 22/23rd. July - Zero 12.30 a.m.

The preliminary arrangements for assembly worked very smoothly, and the party moved out through eight gaps in our wire under the Artillery barrage which dropped at Zero.

On the Right the men pushed forward too eagerly and a 4.5" shell dropped in the midst of the Right Flankers, killing two and wounding several others.

C.S.M. JENKINS showed marked ability and courage in reorganising this party and leading it on to its objectives.

2nd. Lieut. F.S. BOSHELL was killed early in the advance by getting too close up under our barrage.

All objectives were reached by the parties concerned.

Five prisoners were obtained and it is estimated that not less than 50 enemy were killed in dugouts and in fighting exclusive of those killed by the barrage.

The enemy opened fire in under three minutes after Zero.

By Zero plus 24 he had shortened range 700 yards and was dropping shells on a line running East of the Stable Area.

The withdrawal was carried out in accordance with the programme in spite of heavy retaliation.

The spirit of the men was excellent throughout.

Results :-

5 Prisoners obtained. 1 Machine Gun captured.
4 Dugouts located (see attached sketch) Three were occupied and bombed.
1 Trench Mortar ammunition Dump located (see attached sketch).
A quantity of letters and other identifications obtained from enemy dead.
50 at least killed (exclusive of barrage casualties).

Casualties :-

1 Officer killed - 2nd. Lieut. F.S. BOSHELL.
1 Officer wounded - 2nd. Lieut. G. BYSH.
3 Other Ranks Killed.
30 Other Ranks wounded.

Detailed report of Raid Commander is attached.

(Sgd) D.W. POWELL, Lieut. Colonel,
Commanding 1st. Royal Berks. Regt.

24.7.18.

Note. - The fourth dugout cannot be accurately located on Map.

Scale 1:5000

Area Raided
Dugout
T.M. Ammunition Post

Appendix 'B'

Raid Commanders Report.

Report on Operations carried out by B and D Companies
1st. Royal Berkshire Regiment on night 22/23rd. July 1918

Assembly
: Preparations and Assembly were carried out without a hitch and troops were all in position opposite their respective gaps by 12 m.n. i.e. half an hour before Zero.

Attack.
: At Zero the barrage opened and the advance commenced. Waves moved forward according to programme and each objective was occupied immediately the barrage lifted off.

  Enemy were encountered on the 1st. Sunken Road and several were killed, 2 prisoners being sent back.

  The Hut area proved empty except on the left where a dugout was found at F.17.d.1.4. This was bombed and two prisoners were taken, the remainder were killed inside. Both flank parties established themselves without difficulty.

  The Final objective parties followed up the barrage, and the right got in at Zero plus 26 the remainder according to programme. The Stables proved to be empty.

  No enemy were found on the right of the final objective, but as anticipated a dugout was discovered at about F.18.c.00.25. Ten of the enemy were seen to run away from here through our barrage. Two of these were hit and identification obtained. The dugout was bombed and satisfactory noises were heard.

  Withdrawal was commenced at ZERO plus 30 but several more Germans were seen running away and Lieut. DAWSON, Sgt. STACEY, L/Cpl. ELLIOTT and Pte. FOSTER went back to attack them, but failed to catch them. Three more were hit

  On returning to our lines, at about F.17.c.8.5. in the second gun pit from the South a machine gun detachment was found just coming into action. They were immediately attacked and fled into a dugout which was filled with bombs as they refused to come out.
  The gun was captured.

Intelligence -
: (i) Both Sunken Roads were lined with shelters on the Western face. All these had attention.
  (ii) Dumps of Light Mortar Ammunition were found on the second Sunken Road at about F.17.d.1.0.
  (iii) Enemy wire was negligible.
  (iv) The enemy S.O.S. appeared to be two GREEN Lights

Artillery -
: (i)(Our Own)
  The Barrage was excellent, and in every way contributed to the success of the raid.

  (ii) (Enemy)
  German artillery opened at Zero plus 3. It was never intense and chiefly fell on our front line. As the operations proceeded the enemy guns shortened and at Zero plus 30 were shelling East of the second Sunken Road.

Casualties............

Page 2 of Appendix 'B'

Casualties.
4 killed and about 30 wounded - nearly all casualties occurred in No Man's Land and a large proportion were due to over eagerness in following the barrage.

One 4.5" How.shell fell amongst our men at Zero plus 1 and caused casualties. This is the only case I know of, where casualties were caused by our own guns through no fault of our own.

Casualties - Enemy - The enemy undoubtedly suffered very heavily and in dugouts, and in trying to get through our barrage must have lost well over fifty in killed.

Lessons learnt during Raid.

(1) The value of careful preparation over tapes. Men went automatically to their objectives, although visibility was low owing to barrage and control difficult.

(2) The value of a good start. Gaps in the wire were made on compass bearings and tapes laid after careful reconnaissance by day. Troops moved into assembly positions on a time table and all was complete by 12 midnight. This allowed time to correct any hitch that might occur.

(3) The value of a pass word. In the inevitable confusion in the Hut area it was impossible to distinguish friend from foe.

(4) With reference to (3) - the armbands did not show up very well, and it is possible that extra wide bands or some other means might be an improvement.

(5) Whilst it is essentially desirable to keep up close to a creeping barrage we undoubtedly lost men through over eagerness. This was chiefly due to inexperience.
It would be well in rehearsal to insist on a greater distance being kept than is absolutely essential for safety.

(6) So many RED Lights were sent up during the operation that it was difficult to re-organise our own signals for withdrawal. It is questionable whether Very lights of any description are the best method of notifying withdrawal.

(7) The Searchlight as a means of directing stragglers home proved a great success, and was easily distinguishable to all ranks.

(Sgd) V.G.STOKES, Captain,
Commanding Raiding Party.

24.7.18.

SECRET   99th. Infantry Brigade No.
                                                B.M.(S)445

2nd. Division.

                        Raid by 1st. Royal Berkshire Regiment.

1. REASONS FOR RAID.
            Careful reconnaissance of the enemy positions by
            Binocular and the study of aeroplane photographs had
            apparently established the following points :-

    (1)   The enemy had built a main line of trenches from
            F.23.c. through ABLAINZEVELLE CEMETERY to A.13.d. central,
            thence East of the Aerodrome in A.7.d. A big deep trench,
            well supplied with deep dugouts.

    (2)   The main enemy line was built East of a small crest
            line and was evidently intended to sweep the reverse slope
            in the event of attack. This line offered no observation
            to the enemy except at the two buttresses mentioned below.

    (3)   At two points the line crossed to the forward slope,
            forming buttresses to sweep the front of the line -

                The village of ABLAINZEVELLE
                The Redoubt and isolated shell hole work in F.18.a.

    (4)   The position of the Outpost troops in front of the
            enemy main line was uncertain, as dispositions were altered
            each night, and no movement took place by day.

    (5)   The enemy had evidently given orders to avoid losing
            an identification, because offensive patrols had always
            driven the enemy's Outpost troops helter skelter Eastwards

    (6)   The enemy probably had no definite S.O.S. Line and
            his Artillery had been very inactive of late.

    (7)   His barrage, if any, would be expected on the AYETTE-
            BUCQUOY Road or our Front Line.

    (8)   Enemy movement had led us to suppose that he
            reinforced his main line at night.

2. PLAN   The plan evolved was as follows :-

            To place a Standing barrage of Heavy Artillery on
            the enemy main line, with reinforcement of Stokes and
            Newton Trench Mortars and Machine Guns on the known
            buttresses, thus forming a sort of arc round the point to
            be attacked.
            Inside this arc the troops would advance under a
            creeping barrage, moving at the rate of 100 yards every
            3 minutes, with an outer barrage of 4.5" Hows.
            On reaching the outer limit of penetration of the
            raid, the creeping barrage was to rake backwards and forwar
            to the enemy main line so as to catch any of the enemy
            who were bolted by the raiding troops.

                                            As the enemy / 2......

- 2 -

2. PLAN continued.

As the enemy did reinforce his main line, and a good many were bolted from the raided area, the barrage must have been very effective.

The buttresses were easily held under fire and the Raiders were never worried by machine gun fire from a flank. The Stokes Mortar Barrage of 1764 rounds from 9 guns in 65 minutes along a front of 400 yards was annihilating and kept ABLAINZEVELLE absolutely quiet.

3. OBJECTIVE.

The position chosen as objective was the Hutted Camp lying in the fork of the ABLAINZEVELLE - AYETTE Road in F.17.c. and d. and F.23.a. and c., with the road and quarry in the South East corner of F.17.c. as a second objective.

4. TROOPS DETAILED FOR RAID.

The 1st. Royal Berkshire Regt., being the strongest Battalion in the Brigade and best able to afford casualties, was chosen to carry out the raid, and on 3rd. July the Commanding Officer was ordered to work out the necessary details, using two strong companies for the task.

5. PRACTICE

In order to allow opportunity for practice and careful patrolling the raid was planned to take place between 20th. and 24th. July and the Inter-Battalion reliefs were re-arranged accordingly.

6. On 5th. July an outline of the Raid was sent to 2nd. Division and the Artillery, and on 9th. July rough details of the Artillery support required were sent to 2nd. Division and the Field and Heavy Artillery Group Commanders.

7. On 11th. July the C.R.A., 2nd. Division outlined the Artillery support that had been arranged and this was received by 99th. Infantry Brigade on 12th. July.

8. A practice course was taped out near Brigade Headquarters. The 1st. Royal Berks. Regt. came in to Brigade Reserve on night 15/16th. July and Lieut. (A/Captain) V.G. STOKES, M.C., Commanding Raiding Party, started practising his men over the course and working out final details.

9. On 18th. July, 2nd. Division Order No. 344 was issued and the date of the raid was definitely fixed for night 22/23rd. July.

10. On 18th. July the Army Commander Third Army and VI Corps Commander witnessed a practice raid over the tapes and made valuable suggestions which were incorporated in the arrangements.

11. On 19th. July, Right Group (R.F.A.) Operation Order No. 20 was issued detailing the Field Artillery arrangements.

12. On 19th. July, 99th. Infantry Brigade Order No. 244 was issued and Zero hour was fixed for between 12 midnight and 1 a.m. on night 22/23rd. July.

13. On 20th. July M.G. 2/350 was issued by 2nd. Machine Gun Battalion, detailing arrangements for Machine Gun co-operation.

14. On 21st. July, 99th. Infantry Brigade No. B.M.(S)423/1 was issued amending the code of signals to be used by the Raiding party and fixing Zero for 12.30 a.m. on night 22/23rd. July.

15/ page 3........

- 3 -

15. On 21st. July the signals for use by the Raiding party were received and tested the same night. They were found to give far too brilliant a light for the purpose and B.M.(S)423/2 was issued ordering the use of plain 1" RED Very lights in their places.

16. On 21st. July, O.C. 1st. Royal Berkshire Regt. issued his order No.184 detailing raiding arrangements.

17. The Medical arrangements were worked out by A.D.M.S., 2nd. Division and were complete by 21st. July.

18. The raid took place on night 22/23rd. July and all arrangements worked well. Five prisoners were captured, as well as one machine gun, and severe casualties were inflicted on the enemy, of whom it is estimated that 50 were killed by the bayonet and rifle. The Artillery barrage, which was excellent, must have inflicted further severe casualties on the enemy who it is known had two Reserve Companies in his Main Line on which the Heavy Artillery and Machine Gun Barrage fell.

19. The 23rd. Royal Fusiliers established a Lewis Gun post at Fork road F.17. central as soon as the barrage lifted off that point and maintained it as a flank guard until the raid was over, when the post withdrew to BLIZZARD TRENCH.
This co-operation secured the left flank of the Raiding party and did valuable work.

20. The enemy barrage fell at 12.33 a.m. mostly -

(a) in front of our front line.
(b) On the BUCQUOY - AYETTE Road.
(c) In front of our Support line - F.22.b. and F.16.d. and b.

21. Later in the night the JEWEL VALLEY was bombarded with Blue Cross and Lachrymatory gas shells.

22. A searchlight, supplied and worked by Major G.F.WOOD, R.E. A.I.S. Third Army, threw a vertical beam of light on to the clouds from MONCHY, giving a clear mark to the Raiding party on which to withdraw. This light was exposed from Zero plus 27 (12.57 a.m.) to Zero plus 87 (1.57 a.m.) and drew no hostile fire.

23. On withdrawal the Raiding Party reorganised near Battalion Headquarters and later reoccupied the Support and Reserve Positions near CALVERLEY COPSE and in BADEN AVENUE.

24. There was a full moon the whole night, but the sky was cloudy. The weather conditions were consequently ideal.

25. Casualties in the Raiding Party were -

Killed - 2nd.Lieut. F.S.BOSHELL and 3 Other Ranks.
Wounded - 2nd.Lieut. G.BYSH and 30 Other Ranks.
Missing - None.

26. During the raid the 99th. Trench Mortar Battery (increased to 9 guns by the loan of 2 by 6th. Trench Mortar Battery) fired continuously for 1 hour 5 minutes, 1764 rounds being fired during that time.

27/ Page 4....

- 4 -

27. The following are attached as Appendices :-

    A. Report by O.C. 1st.Battln.Royal Berkshire Regt.

    B. Report by Captain V.G.STOKES,M.C.,O.C.Raid.

    C. Copy of B.M. 328 dated 3.7.1918.

    D. Copy of B.M.(S)377 dated 5.7.1918.

    E. Copy of 99th.Infantry Brigade Order No.244 dated 19th.July 1918 with -

        Raid Map
        Artillery Barrage Maps (2) and
        Machine Gun Barrage Map.

    F. Copy of Order No.184 by O.C.,1st.Battalion Royal Berkshire Regt. dated 21.7.1913.

    G. Enlarged Air Photograph of Area raided.

    H. Memorandum to 1st.Royal Berkshire Regt. dealing with points to be considered.

E.Ironside.

Brigadier General,
Commanding 99th.Infantry Brigade

24th.July 1918

Appendix ' C '

1st. Royal Berkshire Regt.

99th. Bde. No. B.M. 328   Date 3.7.18.

    I want to carry out a Raid on a larger scale so as to make no mistake about securing an identification.

    I think that the best thing to do is to clean up the area marked in pencil on the attached map working under a heavy barrage.

    Will you work out the necessary details to put over 2 strong companies ?

    I will arrange to withdraw the 2 Companies for 4 or 5 days before they go over the top - the practice will be carried out between Brigade Headquarters and Reserve Battalion Headquarters over a taped course.

    A Senior Officer must be detailed and work on taping can begin at once.

    We shall probably be out of the line on or about the 28th. of this month and the raid should take place in about 16 days from now, reliefs being arranged to suit this.

    I will see you about this.

                                         (Sgd) E. IRONSIDE,
                                            Brigadier General,
3.7.18.   Commanding 99th. Infantry Brigade

APPENDIX 'D'

SECRET   99th. Infantry Brigade No.
                                      B.M.(S) 377

2nd. Division
1st. Royal Berks. Regt.   )
Right Group R.F.A.   ) For
Sherer's Group R.G.A.   ) information.

OUTLINE of PROPOSED RAID

1. OBJECTIVE. (Raid Map attached).

   (a) To clear out the area marked in BLUE, capture any prisoners, and destroy any deep dugouts or Machine Gun emplacements existing.

   (b) Clear out the enemy Strong Point at 'A' marked in RED.

2. NUMBER OF MEN TO BE EMPLOYED

   2 Companies of the 1st. Royal Berks. Regt. These may be composite.

3. DATE.   The operation to take place about the 22nd. July.

4. ARTILLERY   The operation will take place during the night or early morning, and will be carried out under an Artillery barrage. Details are now being worked out for the Heavy Artillery Support.

5. TRAINING.   The men will be training over tapes near Brigade Headquarters between the 16th. and 20th. inst.

6. REQUIREMENTS   (i) Photographs of the area given on Raid Map. The only ones we have so far of this area are - 7th. June - Very good. - 30th. June - Poor.

   (ii) Certain targets crumped by H.A. (Marked 'C' in GREEN), This is being attended to.

                                      (Sgd) E. IRONSIDE,
                                      Brigadier General,
5th. July 1918   Commanding 99th. Infantry Brigade

SECRET   Copy No..................

99th. Infantry Brigade Order No. 244

Reference Sheet 57 D. N.E. 1/20,000
Edition 5 d. (Local).   19th. July 1918

1.   A Raid will be carried out by the 1st. Royal Berkshire Regt.

   (a) **Strength** - 2 Companies of a minimum number 200.

   (b) **Objective** - To secure prisoners and mop up the area marked A and B. on Raid Map attached.

   (c) **Time.** - Between 12 midnight and 1 a.m. on the night of 22nd./23rd. July. Exact hour will be notified later to all concerned.

2. **Barrages**   The raid will take place under a creeping Field Artillery Barrage and will be protected by a Standing Box Barrage of Heavy Artillery, Trench Mortars, and machine guns. Details of these are contained in Appendices A, B and C. (To be issued later).

3. **Counter-Battery work.**

   Heavy concentrations have been arranged.

4. **Assembly.**   Troops will assemble in the front trenches. No troops will leave the assembly point until the barrage drops. Tapes giving the direction will be laid from the front line trenches, leading through efficient gaps in our wire, which will be made between dusk and the moment the barrage opens.

5. **Disposition of troops during raid.**

   The two remaining Companies of the 1st. Royal Berks. will hold the PICQUET LINE and POSTS. The two Raiding Companies on withdrawal will occupy the PURPLE Front line, but will be held ready to move forward to the support and reserve Company positions at short notice.

   PICQUET 'A' in BADEN AVENUE will be found by the Right of the front line companies.

6. **Signals.** (a) Each of the two Officers going to the Second Objective will fire a BLUE 1½" Very light at the moment of withdrawal from the Second Objective. It is expected that withdrawal will commence within 6 - 10 minutes after reaching the second objective.

   (b) When the Second objective parties have crossed the ABLAINZEVELLE - AYETTE ROAD each of the two Officers will fire 2 BLUE 1½" Very lights in quick succession. This will be the signal for the covering parties on the road to withdraw.

   (c) A Searchlight aimed perpendicularly in the sky will be located in or near MONCHY to give outlying parties a direction upon which to march. This beam will play from ZERO plus 27 minutes to Zero plus 87 minutes.

/ (d)...2....

- 2 -

6. Signals contd.

 (d) The Code word STOKES will be sent out by Advanced Battalion Headquarters to Brigade Headquarters and to the 23rd. Royal Fusiliers to denote parties have crossed our front line on withdrawal. This will be repeated by Brigade Headquarters to 2nd. Division, Right Group, R.F.A., 2nd. Machine Gun Battalion and 112th. Infantry Brigade.

7. Flanks. It is particularly necessary that the flanks be dealt with during the withdrawal and the Standing barrage of Heavy Artillery, Trench Mortars and Machine Guns forming the Standing Outer barrage should fire their most intense fire during the periods :-

 (a) Zero plus 5 minutes to Zero plus 15 minutes (10 minutes).

 (b) Zero plus 30 minutes to Zero plus 50 minutes (20 minutes).

Right Flank. Picquets will be formed by the raiding party.

Left Flank. At Zero, a party of a minimum 1 Officer and 10 Other ranks of the 23rd. Royal Fusiliers with a Lewis Gun will move forward and occupy the road junction at F.17.c.95.95. bringing covering fire against any flash of enemy machine gun which opens up. Careful direction will be obtained so as not to interfere with the Raiding party moving to the Second objective.
In order to bring down the barrage on the road junction at F.17.c.95.95. from Zero to Zero plus 5 minutes, the whole of the Post called " BLIZZARD " and the Flanking party intended to occupy the road junction will be moved Northwards to 'Y' Post at F.17.a.7.4. taken over by the 23rd. Royal Fusiliers on the night of 15/16th. July from 1st. Kings Royal Rifle Corps. At Zero plus 5 minutes the barrage will allow the road junction to be occupied, BLIZZARD POST will be re-occupied at the same time.
The 23rd. Royal Fusiliers will arrange to deal with any isolated machine gun posts known to exist East of the ABLAINZEVELLE - AYETTE ROAD, by Lewis Gun fire. This Left Flank party will withdraw upon orders from O.C. 1st. Royal Berks. who will arrange communication with it.

CHEERING There will be no cheering when charging. The watchword is " TOFREK " one of the Battalion Honours of the 1st. Royal Berks., and will be used if the bayonet is used on a German.

Distinguishing Signs. All Raiders, including the Left Flank party of the 23rd. Royal Fusiliers will wear a narrow white armband on both arms.

10. Synchronisation of watches.

A watch will be sent up to RIGHT Battalion Headquarters at 8 p.m. where O.C. 1st.Royal Berks.Regt. will arrange to synchronise watches with "C" and "D" Companies,2nd. Machine Gun Battalion,and with 99th.Trench Mortar Battery, and (if required) Y/2 Trench Mortar Battery (6" Newtons). No synchronisation of watches will be made by telephone.

11. ACKNOWLEDGE.

Farquharson

Captain,
Brigade Major,
99th.Infantry Brigade

Issued through Signals at 8 a.m. to :-

    23rd.Royal Fusiliers
    1st.Royal Berks.Regt.
    1st.Kings Royal Rifle Corps.
    99th.Trench Mortar Battery
    Captain V.G.STOKES,M.C.(Commanding Raiding party)
    Right Group R.F.A.
    Sherer's Group R.G.A.
    2nd.Machine Gun Battalion
    "C" Company,2nd.M.G.Battalion
    "D" Company,2nd.M.G.Battalion.
    2nd.Division 'G'
    6th.Infantry Brigade
    112th.Infantry Brigade
    War Diary.
    File.

99TH INF. BDE.
(Order No. 246.)
RAID MAP.

First objective —— A.
Second do. ---- B.

Scale 1:5000.

99th INF. BDE.
(Order No. 244)
Appendix A
Creeping Field Artillery Barrage.

Boundary of area to be raided
Boundary of barrage

SCALE 1:5000

18 | 24

23

0-0+2
0+2-0+5
0+5-0+8
0+8-0+11
0+11-0+15
0+15-0+18
0+18-0+21
0+21-0+24
0+24-0+27
0+27 onwards

LEFT GROUP

RIGHT CENTRE GROUP

LEFT GROUP
7th DIV.

99th INF. BDE.
(Order No. 244)
"APPENDIX B"

Reference.
First objective — A
Second — B
H.N. Barrage
18 Pdr Standing
Barrage & O Howitzer
L.T.M. Barrage

99TH INF. BDE.
(Order No 244.)
Appendix "C".
MACHINE GUN
STANDING
BARRAGE.

SECRET　　　　　　　　　　　　　　　　99th. Infantry Brigade No.
　　　　　　　　　　　　　　　　　　　　　B.M.(S)423/1

To all Recipients of

　　　　99th. Infantry Brigade Order No. 244

　　　　　　　　　　Reference 99th. Infantry Brigade Order No.244
dated 19.7.1918 -

1. <u>Para. 1 (c)</u>　　Unless otherwise notified Zero will be 12.30 a.m.
　　　　　　　　　　　on night 22/23rd. July.
　　　　　　　　　　　Any alteration will be notified to all concerned
　　　　　　　　　　　by taking this hour as the basis and adding or
　　　　　　　　　　　deducting the number of minutes.
　　　　　　　　　　　Any such notification will be worded " Reference
　　　　　　　　　　　B.M.(S) 423/1　add (or deduct)＿＿＿＿＿ "

2. <u>Para. 6 (a)</u>　　For " a BLUE 1½" Very Light " read -

　　　　　　　　　　　" A parachute light changing from WHITE to GREEN ".

3. <u>Para. 6 (b)</u>　　For "2 BLUE 1½" Very Lights " read -

　　　　　　　　　　　" 2 parachute lights changing from WHITE to GREEN "

4. ACKNOWLEDGE.

　　　　　　　　　　　　　　　　　　　Farquharson

　　　　　　　　　　　　　　　　　　　　Captain,
　　　　　　　　　　　　　　　　　　　Brigade Major,
21.7.1918.　　　　　　　　　　　　　　99th. Infantry Brigade

S E C R E T   99th. Infantry Brigade No.
                                      B.M.(S)423/2

To all Recipients of

   99th. Infantry Brigade Order No.244

            Reference paras 2 and 3 of B.M.(S)423/1 of
today -

1.   On testing the signal lights at night the parachute was found to be unsatisfactory.

2.   The two paras are accordingly cancelled and paras 6 (a) and (b) of Order 244 will now be amended as follows :-

   Para. 6 (a) For " a BLUE 1½" Very Light " read -

                " a RED Very Light ".

   Para. 6 (b) For " 2 BLUE 1½" Very Lights " read -

                " 2 RED Very Lights "

3.   ACKNOWLEDGE.

                                        Farquharson
                                        Captain,
                                        Brigade Major,
21st. July 1918   99th. Infantry Brigade

SECRET

Appendix 'F'

1st. Royal Berkshire Regiment.

Order No.184 by Lieut.Colonel D.W.POWELL.

Reference Map AYETTE 2.c. 1/20,000

1. **Raid.** A raid will be carried out by the Battalion.

    (a) **Strength** - 'B' and 'D' Companies will each provide 100 Other ranks.

    (b) **Objective.** - To secure prisoners and mop up the area shown in Appendix "A" of 99th.Infantry Brigade Order No.244

    (c) **Zero.** - Between 12 midnight and 1 a.m. night 22/23rd.July. Exact hour will be notified later.

2. **Barrages.** The raid will take place under a creeping Field Artillery barrage and will be protected by a Standing Box Barrage of Heavy Artillery, Trench Mortars and Machine Guns.
Details of these are contained in Appendices A,B and C 99th.Infantry Brigade Order No.244.

3. **Counter-Battery Work.** Heavy concentrations have been arranged.

4. **Assembly.** Eight gaps will be cut in our own wire. These will be labelled, and tapes laid out. Exact location, parties to use same and communication trenches to be used will be notified later to those concerned. No troops will leave the assembly trenches before the barrage drops.

5. **Dispositions.** The attack will be carried out in 3 waves, supported by a reserve and protective parties on either flank.

6. **Withdrawal.**

    (a) Each of the two officers going to the second objective will fire a BLUE 1½" Very light at the moment of withdrawal from the Second Objective. It is expected that withdrawal will commence within 6 - 10 minutes after reaching the second objective.

    (b) When the second objective parties have crossed the ABLAINZEVELLE - AYETTE Road each of the two officers will fire 2 BLUE 1½" Very lights in quick succession. This will be the signal for the covering parties on the road to withdraw.

    (c) A Searchlight aimed perpendicularly in the sky will be located in or near MONCHY to give outlying parties a direction upon which to march. This beam will play from Zero plus 27 minutes to Zero plus 87 minutes.

    (d) The Code Word " STOKES " will be sent out by Advanced parties

/2............

- 2 -   of Appendix 'F'

6. <u>Withdrawal</u> contd.

    (d) <u>contd</u>.

        by Advanced Battalion Headquarters to Brigade Headquarters and to 23rd. Royal Fusiliers to denote parties have crossed our front line on withdrawal. This will be repeated by Brigade H.Qrs. to 2nd. Division, Right Group, R.F.A., 2nd. Machine Gun Battalion, and 112th. Infantry Brigade.

    (e) Raiders will re-cross our front line at such points as are not being shelled, when they will proceed by the shortest route to known rendezvous. On no account will parties wait in front line area.

    (f) The Countersign " WEARY WILLIE " will be used by raiders on being challenged by front line posts.

7. <u>Communication</u>.
    Advanced Battalion Headquarters will be connected by two lines to Rear Battalion Headquarters. They also be connected direct to Right Company 23rd. Royal Fusiliers. Visual will also be established from Advanced to Rear Battalion Headquarters.

8. <u>Cheering</u>   There will be no cheering. The Battle Honour " TOFREK " will be used whenever the bayonet is used.

9. <u>Distinguishing Signs</u>. All Raiders, including the Left Flank party of the 23rd. Royal Fusiliers will wear a narrow white armband on both arms.

10. <u>Synchronisation of watches</u>. A watch will be sent round to Companies at 9 p.m. "C" and "D" Coys, 2nd.M.G. Battln. and 99th. Trench Mortar Battery, and if required Y/2 Trench Mortar Battery will send a representative to Battalion or nearest Coy.H.Qrs. of 1st. Royal Berks. Regt. at 9.15 p.m.

11. <u>Medical arrangements</u>. An advanced Aid Post will be established at Rear Battalion Headquarters. Motor Ambulances will be waiting on track at F.15.central. Stretcher Bearer Relay Posts will be established at about -
    (a) F.17.d.0.0.
    (b) F.17.c.75.20.
    (c) Advanced Battalion Headquarters.
    (d) Right Company Headquarters.

    From the AYETTE - BUCQUOY Road movement will be by wheeled stretchers to Motor Ambulances.

12. <u>Advance Battalion Headquarters</u>.

    Advance Battalion Headquarters will be at No.9 Post F.17.c.1.5.

    Acknowledge.

                        (Sgd) M.P.PUGH, Capt.& Adjt.

<u>NOTE</u> - Zero Hour will be 12.30 a.m. on night 22/23rd. July.

Appendix 'H'

1st. Royal Berks. Regt.

With reference to the proposed raid to be carried out about the 21/22nd. inst.

1. Ensure that there is no mention of it on the telephone at any time from now onwards.

2. The actual number taking part will not be less than 200 counting forward covering parties.

3. The Machine Gun and Field and Heavy Artillery support are being worked out at Brigade Headquarters. The pace of the actual covering and moving artillery barrage can be decided after practice over the tapes.

4. The ground plan of the work is now being taped out on the ground. Any special taping required by the O.C. Raid will be put in as he requires it.

5. Special photographs have been demanded and it is hoped to get them today.

All details must be carefully thought out before the men go over the tapes and they can be elaborated after each days training.
The following points common to all raids require attention :-

(a) Special mark for all taking part. White helmet, armband etc.

(b) Watchword.

(c) Time. It will be full moon and light ~~will~~ all night if weather is fine about 22nd.

(d) Forming up. If very light no men should leave our trenches until barrage drops. Both BADEN and Southern C.T. in 17.c. may be required.

(e) How long raiders in trenches before starting.

(f) Where will raiders be the day before raid.

(g) Arrangements to fill casualties of important people in raid - understudies training.

(h) Pace of barrage. Position of initial barrage and length it remains.

(i) Special signals to denote withdrawal, success of first and second objectives, all party in.

(j) How to deal with possible enemy outlying picquets between our front line and the first enemy road just West of Huts.

(k) Parties to deal with any enemy working parties met with.

/2............

- 2 -   of Appendix 'H'

(l) Searching of buildings for dugouts and carriage of material for destruction. Probably not many dugouts exist under the road NISSEN HUTS and the destruction of huts themselves is not necessary.

(m) Arrangements for sending back prisoners so as not to denude raiding party.

(n) Special identification Police.

(o) Flank protection on Right and left.

(p) Time of wait on 1st.objective.

(q) Minimum number of men necessary for 2nd.Objective and whether this should be optional to O.C.Raid - I think not personally.

(r) Conduct of withdrawal. Direction of withdrawal to avoid barrage.

(s) Checking raiders on return. Rendezvous.

(t) Final ~~objective~~ rendezvous (several) proposed and where raiders stay the next day.

(u) Medical arrangements.

(v) General equipment.

(w) Any special equipment which must be ordered now.

(x) Name of O.C.Raid.

(Sgd) E.IRONSIDE,

Brigadier General,
Commanding 99th.Infantry Brigade

7.7.18.

2nd Division No. G.S. 12/33.

No. 2 M.G. Battalion.

SECRET

The new VI Corps Defence Scheme lays down that the following stores will be kept at each M.G. position.

(a) Range card and Index Board.
(b) 16 filled belts for forward guns and 20 for support and reserve guns.
(c) 5000 rounds of S.A.A. either in belts for forward guns and 10,000 rounds S.A.A. for support and rear guns.

I presume we comply with the above ?

R Clayton
Lieut.-Colonel,
General Staff, 2nd Division.

3rd July, 1918.

2nd Division

Yes above is complied with. Ref. para (c) I presume the words "or boxes" should come after "in belts" or else "boxes" be substituted for word "belts"

3/7/18

H Buchanan, Brevet Lt Col
Comdg No 2 Bn M G C

SECRET

57th. Division N°. 10334

5th. July 1918

IV Corps 'G'
N.Z. Division.
2nd. Division.

> 2nd DIVISION
> GENERAL STAFF
> No. GS 6/15
> Date 6.7.18

Herewith Tracing showing dispositions.

Please acknowledge receipt.

Veaux
G416 and Hablainville copt

for Major General
Commanding 57th. Division.

"A" Form.
MESSAGES AND SIGNALS.

TO 2nd Division G

Sender's Number.	Day of Month.	In reply to Number.	
GA7	2		AAA

Herewith Tracing shewing area harassed by Machine Gun during past week.

> 2nd DIVISION
> GENERAL STAFF
> No. GS 12/32
> Date

From 2nd Batt. M.G. Corps

SECRET

SECRET

S E C R E T   99th. Infantry Brigade No.
                                B.M.(S) 377

2nd. Division.
1st. Royal Berks. Regt.   ) For
Right Group R.F.A.   )
Sherer's Group R.G.A.   ) information.

> 2nd DIVISION
> GENERAL STAFF
> No. GS 13/46
> Date...........

OUTLINE OF PROPOSED RAID.

1. **OBJECTIVE.** (Raid Map attached). (3 copies)

    (a) To clear out the area marked in BLUE, capture any prisoners, and destroy any deep dug-outs or Machine Gun emplacements existing.

    (b) Clear out the enemy Strong Point at 'A' marked in RED.

2. **NUMBER OF MEN TO BE EMPLOYED.**

    2 Companies of the 1st. Royal Berks. Regt. These may be composite.

3. **DATE.** The operation to take place about the 22nd. July.

4. **ARTILLERY.** The operation will take place during the night or early morning, and will be carried out under an Artillery barrage. Details are now being worked out for the Heavy Artillery Support.

5. **TRAINING.** The men will be training over tapes near Brigade Headquarters between the 16th. and 20th. inst.

6. **REQUIREMENTS.** (i) Photographs of the area given on Raid Map. The only ones we have so far of this area are -
    7th. June - Very good.
    30th. June - Poor.

    (ii) Certain targets crumped by H.A. (Marked 'C' in GREEN).

    This is being attended to.

                                        E. Ironside
                                        Brigadier General,
                                Commanding 99th. Infantry Brigade

5th. July 1918

RAID MAP

SCALE 1:5000

RAID MAP
18
SCALE 1:5000
24
A
C
17
23

Berles-au-Bois
Left Bde.
Rabbit Wood
Hanneau Switch Support
Hanneau Switch Front Line
Hanneau Fm.
Adinfer
Valley Wood
Windmill Switch Front Line
Windmill Switch Support
Sugar Factory
Boiry St. Rictrude
Aerodrome Tr.
Billy's Bank
Adinfer Wood
Monchy Switch Res
Monchy Switch Supt
Monchy au Bois
Centre Bde.
Right Bde.
RESERVE
Lotus Lane
Laurel Lane
Lilly Lane
FRONT LINE
Monchy Switch Front Line
Cojeul River
Douchy les Ayette
Ayette
Monchy Switch Support
O.G. Firing Line
O.G. Support
O.G. Reserve
Monchy Switch Front Line
Little Fm.
Ayette Switch
Bull Tr.
PURPLE
Swindon Tr.
Hannescamps
Caruso Copse
Quesnoy Fm.
PURPLE SUPPORT
Sparrow Support
Aah Lane
O.G. Support
O.G. Front Line
Culverley Copse
Buden Trench
Fox Trench
PURPLE
Legende.
Brigade H.Q.
Battalion H.Q.
Scale 1/20,000
Guards H.Q. 1-6-18
Foncquevillers
Stout Trench
Rum Trench
Essarts
Trench
Pigeon Wood
Commecourt
Bradford Tr.
Halifax Tr.
Top Trench
Misty Tr.
Ablainzevelle
SECRET.
37 Div

S.D.R.

SECRET. 2nd Division No. G.S. 13/46/1.

SECRET

37th Division.
----

1. In preparation for a raid to be carried out shortly a shoot on the Southernmost Huts in F.23.a. and c. is being carried out today (July 6th) between 6 p.m. and 8-30 p.m. with Balloon observation.

2. The battery that is shooting (6") is situated at W.24.d.9.5.

3. Up to 100 rounds will be fired, but no shooting will take place after 8-30 p.m.

4. ACKNOWLEDGE.

(sgd) E R Clayton
Lt Col
for Major General,
Commanding 2nd Division.

6th July, 1918.

Copy to 99th Bde.

2nd DIVISION GENERAL STAFF
No. GS 13/46/1
Date 6-7-18

S E C R E T   99th Infantry Brigade
                                              No.B.M.(S)379

2nd. Division.
_____

        Reference attached copy letter No.B.M.(S)378 - As the shoot will be in front of the 63rd. Brigade, will you please have them warned ?

                                                    Brigadier General,
5th. July 1918   Commanding 99th. Infantry Bde.

SECRET

99th.Infantry Brigade No.
B.M.(S)378

23rd.Royal Fusiliers
Sherer's Group.   ) For
2nd. Division.   ) Information.

In preparation for a Raid to be carried out shortly a shoot on the 7 Southernmost Huts in F.23.a. and c. is being carried out tomorrow (6th.) between 6 p.m. and 8-30 p.m. with Balloon Observation.

The Battery that is shooting (6") is situated at W.24.d.9.5. and you should clear all men out of the front line between Nos. 1 and 9 Posts both exclusive during the shoot.

Up to one hundred rounds will be fired but no shooting will take place after 8-30 p.m.

Please arrange to have the shoot observed and report the effect by first run on 7th.

[signature]

Captain,
Brigade Major,
99th.Infantry Brigade

5th.July 1918

2nd Div/gs 13/46/2

2nd Div.
2nd Div. M.G. Bn.   Am(s)383

For the proposed raid I should like the assistance of M.G's for the following

(i) An enfilade standing barrage along the northern edge of the village of ABLAINZEVILLE following the course of the main German trench as far as the northern end of the cemetery at 23.b.6.1

(ii) An enfilade standing barrage along the whole length of C.T. starting at redoubt at 18.a.4.5. and running down to the junction of trenches in 13.d.4.8.

(iii) Redoubt in 18.a.4.5. and the portions of trenches & shell-holes to the S.W. of it as far as 17.b.9.3.

Addressed 2nd Div
+ 2nd Div. M.G. Bn

July 7th
                    E. Ironside.
                         B.G.
                      99 Inf. Bde

2nd Division No. G.S. 13/46/3.

VI Corps.

SECRET

It is proposed to carry out a raid about July 22nd on the Right Brigade Front of this Divisional Sector.

2. OBJECTIVE. (Map attached)

    (a) To clear out the area marked in Blue, capture prisoners, and destroy any deep dug-outs or Machine Gun emplacements existing.

    (b) Clear out enemy's strong point 'A' marked in Red.

3. Number of men to be employed. 2 Companies, 1st Royal Berks Regt.

4. Outline Plan. The operation will take place during the night and will be carried out under Artillery and Machine Gun barrage. Some Heavy Artillery will be required.

5. Practice - will be carried out over tapes near 99th Brigade Headquarters between 16th and 20th July.

6. An estimate of the extra ammunition required will be forwarded later.

7. No special equipment is required.

8. Approximate date July 22nd.

8th July, 1918.

Major-General,
Commanding 2nd Division.

original with "spares" 2nd Division GS 13/46/5

99th Inf. Bde. No. B.M.S. 377/1.

2nd Division
Right Group (For information).

SECRET

Reference proposed raid I have arranged for the following T.M. support :-

1. 99th T.M. Battery 9" Stokes to be located in Sunken Road and ROCKET Trench in 22.b. to put a continuous barrage during the whole operation from the corner of ABLAINZEVILLE at 23.c.4.7. along the Northern end of the Village to where it cuts the road at about 23.central - a distance of about 400yds. About 200 rounds a gun - 1800 in all will be fired during the operation. Ammunition commences going up to-night.
Will you make arrangements with 37th Division ?

   (i) Location of guns is just in their area, Sunken Road about 22.b.5.5. and ROCKET Trench, 22.b.8.5.

   (ii) Safety precautions as to firing on 23.a.4.7.

2. D.T.M.O. with Newton Mortars either in their present positions or moving slightly forward to take on with 2 Mortars the enemy work just West of Redoubt on the Grid line between 18.a. and 17.b.

   About 100 rounds a gun will be fired.

3. D.T.M.O. has been asked to secure the co-operation of 37th Division Newtons to take on the enemy main line just where it leaves the CEMETERY at ABLAINZEVILLE about 23.d.80.95. A permanent barrage on this corner during the whole operations (1 hour at the most).

4. I cannot get Stokes Mortars on to the enemy main trench from where it crosses the ABLAINZEVILLE - AYETTE Road about 23.central to the CEMETERY as I thought I could. This trench will flank the advance of the raid and must be thoroughly neutralised during operations.
The extreme Northerly corner of the CEMETERY about 23.b.65.10 is an important one especially the 2 M.Gs. or T.M. emplacements just West of the road and which can be clearly seen in photographs 4.7.18.6.F.8 require special attention.

5. As regards Heavy Artillery co-operation, from the lV Corps, would it be possible to ensure the following as it is in their area :-

   (a) Neutralisation of Northern points in ABLAINZEVILLE.

   (b) A good crumping during whole of operations of the enemy main line from the point dealt with by 37th Newton Mortars at the ABLAINZEVILLE CEMETERY to the point where it cuts the road almost on the Grid line running E. and W. between 24 and 18.

   (c) Counter-battery work on their Section.

6. As regards our own Heavies, what we require is :-

   (a) Counter-battery work in our area.

   (b) A good crumping during whole operations, along the enemy main line from the point where it cuts the road and Grid line running E. and W. between 24 and 18, the point where it joins the guns of the

lV Corps........

- (2) -

       IV Corps to the junction of trenches about 13.d.5.7, thence along the C.T. running N.W. to the Redoubt situated in 18.a.3.6.

   (c) Neutralisation of bank just East of the above Redoubt which has been already much crumped, this is probably a Coy. H.Q.

7. As regards Field Artillery barrage, this should fulfil the following condition :-

   (a) Clean up the area in front (West) of the hutments and more forward at the pace of the advance to a point covering the first objective.

   (b) Right flank. Cover the block of buildings marked "C" on Raid map, and the small works on the Grid line N. of 23.central.

   (c) Left flank. Cover the enemy trench line West of road running from 17.a.7.0. Northwards to 17.a.6.5. Special attention on the road junction at 17.c.85.90 (where there is a M.G.) until it is attacked.

   (d) There will be a minimum halt on the first objective and the party for the second objective leap-frogging through at once.

   (e) Neutralisation of second objective during capture of first, and continuing until the raid approaches second objective.

   (f) When the move forward to the second objective takes place the Field Artillery barrage to move forward at the pace decided upon and then to rest roughly upon the line of the main German Trench running from the ABLAINZEVILLE CEMETERY to the trench junction at 13.a.5.7, thence along the C.T. to the Redoubt at 18.a.3.6.

   (g) I cannot quite settle the position of the Right flank of this barrage until I see the troops over the tapes. Special measures may have to be taken with regard to the Hutments marked "C".

   (h) As regards the Left flank, it will have to be settled whether the barrage remains upon the trench line running from 17.a.7.0. to 17.a.6.5. or lift so that our left flank guard can clean it up. In case it lifts, the barrage should go well out towards the Redoubt in 18.a.3.6.

   (i) Good photographs of this area are essential to enable us to pick up any M.G. emplacements located West of the enemy main line, and until these come in I cannot give any special points for 4.5" Hows.

                                         (Sgd.) E. IRONSIDE,
                                               Brigadier-General,
9th July, 1918.   Commanding 99th Inf Brigade.

S E C R E T.   99th. Infantry Brigade No.
                                    B.M.(S) 393
2nd. Division.

[Stamp: 2nd DIVISION / GENERAL STAFF / No. G/A 13/46/4 / Date 9.7.18]

In connection with the raid to be carried out by 1st. Royal Berks. Regt. on or about night 21/22nd. inst. it is desired to fire on the Hedge North of ABLAINZEVELLE (F.23.c.70.35. to d.10.95.) with 9 Stokes Mortars from positions in -

    (a) BUCQUOY - AYETTE Road F.22.b.4.2. to 4.4.

    (b) ROCKET TRENCH F.22.b.9.1. to 9.5.

As these positions are not in this Brigade area will you please obtain the necessary permission from 37th. Division ?

9th. July 1918

                                  Brigadier General,
                            Commanding 99th. Infantry Brigade

SECRET

O.C. A. B. C. D. Cos.
5th. 6th. 99th. Inf. Bdes.
37th. M.G. Battalion.
2nd. Division "G".

2nd DIVISION
GENERAL STAFF
No. G.S. 12/37
Date 10.7.18

M.G.2/288.

1. In consequence of a re-numbering of M.G. positions on the Corps front, the following new numbers of guns of this Battalion will come into force on receipt:-

RIGHT CO.

Old No.	New No.
F.1. - F.4.	F.1. - F.4.
F.5. & F.6.	F.5. & F.6.
R.5. - R.8.	S.1. - S.4.
S.1. - S.4.	S.5. - S.8.
R.9. & R.10.	R.5. & R.6.

CENTRE CO.

S.5. & S.6.	F.7. & F.8.
S.7. & S.8.	F.9. & F.10.
S.9. & S.10.	F.11. & F.12.
F.7. & F.8.	F.13. & F.14.
R.11. & R.12.	R.7. & R.8.
R.13. & R.14.	R.9. & R.10.
R.15. & R.16.	R.11. & R.12.
R.17. & R.18.	R.15. & R.16.

LEFT CO.

S.13. & F.14.	F.15. & F.16.
S.15. & S.16.	F.17. & F.18.
S.17. & S.18.	F.19. & F.20.
F.9. - F.12.	F.21. - F.24.
S.11. & S.12.	S.9. & S.10.
R.23. & R.24.	R.17. & R.18.
R.21. & R.22.	R.19. & R.20.

RESERVE CO.

R.1. - R.4.	R.1. - R.4.
R.19. & R.20.	R.13. & R.14.
R.25. & R.26.	R.21. & R.22.

2. Sites for M.G. positions for defence of the PURPLE LINE in depth are numbered as follows:-

RIGHT CO.

No. of Position.	No. of Guns.	LOCATION.
A.1. - A.4.	4	E.17.d.9.7.
A.5. & A.6.	2	F.7.c.4.1.

CENTRE CO.

A.7. - A.10.	4	F.7.b.6.1.
A.11. - A.14.	4	F.1.c.6.6.

LEFT CO.

A.15. & A.16.	2	F.1.b.1.1.
A.17. & A.18.	2	F.1.b.1.3.
A.19. - A.22.	4	X.25.c.1.4.
A.23. & A.24.	2	X.20.c.1.1.

3. Officers Commanding Companies will indent on Battalion Headquarters for necessary new number boards (including those in para.2. above) required for positions.

9.7.18.

H.M. Todd
Major.
for Lieut.Colonel.
Comdg. No.2.Bn. M.G. Corps.

2nd Division No.
G.S. 13/46/4.

SECRET

37th Division.

It is proposed to carry out a raid on or about night 21st/22nd July on the ~~kuxmam~~ hut encampment in F.17.c & d. and F.23.a & b.

In order to fire on the Northern outskirts of ABLAINZEVILLE, it is necessary to place 3" Stokes Mortars in the following positions:-

(a) BUCQUOY - AYETTE Road F.22.b.4.2 to 4.4.

(b) ROCKET TRENCH F.22.b.9.1 to 9.5.

Will you please say if there will be any objection to Stokes Mortars being placed in the above positions.

C.E.Pereira
Major-General,
Commanding 2nd Division.

10/7/18.

Copy to 99th Inf. Bde.

2nd Division No. G.S. 13/46/6.

SECRET.

SECRET

C.R.A. 2nd Division.

With reference to the Raid to be carried out by the 99th Brigade on or about July 22nd, the following is the Heavy Artillery assistance required -

From IV Corps Heavy Artillery.

(a) Neutralisation of Northern points in ABLAINZEVILLE *Special attention being paid to Northern edge of village*

(b) Bombardment of enemy main trench from about ABLAINZEVILLE CEMETERY to grid line between 18 & 24.

(c) Counter battery work.

From VI Corps Heavy Artillery.

(a) Bombardment of enemy trench from grid line between 18 & 24 to junction of trenches about 13.d.5.7, thence to the Redoubt in 18.a.3.6.

Can a plan be arranged please by O.C. Sherer's Group as early as possible ?

10/7/18.

Lieut. Colonel,
General Staff, 2nd Division.

SECRET.

2nd Division No. G.S. 13/46/6.

C.R.A. 2nd Division.

SECRET

With reference to the Raid to be carried out by the 99th Brigade on or about July 22nd, the following is the Heavy Artillery assistance required -

From IV Corps Heavy Artillery.

(a) Neutralisation of Northern points in ABLAINZEVILLE

(b) Bombardment of enemy main trench from about ABLAINZEVILLE CEMETERY to grid line between 18 & 24.

(c) Counter battery work.

From VI Corps Heavy Artillery.

(a) Bombardment of enemy trench from grid line between 18 & 24 to junction of trenches about 13.d.5.7; thence to the Redoubt in 18.a.3.6.

Can a plan be arranged please by O.C. Sherer's Group as early as possible ?

Arrange with 112

10/7/18.

Lieut. Colonel,
General Staff, 2nd Division.

99th Inf. Bde. No. B.M.S. 377/1.

2nd Division
Right Group (For information).

SECRET

Reference proposed raid I have arranged for the following T.M. support :-

1. 99th T.M. Battery 9" Stokes to be located in Sunken Road and ROCKET Trench in 22.b. to put a continuous barrage during the whole operation from the corner of ABLAINZEVILLE at 23.c.4.7. along the Northern end of the Village to where it cuts the road at about 23.central - a distance of about 400yds. About 200 rounds a gun - 1800 in all will be fired during the operation. Ammunition commences going up to-night.
Will you make arrangements with 37th Division ?

   (i) Location of guns is just in their area, Sunken Road about 22.b.5.5. and ROCKET Trench, 22.b.8.5.

   (ii) Safety precautions as to firing on 23.a.4.7.

2. D.T.M.O. with Newton Mortars either in their present positions or moving slightly forward to take on with 2 Mortars the enemy work just West of Redoubt on the Grid line between 18.a. and 17.b.

About 100 rounds a gun will be fired.

3. D.T.M.O. has been asked to secure the co-operation of 37th Division Newtons to take on the enemy main line just where it leaves the CEMETERY at ABLAINZEVILLE about 23.d.80.95. A permanent barrage on this corner during the whole operations (1 hour at the most).

4. I cannot get Stokes Mortars on to the enemy main trench from where it crosses the ABLAINZEVILLE - AYETTE Road about 23.central to the CEMETERY as I thought I could. This trench will flank the advance of the raid and must be thoroughly neutralised during operations.
The extreme Northerly corner of the CEMETERY about 23.b.65.10 is an important one especially the 2 M.Gs. or T.M. emplacements just West of the road and which can be clearly seen in photographs 4.7.18.6.F.8 require special attention.

5. As regards Heavy Artillery co-operation, from the IV Corps, would it be possible to ensure the following as it is in their area :-

   (a) Neutralisation of Northern points in ABLAINZEVILLE.

   (b) A good crumping during whole of operations of the enemy main line from the point dealt with by 37th Newton Mortars at the ABLAINZEVILLE CEMETERY to the point where it cuts the road almost on the Grid line running E. and W. between 24 and 18.

   (c) Counter-battery work on their Section.

6. As regards our own Heavies, what we require is :-

   (a) Counter-battery work in our area.

   (b) A good crumping during whole operations, along the enemy main line from the point where it cuts the road and Grid line running E. and W. between 24 and 18, the point where it joins the guns of the

IV Corps..........

- (2) -

IV Corps to the junction of trenches about 13.d.5.7, thence along the C.T. running N.W. to the Redoubt situated in 18.a. 3.6.

(c) Neutralisation of bank just East of the above Redoubt which has been already much crumped, this is probably a Coy. H.Q.

7. As regards Field Artillery barrage, this should fulfil the following condition :-

(a) Clean up the area in front (West) of the hutments and more forward at the pace of the advance to a point covering the first objective.

(b) Right flank. Cover the block of buildings marked "C" on Raid map, and the small works on the Grid line N. of 23.central.

(c) Left flank. Cover the enemy trench line West of road running from 17.a.7.0. Northwards to 17.a.6.5. Special attention on the road junction at 17.c.85.90 (where there is a M.G.) until it is attacked.

(d) There will be a minimum halt on the first objective and the party for the second objective leap-frogging through at once.

(e) Neutralisation of second objective during capture of first, and continuing until the raid approaches second objective.

(f) When the move forward to the second objective takes place the Field Artillery barrage to move forward at the pace decided upon and then to rest roughly upon the line of the main German Trench running from the ABLAINZEVILLE CEMETERY to the trench junction at 13.a.5.7, thence along the C.T. to the Redoubt at 18.a.3.6.

(g) I cannot quite settle the position of the Right flank of this barrage until I see the troops over the tapes. Special measures may have to be taken with regard to the Hutments marked "C".

(h) As regards the Left flank, it will have to be settled whether the barrage remains upon the trench line running from 17.a.7.0. to 17.a.6.5. or lift so that our left flank guard can clean it up. In case it lifts, the barrage should go well out towards the Redoubt in 18.a.3.6.

(i) Good photographs of this area are essential to enable us to pick up any M.G. emplacements located West of the enemy main line, and until these come in I cannot give any special points for 4.5" Hows.

(Sgd.) E. IRONSIDE,
Brigadier-General,
Commanding 99th Inf Brigade.

9th July, 1918.

2nd Div G.S. 13/46/5 Secret   Am(S)377/1

2nd Div
Right Group (for information)

Reference proposed raid. I have arranged
for the following T.M. support

1. 99th T.M. Bty. 9 Stokes to be located
in Sunken road & ROCKET trench in
22.b to put a continuous barrage
during the whole operation from the
corner of ABLAINZEVILLE at 23.C.4.7.
along the northern end of the village to
where it cuts the road at about 23 Central
a distance of about 400 yards. About
200 rounds a gun 1800 in all will be
fired during the operation
    Ammunition commences going up
tonight
    Will you make arrangements with 37th
Div
    (i) Location of guns is just in their area
Sunken road about 22.b.5.5 &
ROCKET trench 22.b.8.5
    (ii) Safety precautions as to firing on
23.a.4.7.

2. D.T.M.O. with Newton mortars either
in their present positions or moving slightly
forward to take on with 2 mortars the

Ask
37 Div

2

enemy work just west of redoubt on the grid line between 18a and 17b. About 100 rounds a gun will be fired.

3. O.T.M.O. has been asked to secure the cooperation of 37th Div. Mortars to take on the enemy main line just where it leaves the cemetery at ABLAINZEVILLE about 23.d.80.95. A permanent barrage on this corner during whole operation (1 hour at the most)

4. I cannot get Stokes mortars on to the enemy main trench from where it crosses the ABLAINZEVILLE + AYETTE road about 23 central to the cemetery as I thought I could. This trench will flank the advance of the raid and must be thoroughly neutralised during operation.

The extreme northerly corner of the cemetery about 23.b.65.10 is an important one, especially the two M.G. & T.M. emplacements just west of the road & which can be clearly seen in photographs 4.7.18.6 F 8 require special attention

5. As regards Heavy Arty cooperation from the 4th Corps would it be possible to ensure the following as it is in their

area

    (a) Neutralization of batteries points in ABLAINZEVILLE

    (b) A good crumping during whole of operation of the enemy main line from the point dealt with by 37th Newton mortars at the ABLAINZEVILLE cemetery to the point where it cuts the road almost on the grid line running E & W between 24 + 18.

    (c) Counter battery work on their section

6. As regards our own heavies what we require is:—

    (a) Counter battery work in our area

    (b) A good crumping during whole operation along the enemy main line from the point where it cuts the road & grid line running E & W between 24 + 18 the point where it joins the guns of the 4th Corps to the junction of trenches about 13.d.5.7. thence along the ct running N.W. to the redoubt situated in 18.a.3.6.

    (c) Neutralization of bank just E of the above redoubt which has already been much crumped. This is probably a Coy H.q.

4

7. As regards Field Artillery Barrage. This should fulfill the following conditions:—

(a) Clean up the area in front (W) of the battlements & move forward at the pace of the advance to a point covering the first objective.

(b) Right flank. Cover the block of buildings marked C on raid map and the small works on the road line N of 23. central

(c) Left flank. Cover the enemy trench line W of road running from 17. a 7.0. northwards to 17. a. 6.5. Special attention on the road junction at 17. c. 85.90 (where there is an M.G.) until it is attacked

(d) There will be a minimum halt on the first objective & the party to the second objective (approaching through) at once.

(e) Neutralization of 2nd objective during capture of 1st and continuing until the raid approaches 2nd objective

5

(f) When the move forward to the 2nd objective takes place the 3rd Art barrage to move forward at the pace decided upon & then to rest roughly upon the line of the main German trench running from the ABLAINZEVILLE cemetery to the trench junction at 13.a.5.7. thence along the C.T. to the redoubt at 18.a.3.6.

(g) I cannot quite settle the position of the right flank of this barrage until I see the troops over the tapes. Special measures may have to be taken with regard to the shutments marked C.

(h) As regards the left flank it will have to be settled whether the barrage remains upon the trench line running from 17.a.7.0. to 17.a.6.5 or left so that our left flank guard can clean it up. In case it lifts the barrage should go without towards the redoubt in 18.a.3.6

(i) Good photographs of this area are essential to enable us to pick up any M.G. emplacements located west of the enemy main line until these could in I cannot give any special points (?) 4'5" Hows

9th July

E Ironside
BE.
99 Inf Bde

SECRET

2nd D.A. No.B.M. 33/4a.

2/Div G.S. 13/46/10

R.A.,
VI Corps.

The Right Brigade 2nd Division is carrying out a raid on the huts in F.17.c.&.d. and F.23.a.&.b. about the 22nd instant.

Will you kindly ask IV Corps to assist us with Heavy Artillery as follows :-

(1) 2 - Batteries 6" Howitzers.
Neutralizing fire on northern part of ABLAINZEVILLE in the area F.23.c.6.6. - F.23.d.75.90. - F.23.d.8.8. - F.23.c.6.5.

(2) 2 - Batteries 6" Howitzers.
Standing barrage on trench F.23.d.75.90. - F.18.d.7.0.

Rate of fire.
1 round per gun per minute for first 15 minutes.
1 round per gun per 2 minutes for remainder of time.

Total time of raid about 1 hour.

Fuze 101 E. non-delay.

(3) Neutralizing fire during the raid on all enemy batteries in IV Corps Zone likely to fire on the area of the raid.

G.A. Sandys
Brig.General,
C.R.A., 2nd Division.

11th July, 1918.

Copies to :-

2nd Division "G"   } For information.
36th Bde, R.F.A.   }

"A" Form
MESSAGES AND SIGNALS.

Army Form C. 2121
(In pads of 100.)

No. of Message

2nd DIVISION

This message is on a/c of:
GENERAL STAFF

TO: 2nd Division

Sender's Number: 1035
Day of Month: 11
In reply to Number: 64
AAA

With reference to R.A. 2nd Divn B.M./33/1 dated 11-7-18 aaa 18pdrs - about 40 Quas Line 3 for F.23.d.80.95 - A.13.a.5.7 - F.18.a.3.6 read F.23.d.80.95 - A.13.d.5.7 - F.18.a.3.6

From: 2nd D.A.
Place:
Time: 10.15 pm

SECRET.

> 2nd DIVISION
> GENERAL STAFF
> GS 13/46/7
> 11.7.18.

R.A. 2nd Divn. BM/33/4.

2nd Division "G"

Artillery arrangements for the raid will be as follows :-

18-pounders - about 40 guns.

Creeping barrage opening west of the first objective and moving eastwards till it rests as a protective barrage on the Enemy trench F 23 d 80.95 - A 13 & 5.7 - F 18 a 3.6.

Standing barrage on both flanks.

4.5" Howitzers, on Machine-gun and Trench Mortar emplacements as required.

37th Divisional Artillery are being asked to assist on the right flank.

6-inch Trench Mortars, 2 guns, 2nd Div. Arty.

Enemy work in F 17 b.
37th Div. Arty. are assisting with Trench Mortars on the corner about F 23 d 80.95.

Heavy Artillery VI Corps.

6-inch Howitzers. 16 Howitzers. Standing Barrage.
Trench F 18 d 7.0 to A 13 d 4.7 - F 18 c 30.45 and on bank and redoubt in F 18 a.

Heavy Artillery IV Corps are being asked to neutralize the northern part of ABLAINZEVILLE and put a standing barrage on trench F 23 d 75.90. to F 18 d 7.0.

Counter-Battery work.

Neutralizing fire throughout the operation. IV Corps Heavy Artillery are being asked to assist in their zone.

11th July, 1918.

G H Sanders
Brig-General
C. R. A. 2nd Division.

"C" Form.
MESSAGES AND SIGNALS.

| Prefix | Code | Words 13 | Received From Rawl. By | Sent, or sent out At To By | Office Stamp |

Handed in at 7d Office 11.34 Received 11.37

TO 2nd Divn

| *Sender's Number | Day of Month | In reply to Number | |
| G 27 | 13 | G13/46 | AAA |

O- 11th and afree

99 not back

5.45 AM

FROM PLACE & TIME 37 Divn G

2nd. DIVISION "G".
C.R.E.
C.M.G.O.

> 2nd DIVISION
> GENERAL STAFF
> No. GS 12/39
> Date 13-7-18

M.G.2/304.

Herewith PROGRESS REPORT of work on Machine Gun Dug-outs in this Sector:-

LOCATION OF DUG-OUT.	PROGRESS.
F.4.d.1.1.	1 Shaft, 32' down.
F.10.a.3.5.	1 Shaft, 32' down.
F.5.c.5.6.	1 Shaft, 30' down.
F.21.b.8.2.	2 Shafts completed - widening chamber.
F.2.d.8.8.	1 Shaft, 22' down.
F.14.a.9.6.	1 Shaft, 20' down.
F.15.c.7.4.	1 Shaft, 23' down.
F.14.a.7.0.	1 Shaft, 32' down.

LOCATION REPORT.   NIL.

12/7/18.

Lieut.Col.
Comdg. No.2. Bn. M.G.Corps.

2nd Division No. G.S. 13/46/8

SECRET

37th Division.
───────────────

    A raid is being carried out on the Hut Camp in F.17.c. and d. and F.23.a. and b. about ~~June~~ *July* 21st/22nd.

    I should be glad if assistance could be given by the Divisional Artillery covering your front, including 6" Trench Mortars.

    If there is no objection to the proposal, I would suggest that details are arranged between the Divisional Artilleries.

[signature]

Major-General,
Commanding 2nd Division.

11th July, 1918.

SECRET. M.G.2/320.

2nd. DIVISION "G".

> 2nd DIVISION
> GENERAL STAFF
> No. GS 13/46/12
> Date 15.7.18

1. The 99th Infantry Brigade will carry out a Raid on the enemy Trenches about F.17.c. & d. at a date to be notified later.

2. The following will be the Machine Gun arrangements in support of the Raid. Detailed orders will be issued at a later date.

D. COMPANY. (RIGHT).

Number of guns.	Location.	Target.	Remarks.
2 Guns	F.21.a.1.5 (approx)	F.23.c.35.80 to F.23.c.70.78	Indirect Enfilade.
2 Guns	Do.	F.23.c.73.93 to F.23.d.05.88	Do.
2 Guns	Do.	F.23.d.07.98 to F.23.d.40.97.	Do.
2 Guns	F.21.d.50.80 (approx)	F.23.d.4.8 to F.23.d.80.98	Do.

8 Guns, Total.

B. COMPANY. (CENTRE).

Number of Guns.	Location.	Target.	Remarks.
2 Guns	F.10.a.5.0 (approx)	F.18.a.45.37 to F.18.a.70.28	Indirect Enfilade.
1 Gun	F.11.d.00.26	F.18.a.7.2 to A.13.b.0.0	Direct Enfilade.
1 Gun	F.11.d.20.50	Do.	Do.

4 Guns, Total.

A. COMPANY. (LEFT).

Number of Guns.	Location.	Target.	Remarks.
4 Guns	F.5.c.6.8 (approx)	F.18.a.25.41 to F.18.a.50.60	Indirect frontal.

14/7/18.

HM Todd
Major,
for Lieut.Colonel.
Comdg. No.2.Bn. M.G.Corps.

2nd Division No. G.S. 13/46/11.

No.2 M.G. Battalion.

SECRET

Please forward a summary of the orders being issued for the Machine Gun programme for the Raid being carried out by the 99th Inf. Brigade.

14th July, 1918.

E R Clayton
Lieut-Colonel,
General Staff - 2nd Division.

> 2ND BATTALION,
> MACHINE GUN CORPS.
>
> No............
> Date............

2nd Division

Herewith Summary. 99th Inf Bde orders have not been received up to date. BGC 99th Inf Bde has approved of attached M G scheme
H A Buchanan Bunch? Lt Col
Comdg No 2 Bn M.G.C

16/7/18

SECRET

M.G.2/320.

SECRET.

2nd. DIVISION "G".

1.   The 99th Infantry Brigade will carry out a Raid on the enemy Trenches about F.17.c. & d. at a date to be notified later.

2.   The following will be the Machine Gun arrangements in support of the Raid.   Detailed orders will be issued at a later date.

C. COMPANY. (RIGHT).

Number of guns.	Location.	Target.	Remarks.
2 Guns	F.27.a.1.5 (approx)	F.23.c.35.80 to F.23.c.70.78	Indirect Infilade.
2 Guns	Do.	F.23.c.73.93 to F.23.d.05.98	Do.
2 Guns	Do.	F.23.d.07.98 to F.23.d.40.97.	Do.
2 Guns	F.21.d.50.80 (approx)	F.23.d.4.8 to F.23.d.60.98	Do.
8 Guns, Total			

B. COMPANY. (CENTRE).

Number of Guns.	Location.	Target.	Remarks.
2 Guns	F.10.a.5.0 (approx)	F.18.a.45.37 to F.18.a.70.28	Indirect Infilade.
1 Gun	F.11.d.00.24	F.18.a.7.2 to A.13.b.0.0	Direct Enfilade.
1 Gun	F.11.d.20.50	Do.	Do.
4 Guns, Total.			

A. COMPANY. (LEFT).

Number of Guns.	Location.	Target.	Remarks.
4 Guns	F.5.c.6.8 (approx)	F.18.a.25.41 to F.18.a.50.60	Indirect frontal.

W M Todd
Major.
for Lieut.Colonel.
Comdg.   No.2.Bn.   M.G.Corps.

14/7/28.

2nd DIVISION
GENERAL STAFF
No. GS 13/48
Date 15·7·18

S E C R E T.

5th Inf. Bde. No. G.S. 740/94/1.

24TH R.F.
52ND L.I.
2ND H.L.I.
5TH L.T.M.BTY.
6TH INF. BDE.
2ND GUARDS BDE.
2ND DIVISION.

Para. 3. Reference 5th Inf. Bde. No. G.S. 740/94 dated 13/7/18,

ZERO hour will be 8 P.M. and not 10 p.m. as stated.

Acknowledge

14/7/18.

Major,
Brigade Major, 5th Infantry Brigade.

SECRET.   6th Inf. Bde. No. G.S. 740/24.

56th D.T.
56th L.T.
56th R.T.I.
6th L.T.M. Bty.
4th Tnk. Bn.
6th BRIGADE BHQ.
2nd DIVISION.

[stamp: 2nd DIVISION GENERAL STAFF No. GS 13/48 Date 14.7.18]

1. There will be a "CHINESE ATTACK" on the Brigade Front on July 15th.

2. All active guns and Hows. of the Left Group will carry out the following firing programme :-

TIME.	TARGET.	RATE OF FIRE (per gun per minute)
O+ to O+ 4	A.1.d.W.56 - A.2.c.26.86.	4 rds 18 pdrs:2 rds Hows.
O+ 4 to O+ 12	A.1.d.15.40 - A.2.c.30.68	2 " " " :1 " "
O+ 12 to O+ 16	A.1.d.00.75 - A.2.c.18.05	2 " " " :1 " "
O+ 16 to O+ 20	A.1.d.W.56 - A.2.c.26.86	1 " " " :1 " "

3. Zero Hour will be at 10 p.m.

4. 18 pdrs. will fire 50% H.E. and 50% S.S.
    Hows.   "   "   H.E. with 25% Smoke.

5. During the shoot front line posts opposite the area to be fired on may be withdrawn.

6. ACKNOWLEDGE.

                                        [signature]
                                        Major,
                                        Brigade Major, 6th Infantry Brigade.

General Staff,
Third Army
G.12/295. 28/7/18

Third Army.

Vl Corps G.S.50/157.

I submit this report on the raid carried out on the night of the 22/23rd July by the 1st Bn. Berkshire Regiment.

Bg.Genl.Ironsides, Commanding 99th Inf. Brigade, took the greatest pains to ensure that ~~everything~~ *nothing* which could help towards the successfull of this raid was omitted. I think that the highly satisfactory result is mainly due to the careful preparations, the good leading, and the keenness, and resolution all ranks who took part in it.

(Sgd) A, Haldane
Lt. General,
Vl Corps

27th July, 1918

2

G.O.C. Vl Corps

This was a most satisfactory raid. It was evident at the rehearsal I attended that the greatest pains had been taken in the preparations.
The conduct of all ranks in carrying it through is most commendable.

(Sgd) J. Byng.
General,

28/7/18

SECRET 99th. Infantry Brigade No.
　　　　　　　B.M.(S)445

2nd. Division.

      Herewith two copies of Narrative on Raid carried out by 1st. Royal Berkshire Regt. Aeroplane Photographs (Appendix G) are not available at present but will be forwarded later.

25th. July 1918

Brigadier General,
Commanding 99th. Infantry Brigade

SECRET

2nd. Division 'Q'

2ⁿᵈ Div G.S 6/17

99th. Infantry Brigade
No. G/Maps/34

Herewith Map showing present dispositions of this Brigade.

[signature]

Lieutenant,
for Brigadier General,
Commanding 99th. Infantry Brigade

16.7.18.

G.D.No.150/42/G.

2nd Division.

2nd Div G.S. 6/16

Herewith map showing dispositions of 2nd Guards Brigade on right of Guards Division front.

16th July, 1918.

A.C.Wilkinson Capt
General Staff. Guards Division.

Scale 1:20,000.   Note.— New sign for Trenches from information received other than photographs.   BRITISH TRENCHES IN RED   Trenches revised from information received to 14-6-18.   **AYETTE.**   Edition

AYETTE. Edition 2.c Special Sheet. Parts of 51c S.E., 51b S.W., 57d N.E., 57c N.W.

GERMAN TRENCHES IN BLUE
Trenches revised from information received to 24-6-18.

Scale 1: 20,000

Scale 1:20,000. Note:—New Sign for Trenches from information received other than Photographs.   Trenches revised from information received to 10-5-18.   AYETTE. SECRET

Information received to 10-5-18. AYETTE. SECRET Edition 2. Special Sheet. Parts of 51c S.E., 51b S.W., 57d N.E., 57c N.W.

Trenches revised from information received to 24-5-18.

Scale 1:20,000

2nd Division No.G.S.12/40.

99th Inf. Brigade.

SECRET

    New S.O.S. Line for guns F.13.14 is now F.17.b.15.30 - 30.13. Sketch attached.

17th July, 1918.

R Clayton
Lieut - Colonel,
General Staff, 2nd Division.

F

4	5	6
10	11	12
16	17	18

F.13. F.14.

S.O.S LINES
F 13-14.

Ref. Ayette Sheet.
Scale 1:20,000.

"A" Form
MESSAGES AND SIGNALS.

Army Form C. 2121
(In pads of 100)

URGENT

TO: 2nd Div. G.

Sender's Number.	Day of Month.	In reply to Number.	
T.21.	17TH		AAA

New S.O.S. line for
from F13.14 is now
F17B 15.50 — 30.13.
Sketch attached

Copy sent to 99th BDE
B.G.

2nd DIVISION GENERAL STAFF
No. GS 12/40
Date 17-7-18

"MAPS."
2ND DIVISION "G.S." Map corrected

From: No 2 Bn. M.GC.
Place:
Time: 9.30 am.

W. M Todd. Major

Brigade Major,
2nd D.A.

SECRET T.M./48

2nd Divisional Artillery
No. B.M. 33/4c
Date 17. July 18.

Under orders from General Ironside and Colonel Goschen 6" Trench Mortars will carry out the following program during the operation by the 99th Infantry Brigade,

300 rounds about F.18.a.00.45
100 rounds on some other target to be detailed later.

37th Divisional Trench Mortars will barrage enemy main line just where it leaves the Cemetery at ABLAINZEVILLE about F.23.d.30.95 - a permanent barrage on this corner during whole operation,

Total expenditure 2nd, Division :- 400
37th, Division :- 200

2nd DIVISION
GENERAL STAFF
No. G/13/46/14
Date 17.7.18

Soward Roberts.
Captain,
D.T.M.O. 2nd, Division,

17/7/18.

2nd Div "G"

Forwarded.

17/7/18

F.V.Mills.
Major R.F.A.
B.M.R.A. for C.R.A. 2nd Div.

SECRET

3744/40

2nd DIVISION MEDICAL ARRANGEMENTS FOR MINOR OPERATIONS OF 99th INFANTRY BRIGADE.

July 18th, 1918.

Reference Map : BUCQUOY COMBINED SHEET, 1/40,000.

⁂⁂⁂⁂⁂⁂⁂⁂⁂⁂⁂⁂⁂⁂⁂⁂⁂⁂⁂⁂⁂⁂⁂⁂⁂⁂⁂⁂⁂

Casualties will be evacuated from Front line by Wheeled Stretchers on track running from F.16.d. to the road at F.14.c.1.0.

O. C., No. 5 Field Ambulance will lend 5 Wheeled Stretcher carriers to O. C., 1st R.Berks R., for this purpose.

Two Ford cars are placed at the disposal of O. C., No. 5 Field Ambulance. These cars will be sent as near the line as possible on the QUESNOY FARM Road where cases can be transferred from Wheeled Stretchers and taken to Advanced Dressing Station, MONCHY.

1 Bearer Officer from No. 5 Field Ambulance will be at Regimental Aid Post, F.14.d.8.1. to assist the Regimental Medical Officer.

X day and Zero hour will be communicated later.

H.Q., 2nd Divn.
18th July, 1918.

[signature]
Colonel, A.M.S.,
A.D.M.S., 2nd Division.

Copies to :— H.Q., 99th Inf. Bde.
O.C., 1st R.Berks R.
O.C., No. 5 Field Ambulance.
Major ELLIS R.,M.C.,No. 5 F.Amb.
"G.S." 2nd Division.

A.D.M.S.
2nd DIVISION
No. 3744/40
Date 22/7/18

SECRET.

SECRET

Copy No. 13

2nd Division Order No.344.

18th July, 1918.

1. A raid will be carried out by 2 Coys. of 1st Royal Berks Regt. 99th Brigade on the night of July 22nd/23rd.

2. The objectives are as follows:-

   First Objective.- The huts in F.17.c & d and F.23.a & b (vide attached map 'X').

   Second Objective - Enemy's trench about F.18.d.0.4 (marked 'B' on map)

3. The artillery action will be as follows:-

   (a) Right Group. (reinforced by Batteries from 37th Div. Artillery Centre and Left Groups 2nd Div. Artillery).

   (i) At zero will put down a creeping barrage in front of the first objective, moving forward to a point covering the first objective.

   (ii) On the right flank, will cover the block of buildings marked 'C' on map, special attention being paid to the small works immediately North of F.23.central.

   (iii) Left flank - will cover the enemy trench line West of road running from F.17.a.7.0 Northwards to F.17.a.6.5.

   (iv) A standing barrage will be put on to the second objective from zero until the raid approaches.

   (v) When the move forward to the second objective takes place, a creeping barrage will move forward through the second objective and will remain on approximately, the line of the German main trench running from the corner of ABLAINZEVILLE CEMETERY to about A.13.d.5.7 thence to about F.18.a.3.6.

   (vi) Protective barrages will be arranged to protect the raid when at the second objective.

   Detailed arrangements for the above will be made by G.O.C. 99th Brigade with O.C. Right Group.
   The Right Group Guards Div. Artillery is arranging to bombard the enemy's trenches at zero - 10 opposite MOYENNEVILLE.

   (b) Heavy Artillery.

   (i) A bombardment is being carried out by Heavy Artillery IV Corps from Zero of the Northern part of the village of ABLAINZEVILLE and enemy main line from the corner of ABLAINZEVILLE CEMETERY up to grid line F.18.d.7.0.

   (ii) The enemy main trench from the grid line F.18.d.7.0 to trench junction about A.13.d.5.7 thence along the trench running N.W. to the strong point about F.18.a.3.6 is being bombarded by Heavy Arty. VI Corps from Zero.

   (iii) Counter battery work is being carried out by the H.A. of both IV and VI Corps under a programme being drawn up by C.B.S.O. of IV and VI Corps

   Details of Heavy Artillery action are being arranged by VI Corps H.A. in conjunction with C.B.S.O.

P.T.O.

(c) 6" Newton Mortars.

The D.T.M.O. 2nd.Division will engage with 2 mortars the enemy work West of the strong point in the grid line between F.18.a and F.17.b. He will also arrange with the D.T.M.O. of 37th Division to engage the enemy's main line at the Cemetery about F.23.d.8.9 during the whole operation.

4. 99th T.M.Battery, 3" Stokes, will put down a continuous barrage from the corner of ABLAINZEVILLE F.23.c.4.7 along the Northern edge of the village up to the road to about F.23.central.

5. The 2nd M.G.Battn. will arrange -

(a) A machine gun barrage along the Northern edge of ABLAINZEVILLE.
(b) A machine gun barrage to cover the left flank from about F.18.a.2.4 to about A.13.b.0.0.

6. Watches will be synchronised by 2nd Division Signals as follows:-

(a) A watch will be sent to 99th Brigade H.Q. at 6 pm on 22nd July.
(b) Watches will be synchronised with VI Corps H.A. under arrangements to be issued later, and with the Right Group Guards Division Artillery.

7. Zero hour will be notified later.

8. Acknowledge.

E.R.Clayton
Lieut. Colonel,
Issued at 12.30 pm to -   General Staff, 2nd Division.

Copy No.1 to 5th Inf. Bde.
       2   6th Inf. Bde.
       3   99th Inf. Bde.
       4   No.2 M.G.Battn.
       5   C.R.A.
       6   2nd Signal Coy.
       7   37th Division.
       8   Guards Division.
       9   VI Corps.
      10   Shorer's Group H.A.
      11   VI Corps H.A.
      12   IV Corps H.A.
   13-17   G.S.Records.

SECRET

MAP "X"
18/7/18

REFERENCE.
— British Trench
--- German
• M.G.
⊕ T.M.
▫ Post
◊ Dump
⌂ Dug-out
:: Tracks
O.P.
26.7.18

B.M./D.3

<u>Amm. Col</u>

1. Herewith March Table to be attached to Operation Order No: 42 of to day.

The times of starting are arranged to fit in with the crossings of other units and will be strictly adhered to.

2. During daylight no large body of troops will be moved on the roads towards the position of assembly

3. 5 motor ambulances, one for each unit, will be stationed at CROIX DU BAC from 4.pm till 7.pm in case they may be required.

One horse ambulance will be at the position of assembly of each of the trench battalions at 10.30.pm to accompany them on the march. A guide will meet each ambulance on its arrival at battalion billets and conduct it to the 19th Field Ambulance billets.

4. Brigade Headquarters, after reliefs are completed, will be at A.22.a 1.7

5. Please acknowledge receipt by wire.

18/7/15.

Captain,
Brigade Major 19th Infantry Brigade.

Issued with Operation Order No: 42. MARCH TABLE: 19th Infantry Brigade.

UNIT	Place of assembly and starting point	Time of starting	ROUTE.	Billeting area
2nd Royal Welch Frs.	Road junction, H.14.a via road junction H.16.c and CROIX DE ROME.	3.15.pm	FORT ROMPU - BAC ST MAUR Bridge - CROIX DU BAC - Pt.VANUXEEM (A.29.8) - le Pt.MORTIER - road junction A.21.d - road junction A.20.a 5.2	All farms on road between Fme du BOIS LA ROSE Fme A.19. A.14
2nd A. & S. Highlanders	Road junction H.4.d 6.7	3.30.pm	ERQUINGHEM Bridge - cross roads B.27.d - CROIX DU BAC (G.6.c) - Pt.de la BOUDRETTE - road junction G.19.a - road junction G.3.d	Farms in A.28.c.d and G.2.b
Hd.Qrs. and ¼ Battn. 5th Sco.Rifles.	Road junction H.5.b 7.6 (not shown on map) reached by road past Brigade H.Q. and track in H.6.d 7.7	3.30.pm	ERQUINGHEM Bridge - cross roads B.27.d - CROIX DU BAC - Pt.VANUXEEM (A.29.c) - le Pt.MORTIER (G.4.a)	Farms on road from A.27.d to A.21.d
The Maroculans	Farm at H.17.d 2.0	On completion of relief.	Road junctions in H.22.b 9.1 and H.16.c - CROIX DE ROME - FORT ROMPU - BAC ST MAUR bridge - CROIX DU BAC - road junction G.5.b - le SEQUEREAU A.30.c - STEENWERCK - le Gd.BEAUMART A.22.a	Farms on road from A.20.b to A.19.d
1st Middlesex Regiment.	La ROLANDERIE Fme. H.11.c	On completion of relief.	ERQUINGHEM Bridge - cross roads B.27.d - road junction l'HALLOBEAU B.25.c 7.6 - road junction A.18.c 4.2 - STEENWERCK	Farms on road in A.15.a.b.
¼ Battn. 5th Sco.Rifles.	Farm at road junction H.11.d 6.5	On completion of relief.	Road junction H.5.d - ERQUINGHEM Bridge - thence by route as for other half Battalion.	Along road from A.27.d to A.21.d

Issued at 7.15.pm
18/7/15.

W.B.Brodie Captain,

Brigade Major 19th Infantry Brigade.

S E C R E T.　　　　　　　　　　　　　　　　　G.D.No.9/114/G.

No. GS 13/46/13
Date 18.7.18

2nd Division.

With reference to your No.G.S.13/46/13 of July 16th, I am arranging for a demonstration by the Right Group of my Divisional Artillery on the night of July 22nd/23rd.
My C.R.A. will arrange details with yours.

for Major-General,
Commanding Guards Division.

18.7.18.

Copy to: C.R.A.

GUARDS DIVISION

2nd Div No G.S.13/46/13

SECRET

A raid is being carried out by the Right Brigade of this Division on the night of 22/23 July.

I should be glad if a demonstration by the Right Group of the Guards Division could be arranged for that night.

I would suggest that details should be arranged between Cs R.A. of Divisions

16-7-18

Major General
Commanding 2nd Division.

SECRET

M.G.2/346.

2nd. Division "G".
C.R.E. 2nd. Division.
C.M.G.O.

E1 12/41

The following is the WEEKLY PROGRESS REPORT on dugouts under construction in this Sector:-

Location of dugout.	Remarks.
F.4.d.1.1.	1 Shaft completed. - 6 feet on level completed.
F.10.a.3.5.	1 Shaft completed. - 12 feet on level completed and work commenced on upward shaft.
F.5.c.5.6.	2 Shafts and level completed.
F.21.b.8.2.	2 Shafts completed - Passage and chambers completed. Timbering of chambers being proceeded with.
F.2.d.8.8.	1 Shaft and level completed. Work on upward shaft and chamber proceeding.
F.14.a.9.6.	1 Shaft completed. - 8 feet on level completed.
F.15.c.7.4.	1 Shaft completed. - 9 feet on level completed.
F.14.a.7.0.	1 Shaft completed. - 9 feet on level completed.

19/7/18.

Lieut.Col.
Comdg. No.2.Bn. M.G.Corps.

SECRET

2nd DIVISION
GENERAL STAFF
G.1 13/46/16.

SECRET

Third Army.　　　　　　　　　　　　　　　VI Corps
　　　　　　　　　　　　　　　　　　　　　G.S.50/146.

1. The 1st Royal Berkshire Regiment, 99th Infantry Brigade, 2nd Division, are carrying out a raid on the enemy posts North of ABLAINZEVILLE on the night July 22nd/23rd with the object of obtaining identifications and inflicting casualties on the enemy.

2. The strength of the raiding party will be two Companies.

3. The raid will be carried out under a creeping barrage, and a box barrage will be placed round the objectives. Selected targets will be bombarded by the Heavy Artilleries of the VI and IV Corps, who will also neutralise hostile batteries firing on the area to be raided.

4. Machine guns and Trench mortars will co-operate.

5. The raiding party has been practised.

　　　　　　　　　　　　　　　　　　　R.H.Haldane
19th July 1918.
　　　　　　　　　　　　　　　　　　Lieutenant-General,
　　　　　　　　　　　　　　　　　　Commanding VI Corps.

　　　Copies - IV Corps.
　　　　　　　 Canadian Corps.
　　　　　　　 Guards Division.
　　　　　　　 2nd Division.
　　　　　　　 3rd Canadian Division.
　　　　　　　 VI Corps Heavy Artillery.
　　　　　　　 R.A.
　　　　　　　 G.I.

S E C R E T

2nd DIVISION
GENERAL STAFF
No. GS 13/46/5   Copy No. 11
Date

99th. Infantry Brigade Order No. 244

Reference Sheet 57 D. N.E. 1/20,000
Edition 5 d. (Local).   19th.July 1918

1. A Raid will be carried out by the 1st.Royal Berkshire Regt.

   (a) **Strength** - 2 Companies of a minimum number 200.

   (b) **Objective** - To secure prisoners and mop up the area marked A and B. on Raid Map attached.

   (c) **Time.** - Between 12 midnight and 1 a.m. on the night of 22nd./23rd.July. Exact hour will be notified later to all concerned.

2. **Barrages** The raid will take place under a creeping Field Artillery Barrage and will be protected by a Standing Box Barrage of Heavy Artillery, Trench Mortars, and machine guns. Details of these are contained in Appendices A, B and C. (To be issued later).

3. **Counter-Battery work.**
   Heavy concentrations have been arranged.

4. **Assembly.** Troops will assemble in the front trenches. No troops will leave the assembly point until the barrage drops. Tapes giving the direction will be laid from the front line trenches, leading through efficient gaps in our wire, which will be made between dusk and the moment the barrage opens.

5. **Disposition of troops during raid.**
   The two remaining Companies of the 1st.Royal Berks. will hold the PICQUET LINE and POSTS. The two Raiding Companies on withdrawal will occupy the PURPLE Front line, but will be held ready to move forward to the support and reserve Company positions at short notice.
   PICQUET 'A' in BADEN AVENUE will be found by the Right of the front line companies.

6. **Signals.** (a) Each of the two Officers going to the Second Objective will fire a ~~BLUE~~ 1½" Very light at the moment of withdrawal from the Second Objective. It is expected that withdrawal will commence within 6 - 10 minutes after reaching the second objective.

   [margin: parachute light changing from white to green.]

   (b) When the Second objective parties have crossed the ABLAINZEVELLE - AYETTE ROAD each of the two Officers will fire ~~2 BLUE~~ 1½" Very lights in quick succession. This will be the signal for the covering parties on the road to withdraw.

   [margin: 2 parachute lights changing from white to green.]

   (c) A Searchlight aimed perpendicularly in the sky will be located in or near MONCHY to give outlying parties a direction upon which to march. This beam will play from ZERO plus 27 minutes to Zero plus 87 minutes.

   [margin: Red Very lights.]

/ (d)...2....

- 2 -

6. **Signals** contd.

(d) The Code word STOKES will be sent out by Advanced Battalion Headquarters to Brigade Headquarters and to the 23rd. Royal Fusiliers to denote parties have crossed our front line on withdrawal. This will be repeated by Brigade Headquarters to 2nd. Division, Right Group, R.F.A., 2nd. Machine Gun Battalion and 112th. Infantry Brigade.

7. Flanks. It is particularly necessary that the flanks be dealt with during the withdrawal and the Standing barrage of Heavy Artillery, Trench Mortars and Machine Guns forming the Standing Outer barrage should fire their most intense fire during the periods :-

(a) Zero plus 5 minutes to Zero plus 15 minutes (10 minutes).

(b) Zero plus 30 minutes to Zero plus 50 minutes (20 minutes).

Right Flank. Picquets will be formed by the raiding party.

Left Flank. At Zero, a party of a minimum 1 Officer and 10 Other ranks of the 23rd. Royal Fusiliers with a Lewis Gun will move forward and occupy the road junction at F.17.c.95.95. bringing covering fire against any flash of enemy machine gun which opens up. Careful direction will be obtained so as not to interfere with the Raiding party moving to the Second objective.
In order to bring down the barrage on the road junction at F.17.c.95.95. from Zero to Zero plus 5 minutes, the whole of the Post called " BLIZZARD " and the Flanking party intended to occupy the road junction will be moved Northwards to 'Y' Post at F.17.a.7.4. taken over by the 23rd. Royal Fusiliers on the night of 15/16th. July from 1st. Kings Royal Rifle Corps. At Zero plus 5 minutes the barrage will allow the road junction to be occupied, BLIZZARD POST will be re-occupied at the same time.
The 23rd. Royal Fusiliers will arrange to deal with any isolated machine gun posts known to exist East of the ABLAINZEVELLE - AYETTE ROAD, by Lewis Gun fire. This Left Flank party will withdraw upon orders from O.C. 1st. Royal Berks. who will arrange communication with it.

CHEERING There will be no cheering when charging. The watchword is " TOFREK " one of the Battalion Honours of the 1st. Royal Berks., and will be used if the bayonet is used on a German.

Distinguishing Signs. All Raiders, including the Left Flank party of the 23rd. Royal Fusiliers will wear a narrow white armband on both arms.

10. Synchronisation of watches.

A watch will be sent up to RIGHT Battalion Headquarters at 8 p.m. where O.C. 1st.Royal Berks.Regt. will arrange to synchronise watches with "C" and "D" Companies, 2nd. Machine Gun Battalion, and with 99th.Trench Mortar Battery, and (if required) Y/2 Trench Mortar Battery (6" Newtons). No synchronisation of watches will be made by telephone.

11. ACKNOWLEDGE.

Farquharson
Captain,
Brigade Major,
99th. Infantry Brigade

Issued through Signals at 8 a.m. to :-

```
23rd.Royal Fusiliers
1st.Royal Berks.Regt.
1st.Kings Royal Rifle Corps.
99th.Trench Mortar Battery
Captain V.G.STOKES, M.C.(Commanding Raiding party)
Right Group R.F.A.
Sherer's Group R.G.A.
2nd.Machine Gun Battalion
"C" Company, 2nd.M.G.Battalion
"D" Company, 2nd.M.G.Battalion.
2nd.Division 'G'
6th.Infantry Brigade
112th.Infantry Brigade
War Diary.
File.
```

SECRET

> 2nd DIVISION
> GENERAL STAFF
> No. G.S. 13/46/19
> Date

99th. Infantry Brigade No.
B.M.(S)423

To all Recipients of
99th. Infantry Brigade Order No.244

      Herewith " Raid Map " and Appendices A, B, and C to accompany 99th. Infantry Brigade Order No.244.

ACKNOWLEDGE.

Done 20/7/18

Farquharson
Captain,
Brigade Major,
99th. Infantry Brigade

19.7.18.

99th INF. BDE.
(Order No. 244.)
RAID MAP.

First objective --- A.
Second do --- B.

SCALE 1:5000.

99th INF. BDE.
(Order No. 244.)
Appendix "A"

Creeping
Field Artillery
Barrage.

Boundary of area to be raided —————
Boundary of barrage. ———

SCALE 1:5000

99th INF. BDE.
(Order No.244.)
APPENDIX "B"

Reference:
First Objective --- A
Second do --- B
H.A. Barrage
18 Pdr. Standing
Barrage & Howitzers
L.T.M. Barrage

ABLAINZEVELLE

99th INF. BDE.
(Order No. 244.)
Appendix "C".
—
MACHINE GUN
STANDING
BARRAGE.

"A" Form.
MESSAGES AND SIGNALS.

Army Form C.2121 (in pads of 100).

TO 2nd Division

Sender's Number: G1314/1
Day of Month: 20th

Herewith map showing dispositions of our left Brigade since reorganisation.

2nd DIVISION GENERAL STAFF
No.
Date

From 62 Division

Alexander
Captain
Comg 62 (WR) Div

SECRET.

SHEETS 57ᴅ. N.E. 2 & 4. (Parts of)   SCALE 1:10,000.   14-5-18.

Reference.
Trenches now in Use ————
Trenches proposed to be adopted in Defence System ----
Post .... 4. | Dugout .... ◠

LEGEND
Coy. Area
Pln. "
Posts
Battle Position
Batn. H.Q.
Coy. "

Corps Topo Section.   MAP No. 151.

SECRET

2nd DIVISION
GENERAL STAFF
No. GS 78/208
Date 21-7-18

Copy No. 2

VI CORPS ORDER NO. 340.

20th July 1918.

1. The 160th Brigade A.E.F. will move by march route from present billets in the LUCHEUX area to the VI Corps reserve Divisional area on the 22nd July and will be disposed in accordance with Table "A" Attached.

   No restrictions as to time or route.

2. The following intervals will be maintained on the march:-

   500 yards between Battalions.
   100   "   "   Companies.
   200   "   "   tail of Battalions and Transport.

3. Administrative instructions will be issued separately.

4. Completion of move will be reported to Headquarters, VI Corps.

5. ACKNOWLEDGE.

Done G 560.

C.C. McKenzie, Maj.
for B.G.G.S.

Issued at:- 11.50 p.m.

Distribution:-

    Copy No. 1 Guards Division.
           2 2nd Division.
           3 3rd Canadian Division.
           4 80th Division U.S.A.
           5   "   "   "
           6 160th Infantry Brigade A.E.F.
           7   "   "   "   "
           8 Third Army.
           9 IV Corps.
          10 Canadian Corps.
          11 VI Corps R.A.
          12 VI Corps Heavy Artillery.
          13 4th Tank Brigade.
          14 A.D.A.S. VI Corps.
          15 A.P.M.   "
          16 D.D.M.S.   "
          17 G.I.   "
          18 "Q"   "
          19 File.
          20 War Diary.

2nd DIVISION
GENERAL STAFF
No.
Date.

TABLE "A" — To accompany VI Corps Order No. 340.

H.Q. 160th A.E.F. Infantry Brigade   BAVINCOURT CHATEAU

H.Q. 319th Infantry Regiment   LA BAZEQUE
    One Battalion   LA CAUCHIE
    Two Battalions   LA BAZEQUE area

H.Q. 320th Infantry Regiment   SAULTY CHATEAU
    One Battalion   BAVINCOURT
    Two Battalions   SAULTY

N.B.
Detailed billeting list will be issued with administrative instructions.

2nd Division No.
G.S. 1675.

5th Inf. Bde.
6th Inf. Bde.
99th Inf. Bde.

1. The 319th American Regiment will be attached to the Division shortly.

2. About 15 officers, 30 Sergts. 45 Corporals and 15 Runners will be attached to each Brigade in the line for 48 hours from various dates which will be notified later.

3. After individual attachments have been completed, it is probable that complete platoons will go into the line to hold definite portions of the front line. About 4 or 5 platoons will be attached to each British Infantry Brigade at a time and probably will remain in for 48 hours

4. As soon as further details are known, a definite programme will be forwarded.

20/7/18.

Lieut. Colonel,
General Staff, 2nd Divn.

"C" Form.
MESSAGES AND SIGNALS.

Army Form C. 2123.
(In books of 100.)
No. of Message _____

Prefix **OH** Code _____ Words **16** Received. From **MGO** By **MC** Sent, or sent out. At _____ m. To _____ By _____ Office Stamp.

Charges to Collect _____
Service Instructions _____

Handed in at **KOPO** Office **647** m. Received **655** m.

TO **2 M.G** **George G** **372**

*Sender's Number **C7350** Day of Month **20** In reply to Number _____ AAA

Ref.		2/356	para
30		70	Read
		2/350	
	Ref. M.G.	Batt. order	
	for 99	Batt. Raid	

FROM PLACE & TIME: **Luke. 6.50pm 2 M.G**

* This line should be erased if not required.

SECRET.

2nd DIVISION GENERAL STAFF
No. GA 13/46/18
D... 20.7.18

M.G.2/350.

A. B. D. Cos. No.2.Bn. M.G.C.)
99th. Infantry Brigade.)
6th. Infantry Brigade.) For
5th. Infantry Brigade.) information.
2nd. Division "G".)

1. Raid by 1st. Royal Berkshire Regt. will be carried out on night 22nd/23rd. July between 12.midnight and 1.a.m. Exact hour will be notified later.

2. Machine Gun supporting fire will be as detailed in M.G.2/230. issued to Companies on 14th. July.

3. Rate of Fire will be as follows:-
   Zero to Z plus 15.   Medium.   (1 belt in 2 minutes).
   Z plus 15 to Z plus 40.   Slow.   (1 belt in 4 minutes).
   Z plus 40 till Artillery fire dies down.   Medium.   (1 belt in 2 minutes).

4. The following guns will be used by Companies to support the raid:-
   D. Co. (Right).   F1, F2, S3, S4, S5, S6, S7, S8.
   B. Co. (Centre).   F9, F10, F13, F14.
   A. Co. (Left).   F15, F16, S9, S10.
   Firing positions for the above will be constructed on nights of 20th/21st. and 21st/22nd. and guns moved into positions at "Stand To" on night 22nd/23rd. They will return to their Battle Positions on completion of raid.

5. Watches will be synchronised as follows:-
   (a). D. Co. at Headquarters 1st. Royal Berkshire Regt. at 8.p.m. on 22nd. July.
   (b). B. Co. at 99th. Brigade Headquarters at 6.p.m. on 22nd. July.
   (c). A. Co. A watch will be sent to A. Company Headquarters at 7.p.m. 22nd. July, from Machine Gun Battalion Headquarters.
   No synchronisation of watches will be made by telephone.
   Machine Gun barrage will open at Zero hour with Artillery barrage.

6. **Ammunition.**
   (a). 24 Filled belts for each Machine Gun supporting raid will be taken up to positions on night 21st/22nd. These will be taken from Company Mobile Reserve and Ammunition at M.G. Battle Positions will not be used.
   (b). Empty belts will be returned to Battalion Headquarters on the night of 23rd/24th. and will be refilled by details under Battalion arrangements and returned to Company Transport.

20/7/1918.

W.M.Todd. Major
for Lieut.Colonel.
Commanding No.2.Bn. M.G. Corps.

SECRET

37th Division No. G. 9368

2nd DIVISION
GENERAL STAFF
No. G.S 13/46/19
Date 20-7-18

20th July 1918.

63rd Inf.Bde.
112th
C.R.A.
D.H.S.C.
37th Signal Co.

1. A raid is to be carried out by 2 companies 1st Royal Berkshire Regt (2nd Division) on the night 22/23rd July.

2. The objectives are as follows:—
   First objective. Huts in F.17.c. and d. and F.23.a. and b.
   Second objective. Enemy trench about F.18.d.0.4.

3. The raid is to be carried out under a creeping barrage.
   37th Div.Arty will co-operate under arrangements already made by G.O.C.R.A.

4. 6" Newton Mortars of 37th Division will engage the enemy's main line at the CEMETERY about F.23.d.8.9. during the whole operation, under arrangements made by C.R.A.

5. 2nd Division are placing a Stokes Mortar and Machine Gun barrage along the northern edge of ABLAINZEVELLE throughout the operation. Their Stokes Mortars will be firing from positions about ROQUET TRENCH. The accommodation they require will be arranged by G.O.C. 112th Inf.Bde.

6. Watches will be synchronised at 99th Brigade H.Q. at 6.0pm 22nd July.

7. As the operation extends partially over the front of this Division, all front line posts of the Left Battalion, 112th Inf.Bde., as well as Artillery and machine gunners covering that battalion, will be specially warned. This warning will be given as late as it is possible to ensure receipt. Patrols will not be sent out by the 112th Inf. Bde. North of the grid line between Squares F.23. and F.29. between Zero minus half an hour and daylight.

8. Zero hour will be notified later.

Lieut-Colonel
General Staff, 37th Division.

✓ Copy to 2nd Division.

SECRET

SECRET.

2nd Division No. G.S 1675/2.

5th Inf. Brigade.
6th Inf. Brigade.
99th Inf. Brigade.
~~G.R.A.~~
~~"Q"~~ (for information)
~~319th Regt. 160th Inf.Bde. A.E.F.~~ (For information)

---

1. The training of the 319th American Regiment will be carried out as follows:-

   Period 'A'   By individuals.
   "   'B'   By Complete Platoons.
   "   'C'   By Complete Battalions.

2. Period 'A' will be completed in 6 days.

   (i) <u>July 23rd to 25th.</u>
   3 Officers, 3 N.C.Os., 3 Runners, Regimental Staff, 319th Regiment, attached to 99th Inf. Brigade.

   1st Battalion.-
   15 Officers, 30 Sergeants, 45 Corporals, 15 Runners attached to 5th Inf. Brigade.

   2nd Battalion.-
   15 Officers, 30 sergeants, 45 Corporals, 15 Runners, attached to 6th Inf. Brigade.

   (ii) <u>July 25th to 27th.</u>
   3 Officers, 3 N.C.Os., 3 Runners, Regimental Staff, 319th Regiment attached to H.Q.6th Inf. Brigade.

   1st Battalion - 15 Officers, 30th Sergeants, 45 Coporals, 15 Runners, attached to 5th Inf. Brigade.

   3rd Battalion - 15 Officers, 30 Sergeants, 45 Coporals, 15 Runners, attached to 99th Inf. Brigade.

   (iii) <u>July 27th to 29th.</u>
   3 Officers, 3 N.C.Os., 3 Runners, Regimental Staff, 319th Regiment, attached to H.Q. 5th Inf. Brigade.

   2nd Battalion - 15 Officers, 30 Sergeants, 45 Corporal, 15 Runners attached to 6th Inf. Brigade.

   3rd Battalion - 15 Officers, 30 Sergeants, 45 Corporals, 15 Runners, attached to 99th Inf. Brigade.

3. During the periods mentioned in para 2 the details from battalions of the 319th Regiment will be attached to British Battalions in the front line.

4. Details regarding guides rations etc. will be issued later.

5. Period 'B', i.e., Attachment by complete platoons, will begin on the 29th or 30th July. Separate instructions will be issued.

E R Clayton

21st July, 1918.

Lieut-Colonel,
General Staff, 2nd Division.

2nd DIVISION
GENERAL STAFF
No. G1 1675/2
Date 21.7.18

American File
BQS

S E C R E T.

VI Corps
G.S. 54/29.

Guards Division.
2nd Division.
160th Inf. Bde. A.E.F.
C.E., VI Corps.
S.M.T.O., VI Corps.

1. Phase "A" of the training of the 160th Brigade A.E.F. will be completed on July 22nd., and Phase "B" will commence on the 23rd July.

2. For Phase "B" formations and units of the 160th American Brigade will be attached as follows :-

   Guards Division.   160th Infantry Brigade H.Q.
                                      320th Regiment.
                                      315th M.G. Battalion.
                                      320th M.G. Company.

   2nd Division.   319th Regiment.
                                    319th M.G. Company.

3. During Phase "B", the training of American units in the line will be carried out as follows :-

   Period (a) By individuals.
   Period (b) By complete platoons.
   Period (c) By complete Battalions.

4. Period (a) above will be completed in 6 days, during which time parties of Officers and N.C.Os. will be attached to units in the line for 48 hours.

   Period (b) should be completed in 14 days from completion of period (a), during which all platoons in each American Battalion will be attached, as platoons, to Companies of British Infantry. These attachments will be synchronised, as far as possible, with British reliefs, except that no American platoon will be in the line for more than four days.

   Period (c) will commence immediately on completion of period (b). During this period each American Battalion will do a tour of duty in the line as a Battalion, its moves being synchronised, whenever possible, with the normal reliefs of the British Battalions.

   This period is to be completed as quickly as circumstances permit.

   Under normal conditions the whole of Phase "B" should be completed in from 4 to 5 weeks from 23rd July.

5. The period (a) attachment will be carried out as follows :-

Guards Division.

July 23rd to July 25th.

3 Officers, 3 N.C.Os., 3 Runners, Regimental Staff, 320th Regiment.
2nd Battn., 15 officers, 30 Sgts., 45 Corporals, 15 Runners.
3rd Battn., 15 officers, 30 Sgts., 45 Corporals, 15 Runners.

July 25th to 27th.

3 Officers, 3 N.C.Os., 3 Runners, Regimental Staff, 320th Regiment.
1st Battn., 15 officers, 30 Sgts., 45 Corporals, 15 Runners.
3rd Battn., 15 officers, 30 Sgts., 45 Corporals, 15 Runners.

July 27th to 29th.

3 Officers, 3 N.C.Os., 3 Runners, Regimental Staff, 320th Regiment.
1st Battn., 15 officers, 30 Sgts., 45 Corporals, 15 Runners.
2nd Battn., 15 officers, 30 Sgts., 45 Corporals, 15 Runners.

2nd Division.

July 23rd to 25th.

3 Officers, 3 N.C.Os., 3 Runners, Regimental Staff, 319th Regiment.
1st Battn., 15 officers, 30 Sgts., 45 Corporals, 15 Runners.
2nd Battn., 15 officers, 30 Sgts., 45 Corporals, 15 Runners.

July 25th to 27th.

3 Officers, 3 N.C.Os., 3 Runners, Regimental Staff, 319th Regiment.
1st Battn., 15 officers, 30 Sgts., 45 Corporals, 15 Runners.
3rd Battn., 15 officers, 30 Sgts., 45 Corporals, 15 Runners.

July 27th to 29th.

3 Officers, 3 N.C.Os., 3 Runners, Regimental Staff, 319th Regiment.
2nd Battn., 15 Officers, 30 Sgts., 45 Corporals, 15 Runners.
3rd Battn., 15 officers, 30 Sgts., 45 Corporals, 15 Runners.

2.

6. S.M.T.O., VI Corps, will detail lorries as under for the conveyance of above personnel to and from the line :-

Parties attached to Guards Division.

Lorries to report at Headquarters, 320th Regiment, A.E.F., SAULTY CHATEAU, at 3 p.m. on July 23rd, 25th & 27th.

July 23rd.   5 lorries to convey personnel of 2nd Battn., 320th Regt., to X.1.d 6.0, Sheet 51.c., 1/40,000.
5 lorries to convey personnel of 3rd Battn., 320th Regt., to R.34.e 6.0, Sheet 51.c., 1/40,000.

July 25th.   5 lorries to convey personnel of 1st Battn., 320th Regt., to X.1.d 6.0.
5 lorries to convey personnel of 3rd Battn., 320th Regt., to R.34.e 6.0.

Lorries to wait at debussing point to convey back personnel returning from the line.

July 27th.   5 lorries to convey personnel of 1st Battn., 320th Regt., to X.1.d 6.0.
5 lorries to convey personnel of 2nd Battn., 320th Regt., to X.1.d 6.0

Lorries to wait at debussing point to convey back personnel returning from the line.

July 29th.   10 lorries to be at X.1.d 6.0 at 7.30 pm. to convey back personnel of 1st and 2nd Battns., 320th Regt., A.E.F., returning from the line.

Guards Division will arrange for guides to be at debussing points on 23rd, 25th and 27th instant at 6 p.m.

Parties attached to 2nd Division.

July 23rd, 25th, 27th - 10 lorries to be at 2nd Divisional Headquarters at 3 p.m. on each date.

Officer Commanding 319th Regiment A.E.F., will arrange direct with G.O.C., 2nd Division, all details regarding the transport of personnel up to the forward area on these dates. S.M.T.O., VI Corps, will arrange direct with 2nd Division the rendezvous and time for lorries to convey personnel of the 319th Regiment A.E.F. from the line on July 29th.

7. American personnel will bring their rations with them during period (a) attachment.

4.

8. Further instructions will be issued regarding the attachment of the 160th Infantry Brigade, A.E.F., for the period (b) and (c), above.

9. On arrival in the VI Corps area, instructions will be issued regarding the attachment of the personnel of 315th M.G. Battalion and 319th and 320th M.G. Coys., A.E.F., to British M.G. units in the line.

10. Instructions will be issued later regarding the attachment of the following units :-

    (A) Engineer Train and Battalions to Field Coys., R.E. and Pioneer Battalions.

    (B) Pioneer Platoons of Headquarter Companies A.E.F. to Field Companies R.E. of the British Division to which their respective Regiments are affiliated.

    (C) Personnel of the Signal Battalion, Trench Mortar Battery, &c.

11. Further instructions regarding the attachment of Commanders and Officers of the American Brigade and Regimental Headquarters will be issued later.

C.C.M. Kennedy Maj.
for B.G.G.S.

VI Corps,
21st July, 1918.

Copies to :-

    3rd Canadian Division.
    80th American Division.
    Third Army.
    "Q" VI Corps.
    R.A.   "
    D.D.M.S. "
    A.D.A.S. "
    C.M.G.O. "
    C.A.   "

> 2nd DIVISION
> GENERAL STAFF.
> No. GS 13/46/20
> Date. 21-7-18

S E C R E T   99th. Infantry Brigade No.
                                         B.M.(S)423/1

To all Recipients of

     99th. Infantry Brigade Order No. 244
___

                  Reference 99th. Infantry Brigade Order No.244
dated 19.7.1918 -

1. **Para. 1 (c)**   Unless otherwise notified Zero will be 12.30 a.m.
                     on night 22/23rd. July.
                     Any alteration will be notified to all concerned
                     by taking this hour as the basis and adding or
                     deducting the number of minutes.
                     Any such notification will be worded " Reference
                     B.M.(S) 423/1   add (or deduct) _____ "

2. **Para.6 (a)**   For " a BLUE 1½" Very Light " read -

                     " A parachute light changing from WHITE to GREEN "

3. **Para.6 (b)**   For " 2 BLUE 1½" Very Lights " read -

                     " 2 parachute lights changing from WHITE to GREEN "

4. ACKNOWLEDGE.

                                                     Farquharson

                                                     Captain,
                                                  Brigade Major,
                                              99th. Infantry Brigade

21.7.1918.

O 117 was passed to 99th Brigade on 20th

> 2nd DIVISION
> GENERAL STAFF
> No. GS 972/9/1
> Date 22-7-18

Amendment No.1. to VI Corps Heavy Artillery
Operation Order No.117 of 19th July, 1918.

(a) In para. 3 (b) ii and in Table A.

Delete rate of fire given in both cases and substitute the following :-

    Zero to Zero plus 15 ...   Rapid.

    Zero plus 15 to Zero plus 30 ...   Normal.

    Zero plus 30 to Zero plus 50 ...   Rapid.

    Zero plus 50 to Zero plus 1 hour ...   Normal.

(b) In Table A in column headed Time

    for "Zero to Zero plus 40" substitute "Zero to Zero plus 1 hour".

[signature]
Major R.A.,

21/7/18.   Brigade Major, Heavy Artillery, VI Corps.

To all recipients of VI Corps H.A. Operation Order No. 117.

S E C R E T.

2nd DIVISION GENERAL STAFF
No. GS 972/9/2
Date 22.7.18

F.H.G. 22/74.

Reference para. 7 of O.O. No.117. of 19/7/18.
Unless otherwise notified Zero will be ~~2.30~~ a.m. on night 22nd/23rd July.   12-30

Any alteration will be notified to all concerned by taking this hour as the basis and adding or deducting the number of minutes. Any such notification will be worded "Add or deduct........minutes.

ACKNOWLEDGE.

one 9.581.   W.S. Mascall.
                                    Major R.A.,
22/7/18.   Brigade Major, Heavy Artillery, VI Corps.

Copies to :-

Shoror's Group.
Phipps'   :
Gray's   :
32nd Bde R.G.A.
86th   :   :
C.B.S.O.
Sigs. H.A.
I.O.
VI Corps.
VI Corps R.A.
2nd Division.
2nd D.A.
Guards Division.
Guards D.A.
3rd Canadian Division.
3rd Canadian D.A.
IV Corps H.A.
War Diary.
File.

SECRET

2nd Div No G.S.13/46/21

99th Inf Brigade

SECRET

During the raid to be carried out by the 99th Inf Brigade, special arrangements will be made to search the huts in F.17 and 23, so as to ascertain whether the enemy is accumulating any store of Trench Mortar or other ammunition there.

If ammunition is found, an estimate should be made of the amount.

21-7-18

E R Clayton
Lieut Colonel
General Staff 2nd Division.

SECRET.   2nd Division No. G.S.13/46/22

Reference 2nd Division Order No. 344 dated 18th July,1918, Para 7
Unless otherwise notified ZERO will be 12.30 a.m. on night of
22nd/23rd July.   Any alteration will be notified to all concerned
by taking this hour as the basis, and adding or deducting the
number of minutes. Any such notification will be worded "Add or
deduct...... minutes ".

ACKNOWLEDGE.

                                        E.R. Clayton
                                        Lieut-Colonel,
21st July,1918.   General Staff, 2nd Division.

Copy No.1, to C.R.A.
       2   2nd Signal Coy.
       3   37th Division
       4   Guards Division
       5   Vl Corps
       6   Vl Corps H.A.
       7   lV Corps H.A.
       8   Office.

2nd Div. G.

[stamp: 2nd DIVISION GENERAL STAFF Date 13/6/23]

Herewith copy of 36 Bde OO
No 2Q with tracing attached

[stamp: 36th BRIGADE, R.F.A. No. 793 Date 2.7.18]

P.W. Ramey
Capt RFA
Adjt 36 Bde

Light Group Operation Order No.20   Ref. 1/20,000 Map Sheet AYETTE
                                     Edition 2c.

19th July, 1918.

1.   The 1st Royal Berks are carrying out a raid probably night 22/23rd July.

2.   The objective is the area enclosed by the black line on attached tracing. No infantry posts will be inside this area. The final objective is the Quarry at F 18 c 0.3.

3.   The raiders are assembling in our front line which they are not leaving till Zero   The posts at F 17 d 2.9 and F 17 a 7.2 will be evacuated before zero and our most Southern post will then be at F 17 a 7.4.

4.   18-pr Creeping barrage will be formed by :-
     2 Batteries, 37th Divl. Arty.
     Right and Centre Groups 2nd Divl. Arty. (less "T" Battery R.H.A).
     Left Group, 2nd Divl. Arty., consisting of :-
     "F" Battery R.H.A......4 guns.
     400th   ,,   R.F.A......4 guns.
      70th   ,,   R.F.A......6 guns.
     C/34th ,,   R.F.A......2 guns.

It will be as shown on attached tracing. On reaching the continuous line, batteries will search forwards and backwards between the above line and the trench running from ABLAINZEVILLE Cemetery to A 13 d 4.7 to F 18 a 5.5.
     In searching particular attention will be paid to traces of new work on latest intelligence map and photographs.
     The Left Group will pay special attention to the workings in F 18 a

5.   4.5" Howitzer Targets.
                       .....(a)..... *Left Group. 37th D.A.*

Number of Guns.	Time.	Task.
2 Batteries	Zero to Stop	Bombard Trench from F 23 d 1.9-F 23 b 7.0
1 Battery.	Zero to Stop	Bombard block of Stables at F 23 b 1.2 to F 23 b 1.4.
		.....(b)..... *Right Group 2nd D.A.*
1 Section	Zero-Zero plus 21.	On Quarry at F 18 c 0.3.
1 Section	Zero-Zero plus 5	On huts at F 17 d 05.05 This Section will be at disposal of Battalion Commander, *after zero + 5.*
1 Section	Zero-Zero plus 8	On work at F 23 b 15.65
		On completion of above tasks two sections will engage following T.M. using Chemical shell if conditions are favourable - F 23 d 55.98, F 23 d 55.70.
		....(c)....
Centre Group. 1 Battery	Zero-Zero plus 8	Block of Stables at F 17 d 25.50.
	Zero plus 8 to Stop.	Following T.Ms. in ABLAINZEVILLE, F 23 d 70.70, F 23 d 18.95, F 23 d 68.99, F 23 c 61.93

(d) Loft Group.

Page 2.

5. **4.5" Howitzer Targets (Continued).** ....(d)....

Number of Guns.	Time	Task.
Left Group.		
1 Section.	Zero-Zero plus 5	Road & Bank Junction at F 17 d 05.50
	Zero plus 5 to Stop.	Work at F 18 a 5.5 to F 18 a 55.70.
3 Sections	Zero to Stop	Work at F 18 a 5.5 to F 18 a 55.70

6. **"T" Battery R.H.A.**
Standing Barrage on new works and organized shell-holes about F 18 a 0.6.
If the wind is favourable 20% smoke shell will be used to obscure the view from these works up the valley in a S.W. direction.

7. **6-inch Newtons.**

   37th Division.

   Zero to Stop standing barrage on N. corner of Cemetery about F 23 b 65.05.

   2nd Division.

2 Mortars.	Zero to Stop	On work at F 18 a 0.6 to F 18 a 0.7
1 Mortar.	Zero to Stop	Trench at F 18 a 3.5
1 Mortar.	Zero-Zero plus 3	Road junction at F 17 c 95.95.

8. **AMMUNITION.** Batteries at over 4,500....H.E.
   (106 fuzes will be used with H.E. where possible except within 300 yards of our own infantry.)

   Batteries under 4,500 Shrapnel only.

9. **RATES OF FIRE.**

   Zero - Zero plus 15   INTENSE.
   Zero plus 15-Zero plus 18 NORMAL.
   Zero plus 18-Zero plus 19 INTENSE.
   Zero plus 19-Zero plus 24 RAPID.
   Zero plus 24-Zero plus 27 INTENSE
   Zero plus 27-Zero plus 60 SLOW with ½ 1-minute bursts
                                of INTENSE at irregular intervals.

   Zero plus 60 STOP.

10. Arrangements for synchronization of watches and the zero date and time will be notified later.
11. H.A. are co-operating in bombardment of trenches, and C.B. work.
12. D/38 Battery will provide a Liaison Officer at Advanced Battalion H.Q in No.10 Post, who will have a telephone wire to control the Section of Hows put at the disposal of Battalion Commander. See para. 5 (3)

Copies to :-
   Inf.Bde.   16 Batteries.
   D.A.   2 T.M.Batteries
   3 Groups.   H.A. (Sherers Group)
       Spare

Rubanes Capt for Lt-Col.R.F.A.
Commanding Right Group.

use with Artillery Maps.

F

Left Group

←0+2-0+5
←0+5-0+8
←0+2-0+5
←0+8-0+11
17
←0+11-0+15
←0+15-0+18
←0+18-0+21
18
←0+21-0+24
←0+24-0+27
←0+27 Onwards

Right and Centre Groups

←4·8→
←0-0+2
←15→
←16→
←7'1→

Left Group. 37ᵀᴴ Div.

0-0+2
0+2-0+5
0+5-0+8
0+8-0+11
23
0+11-0+15
0+15-0+18
0+18-0+21
0+21-0+24
0+24-0+27

24

—— Boundary of Area to be Raided
—— Boundary of Barrage.

SECRET

99th. Infantry Brigade No.
B.M.(S)423/2

Amendments made BQC

[Stamp: 2nd DIVISION GENERAL STAFF No. GS 13/46/24 Date 22-7-18]

To all Recipients of

99th. Infantry Brigade Order No.244

Reference paras 2 and 3 of B.M.(S)423/1 of today –

1. On testing the signal lights at night the parachute was found to be unsatisfactory.

2. The two paras are accordingly cancelled and paras 6 (a) and (b) of Order 244 will now be amended as follows :-

   Para.6 (a) For " a BLUE 1½" Very Light " read –
   " a RED Very Light ".

   Para.6 (b) For " 2 BLUE 1½" Very Lights " read –
   " 2 RED Very Lights "

3. ACKNOWLEDGE.

Done. BQC

Farquharson
Captain,
Brigade Major,
99th. Infantry Brigade

21st. July 1918

SECRET.

2nd DIVISION
GENERAL STAFF
No. GS 1675/7
Date 24-7-18

Guards Division.
2nd Division.
160th Inf. Bde. AEF.

VI Corps G.S. 54/32.

Reference VI Corps G.S. 54/29 dated July 21st.

1. Period (b) of the Training of 160th Inf. Bde., A.E.F. will commence on July 27th and must be completed by August 9th.

2. Not more than one American Inf. Battn. from each Infantry Regiment is to be in the line at the same time.
   The remaining two Battalions of each Infantry Regt., are so disposed that in case of attack they can man the Fourth System (G.H.Q. Line).

3. American platoons are to be attached to front line battalions and must be in the actual front line for part of their attachment.

4. No American patrol is to be sent out unless accompanied by at least one N.C.O. and two privates from the British Company to which they are attached.

5. Instructions regarding the supply of rations to the 160th Inf. Bde. A.E.F. have been issued by VI Corps "Q" under VI Corps Nos. S.Q.406/1 dated 22nd July and S.Q.406/1 dated July 23rd.
   The transport of American Battalions will be instructed in the conveyance of rations to the Front Line.

6. All other details regarding the attachments will be arranged direct between the Division and the affiliated American Infantry Regiment.

7. Guards Division will arrange for the attachment of the Commander and Staff of 160th Inf. Bde., A.E.F., direct with the Brigade. It is suggested that this attachment should be to both Divisional and Brigade Headquarters.

8. Guards and 2nd Divisions will arrange direct with their affiliated Regiment for the attachment of the Commander and Officers of the Regimental Headquarters to a Brigade Hd.Qrs.

9. The accommodation vacated by American Battalions, whilst in the line, will be available for the use of the Division to which they are attached.

10. Guards and 2nd Divisions will report to Corps Hd.Qrs., as soon as possible, to what battalions American Platoons are to be attached, and the dates when each attachment begins and ends.

R H Kearsley
B.G.G.S.

VI Corps.
23rd July, 1918.

Copies to :- 80th American Div.
Third Army.
"Q" VI Corps.
D.D.M.S. "
A.D.A.S. "
C.A. "

HEADQUARTERS 319TH INFANTRY,
AMERICAN EXPEDITIONARY FORCES
23rd July 1918

2nd DIVISION
GENERAL STAFF
No. GS 1675/5
Date 23-7-18

MEMORANDUM:- To the C. O., 2nd Division:-

1. In accordance with 2nd Division Memo of July 21st and 22nd, 1918, the following officers and enlisted men will report at 2:45 P.M. to-day for tour of duty at the front line:

REGIMENTAL HEADQUARTERS

Major James L. Montague	2nd in Command.
Capt. Byron Van Etten	Regimental Adjutant.
1st Lt. Frank N. Youngman	Regimental Gas Officer
Sergt. John R. Canning	Signal Platoon
Sergt. Thomas Phillips	One Pound Gun Platoon
Sergt. Marion L. Grier	Trench Mortar Platoon.
Pvt. 1st Cl. Gus Steinke	Runner
Pvt. Michael Conroy	Runner
Pvt. Wm. Hauseman	Ruhher

FIRST BATTALION

Major Hugh H. Obear	Bn. Commander
1st Lt. Hynes Sparks	Bn. Adjutant.
Capt. William F. Passer	Bn Surgeon.
1st Lt. W. Brown Baxley	Bn. S.O.S. Officer
2nd Lt. Henderson N. Horsley	Bn. Transport Officer.
2nd Lt. James G. Gibson	Bn. Lewis Gun Officer
Capt. Perry W. Huston	Co. Comdr., Co. A.
2nd Lt. David B. Payne	Pltn. Comdr., Co. A.
1st Lt. John McK. Mitchell	2nd in Comd., Co. B.
2nd Lt. William H. Johnson	Pltn. Comdr., Co. B.
1st Lt. Elliott M. Braxton, Jr.	Pltn. Comdr., Co. C
2nd Lt. Robert J. T. Paul	Pltn. Comdr., Co. C.
2nd Lt. Narvin Ash	Pltn. Comdr., Co. C
Capt. Julien H. Addison	Co. Comdr., Co. D.
2nd Lt. Arthur L. Moore	Pltn. Comdr., Co. D.

Co. A:
1st Sgt. Alphie E. Johnston	1st Sgt. Co.
Sgt. George E. Marvin	Pltn. Sgt.
Sgt. Norman B. Wolfe	Pltn. Sgt.
Sgt. Melvin C. Harris	Actg. Pltn. Sgt.
Sgt. John P. O'Neill	Actg. Pltn. Sgt.
Sgt. George W. Bjornberg	Lewis Gun Sgt.
Sgt. Frank K. Poland	Lewis Gun Sgt.
Col. Andy G. Hafner	Lewis Gunner
Col. Paul G. Reinehr	Newis Gunner
Col. Edwin E. Ziegenhein	Lewis Gunner
Col. Orin C. Frank	Grenadier
Col. John M. Benson	Grenadier
Col. Frank R. Curtis	Grenadier
Col. Christie F. Weller	Grenadier
Col. Henry W. Jarrett	Rifleman
Col. Stanley B. Boyle	Rifleman
Col. Joseph A. Hensler	Rifleman
Col. Leonard A. Rafferty	Bomber
Pvt. 1st Cl. Harry E. Van Divner	Runner
Pvt. 1st Cl. Louis E. Erk	Runner
Pvt. 1st Cl. Mark J. Gallagher	Runner.

Co. B:	Sup. Sgt. Hyman Silverblatt	Co. Sup. Sgt.
	Sgt. Harold Wilkinson	Pltn. Sgt.
	Sgt. Paul Lillocotch	Rifle
	Sgt. Lawrence May	Pltn. Sgt.
	Sgt. Frank Mowery	Pltn. Sgt.
	Sgt. Ronald A. Friend	Auto.
	Sgt. William Smith	Auto.
	Col. Orville Grier	Auto.
	Cpl. Arthur Pearson	Rifle Gren.
	Col. Harry Monz	Rifle
	Col. William Mayer	Rifle
	Cpl. Otto Schmidt	Hand. Gren.
	Col. Orville Spindler	Auto.
	Cpl. Frederick Geisner	Rifle Gren.
	Col. James Sutton	Auto.
	Col. George Longhenry	Hand Gren.
	Cpl. Frank Limberger	Auto.
	Cpl. James Watson	Rifle
	Pvt. Howard Alexander	Runner
	Pvt. Carl Dunn	Pltn. Runner
	Pvt. Jesse L. Moore	Pltn. Runner
Co. C:	1st Sgt. Bernard E. Golden	1st Sgt. Co.
	Sgt. Fred W. Guy	Pltn. Sgt.
	Sgt. Emil A. Wagner	Rifle Sgt.
	Sgt. Ambrose C. Karcher	Rifle Sgt.
	Sgt. William Atkinson	Auto. Sgt.
	Sgt. John Atkinson	Rifle Sgt.
	Sgt. Frank J. Urbany	Auto. Sgt.
	Cpl. Byron Lynch	Rifle Grenadier
	Cpl. William Gall	Auto. Cpl.
	Cpl. Ferdinand F. Blume	Bomber
	Cpl. Fred J. Kuttler	Auto.
	Cpl. Charles Gawrincki	Bomber
	Cpl. Denver Smith	Rifle.
	Cpl. William Gray	Rifle
	Cpl. Roy Tanner	Auto.
	Cpl. Emery B. Dayton	Bomber
	Cpl. Cuneo	Rifle
	Cpl. Frederick Niedermeyer	Auto.
	Pvt. D. C. Warner	Pltn. Runner
	Pvt. Schuyler Coddington	Co. Runner
	Pvt. Frank J. Ferrell	Pltn. Runner
Co. D:	Sup. Sgt. Herbert F. Cooley	Co. Sup. Sgt.
	Sgt. Ralph A. Blaugher	1st Pltn. Sgt.
	Sgt. Harry Weston	Auto. Sgt., 2nd Pltn.
	Sgt. Clifford C. Hopkins	Auto. Rifle
	Sgt. Ernest D. Swarner	Pltn. Sgt.
	Sgt. John E. Crouch	Pltn. Sgt.
	Sgt. John J. Cloherty	Auto. Rifle
	Cpl. George Everett	Hand Bomber
	Cpl. John McMahan	Gas
	Cpl. Joseph A. Mooney	Gas
	Cpl. Harry L. Easton	Hand Bomber
	Cpl. Robert D. Adans	Gas & Musk.
	Cpl. William D. Nixon	Hand Bomber & Lewis Gun.
	Cpl. Pasquale Fusco	Hand Bomber
	Cpl. Frederick W. Howden	Auto.
	Cpl. Pietro Carrol	Rifle Grenadier
	Cpl. Fred E. A. Barthol	Auto.
	Cpl. George Baer	Auto.
	Pvt. Ray N. Huggins	Runner
	Pvt. Curtis E. Gerber	Runner
	Pvt. George W. Lee	Runner

Sgt. Kleber — S.O.S.
Sgt. Kennedy, Ray L. — Med.
Cpl. Hagerty, James C. — S.O.S.
Pvt. Hines — Runner S.O.S.
Cpl. Wm. J. Hauser — Runner Bn. Hq.
Pvt. 1st Cl. James E. Laughlan — Med. Runner.

SECOND BATTALION

Captain Rembrandt P. Keezell, — 2nd in Command.
Captain Millard J. Arnold — Co. Comdr., Co. E.
1st Lt. Clarence L. O'Neill — Pltn. Leader, Co. E.
2nd Lt. Richard C. Cruit, — Pltn. Leader, Co. E.
1st Lt. Preston Parsons, — Pltn. Leader, Co. E.
1st Lt. Paul J. Rutan, — Co. Comdr., Co. F.
1st Lt. Wesley Wright, — Pltn. Leader, Co. F.
2nd Lt. Stephen Y. McGiffert — Pltn. Leader, Co. F
2nd Lt. Henry B. Curry, — Pltn. Leader, Co. E.
2nd Lt. Van Dyck Clark, — Pltn. Leader, Co. G.
2nd Lt. Clyde A. Trotter, — Pltn. Leader, Co. G.
1st Lt. John J. Noone, — Co. Comdr., Co. H.
2nd Lt. Austin L. Brawn, — Pltn. Leader, Co. H.
2nd Lt. Fred W. Glaser, — Pltn. Leader, Co. H.
1st Lt. George M. Kiner, — Dental Officer.

Co. E:
Sgt. Stephen Thomas, — Pltn. Sgt.
Sgt. John Heinauer, — Rifle Sgt.
Sgt. Michael B. Girod — Pltn. Sgt.
Sgt. Arron L. Jeffries — Rifle Sgt.
Sgt. John F. Hogsett — Pltn. Sgt.
Sgt. Ralph B. Bygate — Sup. Sgt.
Sgt. Robert G. Morris — Rifle Sgt.
Cpl. Joseph Temosky — Auto Rifle.
Cpl. Fillmore Withers — Lewis Gun
Cpl. Henry S. Robson — Auto. Rifle
Cpl. William W. Webb — Gas N.C.O.
Cpl. Delbert A. Fike — Rifleman
Cpl. Clyde S. Sawhill — Rifle Grenade
Cpl. Harry J. Lenihan — Auto Rifle
Cpl. Jos. Spina, — Bomber
Cpl. Lewis Grier — Lewis Gun
Cpl. Earl Harford — Bomber
Cpl. Francis X. Sissmore — Rifle Grenadd
Cpl. William M. Young — Rifle Grenade

Co. F:
Sgt. Thos. H. Morgan — Auto Rifle
Sgt. Maurice J. Haupt — Rifle Sgt.
Sgt. Harry A. Scholl — Rifle Grenadier
Sgt. John E. Baher — Lewis Gunner
Sgt. Albert Smith — Pltn. Sgt.
Sgt. Edwin Mohr — Auto Rifle
Cpl. Robert S. Sleeth — Rifleman
Cpl. George P. Reiter — Rifle Grenadier
Cpl. Boleslaw Napierkawski — Rifle Grenadier
Cpl. John J. Steinhagen — Bomber
Cpl. Edward L. Peters — Rifle Grenadier
Cpl. John M. Bretschneider — Bomber
Cpl. Earl A. Reichard — Auto Rifleman
Cpl. Glen E. Stone — Bomber
Cpl. Paul Troetschall — Auto Rifle
Cpl. Thomas A. Burkes — Bomber
Cpl. William P, Alter — Auto Rifle.

Co. G: Sgt. Millard F. Tatem — Pltn. Sgt.
Sgt. John H. Wesoloski — Auto Rifle
Sgt. Robert B. Patterson — Auto Rifle
Sgt. Robert H. Scott — Mess Sgt.
Sgt. Daniel T. Downes — Rifle Sgt.
Sgt. Bennet A. Enrietta — Rifle Sgt.
Sgt. Iver Rees — Auto Rifle
Sgt. Francis Ashmead — Auto Sgt.
Cpl. Patrick McGraw — Gas N.C.O.
Cpl. Joseph H. Brooks — Auto Rifle
Cpl. John Skilsky — Rifleman
Cpl. John W. Marlow — Auto Rifleman
Cpl. Thomas G. Kerns — Auto Gren.
Cpl. William J. Hastings — Auto Rifleman
Cpl. Stephen J. Wolfinger — Rifle Gren.
Cpl. Carl O. Mattson — Bomber
Cpl. William E. Cousins — Rifleman
Cpl. George M. Wolf — Rifleman
Cpl. James Gibson — Auto Rifleman

Co. H: Sgt. Herman E. Johnson — Rifle Sgt.
Sgt. Albert Rotter — Pltn. Sgt.
Sgt. Alexander Leckie — Pltn. Sgt.
Sgt. Dennie Karpovitch — Pltn. Sgt.
Sgt. Harold Weaver — Gas N.C.O.
Sgt. Charles M. White — Auto Sgt.
Sgt. Carl Heumme — Rifle Sgt.
Cpl. John J. Shedlock — Bomber
Cpl. Cark W. Kill — Lewis Gunner
Cpl. George R. Burkes — Lewis Gunner
Cpl. Francis E. O'Malley — Bomber
Cpl. Frank Cervanack — Lewis Gunner
Cpl. Oscar W. Janda — Rifle Gren.
Cpl. Milton L. Pratt — Rifleman
Cpl. Albert A. Huth — Lewis Gunner
Cpl. Peter Livingstone — Rifleman
Cpl. John Mulligan — Rifleman
Cpl. Collin C. Lease — Bomber

Pvt. Thomas R. Bache — Runner
Pvt. William J. McMarlin — Runner
Pvt. William A. Scott — Runner
Pvt. Robert Daniels — Runner
Pvt. John Berent — Runner
Pvt. John Slater — Runner
Pvt. Edward L. Burns — Runner
Pvt. Peter Hopper — Runner
Pvt. Robert Jordan — Runner
Pvt. Walter S. Chuck — Runner
Pvt. Paul Ringler — Runner
Pvt. Charles Donohoe — Runner
Pvt. George G. Russell — Runner
Pvt. Henry B. Dexter — Runner
Pvt. Massion Permigiano — Runner

By order of Colonel Cocheu:

BYRON VAN ETTEN
Captain, 115th Infantry,
Adjutant.

2nd Division No. G.S.13/46/25.

VI Corps.

SECRET

      With regard to the enquiry made by the Army Commander; during the raid carried out by this Division on night July 22/23rd one small dump of "PINEAPPLE" was found by the raiders in the huts in F.17.c. and d. There was no evidence of a dump of Trench Mortar Ammunition.

23rd July, 1918.

Major-General,
Commanding 2nd Division.

SECRET.   2nd Division No.G.S.13/51.

5th Inf. Brigade.
6th Inf. Brigade.
99th Inf. Brigade.

      For the moment the identifications required have been obtained.

      The G.O.C., however, wishes Brigadiers to continue to prepare raids, so that further identifications may be obtained if required without undue delay.

      As much warning as possible will be given of any raids which Brigades will be called on to make.

23rd July, 1918.
                                        Lieut-Colonel,
                                General Staff, 2nd Division.

SECRET.
****

Headquarters,
2nd Division 'G'.

2nd DIVISION
GENERAL STAFF
No. G/13/52
Date 23.7.18

The 1st Battn. 'The King's' Regiment are anxious to carry out a small raid (strength 1 Company) on the enemy's advanced posts in F.12.a. and F.6.c. on the night 28th/29th July.

In addition to Artillery support of the CENTRE Group, can adequate counter-battery co-operation be provided by the Corps from ZERO + 5 to ZERO + 30.

Please reply early if this meets with the G.O.C's approval, so as detailed arrangements can be taken in hand.

23/7/18.

Brigadier General,
Commanding, 6th Infantry Brigade.

2nd Div GS 13/53

S E C R E T .　　　　　　　　　　5th Inf. Bde. No. G.S. 740/115.

2ND DIVISION.

    It appears no recent photographs are available of the area shaded on attached sketch.

    Ground observation of this area is impossible, and our only means of getting information of it is by patrolling and from photographs.

    A special enterprise is being considered here, and ~~the~~ *it is* ~~B.G.C. therefore~~ desired that photographs on as large a scale as possible be taken and forwarded early.

                                      [signature]

                                        Brigadier General,
24/7/18.   Commanding 5th Infantry Brigade.

BRITISH FRONT LINE

S.26.a. S.27.c.

ENEMY OUTPOST LINE

A.2.b. A.3.a.

AYETTE - MOYENNEVILLE ROAD

S E C R E T.
****

Headquarters,

    2nd Division 'G'.

    Reference your No. G.S. 13/25 of 13/6/18.

    The following is the information required with reference to the proposed Raid by 1st KING'S Regt.

(1) Enemy's advanced posts in F.12.a. and F.6.c.

(2) 120 men of 1st KING'S Regt.

(3) Attached.

(4) The necessary reconnaissance will be carried out nightly in 'NO MAN'S LAND' from night 25/26th July.

(5) See para.4 of the attached.

(6) No. Right and Left Groups have been asked to co-operate.

(7) Nil.

(8) Night 28th/29th July.

                              Brigadier General,

24/7/18.   Commanding, 6th Infantry Brigade.

Nothing attached.

2nd Division No.G.S.1695/10.

99th Inf. Brigade.

1. Colonel COCHEU and Captain ROSSIRE, 319th Regiment with 2 orderlies will be attached to 99th Brigade H.Q. on Sunday July 28th.

2. A car will be at H.Q. 319th Regiment at 3 p.m. to convey the above mentioned officers.

Sgd. E. R. Clayton
Lieut-Colonel,
General Staff, 2nd Division.

25th July, 1918.

Copy to 319 Regt AEF
Camp Commandant.

"A" Form
MESSAGES AND SIGNALS.

Army Form C. 2121
(In pads of 100.)

SECRET

Sent At 9..m. 3/52/2

TO: HdQrs 2nd Divn G

Sender's Number: BA261
Day of Month: 25th

Herewith letter which should have been attached to my GS.1103/8/19 of yesterday aaa Error regretted

From 6th Inf Bde

VERY SECRET.

Copy No. 1

6th Infantry Brigade

1. It is proposed to carry out a raid on the enemy Advanced posts in F.12.a. & F.6.c. i.e. from AERODROME ROAD to N. of the MOYENNEVILLE ROAD during the next tour of the Bn in the line, Subject to the approval of the Brigade Commander.

2. The rough outline of the Scheme is as follows:-
   (a) To definitely locate by reconnoitring patrols the exact position of these posts & then to arrange a Stokes Mortar bombardment with 16 guns on these posts, leaving the gaps to be covered by 6 Vickers guns firing from our OUTPOST LINES diagonally across these gaps. The Vickers guns will fire over the enemy outpost line, More for moral than actual effect. Every available 18 pdr. to put down a Standing Barrage at ZERO, roughly 200 yards EAST of the enemy OUTPOST LINE to prevent the enemy from escaping. Only direct action H.E to be used. To further thicken this back barrage, 6 Vickers guns to fire from about X.30.c. due SOUTH thro' F.6.c.8.0 & F.12.a.7.0. thus Sweeping a long narrow zone with rapid fire till ZERO + 3. This Should prove demoralizing

3. All 4.5. Howitzer batteries available, to fire on enemy works, approximately along the line F.18.a.3.7. to A.2.c.3.3., as it is possible the enemy has arranged his machine guns along this line So as to cover the gaps between his posts. There will of course be enemy machine guns out in front of AERODROME TRENCH, and more exact information regarding these posts will be given to the Artillery when the latest photographs have been Studied.   X. 6" T.M. Battery will barrage the MOYENNEVILLE ROAD.

4. It is requested that provisional arrangements may be made for the Cooperation of the Corps Heavy Artillery in Counter battery work from ZERO + 5. onwards for 25 minutes

5. I should be glad if the registrations of the Field Artillery could be Spread over the next 4 days, So as to minimize any risk of our intentions being disclosed.   The registrations should be

Sheet 1. Continued

Sheet 2. Continued.

should be.
Complete by the evening of the 26th inst.
The Stokes Mortars must of necessity with-hold their registrations until the detailed reconnaissance has been carried out in "NO MAN'S LAND" Positions could however be selected at once along the whole front of attack

6. The raid will be carried out by 1 Company formed in Section Groups.
In view of the moonlight; faces, hands & bayonets will be blackened. Buttons will be painted with luminous paint & white arm bands with khaki covers will be worn as before; Balaclava Caps will be worn instead of Steel helmets & the distribution of the Section groups on a wide front will lessen the chances of discovery

The very heavy Stokes Mortar barrage i.e. 384 rounds in 1 minute should be effective in neutralizing any resistance from the enemy OUTPOST LINE.

7. Code name for this Operation will be "ARCHIBALD"

H H King
Lieut Colonel,
Commanding 1st Bn "The King's" Regt.

23.7.18

Copies to.
1. 6th Infantry Brigade
2. — do —
3. OC "A" Company
4. File.

SECRET
Urgent. ES 12/43.

G.S.O. I

2nd Division

Ref our conversation over telephone this evening I am forwarding herewith draft of my orders for redistribution of M.G defence in order to withdraw the 3 guns of Reserve company now in the line.

H.D Buchanan-Dunlop Capt
comdg No. 2 Coy M.G.C.

28/7/18

SECRET

2nd. BATTALION, MACHINE GUN CORPS, ORDER No. 22.

Ref. Map. AYETTE. 1/20000.

1. On the night of the 27th/28th. July. 1918. the Machine Guns of C. Company will be withdrawn from the following positions:-
   - R.1. & 2.   F.19.a.5.6.
   - R.3. & 4.   F.13.c.45.15.
   - R.13. & 14.   F.3.a.00.00.
   - R.21. & 22.   X.28.a.50.35.

2. These positions will be taken over as follows:-
   - (a). R.1. & 2.   -   Will not be taken over.
   - (b). R.3. & 4.   -   Will be taken over by 2 guns of D. Company from S.1. & S.2. positions at F.14.d.70.68.
   - (c). R.13. & 14. -   Will not be taken over but will become an alternative position for the 2 guns of B. Company at R.15. & 16 positions at F.3.d.00.36.
   - (d). R.21. & 22. -   Will be taken over by 2 guns of A. Company from R.19. & 20. positions at X.27.d.8.4.

3. The above 8 guns of C. Company when withdrawn will be stationed at Battalion Headquarters at W.26.d.8.3. and will form a mobile reserve ready to occupy the following reserve positions if required:-
   - A.11. 12. 13. 14.   F.1.c.6.6.
   - A.15. & 16.   F.1.b.1.1.   (With 2 guns only).
   - A.23. & 24.   X.20.c.1.1.

4. The 8 guns of C. Company at present stationed at E.11.b.5.6. will not move. They will be prepared to occupy the following reserve positions if required:-
   - A.1. 2. 3. 4.   E.17.d.9.7.
   - A.5. & 6.   F.7.c.4.1.
   - A.7. 8. 9. 10.   F.7.b.6.1.   (With 2 guns only).

5. The Officer Commanding C. Company will continue to provide labour for work on dugouts now under construction at the following positions:-
   - F.14.a.7.0.
   - F.14.a.9.6.
   - F.2.d.8.8.

6. All details in connection with the handing over of positions, in accordance with para.(2). will be arranged between the Officer Commanding C. Company and the Company Commanders concerned.

25/7/18

Lieut.Colonel.
Comdg. 2nd. Bn. M.G. Corps.

2nd Division No. G.S. 12/43.

No. 2 M.G. Battalion.

SECRET

The Machine Gun defence of the Divisional Sector will be re-organised on the night of July 27th/28th as follows :-

The following guns will be withdrawn -

    F.13.c.   FARM TRENCH   ...   2 guns
    F.14.d.8.4. SUNKEN ROAD ..   2 guns
    F.2.a.0.0.   ...   ...   2 guns
    K.27.d.7.1. ...   ...   2 guns

2.   When the above re-adjustment has taken place the 2nd M.G. Battalion will have one complete Company out of the line, of which 8 guns will be in immediate reserve about the Old German Front Line, and 8 guns will be withdrawn to near the Battalion Headquarters, about W.28.d.

E R Clayton
Lieut-Colonel,
General Staff, 2nd Division.

25th July, 1918.

Copies to :-

    5th Inf. Brigade
    6th Inf. Brigade
    99th Inf. Brigade
    C.R.A.
    C.R.E.
    2nd Signal Coy.
    VI Corps.

SECRET

2nd Division No. G.S. 13/52/2.

VI Corps.

      It is proposed to carry out a raid shortly on the front of this Division.

2. (i) <u>Objective</u>.   Enemy advanced posts in F.12.a. and F.6.c.

   (ii) One Company 1st King's Regiment.

   (iii) A Stokes Mortar barrage will be put down on the objective. In addition a Machine Gun barrage will be put down between the Posts to be raided, while a Field Artillery barrage will be placed 200yds. in front of the objective. After the bombardment has lasted about a minute the raiding party will rush the objective.

   (iv) No practice is at present arranged.

   (v) The ammunition will come out of the ordinary allotment.

   (vi) No special equipment is required.

   (vii) Arrangements are being made for counter-battery work on the night of the raid.

   (viii) Night of July 28th/29th.

(sgd) C.E.Pereira

25th July, 1918.

Major-General,
Commanding 2nd Division.

VI Corps H.A.

2nd Div No G.S.13/52/3

SECRET

1. A raid is being carried out by one Company of the 1st King's Regiment on the night of July 29/30th.

2. ZERO Hour will be notified later, but will probably be about 11 pm.

3. The objective is the line of enemy advanced posts in F.12.a. and F.6.c.

4. It is requested that Counter Battery fire may be arranged to keep down the enemy's Artillery fire from Z plus 5 to Z plus 30.

5. Will you kindly forward in due course, a copy of the Counter Battery Programme for this operation?

July 26th 1918

Major General
Commanding 2nd Division

Copy to
6th Inf Brigade
C.R.A. 2nd Division
SHERER'S Group H.A.

2nd Division No. G.S. 13/52/4.

VI Corps.

SECRET

Reference 2nd Division No. G.S. 13/52/2, dated 25th July, 1918.

The date of the raid to be carried out by the 1st King's Regiment will be the night of July 29th/30th, instead of as stated in the above quoted letter.

26th July, 1918.

Major-General,
Commanding 2nd Division.

2nd Division No. G.S.13/55.

5th Inf. Brigade. 8
6th Inf. Brigade. 8
99th Inf. Brigade. 8
C.R.A. 31
C.R.E. 4
No.2 M.G.Battn. 2
10th D.C.L.I. 2
2nd Signal Coy. 2
A.D.M.S. 4
"Q" 1
A.P.M. 1
Camp Commandant. 1
2nd Div. Gas Officer. 1
2nd Div. Train. 1
D.A.D.V.S. 2

    There has been far too much open discussion about the raids that have recently taken place before they were actually carried out. All ranks from the Divisional Staff downwards must ensure that secret operations are kept secret and that they are only discussed with those concerned under strict secrecy.

2.   It is an essential part of the training of all ranks to keep their eyes open and their mouths shut. One object of all raids is to extract from prisoners the results of profitless gossip that makes public concerns that should be kept secret.

3.   If all ranks are trained to observe secrecy about raids they will be able to observe secrecy about more important operations, and one important source of enemy information through prisoners or agents at home or out here will be closed.

4.   Many a British life has been sacrificed out here because people will gossip about secret matters.

5.   A fruitful source of leakage of information is the discussion of operations or secret matters by officers at meals, in the presence of their servants.

Major-General,
Commanding 2nd Division.

26th July, 1918.

American file

2nd Division No. G.S. 1675/11

319th Regt.
5th Inf. Brigade
6th Inf. Brigade
99th Inf. Brigade
"Q" 2nd Division
A.D.M.S.
2nd Div. Gas Officer
S.S.O.
A.P.M.

SECRET

1. Period "B" attachment of Platoons of 319th Inf. Regiment to Companies of 2nd Division, will begin on July 28th, and will be carried out as under :-

    From July 28th to August 1st ... ... 1st Battalion
    From August 1st to August 5th .. ... 2nd Battalion
    From August 5th to August 8th .. ... 3rd Battalion

2. The 1st Battalion will be attached as under from July 28th to August 1st :-

    To 5th Inf. Brigade - 'A' Coy. complete.
    Coy. H.Q., and 2 Platoons of 'D' Coy.
    Battalion H.Q. (for composition vide Appendix "A").

    To 6th Inf. Brigade - 'B' Coy.

    To 99th Inf. Brigade - 'C' Coy. and 2 Platoons of 'D' Coy.

3. The attachment of the 2nd and 3rd Battalions will be carried out on similar lines, under orders which will be issued later.

4. All movement to and from the trenches will be by Platoons. A distance of 200 yds. will be maintained between Platoons. Brigades will arrange guides direct with the attached Companies on the scale of one guide per Platoon, and one guide per Company and Battalion H.Q.

5. During the attachment in the line, no American patrols are to be sent out unless accompanied by at least 1 N.C.O. and 2 Privates from the British Coy. to which they are attached.

6. One specially selected British Subaltern and one Sergeant will be attached to each American Platoon in an advisory capacity, and will go into the line with it.

7. During period "B" American Platoons will be in the front line for part of the period in the trenches. Every opportunity will be taken of training the transport in the conveyance of rations to the front line.

8. The Battalion Transport of the 1st Battalion 319th Regiment will move to HUMBERCAMP on the 28th July and be attached to Battalions of the 5th Infantry Brigade under arrangements to be made between Battalion Commander 1st Battalion and 5th Infantry Brigade.

9. Brigadiers will report what changes they propose to make in the disposition of troops in the line. The only extra accommodation available is that which will be vacated by the American Battalions.

P.T.O.

-2-

10. Instructions regarding rations are being issued by 2nd Division "Q".

11. ACKNOWLEDGE.

E. R. Clayton
Lieut-Colonel,
General Staff, 2nd Division.

26th July, 1918.

No. 2 M.G. Battalion)
C.R.A.)
C.R.E.)
2nd Signal Coy. R.E.) For information.
10th D.C.L.I.)
2nd Div. Train.)
37th Division.)
Guards Division.)
VI Corps.)

APPENDIX "A"

COMPOSITION OF BATTALION HEADQUARTERS.

Battalion Commander
Second in Command
Adjutant
Lewis Gun Officer
Scouting, Observation and
    Sniping Officer (Intelligence)
Gas Officer
Supply Officer
Transport Officer
2 Medical Officers
1 Dentist
} 11 Officers

1 Sergeant Major
Cook
Assistant Cook
3 Runners
28 Scouts, Observers and Snipers
18 Signallers
} 52

COMPOSITION OF COMPANY HEADQUARTERS

Company Commander
Second in Command
} 2 Officers

First Sergeant
Supply Sergeant
Mess Sergeant
Company Clerk
2 Buglers
4 Cooks
4 Signallers
4 Mechanics
} 18 O.Rs.

SECRET

2nd. Division "G".
C.R.E., 2nd. Division.
C.M.G.O., VI Corps.

M.G.2/394.

2nd Div G/12/144.

The following is the WEEKLY PROGRESS REPORT on dugouts under construction in this Sector:-

Location of dugout.	Remarks.
F.4.d.1.1.	DOWN shaft completed – Passage completed – UP shaft 10' completed – Work on chambers being done.
F.10.a.3.5.	DOWN shaft, Passage and UP shaft nearly completed.
F.5.c.5.6.	DOWN shaft, Passage and UP shaft completed.
F.21.b.8.3.	Two shafts and Two chambers completed. Third shaft 14' down.
F.2.d.8.8.	DOWN shaft, Passage and UP shaft completed. Work in progress on steps and chamber.
F.4.a.9.6.	DOWN shaft and Passage completed. 12' of UP shaft completed.
F.5.c.7.4.	DOWN shaft and Passage completed. 8' of UP shaft completed.
F.1.a.7.0.	DOWN shaft and Passage completed. 10' of UP shaft completed.

26/7/1918.

Lieut. Colonel.
Commanding 2nd. Bn. M.G.Corps.

D.O.Map corrected.

SECRET.

2nd DIVISION GENERAL STAFF
No. G13/52/5.

Copy No. 8

6th Infantry Brigade Order No. 375.

27th July, 1918.

1. 1st Battn. KING'S Regiment will carry out a Raid on the enemy's Outpost Line in F.12.a. and F.6.c. on the night of 29th/30th July, 1918.
    Strength of Raiding Party - 1 Company.
    Object - To secure identifications and to kill as many of the enemy as possible.

2. The Raid will be supported by Field and Heavy Artillery and by 6th T.M. Battery, as under :-

    (a) The 18 pdr. barrage will be put down as follows :-
        ZERO to ZERO + 2.   200 yards East of the line of enemy Posts from F.12.c.60.65, to F.6.c.80.55.

        ZERO + 2.   The barrage will lift 200^x

        ZERO + 20.   The barrage will cease.

    (b) 4.5" Howitzers.
        ZERO to ZERO + 20. Bombardment of the enemy's works between F.18.a.0.3. and A.2.c.3.6.

    (c) Corps H.A. have been asked to co-operate in counter-battery work from ZERO + 5.

    (d) 6th T.M. Battery with the addition of 8 guns will place an intense barrage on the Posts to be raided from ZERO to ZERO + 1.

3. A Machine Gun barrage has been arranged to cover the Valley in F.17.d.

4. The following will be the action of the Infantry :-

    ZERO + 1.   The Raiding Parties will rush the enemy's Posts.

    ZERO + 6.   The Raiding Parties will withdraw to our lines.

5. The withdrawal will be signalled by the following means :-
    Klaxon Horns, Railway Hooters and Rockets.

6. O.C. 1st KING'S Regt. will arrange for synchronisation of watches with all concerned.
    2nd Division "G" will please arrange with Corps H.A. in this respect.

7. ZERO hour will be notified later.

8. ACKNOWLEDGE

R. Bryans
Captain,
Brigade Major, 6th Infantry Brigade.

Issued at 9 p.m.

Copy No. 1 - 17th R. Fusiliers
        2 - 1st King's Regt.
        3 - 2nd S. Staffs Regt.
        4 - 6th T.M. Battery.
        5 - 5th Fd. Coy., R.E.
        6 - 5th Inf. Brigade.
        7 - 99th Inf. Brigade.
        8 - 2nd Division 'G'
        9 - Centre Group RFA.
        10 - SHERER'S Group.
        11 - No.2 Bttn. M.G. Corps
        12 - 'X' T.M. Battery.
        13 - 'Y' T.M. Battery.
        14 - D.T.M.O.
        15 - Staff Captain.
        16 - Bde. Signals.
        17 - Bde. Int. Officer.
        18 - Office.
        19)
        20) - War Diary.

SECRET.

M.G.2/400.

2nd DIVISION GENERAL STAFF
No. GS 13/52/6
Date 28/7/18

O.C. A. B. D. Co.
O.C. 1st. Bn. "The Kings'" Regt.)
5th. Infantry Brigade.)
6th. Infantry Brigade.) For information.
99th. Infantry Brigade.)
2nd. Division "G".)

1. A Raid will be carried out by 1st. Bn. "The Kings'" Regt. on Enemy Outpost Groups at about F.12.a.35.20., F.12.a.45.75., F.12.a.45.80., F.6.c.35.30., F.6.c.60.35., F.6.c.70.35.

2. The Raid will take place on night of 29th/30th. July and will be supported by Artillery, Trench Mortar, and Machine Gun fire. Zero hour will be communicated to M.G. Cos. later.

3. (a). M.G. Standing Barrages will be placed as follows:-

No. of Guns.	LOCATION. (Approx).	TARGET.	Guns to be used.	Company.
4.	F.21.b.7.2.	F.18.a.5.3. to F.18.a.25.65.	F.1. - F.4.	D.
4.	F.15.b.4.3.	F.17.b.8.4. to F.17.b.75.83.	S.5. - S.8.	D.
2.	F.5.c.8.6.	F.18.a.05.80. to F.18.a.22.88.	F.13. & 14.	B.
4.	F.5.a.8.6.	F.17.b.62.25. to F.18.a.02.35.	F.15. & 16.) S.9. & 10.)	A.

(b). Rate of Fire will be:-

Zero to Zero plus 1.	Rapid.
Zero plus 1. to Zero plus 6.	Medium.
Zero plus 6. to Zero plus 10.	Rapid.
Zero plus 10. to Zero plus 15.	Medium.
Zero plus 15. to Zero plus 20.	Slow.

Great care must be taken to ensure that guns open fire promptly with Artillery at Zero hour.

4. Ten Belts per gun will be taken up to positions from Transport Lines on night 28th/29th. These will be returned to Battalion Headquarters on night 30th/31st. and refilled under arrangements to be made by Battalion Headquarters.

5. Arrangements for raid and the fact that a raid will take place must be kept secret as long as possible. Only Section Officers who will take part in operation are to be informed.

6. Os. Cdg. Companies will send a representative to Headquarters, 1st. Bn. "The Kings'" Regt. - F.9.a.8.3. (old gun pits) four hours before Zero to synchronise watches.

7. ACKNOWLEDGE.

Done G. 634
AQC

W.M. Todd. Major
for Lieut. Colonel.
Comdg. 2nd. Bn. M.G. Corps.

27/7/1918.

SECRET

2nd Div No G.S.1675/13

319th Regt A.E.F.
2nd M.Gun Battn

1. The 319th M.Gun Coy A.E.F. (MONDICOURT Area) will commence periods of attchment for training with the 2nd M.Gun Battalion, starting 28-7-18.

2. The attachment will be divided into three periods of four days.

    First Period - From July 28th to Aug 1st
    Second   "   - From Aug 1st to Aug 5th
    Third   "   - From Aug 5th to Aug 9th

3. One Officer and 50 O.Rs of 319th M.Gun Coy will be attached during each period

4. 319th M.Gun Coy will arrange its own details as regards rations and will keep one Limbered G.S.Wagon and Quartermaster at 2nd M.Gun Battalion Transport lines, HUMBERCAMP for the purpose of drawing and delivering rations.

5. 2nd M.Gun Battalion will arrange for guides to meet each party from 319th M.Gun Coy at 3 pm on 28th July, 1st Aug, and 5th Aug., outside Division Headquarters V.23.c.7.7

6. 2nd Division M.Gun Battalion Headquarters is at W.26.d.8.3.

7. 2' M.G. Battn to acknowledge

27-7-18

E R Clayton
Lieut Colonel
General Staff 2nd Division.

Copy to "Q" 2nd Division
       VI Corps for information.

"A" Form.
MESSAGES AND SIGNALS.

Army Form C. 2121
(In pads of 100.)

TO 2nd Division G G 12/45

Sender's Number.	Day of Month.	In reply to Number.	AAA
G 8	27		

Herewith tracing shewing areas harassed by machine guns from 15th inst to 25th inst.

RA Wee
B.G.R.A. 2nd Div
27.7.18

2ND BATTALION,
MACHINE GUN
CORPS.

From 2nd MG Battn

SECRET.

NOTE.—(1). These traces are intended to facilitate the communication of information as to the position of targets, which have been located on a squared map.
(2). The squares on this trace are 500 yards in length on the 1/10,000 scale, 1,000 yards in length on the 1/20,000 scale, and 2,000 yards in length on the 1/40,000 scale.
(3). The squares and numbers must also be fitted to the squares of the map showing the targets, which are then drawn on the trace. Sufficient letters and numbers must also be added to enable the recipient to place the trace in the correct position on his own map. A little detail may also be traced, but this is not essential. The name and scale of the map to which the trace refers must be always given. The trace can be used for the 1/10,000, 1/20,000, or 1/40,000 scale.

G.S.G.S. 3033.

Tracing taken from Sheet _____ of the 1: _____ map of _____

Signature _____ Date _____

Identification Trace for use with Artillery Maps.

TO BE SUPERIMPOSED ON
AYETTE. U.T.S.J.45 MOYENNEVILLE U.T.S.J76
SCALE 1:10,000.

X5   FA

SECRET

TO BE SUPERIMPOSED ON
AYETTE SHEET
Scale 1:20,000

No. 2 BN. M.G.C.

2nd Div No G.S.13/54

VI Corps

    As requested.

    I forward a second copy of the Narrative of Raid carried out by 1st R.Berks Regt., on night 22/23 July.

28-7-18

                  Major General
          Commanding 2nd Division.

SECRET

2nd Division No.G.S.13/54.

V1 Corps.

A report on a raid by 2 companies of the 1st Royal Berks, 99th Inf. Brigade, is forwarded herewith.

This raid was skilfully prepared by Brigadier General IRONSIDE and well carried out.

The concentration of heavy artillery in counter-battery work from Zero onwards kept down the enemy's retaliation.

This raid showed that no preparations ~~have been made~~ for offensive operations have been begun by the enemy near the huts. Only a small dump of trench mortar ammunition was found.

Some useful points in the preparation of raids are brought to notice in the report by Captain STOKES, Commanding the Raiding Party.

26th July, 1918.

Major-General,
General Staff, 2nd Division.

SECRET.

5th Inf. Bde. No. G.S. 740/121.

2nd Div G.S. 13/56

2ND DIVISION.

1. Herewith 2 pocket books and shoulder strap of the German Officer killed this morning.

2. These further details are to hand with regard to his capture.
   At 2.25 a.m. this morning an enemy party raided our Front Line at L.4. and L.5. Posts. He made an entry, causing three casualties (wounded) by bombing. Immediate counter-attacks from the flanks drove him out, and 1 dead Officer was left in our hands. None of our men are missing.

3. A full report has been called for and will be forwarded as soon as received.

4. The Battalion concerned has specially asked that the enclosed may be returned to them, and I would be obliged if you will return them to this Office as soon as they are finished with.

28/7/18.

Brigadier General,
Commanding 5th Infantry Brigade.

2nd DIVISION
GENERAL STAFF
No. GS 972/14
Date 28-7-18

SECRET   VI CORPS COUNTER BATTERY.   F.H.C.5/428.

Operation Order No. 3. – July, 1918.

1. In cooperation with a raid by the 2nd Division on the night 29/30th July, the following Counter Battery cooperation will be carried out :-

2. SCHEDULE OF NEUTRALIZATION

   63 Brigade.
   430 S.B.   -   A.Y.16.   -   A.21.b.5.7. to 5.9.

   Phipps Group.
   206 S.B.   -   A.4.c.3.2.
   125 S.B.   -   A.15.b.05.55.   -   A.16.c.9.6.
   263 S.B.   -   A.X.26.   -   A.X.25.
   281 S.B.   -   A.X.34.
   250 S.B.   -   A.X.40.   -   A.X.41.
   320 S.B.   -   A.10.a.65.22.   -   A.10.c.2.7.

   Shorers Group.
   34 S.B.(S)   -   A.Z.16.
   77 S.B.   -   A.Y.13.   -   A.Y.20.
   103 S.B.   -   A.Y.9.   -   A.26.c.4.2. to 3.7.
   342 S.B.   -   A.Y.8.   -   A.Y.17.
   336 S.B.   -   A.Y.1.   -   A.Y.15.
   276 S.B.   -   A.21.a.4.3.   -   A.20.b.5.9.
   24 H.B.   -   A.Z.10.   -   A.Z.13.
   152 H.B.   -   A.Y.21.

3. TIMES – Zero plus 5 minutes to Zero plus 30 minutes.

4. RATES OF FIRE –

   Zero plus 5 minutes to Zero plus 10 minutes – RAPID
   Zero plus 10 minutes to Zero plus 20 minutes – NORMAL.
   Zero plus 20 minutes to Zero plus 30 minutes – SLOW.

   One section will engage each hostile battery.

5. 6" Howitzers will fire N.C. from Zero plus 5 minutes to Zero plus 30 minutes, if weather conditions per-mit; –
   Rate of fire – Zero plus 5 to Zero plus 15 mins. INTENSE
   Zero plus 15 to Zero plus 30 mins SLOW.

6. 60-pdrs will fire shrapnel if possible.

7. Watches will be synchronized with Counter Batteries on the evening of the 29th.

8. Zero hour will be communicated in due course in hours and minutes plus or minus from midnight 29/30 July, 1918.

9. ACKNOWLEDGE BY WIRE.

23/7/18.

Capt RH for Lt. Colonel.,
C.B.S.O., VI Corps.

Copies to :-
63 Brigade   -   2   2nd D.A.   -   1
Phipps Group   -   8   S.O.R.A., VI Corps 4
Shorers Group   -   10   B.M., VI CHA   -   2
2nd Division.   -   1   File   -   4

SECRET

2nd Division No.
G.S.1675/21.

5th Inf. Bde.
6th Inf. Bde.
99th Inf. Bde.
319th Regt. A.E.F. (3)

In continuation of 2nd Division wire G.632 dated 27th inst.

1. Platoons of the 1st Battn. 319th Inf. Regt. proceeding to the line for attachment, will entrain to-day at LA BAZEQUE Light Railway Siding (V.22.c.8.5).

2. The first train will leave LA BAZEQUE at 5 pm and should arrive at detraining point about 6 pm.
There will be 5 minutes interval between trains.

3. There will be 5 trains in all.

4. 'A' Coy. and 2 platoons 'C' Coy. proceeding to 5th Brigade will entrain first, followed by 'B' Coy. proceeding to 6th Brigade and finally 'D' Coy. and the two platoons 'C' Coy. which are allotted to 99th Brigade.

5. All parties will detrain at MONCHY Dump where Brigades will arrange for guides to meet the platoons attached to them.

R Clayton
Lieut. Colonel,
General Staff, 2nd Division.

28/7/18.

Copy to "Q" for information.

SECRET.   — 1 —   2nd Division No.G.S.12/43/1.

No. 2. M.G.Battn.

SECRET [stamp]

It is to be understood that the Machine Gun Coy., now out of the line will, immediately there seems to be any possibility of an enemy attack, be required to at once occupy positions in or about the PURPLE LINE.

Will you please forward your proposals as to where these guns will be located. for battle.

E R Clayton Lieut-Colonel,
General Staff, 2nd Division.

28th July, 1918.

— 2 —

2nd Division

Please see my order No. 22 sent you on 26/7/18

H Dunham Lieut Col
Comdg No 2 45 MGC

SECRET

2nd DIVISION
GENERAL STAFF
GS 12/43/1
28.7.18

GENERAL STAFF, VI CORPS.
GS 31/65

2nd Division.

Reference 2nd Div. No. G.S. 12/43 dated 25th July.

The Corps Commander agrees to the withdrawal of one complete M.G. Company as detailed in para. 1. of above quoted letter, but wishes it to be clearly understood that the Company so withdrawn, is not to be held as a mobile reserve, but is to have definite positions assigned which will be occupied in the event of an attack being imminent.

VI Corps
27th July 1918.   Copy to,- C.M.G.O.

Alex Kennedy Maj
for B.G.G.S.

SECRET

2nd. DIVISION "G".

2nd DIVISION
GENERAL STAFF
No. GS 12/46
Date 28.7.18

M.G.2/395.

LOCATION REPORT.

RIGHT COMPANY.	- Headquarters.	F.13.c.95.90.
No. of Position.	No. of Guns.	Location.
F.1. - F.4.	4.	F.21.b.95.22.
F.5. - F.6.	2.	F.16.a.65.34.
S.3. - S.4.	2.	F.14.d.70.68.
S.5. - S.6.	2.	F.15.c.50.05.
S.7. - S.8.	2.	F.15.c.90.60.
R.3. - R.4.	2.	F.13.c.45.15.
R.5. - R.6.	2.	F.14.b.40.56.

CENTRE COMPANY.	- Headquarters.	E.11.b.5.6.
F.7. - F.8.	2.	F.10.c.3.8.
F.9. - F.10.	2.	F.10.a.30.48.
F.11 - F.12.	2.	F.4.d.1.5.
F.13. - F.14.	2.	F.5.c.40.50.
R.7. - R.8.	2.	F.9.c.06.50.
R.9. - R.10.	2.	F.9.c.10.78.
R.11 - R.12.	2.	F.8.b.45.28.
R.15 - R.16.	2.	F.3.d.00.36.

LEFT COMPANY.	- Headquarters.	X.28.a.60.35.
F.15. - F.16.	2.	X.29.c.72.18.
F.17. - F.18.	2.	X.29.c.60.65.
F.19. - F.20.	2.	X.24.c.28.25.
F.21. - F.24.	4.	S.25.b.4.6.
S.9. - S.10.	2.	X.28.d.9.7.
R.17. - R.18.	2.	X.28.c.15.20.
R.21. - R.22.	2.	X.28.a.50.35.

RESERVE COMPANY.	- Headquarters.	W.27.c.8.5.
	8 Guns.	E.11.b.5.6.
	8 Guns.	W.27.c.8.5.

27/7/1918.

Major.
for Lieut.Colonel.
Comdg. 2nd. Bn. M.G.Corps

SECRET

2nd Division No. G.S. 1675/19.

160th Inf. Bde. A.E.F.
319th Regt. A.E.F.
315th M.G. Battn. A.E.F.
319th M.G. Coy. A.E.F.
No. 2 M.G. Battalion

'C' and 'D' Companies of 315th M.G. Battalion, A.E.F. and 319th M.G. Company, A.E.F. at present located at MONDICOURT, will be attached to the 2nd M.G. Battalion in 2 parties as under :-

    'A' party — from July 30th to August 1st.
    'B' party — from August 2nd to August 4th.

2.   Each party will consist of the following personnel from each of the three above M.G. Companies :-

    2 Officers, 7 Sergeants, 6 Gun Commanders, 6 Nos. 1, 6 Agents (Runners) and Signallers.

3.   On each day the party for the 2nd Division will be conveyed in 4 lorries which will report at the Area Commandant's Office, MONDICOURT at 2 p.m. (4 lorries are being detailed from the conveyance of a similar party to the Guards Division at the same time).

4.   American personnel will bring with them rations for the period of attachment.

5.   Further details will be arranged by O.C., 2nd M.G. Battalion with O.C., 315th M.G. Battalion, A.E.F.

                                      E R Clayton
28th July, 1918.   Lieut-Colonel,
                              General Staff, 2nd Division.

Copies to :-

    5th Inf. Brigade
    6th Inf. Brigade
    99th Inf. Brigade
    "Q" 2nd Division

Guards Division. (3)
2nd Division. (3)
160th Infantry Brigade A.E.F. (10)
S.M.T.O. VI Corps.

SECRET.

VI Corps
G.S.54/35.

Reference VI Corps G.S. 54/29, dated July 21st.

1. The 315th M.G. Battalion, 319th and 320th M.G. Companies, American Expeditionary Force, have arrived in the VI Corps area and are located at MONDICOURT.

2. For Phase "B" these units will be attached as follows and not as stated in above-quoted letter.

   To Guards Division

   315th M.G. Battalion, less "C" and "D" Companies.
   320th M.G. Company.

   To 2nd Division

   319th M.G. Company.
   "C" and "D" Companies, 315th M.G. Battalion.

3. Two parties will be sent from each Machine Gun Company A.E.F. for attachment to British Machine Gun Companies in the Line.

   "A" Party - from evening July 30th to evening August 1st.

   "B" Party - from evening August 2nd to evening August 4th.

   On each occasion the party from a Machine Gun Company A.E.F. will consist of the following:-

   2 Officers.
   7 Sergeants.
   6 Gun Commanders.
   6 Nos. 1.
   6 Agents (runners).
   and Signallers.

4. S.M.T.O. VI Corps will detail eight lorries to report at the Area Commandant's office, MONDICOURT, by 2 p.m. on July 30th; four lorries for the conveyance of personnel to the 4th Battalion Guards M.G. Regiment, the remaining four lorries for the conveyance of personnel to the 2nd Battalion M.G. Corps.

   A similar number of lorries will be required on August 1st, August 2nd and August 4th. Details regarding these will be issued later.

5. American personnel will bring rations with them for the period of their attachment.

6. All other details regarding attachment will be arranged direct between the Officer Commanding 315th M.G. Battalion A.E.F. and the Officers Commanding 4th Battalion Guards M.G. Regiment and 2nd Battalion M.G. Corps.

(2)

7.   The Officer Commanding 4th Battalion Guards M.G.
Regiment will also arrange for the following personnel of
Battalion Headquarters, 315th M.G. Battalion A.E.F., to
be attached for 48 hours to the Battalion Headquarters
of the 4th Battalion Guards M.G. Regiment.

     Battalion Commander.
     Adjutant.
     Supply Officer.
     Transport Officer.
     Medical Officer.
   6 Signallers.
   8 Transport men.
   5 Medical men.

VI Corps.
27th July 1918.

     R h Watson Major
     for B.G.G.S.

    Copies - 80th American Division.
      Third Army.
      "Q".
      DDMS.
      CMGO.

2nd Div No G.S.13/56/1

5th Inf Brigade
_____

      Reference 5th Inf Brigade No G.S.740/123:

    I am very pleased with the prompt action of No 5 Post, which gave us a valuable identification and prevented the enemy from securing one.

29-7-18

                                Major General
                        Commanding 2nd Division.

5TH INFANTRY BRIGADE.

About 2 a.m. this morning the enemy put down a slight barrage on most of the Brigade Front. This barrage was apparently so slight that working parties were not interfered with e.g., one in TYNE AVENUE. Between Posts. 6 and 9 the trench received several direct hits from 5.9's where the barrage was apparently slightly heavier.

About 2.30 a.m. 12 Germans under an Officer rushed from our wire into our trench between Posts 4 and 5. One or more men were left as a block at this point and the remainder of the party rushed down the trench and along the parapet to NO. 4 Post. This was a L.G. Post and the Lewis Gunner there fired at the enemy as they were rushing into our trench but once they had got in or on to our parapet he states he could no longer shoot at them. The Germans pulled this man out of the trench along with his Lewis Gun and started to go back. The remainder of this man's Post appear to have retired further down the trench, but returned later. Having got this man out of the trench, he and the Germans came under the fire of No. 5 Post (rifle post), the men of which had got out of the Post, some in front of the parapet, others behind the parados. (One man of this Post was slightly wounded by a bomb as the Germans entered).

This caused the Germans to lie down and a bomb thrown by a man of No. 4 Post landed in the middle of them which made them double away, leaving their prisoner and the Lewis Gun between our trench and wire. (The man captured by the Germans and another of this Post were slightly wounded by bombs).

At the time this happened, the N.C.O. i/c of No. 4 Post was absent posting a relief to a listening Post in front of No. 5 Post. The fact that the listening Post was being relieved at the time, may account for the Germans not being seen or heard until they actually rushed into our trenches.

The German Officer was apparently shot on our parapet as he was pulling out the Lewis Gunner. Apparently other Germans were hit, but these were evidently got away, and subsequently search failed to find any trace of them.

A protective patrol had spotted a party, probably the raiding one, and was following it from our right posts when the shelling started, and the Germans rushed in.

28/7/18.

(sd) W.L.BRODIE, Lt. Col.,
Commanding 2ND HIGHLAND LIGHT INFANTRY.

- 2 -

2ND DIVISION.   5th Inf. Bde. No. G.S.740/123
24TH R.F.)
52ND L.I.) for information.
2ND H.L.I.)

I consider the action taken by the garrison of NO. 5 Post shewed good initiative and is praiseworthy.

28/7/18.

Brigadier General,
Commanding 5th Infantry Brigade.

SECRET

2nd Division No.
G.S. 1352/8.

VI Corps H.A.

Reference 2nd Division G.S. 1352/3 dated 26/7/18. Zero hour for the raid to be carried out by the 1st King's Regt. to-night 29/30th July, will be 10.40 pm.

2. Please acknowledge.

29/7/18.

E R Clayton
Lieut. Colonel,
General Staff, 2nd Division.

2nd Division No.
G.S. 1352/8

VI Corps.
Guards Division.
37th Division.

SECRET

A raid is being carried out to-night on the enemy's advanced posts in F.12.a & c by 1 Coy. of the 6th (Centre) Brigade of this Division.
Zero hour is 10.40 pm.
A counter-battery programme is being carried out at the time of the raid by VI Corps Heavy Artillery.

29/7/18.

R Clayton
Major-General,
Commanding 2nd Division.

2nd Division No.
G.S.1347/8.

6th Inf. Bde.
———————————

Reference 2nd Division G.S.1347/7 dated 24th July.

Herewith the remarks of the Army Commander on the raid recently carried out by the 1st King's Regt. Please forward this paper to ~~that~~ the Battalion.

Lieut. Colonel,
General Staff, 2nd Division.

29/7/18.

2nd Division No. G.S. 13/47/7.

G.O.C.
    6th Infantry Brigade.

    It is a very great pleasure to me to forward the high praise which the Army Commander gives to Capt. MACE's Company.

                                            C. E. Pereira

24th July, 1918.
                                          Major General,
                               Commanding 2nd Division.

2nd Division No. G.S. 13/47/6.

VI Corps
———

The attached report by the O.C. 1st King's Regiment, and remarks by G.O.C. 6th Infantry Brigade on a raid carried out on the night 14th/15th July, are forwarded for information.

2. (a) The scheme of the raid was as follows :-
    Objective - the enemy's line of posts as shewn on attached map.

    (b) Troops carrying out the raid - 'D' Company, 1st King's Regiment, strength 4 Officers 136 O.Rs.

    (c) The raiding party began to form up in No Man's Land at Zero minus 60. Flank detachments were put out. The Sections detailed to take the various parts of the enemy's outpost system are shewn on attached map.

    (d) <u>Artillery arrangements</u>. At zero, 4 18-pdr. batteries and 1 Stokes Mortar Battery put down a barrage as shewn on sketch of the enemy's outpost line.
    2 Batteries 18-pdrs., 1 6" Newton Battery and 2 Batteries 4.5" Hows. put down a thin protective barrage on the flanks of the raid and approximately 350yds. in front of the objective.
    Shortly after zero a counter-battery bombardment was carried out by VI Corps H.A.

    (e) The intention was for the Infantry to push through the gaps in the barrage and attack the enemy's posts from the flanks and rear.

3. The arrangements seem to have worked perfectly owing to the careful reconnaissance carried out on the two previous nights and to the good arrangements made by the Battalion Commander.
    9 prisoners were captured and it is believed that a similar number of the enemy were killed, while only 4 or 5 got away.

4. The counter-battery work carried out by the Heavy Artillery was fully justified as the enemy retaliation was very feeble and consequently the casualties to the raiding troops were light.

18th July, 1918.

Major-General,
Commanding 2nd Division.

CONFIDENTIAL.

2nd Division No.G.S.13/47/4.

G.O.C.
2nd Division.

5th Inf. Brigade.G.S.1103/8/14.

The attached report of the raid carried out by the 1st battalion 'The King's' Regiment is forwarded.

I have little to add, as I left the entire arrangements in the hands of Lieut-Colonel KING, and Lieut-Colonel WICKHAM to whom the greatest credit is due.

The success of the operation was undoubtedly the very accurate reconnaissance that was carried out on the two previous nights, under the personal supervision of Captain MACE.

The gaps in the barrage, allowed the Raiders to approach close to their objective, and thus minimized the chance of the garrison escaping, this can only be done after careful reconnaissance and perfect liaison between the artillery and Infantry.

The support of the artillery and Trench Mortar Batteries afforded the greatest assistance, all Commanders were most indefatigable in their arrangements and the success of the enterprise is very largely due to their efforts.

I propose to submit names for Immediate Reward.

(Sgd) F.G.Willan,
Brigadier General,
Commanding, 6th Infantry Brigade.

15/7/18.

SECRET.

Headquarters,
    6th Infantry Brigade.

The following particulars are forwarded regarding the Raid carried out by 'D' Company (Captain E.R.MACE) of the Battalion under my Command on the night 14th/15th July, 1918.

1. A thorough reconnaissance of the ground and enemy Posts was carried out on the nights 12/13th and 13/14th July. All leaders and Scouts went out for several hours. Each night several Boche were seen and heard. Posts were definitely located and lines of approach decided.

2. The strength of 'D' Company on 14th July:-
    4 Officers, 148 Other Ranks with 8 Lewis Guns, of these the following went over the parapet:-
    4 Officers 136 Other Ranks with 8 Lewis Guns.

3. The normal organisation of a Company was adhered to. The Raiders were formed into 8 parties. Each party was a complete Rifle Section and had 2 trained Battalion Scouts attached as guides in "NO MAN'S LAND". 2 L.G. Sections were disposed in rear, and in echelon on each flank.

4. A full hour was taken in creeping forward into the positions of deployment in "NO MAN'S LAND". This advance was not detected. No equipment was worn except a bandolier of S.A.A. and a Box Respirator. Balaclava caps were worn instead of steel helmets. All Raiders except Officers carried a rifle and bayonet. Officers carried revolvers only.

5. The combined F.A. and STOKES Mortar barrage was excellent. The registrations had been so accurate, that the various section groups of their own accord got inside the Boche wire where gaps had been arranged before ZERO HOUR.
    This confidence in the Artillery was brought about by a close liaison and the very active interest taken by all the Battery Commanders in their registrations which was not unnoticed by the Raiders.

6. The "LIFT" of 200 yards at ZERO + 1 was pronounced, and strikingly co-ordinated by the Artillery. Every gun and Mortar appeared to stop and lift together. The Raiders rushed the Posts from their lying up positions on the flanks without any hesitation. 9 prisoners were secured, and 9 more dead were seen in the Posts. There were probably many more, but the night was too dark to see far.

7. Our casualties in the Raiding Party were, 1 Officer slightly wounded (at duty). 1 O.R. severely wounded, 5 O.Rs. slightly wounded, 2 O.Rs. of a flank Company were wounded.

8. The withdrawal was carried out successfully. The Rocket Signal and 'Railway Hooters' were useful.
    The Boche retaliation was negligible. It is considered that this was due to the steady and effective counter-battery work carried out by the Corps Heavy Artillery from ZERO + 7 onwards. Approximately 900 rounds were fired by the Heavies.

9. The success of the raid may be attributed to the following:-
    (a) Two nights reconnaissance of ground very thoroughly carried out by Captain E.R.MACE personally, with all his Sections Leaders and Scouts.

    (b) A very accurate barrage which gave great confidence to the Raiders from the start.

(c) An organisation which kept Officers, N.C.Os. and men in their own Platoons and Sections and thus engendered the keenest competition. The only personnel attached were the trained Scouts.

(d) The attacks being launched from the flanks of Posts. The effective counter-battery work by the Corps Heavy Artillery, on all known hostile batteries, which could fire on the Sector, undoubtedly saved the Raiders many casualties in the withdrawal.

I wish to bring to the notice of the Brigade Commander the excellent work done by Captain E.R.MACE, who spent two nights in "NO MAN'S LAND" reconnoitring and then personally led two Sections in the Raid with great dash and pluck, and was himself responsible for the capture of 6 prisoners. His work was thorough from start to finish and I strongly recommend him for an Immediate Reward of the MILITARY CROSS. A few further recommendations will be submitted when fuller details are available.

15th July, 1918.

(sgd) D.M.KING, Lieut-Colonel,
Commanding, 1st Bn. "The King's" Regiment

2nd Div G.S 13/47/5

Headquarters,

2nd Division 'G'.
========================

Reference telephone conversation with G.S.O. 1.

    Herewith map, to accompany the account of the Raid carried out by 1st KING'S Regt., forwarded under this Office No. G.S. 1103/8/14 of 16/7/18.

R Bryans Capt
for Brigadier General,
Commanding 6th Infantry Brigade.

16-7-18.

2nd Division No,
G.S.13/47/4.

G.O.C. 6th Inf. Bde.

      I have received the report of the raid carried out by the 1st King's and I consider that the plan was an extremely good one and the execution of the plan most skillfully carried out. I should like my personal congratulations to be sent to Capt. MACE and to "D" Company of the 1st King's. I think the value of the raid is greatly increased owing to the fact that it was carried out by a complete Company with Section Commanders leading their own men. I should very much like to see "D" Coy on parade when they come out of the line.

                                                                         Major General,
16/7/18.   Commanding 2nd Division.

Legend (as annotated on map)

- Sections marked
- Scouts
- Officers
- Route Taken
- Halt for Barrage
- Lewis Guns

Totals.
Raiding Party
4 Officers 98 OR
LGs   38
4 Off.   136 OR

Annotations on map

- No 1 Section 1 NCO + 1/10R
- No 2 Section 1 Off + 1/8 OR
- No 3 Section 1 Off + 1/2 OR
- No 4 Section 1 NCO + 1/10 OR
- No 5 Section 1/Liverpool
- No 7 Section 1 Off + 1/2 OR
- No 8 Sect 1 NCO + 1/2 OR
- 2 Scouts 4 LGs 1 NCO + 1/8 OR

- Arty Barrage — 3 Prisoners Identified. Very Light Mags here. Shot at — nothing found here.
- GAP in BARRAGE — 5 Prisoners Identified
- Arty Barrage — 1 Prisoner Identified
- GAP in BARRAGE — Post unsuccessful
- Arty Barrage — Poor eventual IDENTIFICATION obtained

- Work on Shell Holes
- Post & Barricade
- New Work at Camouflage
- Aerodrome
- Work on Shell Holes
- Mushroom Bush

Legend (side)

- M.G.   O.P.
- T.M.   Dug out
- Post   Infy Track
- Sniper   Hesbarc

- position of deployment — (red)
- Line of Advance — (dashed red)
- Barrage at Z — (blue)

ENLARGEMENT from G.T.S. MAPS: 575 & 370.   SCALE 1/5000.

G.O.C.

2nd Division.   2nd Div GS 13/47/4

The attached report of the Raid carried out by the 1st Battalion 'The King's' Regiment is forwarded.

I have little to add, as I left the entire arrangements in the hands of Lieut-Colonel KING, and Lieut-Colonel WICKHAM, to whom the greatest credit is due.

The success of the operation was undoubtedly the very accurate reconnaissance that was carried out on the two previous nights, under the personal supervision of Captain MACE.

The gaps in the barrage, allowed the Raiders to approach close to their objective, and thus minimized the chance of the garrison escaping, this can only be done after very careful reconnaissance and perfect liaison between the Artillery and Infantry.

The support of the Artillery and Trench Mortar Batteries afforded the greatest assistance, all Commanders were most indefatigable in their arrangements and the success of the enterprise is very largely due to their efforts.

I propose to submit names for Immediate Reward.

15/7/18.   Brigadier General,
                 Commanding, 6th Infantry Brigade.

2nd Div G.S.13/47/2/O/326/1.

Copy.

SECRET.

1. On the night 14th/15th July, 1918, 1st Bn. King's Regt. will carry out a raid on the enemy's Outpost line from F.11.d.3.1. to F.12.a.4.3.
   Object :- To secure an identification.

2. The raid will be carried out by two main groups against the following posts :-

   "A" Group.... Posts at F.11.d.4.2. and F.11.d.5.4.
   "B" Group.... Posts at F.12.c.20.55, F.12.a.00.15, F.12.a.4.2.

   Each raiding Group will consist of 4 rifle sections and 2 L.G. sections (2 guns each).

3. The raid will be supported by 8 Batteries 18-pdrs. 4 Batteries 4.5" Hows. 6th L.T.M. Battery and "Y" T.M. Battery.
   These Batteries will be distributed as follows :-

(a) CENTRE GROUP.
   "F" Battery, R.H.A.   (6 Guns) F.11.d.80.50.to F.12.c.10.80.
   "T" Battery, R.H.A.   (4 Guns) F.11.d.80.50.to F.11.d.55.40.
   400th   ., R.F.A.   (4 Guns) A.12.c.10.70.to F.12.c.30.80.
   401st   ., (Adv.Sec) (2 Hows) F.12.c.30.80.to F.12.c.60.45.
   401st   .,   (4 Hows) F.12.c.50.82.to F.13.c.75.31.
   COMPO   .,   (4 Guns) F.12.c.80.90.to F.12.a.35.15.

(b) Right Group.
   6 Forward 18-pdrs.   F.11.d.30.10.to F.11.d.55.40.
   9th Battery, R.F.A.   (4 Guns) F.17.b.80.70.to F.17.b.80.80.
   16th   .,   (4 .,) F.17.b.80.80.to F.17.b.90.55.
   47th   .,   (6 Hows) F.17.b.90.55.to F.18.a.30.60.
                                   to F.18.a.45.80.
   D/36th   .,   (6 .,) F.18.a.45.80.to F.18.c.80.80.

(c) Left Group.
   1 18-pdr. Battery.   (6 Guns) F.12.a.80.80.to F.12.a.40.60.to
                                   A.7.a.00.00.
   1   .,   (6 .,) A.7.a.00.00.to F.12.c.80.90.
   1 4.5" How. Battery. (4 Hows) F.12.c.80.90.to F.12.c.80.80.

(d) Y/ T.M.Battery.   F.17.b.00.70.to F.17.b.50.80.

4. At zero hour..... Batteries will open at an intense rate on the above barrage lines.

   At zero plus 1 minute. "F", "T", 400th, COMPO, and 6 forward guns of right group will left 200 yards.

   At zero plus 2 minutes. "F", "T", COMPO, and 6 forward guns of Right Group will lift 100 yards, 400th Battery will lift 50 yards.

   At zero plus 20 minutes. All artillery and T.M's will cease fire.

5. Any further necessary registration will be carried out with as few rounds as possible.
   401st Battery must take particular care to register their targets.

6. The following will be the action of the Infantry :-
)Zero minus 25 minutes. The raiding parties will moveforward in section Groups and approach the enemy outpost line.
   Zero minus 15 minutes. L.G. sections will move forward to positions in echelon on the flanks.

P.T.O.

Zero plus 1 minute.   The raiding parties will rush the enemy outpost line.

Zero plus 10 minutes.   The raiding parties will withdraw to our lines.

12-7-18.
                                    Sd/- W.G.SCOTT BROWN, Capt,R.F.A.
                                    Adjt. 14th. Brigade, R.H.A.

SECRET.   14th. Bde R.H.A. No.C.326/2.
                                           2nd D.A. No. B.M. 33/6a.

All recipients of
14th Brigade R.H.A. C.No.326/1.

1.   Reference Para 3 (a).

        Amend as follows :

        "F" Battery R.H.A.   (6 Guns). F.11.d.30.10. to F.11.d.55.40.

        "T" Battery R.H.A.   (4 Guns). F.11.d.70.50. to F.11.d.55.40.

        400th Battery R.F.A. (4 Guns). F.12.c.10.70. to F.12.c.25.80.

        COMPO (4 Guns).   F.12.a.35.10. to F.12.a.40.40.

        This new distribution will leave two gaps for the raiders
in which there will be no firing.

                (1)   F.11.d.70.50. to F.12.c.10.70.
                (2)   F.12.c.25.80. to F.12.a.35.10.

2. RATE OF FIRE.

        The rates of fire for all Artillery will be as follows :

        Zero to Zero plus 6 ....INTENSE.
        Zero plus 6 to Zero plus 10...............NORMAL.
        Zero plus 10 to Zero plus 11..............INTENSE.
        Zero plus 11 to Zero plus 15..............NORMAL.
        Zero plus 15 to Zero plus 20..............SLOW.
        At Zero plus 20...........................Cease Fire.

        6" Newton Mortars and Stokes Mortars will fire at
corresponding rates.

3. AMMUNITION.

        The 18.pdr Batteries of the Centre Group also the Six
forward 18.pdrs. of the Right Group will fire.

                AX 101 E. (direct action).

        All other 18.pdrs Batteries.
                50% A.
                50% AX. 101 E. (direct action).

        All 4.5" How. Batteries will fire :

                BX. 101 E. (direct action).

4. Zero hour will be notified later.

13th July. 1918.   Sd. W.G.SCOTT BROWN. Capt. R.F.A.
                                        Adjutant 14th Brigade. R.H.A.

SECRET.   2nd Division No.
                                       G.S.   13/47.

VI Corps.   **SECRET**

1.   1st King's Regt. 6th Inf. Bde. will carry out a raid on the night July 14th/15th.

2. (i) Objective, enemy's outpost line from F.11.d.3.1 to F.12.a.4.3.

  (ii) Approximate strength, 2 platoons.

 (iii) At zero - 25 the raiding party will form up outside our wire.
       At zero a barrage will be put down on the part of the enemy's line to be raided for one minute together with a barrage on each flank. At zero plus 1 the barrage will lift 200 yds. and the raiding party will rush the objective.

  (iv) No special practice will be carried out.

   (v) No extra ammunition is required.

  (vi) No special equipment is required.

 (vii) Date, July 14th/15th.

                                          Sgd C.E.Pereira
                                          Major-General,
12/7/18.   Commanding 2nd Division.

Prefix	Code	m.	Words	Charge	This message is on a/c of :	Recd. at	m.
Office of Origin and Service Instructions.			Sent			Date	
			At	m.	Service.	From	
			To				
			By		(signature of " Franking Officer.")	By	

TO { Am Col

Sender's Number	Day of Month	In reply to Number	AAA
PM/47	31		

The relief order should have been dated 30th July and issued Y. P.M. AAA. Relief takes place to-night AAA. addressed all units concerned AAA acknowledge

Priority RR

From / Place: 19th Inf. Bde.
Time: 9.30 am

H S Rains
Major

The above may be forwarded as now corrected (Z)

Censor. Signature of Addresser or person authorised to telegraph in his name

*This line should be erased if not required.

2662 M. & Co. Ltd. Wt W329/519—100,000. 6/14. Forms C2121/10.

6th Bde. No.GS.1103/3/21.

SECRET

To all recipients of 6th Brigade Order No. 375.

Reference para.7 -

ZERO hour will be at 10.40 p.m.

ACKNOWLEDGE.

29/7/18.

Bryan Captain,
Brigade Major,
6th Infantry Brigade.

SECRET.   Copy No........

6th Infantry Brigade Order No. 375.

27th July, 1918.

1.   1st Battn. KING'S Regiment will carry out a Raid on the enemy's Outpost Line in F.12.a. and F.6.c. on the night of 29th/30th July, 1918.
   Strength of Raiding Party - 1 Company,
   Object - To secure identifications and to kill as many of the enemy as possible.

2.   The Raid will be supported by Field and Heavy Artillery and by 6th T.M. Battery, as under :-

   (a) The 18 pdr. barrage will be put down as follows :-
       ZERO to ZERO + 2.   200 yards East of the line of enemy Posts from F.12.c.60.65. to F.6.c.80.55.

       ZERO + 2.   The barrage will lift 200^X

       ZERO + 20.   The barrage will cease.

   (b) 4.5" Howitzers.
       ZERO to ZERO + 20. Bombardment of the enemy's works between F.18.a.0.3. and A.2.c.3.6.

   (c) Corps H.A. have been asked to co-operate in counter-battery work from ZERO + 5.

   (d) 6th T.M. Battery with the addition of 8 guns will place an intense barrage on the Posts to be raided from ZERO to ZERO + 1.

3.   A Machine Gun barrage has been arranged to cover the Valley in F.17.d.

4.   The following will be the action of the Infantry :-

   ZERO + 1.   The Raiding Parties will rush the enemy's Posts.

   ZERO + 6.   The Raiding Parties will withdraw to our lines.

5.   The withdrawal will be signalled by the following means :- Klaxon Horns, Railway Hooters and Rockets.

6.   O.C. 1st KING'S Regt. will arrange for synchronisation of watches with all concerned.
   2nd Division "G" will please arrange with Corps H.A. in this respect.

7.   ZERO hour will be notified later.

8.   ACKNOWLEDGE

R. Ryans   Captain,
Issued at 9 p.m.   Brigade Major, 6th Infantry Brigade.

Copy No.1 - 17th R. Fusiliers   11 - No.2 Bttn. M.G.Corps
       2 - 1st King's Regt.   12 - 'X' T.M. Battery.
       3 - 2nd S. Staffs Regt.   13 - 'Y' T.M. Battery.
       4 - 6th T.M. Battery.   14 - D.T.M.O.
       5 - 5th Fd. Coy., R.E.   15 - Staff Captain.
       6 - 5th Inf. Brigade.   16 - Bde. Signals.
       7 - 99th Inf. Brigade.   17 - Bde. Int. Officer.
       8 - 2nd Division 'G'   18 - Office.
       9 - Centre Group RFA.   19)
      10 - SHERER'S Group.   20) - War Diary.

S E C R E T.

VI Corps
G.S.54/38.

Guards Division.
2nd Division.
160th Inf.Bde. A.E.F.
S.M.T.O., VI Corps.

Reference VI Corps G.S.54/35 dated 27th July, para. 4.

S.M.T.O., VI Corps will detail lorries as follows for the conveyance of personnel of Machine Gun Companies A.E.F. to and from the line :-

August 1st.   4 lorries to be at X.1.d 5.0 (RANSART - BELLACOURT Road) at 3.30 p.m.
              4 lorries to be at 2nd Bn. M.G. Corps H.Q., W.26.d 8.5 (BIENVILLERS - BERLES Road) at 7 p.m.

August 2nd.   8 lorries to report at Area Commandant's office MONDICOURT, at 2 p.m.

August 4th.   4 lorries to be at X.1.d 5.0 (RANSART - BELLACOURT Road) at 3.30 p.m.
              4 lorries to be at 2nd Bn. M.G. Corps H.Q., W.26.d 8.5 (BIENVILLERS - BERLES Road) at 7 p.m.

R.H.Watson Major
for B.G.G.S.

VI Corps.
29th July, 1918.

Copies to :-

80th Division A.E.F.
"Q" VI Corps.
C.M.G.O.

SECRET   office

PRESSING

2nd Divn. No. 1675/24.

6th Inf. Bde.
319th Regt. A.E.F. (2 copies).

    2nd Division No. G.S.1675/16 dated 27/7/18 is cancelled.
    319th T.M.Bty. will be attached to the 6th Trench Mortar Bty. from July 30th to August 5th.
    All personnel of 319th T.M.Bty. A.E.F. going up to the line for attachment will report at 3 pm on 30th July at HUMBERCAMP Church, where a guide from 6th Inf. Bde. will meet them.
    The party will then march to bivouacs arranged by 6th Inf. Bde., about E.4,a.
    Personnel of 319th T.M.Bty. A.E.F. will then be attached to guns of 6th T.M.Bty. in the line under arrangements to be made direct between O.C. 319th T.M.Bty. A.E.F. and O.C. 6th T.M.Bty.
    Period of attachment will be completed by the evening of August 5th.
    All personnel of the 319th T.M.Bty. will bring two days rations with them, and will be rationed by the 6th Inf. Bde. from 1st to 5th August inclusive. Ration strength of the 319th T.M. Bty. A.E.F. will be - 1 officer 40 O.Rs.

E R Clayton
Lieut. Colonel,
General Staff, 2nd Division.

29/7/18.

Copies to :-

    160th Bde. A.E.F.   )
    "Q" 2nd Divn.   ) for information.

Guards Division.
2nd Division.
160th Infantry Brigade A.E.F.

GENERAL STAFF
No. GS 1675/28
Date 30.7.18
2nd DIVISION

VI Corps No.
G.S.54/39.

Reference VI Corps G.S. 54/29, dated July 21st, and G.S. 54/35, dated July 27th.

1. The individual attachment of personnel of American M.G. Companies will be completed on August 4th.

2. Platoons, complete with guns, &c., from American M.G. Companies, will then be attached to British M.G. Battalions. Three platoons at a time will be attached to each British M.G. Battalion, and will be distributed amongst the M.G. Companies in the line. Each platoon will be attached for four days.

3. These attachments will commence on August 5th and will finish by August 20th, by which date every American M.G. Platoon must have completed its attachment.

4. All details will be arranged direct between Guards and 2nd Divisions and O.C. 315th M.G. Battalion A.E.F.

5. Arrangements will also be made by Guards and 2nd Divisions for American M.G. Company Commanders to be attached for four days to their opposite numbers in British M.G. Battalions.

In addition Guards Division will arrange for the Commander and Staff of 315th M.G. Battalion A.E.F. to be attached for four days to Headquarters, 4th Battalion Guards M.G. Regiment.

VI Corps.
30th July 1918.

RhWatson Major
for B.G.G.S.

Copies - 80th Division A.E.F.
"Q" VI Corps.
C.M.G.O.

SECRET.   2nd Division No. G.S.1675/27.

319th Regiment A.E.F.
5th Inf. Brigade.
6th Inf. Brigade.
99th Inf. Brigade.
_____

In continuation of 2nd Division No. G.S.1675/11, dated 26th July, 1918.

1. The 1st Battalion 319th Regiment will be withdrawn from the line on August 1st. Trains for the conveyance of the battalion to LA BAZEQUE will be at MONCHY Siding at 12 midnight August 1/2nd.

2. The 2nd Battalion 319th Regiment, A.E.F., will be attached as under from August 1st to August 5th;-

    To 5th Infantry Brigade.

    "E" Coy. complete, 2 platoons "H" Coy.

    To 6th Infantry Brigade.

    "F" Coy. and Battalion Headquarters.

    To 99th Infantry Brigade.

    "G" Coy. complete, Headquarters and 2 platoons of "H" Coy.

3. The strength of the American Platoons will be 1 officer, and between 34 and 40 other ranks, with 2 Lewis Guns.

4. Personnel of the 2nd Battalion 319th Regiment will proceed from FARM DUMP to MONCHY R.E. DUMP on the 1st August by train; the first train leaving at 5 p.m.

5. All movement to and from the trenches will be by platoons. A distance of 200 yards will be maintained between platoons.

    Brigades will arrange guides direct with the attached Companies on the scale of one guide per platoon, and one guide per Company and Battalion H.Q.

6. During the attachment in the line, no American patrols are to be sent out unless accompanied by at least 1 N.C.O. and 2 privates from the British Coy. to which they are attached.

7. One specially selected British Subaltern and one Sergeant will be attached to each American Platoon in an advisory capacity, and will go into the line with it.

8. During period "B" American platoons will be in the front line for part of the period in the trenches. Every opportunity will be taken of training the transport in the conveyance of rations to the front line.

9. The Battalion Transport of the 2nd Battalion 319th Regiment will move to HUMBERCAMP on the 1st August, taking over the lines now occupied by the Battalion Transport of the 1st Battalion 319th Regiment. The Transport of the 1st Battalion will be clear of the lines at HUMBERCAMP by 2-30 p.m. and will proceed to the standings formerly occupied at LA BAZEQUE.

                                                P.T.O.

-2-

The transport of the 2nd Battalion will be attached to Battalions of the 6th Inf. Brigade under arrangements to be made between the Battalion Commander 2nd Battalion 319th Regiment and 6th Inf. Brigade.

10. Brigadiers will report what changes they propose to make in the disposition of troops in the line. The only extra accommodation available is that which will be vacated by the American Battalions.

11. Instructions regarding rations are being issued by 2nd Division "Q".

12. For composition of American Battalion and Company H.Q. see Appendix "A", 2nd Division No.G.S.1675/11, dated 26th July.

13. Brigades and 319th Regiment to acknowledge.

E.R. Clayton
Lieut-Colonel,
General Staff, 2nd Division.

30th July, 1918.

Copy to C.R.A.
"Q" 2nd Division.
160th Brigade, A.E.F.   } For information.
VI Corps.

SECRET

RELIEF ORDERS.   Copy No. 9

31st July, 1915.

Reference attached map (issued to five Inf. Bns. only)

1. From to-morrow night, the front held by the Brigade will be from FAUQUISSART - TRIVELET road (inclusive) to the SAILLY - FROMELLES Road (exclusive).

2. The 1st Bn. The Cameronians will, tomorrow evening, take over from the 2nd Bn. East Lancashire Regt. (24th Infantry Brigade), sub-sections 1.P., 1.Q., 1.R., on the present left of the Brigade front, with the supporting posts L.A., 1.X., and 1.B. in rear.
   Details of relief have been arranged between Officers Commanding Battalions concerned.

3. The 3rd Battery, R.F.A. will cover the line held by the 1st Bn. The Cameronians.

4. Besides S.A.A., Sniperscopes, megaphones, rifle grenade stands, catapults, water tanks, gongs, grenades, green signal rockets and Very pistol ammunition, are trench stores, and will be handed over by the Officer Commanding 2nd East Lancashire Regiment.
   Periscopes, Very pistols, and Vermorel Sprayers will not be handed over.
   Officers Commanding 1st Bn. Middlesex Regiment, and 5th Scottish Rifles will hand over to 1st Bn. The Cameronians by 4 pm tomorrow, 3 and 2 Vermorel Sprayers, respectively.

5. The 2nd Bn. Royal Welch Fusiliers will relieve the garrisons in posts 11, 12, 13, 14, 17, and 18 in the RUE DU BACQUEROT by 6 pm tomorrow.
   The remainder of the battalion (less 1 Company), with machine guns will relieve the 1st Bn. The Cameronians in billet line, by 8 pm.
   Detailed arrangements to be made between Commanding Officers concerned.
   Headquarters and 1 Company, 2nd Bn. R.Welch Fusiliers will remain in LAVENTIE.

6. Headquarters of Battalions in trenches will be as follows:-
   5th Scottish Rifles.   M.12.c.5.6.
   1st Middlesex Regt.   M.6.d.2.1.
   1st Cameronians.   M.6.d.6.4.

7. Rocket signals by night for the Brigade will be Green from evening of 31st July, inclusive.

8. At 6 am, 1st August, the 2nd Argyll & Sutherland Highrs. will be in Brigade reserve, the Brigade finding no Divisional reserve battalion.

9. On completion of relief, O.C., 19th Infantry Brigade will assume command of the line mentioned in para. 1 above.

                                    Major,
                        Brigade Major, 19th Infantry Brigade.

Issued at 7 am.
Copy. No. 1 Filed.
      "   2 Staff Captain.   Copy. No. 8. 10th Fd. Amb.
      "   3 2nd R.Welch Fus.   "   9. 19th Bde. Ammn.Col.
      "   4 1st Cameronians.   "   10. 19th Bde. Train.
      "   5 1st Middlesex R.   "   11. Bde. Transport Off.
      "   6 2nd A. & S. Highrs.   "   12. 24th Inf. Bde.
      "   7 5th Scottish Rifles.   "   13. 8th Division.
                                             "   14. G.O.C., R.A., 8th Div.
                                             "   15. 9th Bde. R.F.A.

SECRET.

RELIEF ORDERS
of
19th Infantry Brigade.

Copy No. 9

31st July, 1915.

Reference: 1/40,000 map, sheet, 36.

1. After completion of relief tomorrow evening (1st August) the front line held by the Brigade will extend from Communication trench No. 10 (exclusive) (N.13.c.5.9.) to the SAILLY - FROMELLES Road, exclusive (N.9.c.6.8.).
   The southern boundary of the Brigade area will be RUE MASSELOT - Road Junction M.10.d. - LAVENTIE - LAVENTIE STATION - NOUVEAU MONDE - (all inclusive).
   2½ battalions will be in front line and 2½ battalions in Brigade reserve.

2. Tomorrow evening (1st August) the 5th Scottish Rifles will hand over the trench line from FAUQUISSART - TRIVELET road (inclusive) to No. 10 Communication trench (inclusive) and Posts E.4, F.1, to units of the BAREILLY Brigade (MEERUT Division).
   On completion of relief, 2 Companies, 5th Scottish Rifles will move to billets in LAVENTIE.
   Details of relief have been arranged by the Officers Commanding units concerned.

3. The 2nd Bn. R.Welch Fusiliers will, tomorrow evening, 1st August, hand over posts 11, 12, and 13 on the RUE DU BACQUEROT to units of the BAREILLY Brigade.
   Details to be arranged between Officers Commanding units concerned.
   On completion of relief, 2nd R.Welch Fusiliers will have 2 companies and 4 machine guns on the RUE DU BACQUEROT and 2 companies with Headquarters in LAVENTIE.

4. The 2 Companies, 2nd R.Welch Fus. on the RUE DU BACQUEROT will find the garrisons for posts as follows:-
   Post No. 14 (CELLAR)   - 1 Section.
   Post No. 17 (DEAD END) - 2 Sections.
   Post No. 18 (PICANTIN) - 2 Sections.
   The remainder of the two companies will be billetted as laid down in para 4 of Secret memorandum O.8 of 24th July, 1915.
   The Machine guns will not be placed in the posts.

5. Picks, shovels, periscopes, Very pistols, Vermorel sprayers, and latrine buckets will not be handed over to relieving units.

6. Artillery support on the Brigade front will be given by the 9th Brigade, R.F.A. until 10 pm, from which hour it will be given by the 90th Brigade, R.F.A.

2nd August

W.B. Roame
Major,
Brigade Major, 19th Infantry Brigade.

Issued at 5 pm.
Copy No. 1 Filed.
"   2 Staff Captain.
"   3 2nd R.Welch Fus.
"   4 1st Cameronians.
"   5 1st Middlesex Regiment.
"   6 2nd A. & S. Highrs.
"   7 5th Scottish Rifles.
"   8 19th Fd. Amb.
"   9 19th Bde. Ammn. Col.
"   10 19th Bde. Train.
"   11 Bde Transport Officer.
"   12 Bareilly Brigade.
"   13 9th Division.
"   14 9th Bde. R.F.A.

2nd Division No. G.S. 1675/3.

5th Inf. Brigade.
6th Inf. Brigade.
99th Inf. Brigade.

The G.O.C. wishes particular care to be taken that American Platoons holding the line are warned when patrols are out at night. A case has occurred that in spite of this warning a returning patrol was fired on.

Lieut-Colonel,
General Staff, 2nd Division.

31st July, 1918.

2nd Division.

This note for information of M.G. Coy. & and follows later.

Last night Lt. Hart & 24 R.F. took over a U.S.A. line & Lt. BAXLEY & patrol. He warned flank parties, took the extra precaution of front out sentries in no man's land to covering party returning but they failed in. When patrol was coming in Lt. R.3 returned & U.S.A. sentries from blue trench & were surprised. The party opened fire & wounded Lt. BAXLEY 1/7/5 319th Infantry R.3 tenderly in the neck. Lt. Hart is a most experienced patrol leader.

W. Abram Br.
Guilf. 3rd 7/5.

31. viii – 18.

Defence Scheme July 1918.

LIST OF CONTENTS.

Paragraph 1.   Boundaries.
          2.   Organisation of Defences.
          3.   Probable forms of attack.
          4.   Method of holding the line.
          5.   Distribution of troops.
          6.   Action in case of a threatened attack.
          7.   Anti-Tank defence.
          8.   Sector Guides.
          9.   Action of working parties.
         10.   Anti-Aircraft defence.
         11.   S.O.S. Signals.

LIST OF APPENDICES.

Appendix A.   Artillery.
         B.   Occupation of Purple Line.
         C.   Action of tanks in event of enemy attack.
         D.   Arrangements for Demolitions.
         E.   Action in case of enemy shelling with Yellow Cross Gas.
         F.   Defence against Cloud Gas attack.
         G.   Communications.
         H.   Administrative arrangements.

MAPS.

Map A.   General Map.
    B.   Disposition of troops
    C.   Disposition of Machine Guns.
    D.   Track Map.

DEFENCE SCHEME

SECRET.

RIGHT DIVISION VI CORPS.

Copy No...../......

1. The front held by the Division is from F.23.a.0.6 to S.27.a.1.0.

    <u>Right Boundary</u> - F.23.a.0.6 - F.20.a.1.5 - E.24.b.05.65 - E.24.a.3.7 - E.16.d.30.15.

    <u>Left Boundary</u> - S.27.a.1.0 - S.27.a.0.1 - X.22.c.6.0 - X.20.c.4.2 - W.21.c.9.3.

    Boundary between Right and Centre Brigades:- Front line at F.11.d.10.45 - F.10.d.6.5 - trench junction F.10.d.5.8 - thence along North of AYETTE AVENUE (inclusive to Right Brigade) to trench and road crossing at F.9.b.9.3 - F.9.c.7.6 thence an East and West line to E.11.c.7.6.

    Between Centre and Left Brigades:- Front line at F.6.a.3.4 - trench and road crossing F.5.b.7.5 - South of MEAL TRENCH (inclusive to Left Brigade) to F.5.a.0.8 ~~thence due West.~~ F.3.A.6.2 (LILY LANE inclusive to Centre Brigade) F.2.B.8.5 - F.1.B.2.2 thence

    These boundaries are shown on the attached map 'A'. Due West.

2. <u>ORGANIZATION OF DEFENCES.</u>

    The defences in the Divisional area are organized as follows:-

    (a) <u>Front or Outpost Line</u> - consisting of

        (i) Front line with, in places, an observation line pushed out in front.

        (ii) Support and Reserve Lines.

    (b) <u>The Second or Purple System</u> - consisting of

        (i) Purple Front line, continuously dug and wired.

        (ii) Purple Support.

        (iii) QUESNOY FARM trenches.

        (iv) The Purple Reserve.

    (c) The AYETTE SWITCH running from the defences about F.10.d.5.7 to the Purple System at F.9.c.5.4.

    (d) The WINDMILL SWITCH. From the front system in F.8.b to the Purple System South of HENDECOURT.

    (e) <u>MONCHY SWITCH.</u> OLD BRITISH and OLD GERMAN FRONT LINES.

    (f) Third or Red System.

    > The Division is responsible for construction and maintenance of all defences in or East of the Purple Reserve. Trenches in the Purple System now being constructed under the C.E., VI Corps will be handed over to the Division when completed.
    > The Division is not responsible for defences in rear of the Purple System.

DEFENCE SCHEME   SECRET.

RIGHT DIVISION VI CORPS.   Copy No..........

1.   The front held by the Division is from F.23.a.0.6 to
     S.27.a.1.0.

     Right Boundary - F.23.a.0.6 – F.20.a.1.5 – E.24.b.05.65 –
                        E.24.a.3.7 – E.16.d.30.15.

     Left Boundary   - S.27.a.1.0 – S.27.a.0.1 – X.22.c.6.0 –
                        X.20.c.4.2 – W.21.c.9.3.

     Boundary between Right and Centre Brigades:- Front line at
     F.11.d.10.45 – F.10.d.6.6 – trench junction F.10.d.5.8 – thence
     along North of AYETTE AVENUE (inclusive to Right Brigade) to
     trench and road crossing at F.9.b.9.3 – F.9.c.7.6 thence an East
     and West line to E.11.c.7.6.

     Between Centre and Left Brigades:- Front line at F.6.a.3.4 –
     trench and road crossing F.5.b.7.5 – South of MEAL TRENCH
     (inclusive to Left Brigade) to F.5.a.0.2 – ~~thence due West.~~ F.3.A.6.2
     (LILY LANE inclusive to Centre Brigade) F.2.B.8.5 – F.1.B.2.2 thence
     These boundaries are shown on the attached map 'A'. Due West.

2. ORGANIZATION OF DEFENCES. *

     The defences in the Divisional area are organized as follows:-

     (a) Front or Outpost Line - consisting of

         (i) Front line with, in places, an observation line pushed
              out in front.

         (ii) Support and Reserve Lines.

     (b) The Second or Purple System - consisting of

         (i)   Purple Front line, continuously dug and wired.

         (ii) Purple Support.

         (iii) QUESNOY FARM trenches.

         (iv) The Purple Reserve.

     (c) The AYETTE SWITCH running from the defences about F.10.d.5.7
         to the Purple System at F.9.c.5.4.

     (d) The WINDMILL SWITCH. From the front system in F.8.b to
         the Purple System South of HENDECOURT.

     (e) MONCHY SWITCH. OLD BRITISH and OLD GERMAN FRONT LINES.

     (f) Third or Red System.

         * A Secret letter on this subject will be issued to
           Brigades, C.R.A. and M.G.Battalion.

                                                          P.T.O.

3. PROBABLE FORMS OF ATTACK.

It seems probable from recent experience that the enemy will avoid ADINFER WOOD in the case of an attack in strength.

The most probable forms of attack are -

(a) An attack with QUESNOY FARM Ridge as the objective, which would take place after the outpost troops of the Division on our right on HENLEY HILL had been driven in, and which would probably be combined with a large operation against ESSARTS.

(b) An attack against the high ground N. of AYETTE held by the Left Brigade.

The above might be combined with a movement up the COJEUL Valley between QUESNOY FARM Ridge and ADINFER WOOD, in order to penetrate the Purple Line and to threaten the QUESNOY FARM Ridge from the rear.

Indications of the enemy's intentions may be obtained from his gas shelling.

Special arrangements will be made by the Centre and Left Brigades to watch for and to report Yellow Cross gas shelling on ADINFER WOOD and the COJEUL Valley if an attack seems probable.

4. METHOD OF HOLDING THE LINE.

The front line is to be held as a fighting line from which there is to be no voluntary retirement.

In the event of an attack on the front line by -

(a) A raid.
(b) A local attack against some Tactical Feature,

the enemy is to be immediately counter-attacked by the supporting troops, and our line restored. Such counter-attack being made immediately, from the flanks, and from the support trenches if possible. Should the immediate counter-attack fail, a deliberate counter-attack will be organised from the troops in Divisional Reserve.

In the event of an attack with great weight bringing about a break through on a large scale, troops in supporting and reserve positions must hold their ground, and break up the enemy's attack by fire. It will be useless to fritter away supporting platoons by local counter-attacks.

Our attitude is not to become one of passive defence. Identifications must be frequently obtained by patrols. Schemes for raids must be prepared. The enemy must be harassed and caused loss by every possible means.

5. DISTRIBUTION OF TROOPS.

Divisional Headquarters - V.27.c.7.7, LA BAZEQUE.
Adv. Divisional H.Q. - old dugouts W.20.c.1.9 (Cars to W.19.c.9.3 - thence on foot along buried cable track).

Right Bde......

- 3 -

Right Brigade.   Headquarters - E.4.c.2.4.
                 2 Battns. forward system.
   Right Battn. H.Q. ~~F.15.c.2.1~~. Left Battn. H.Q. F.9.b.6.1.
      F.20.B.6.8
   1 Battn. Brigade Reserve, H.Q. E.5.d.4.3.

Centre Brigade.   Headquarters E.4.a.6.3.
                Battle H.Q. - E.5.d.3.3.
                2 Battns. forward system.
         (1 Battn. E. of DOUCHY. 1 Battn. in Support).
   Front Battn. H.Q. F.9.a.8.4. Support Bn. H.Q. F.1.c.0.0.
   1 Bn. in Divl. Reserve about MONCHY, H.Q., E.5.d.2.3.

Left Brigade.   Headquarters W.23.c.1.9.
                2 Battns. forward system.
   Right Battn. H.Q., X.27.b.9.5. Left Battn. H.Q. X.24.c.2.0.
   1 Battn. in Brigade Reserve H.Q., X.19.c.8.2.

      The dispositions of Battns. are shewn on attached map 'B'.

      In the Right and Left Brigade areas, 2 Battalions are allotted for the defence of the Front System. These Battalions are organised in depth. The Third Battalion in the Right and Left Brigade areas is definitely allotted for the defence of the Purple Line and will not be moved forward of the Purple Front Line without sanction from Divisional H.Q.

      In the Left Brigade area, the Reserve Coy. from each of the front Line Battalions is located in or about the Purple Line. If moved forward of the Purple Line owing to the tactical situation, these Coys. will be at once replaced from the Battn. in Brigade Reserve.

      In the Centre Brigade area, one Battn. situated in the trenches S. of MONCHY is in Divisional Reserve. Two Companies of the Support Battalion will be definitely considered as the garrison of the Purple System and will not be moved forward of the Purple Front Line without sanction from Divisional H.Q.

      The 2nd M.G. Battalion is disposed in depth, in groups which approximately correspond with the Brigade areas.

      As soon as certain reorganisation is completed, the fire from about 30 guns will be available to put down a barrage, either direct or indirect, for the defence of the Front Line. This barrage is designed to fill gaps in the Field Artillery barrage.

      The Field Artillery is organised in 3 Groups -

   Right Group, Headquarters E.5.d.25.30
   Centre   "   "   W.24.b.25.65
   Left   "   "   W.18.b.50.00

      The Battle H.Q. of the Groups is with the Infantry Brigade which they cover.
      The Batteries of each Group cover approximately the front of an Infantry Brigade.

Heavy T.Ms.   There are no Heavy T.Ms. in the area.

6" Newtons.   6" Newton Mortars are located as follows:-

   (a) In the front system - 2 in F.16.b., 2 in F.11.c.
                           and 4 at X.29.d.0.0.

   (b) In the second system - 4 in F.13.c., F.14.a., and
                        F.8.a.

                                   6.   <u>Action in case</u> ....

- 4 -

6. ACTION IN CASE OF A THREATENED ATTACK.

Right Brigade. The Reserve Coy. of the Left Battn. will occupy the AYETTE SWITCH from about the Purple Front Line to about the DOUCHY - BUCQUOY Road.

Left Brigade will move forward the Reserve Coy. of the Left front Battn. to WINDMILL SWITCH in X.29, getting touch with the Divn. on the left about X.23.c.4.0. This Coy. will be replaced, vide para.5.

The Battn. in Divisional Reserve will be prepared to move at short notice.

10/D.C.L.I. (Pioneers) will concentrate about MONCHY MILL SOUTH at their present billets, and will be prepared to move at short notice.

The Field Coys. R.E. will assemble as follows -

Namely 226th Field Coy. near 5 Bde. Headquarters.
5th and 483rd Field Coys. South of MONCHY.

under the orders of the C.R.E., and will be prepared to move at short notice.

Artillery.

If, owing to hostile artillery fire, or for any other reason, an enemy attack seems probable, the Artillery, both Heavy and Field, will open annihilating fire on the order of -

Divisional Headquarters
Divisional Artillery Headquarters.
Artillery Group Headquarters

and, in exceptional circumstances, Inf. Brigade Headquarters.

In order to deal with a surprise hostile attack, for the first 15 minutes annihilating fire will consist of fire on approx. S.O.S. lines at a slow rate, after which if no attack develops, guns will lift on to various targets, viz. Field Arty., occupied trenches and shell holes and places likely to be occupied or made use of in case of attack. Heavy Arty. (not engaged in counter-battery work) on likely points of concentration.

The Heavy Artillery S.O.S. lines on the Divisional front are arranged to fire on the valleys -

(a) Between A.13.d and A.2.d.
(b) Between A.19.d and A.9.d.

In the event of a heavy bombardment opening about 3 or 4 hours before dawn, gas shell will be put down in the above valleys which are likely places of assembly for the enemy, in order to delay and disorganize his troops while forming up.. This bombardment will be timed for about 3 hours before sunrise.

7. ANTI-TANK DEFENCE.

Anti-Tank guns are in position at:-

F.9.c.8.4.
F.14.b.0.5.
F.4.a.4.5.
X.23.a.1.1.

Anti-Tank trenches.....

Anti-Tank trenches have been dug across the roads at:-

        F.11.c.8.7.
        F.11.b.5.4.
        F.5.d.5.1.

8. **Sector Guides.**

    Brigades and 10/D.C.L.I. each provide 8 guides. These guides are intended to guide up reinforcing troops from the Red System to any part of the Divisional Sector in the case of guides from the 10/D.C.L.I. and in their own Brigade areas, in the case of guides provided by Brigades.

    Capt. R.G.FINLAY, Divisional Headquarters, is the Sector Guide Commandant.

    Brigades and 10/D.C.L.I. are ready to furnish guides as above at short notice.

9. **Action of Working Parties.**

    In the event of an enemy attack, Infantry working parties will place themselves under the orders of the nearest Company or Battn. Commander, who will be responsible that as soon as the situation permits the parties are sent back to their own units.

    Men of the 174th Tunnelling Coy. will be sent to rejoin their unit.

10. **Anti-Aircraft Defence.**

    (a) The Anti-Aircraft Sections are responsible for defence against enemy aircraft at a height exceeding 3000 feet.

    (b) Below 3000 feet, Commanders OF UNITS are responsible for their own defence. For this purpose Vickers or Lewis Guns should be placed in pairs, each pair when possible being about 1000 yds. apart.

    (c) Should the enemy use low flying aeroplanes with which to engage the attention of trench garrisons so as to cover an attack, all ranks must understand that the garrisons of the front trenches will engage the hostile infantry while the troops in support and reserve deal with the hostile aeroplanes.

    (d) Enemy aircraft will not be engaged with Rifle or Machine Gun fire unless the markings are recognisable, and the struts of the aeroplane are visible to the naked eye.
        At night only when -
        (i) The aeroplane can be seen against the sky, or
        (ii) The struts can be seen when the aeroplane is in the beam of a searchlight.

    (e) Certain 18-pdr. guns are detailed to engage low flying aeroplanes with a false angle of sight on S.O.S. lines. The call for this will be "Aeroplane attack".

11. **S.O.S. Signals.**

    (a) The S.O.S. Signal from July 4th is a Rifle Grenade bursting into GREEN over GREEN.
    The S.O.S. Signal for the Division on our Right (IV Corps) is a Rifle Grenade bursting into RED over GREEN over RED.

    (b) The S.O.S. Signal fired from a reconnoitring aeroplane is a red parachute light meaning -
        "The enemy is advancing to the assault".

E.R. Clayton
Lieut-Colonel,
General Staff, 2nd Division.

July 4th 1918.

2ND DIVISION DEFENCE SCHEME.

APPENDIX "A"   ARTILLERY

1. ARTILLERY POLICY.

Main positions will be kept well to the rear, and one or two guns per battery forward. Every possible effort will be made not to disclose Main positions, and all sniping and harassing fire etc- will be done from the forward positions - the guns being moved about if found by the enemy.

Each Main Battery position will have a "Home" O.P. near it, with telephone wire laid to it, and arrangements should be made for the siting of Battery Lewis guns and rifles for close defence.

Each Battery will also have an alternative position reconnoitred, and as far as possible prepared for occupation.

2. ANTI-TANK DEFENCE.

The defensive arrangements in this area consist of :-
(a) 4 Single 18-pdr. guns in the forward area. 300 rounds per gun are ~~will be~~ maintained at each ~~18-pr~~ position, ~~and great care should be taken to see that the parts of the gun and all ammunition etc. are kept in good order.~~

(b) Guns run out from Battery positions (arrangements to be made beforehand) to engage tanks that have broken through the first defences.

(c) One 18-pr. Battery of the Brigade in Mobile Reserve at POMMIER.

3. LIAISON ARRANGEMENTS.

The Divisional Front is held by three Infantry Brigades, each supported by a Field Artillery Group. Group Commanders are responsible for keeping the closest touch with their Infantry Brigades. In cases where the Group Headquarters and Infantry Brigade Headquarters are not at present sited together, the Battle Headquarters of the Artillery Group H.Q. will be the same as that of the Infantry Brigade H.Q. with which they are affiliated. The occupation of this H.Q., testing Communications etc. etc., should be practised.

A Liaison Officer will be provided with each battalion H.Q. under Group arrangements.

A Heavy Artillery Group (consisting of ~~two~~ mixed Brigades) is affiliated to this Division, and in addition, Field Artillery Groups have direct wires to certain Heavy Batteries who fire on their front.

Two Batteries of 6-inch Newton Trench Mortars are in action on the Divisional Front.

4. S.O.S.

The S.O.S. signal or message will only be sent when the enemy is actually advancing to attack our trenches. It will be sent through every available means of communication in addition to the rocket; the latter signal being continued till answered by the guns.

2ND DIVISION DEFENCE SCHEME APPENDIX "A" (Continued).   Page 2.

S.O.S. (continued)

It will be passed on in the following order by Stations receiving it :-
(1) Batteries.
    (a) To Batteries on their flanks.
    (b) To Brigade Headquarters.

(2) Groups.
    (a) To their Batteries.
    (b) To Groups on both flanks.
    (c) To Divisional Artillery Headquarters.

(3) *Divisional Artillery*
    (a) To Groups.
    (b) To Heavy Artillery Group affiliated to Division.
    (c) To Divisional Artilleries on flanks.
    (d) To Division "G"
    (e) To Corps R.A.

On receipt of the Signal or message all guns and Trench Mortars covering the front attacked will at once open fire on their S.O.S. lines at rates as follows:-

	18-prs.	4.5"Hows.
First 5 minutes	INTENSE	RAPID
Next 5 minutes	NORMAL	RAPID
Next 20 minutes	SLOW	NORMAL

Then Stop unless signal is repeated.

Ammunition....18-prs......75% Shrapnel, 25% H.E.
            4.5" Hows....106 Fuze.

The Divisional front is divided into 3 S.O.S. sections, reading from Right to Left, each S.O.S. section corresponding to a Brigade front.
S.O.S. Code words will be as under :-

    99th Infantry Brigade front.........QUESNOY.
    6th Infantry Brigade front.........AYETTE.
    5th Infantry Brigade front.........OSTRICH.

The terms "Right" "Centre" and "Left" will only be used to refer to the three Divisions in the Corps. Thus "S.O.S. RIGHT" means an attack on the whole 2nd Divisional front; and "S.O.S. QUESNOY" means an attack on the 99th Infantry Brigade front.

5. ANNIHILATING FIRE.

Annihilating fire will be carried out by both Field and Heavy Artillery should there be indications that the enemy is about to attack. It will consist of bursts of Normal or Rapid fire (for not more than 10 minutes continuously) searching all hidden approaches and likely places of assembly to a depth of 2,000 yards from our line. All batteries will return periodically to their S.O.S. Lines.

For the first 15 minutes, this fire will be directed on or near S.O.S. lines.

The following procedure will be adopted on the opening of an intense Hostile Bombardment :-
All guns and howitzers open on S.O.S. lines at rapid rate for 15 minutes. Heavy Artillery howitzers S.O.S. lines to be continuous just beyond Field Artillery S.O.S. lines.

                                                  From plus 15....

                                                      To page 3.

2nd DIVISION DEFENCE SCHEME. (Appendix "A")   PAGE 2 A

6. COUNTER PREPARATION AND ANNIHILATING FIRE.

(a) As soon as there are indications that the enemy is preparing for an offensive, counter measures begin, and orders will be issued for increased C.B. work and harassing fire, and concentrations on T.M. positions etc. etc.

(b) <u>Counter-Mortar Bombardment.</u> Should the date of the enemy's attack be learned beforehand, a bombardment of likely T.M. positions will be ordered to take place on the previous night probably before midnight. This bombardment will consist of 2 periods of 20 minutes each at Normal rates, with an interval of 30 minutes in between the periods. Zero hour for beginning of first period will be notified by Divisional Headquarters.

Ammunition.   All Howitzers :-   50% 106   18-pounders 75% H.E.
                                  25% Delay   25% Shrap.
                                  25% Non-delay.

Mustard Gas shell will be used for the first period if available and weather conditions are suitable.

Field Artillery will search the whole area within 600 yards of our front line, and the Heavy Artillery the area from 600 yards to 1200 yards from our front line.

(c) <u>Annihilating Fire.</u> The primary object of annihilating fire is to crush the enemy's infantry while they are assembling or after they have assembled before their assault. It may be put down by order of the Corps, Div.H.Q., Div.Arty.H.Q., or R.F.A.Group H.Q. in conjunction with the Infantry Brigadier. The time to open fire will be judged by the intensity of the enemy's bombardment or from information received of an impending attack.

The area from our front line of outposts to a depth of 1500 yards (extended in the centre of the area to include the Valley N.W. of COURCELLES) will be thoroughly searched by Field and Heavy Artillery according to the belts shown on S.O.S.Map, attached.

The following procedure will be adopted when Annihilating Fire is ordered :- All guns and howitzers will open on their S.O.S.Lines for ten minutes at Normal rate searching back to the boundary of their annihilating fire belt. After the first ten minutes, the Field Arty. will continue to search their belt by a series of creeping barrages each of ten minutes duration at a Normal rate, paying special attention to any likely assembly places.

The series of barrages should cover the whole Group sector, each barrage being concentrated on selected areas by the Group Commander. Ammunition expenditure to average 40 rounds per gun (50% A; 50% AX) and 30 rounds per 4.5" How. (75% 106 and 25% Non-delay) per hour.

<u>Heavy Artillery.</u> The Heavy Artillery will search their belt by a series of creeping barrages each of from 15 to 20 mins. duration at Normal rate, omitting the area more than 1500 yards from our outpost line as far as the beginning of the valley N.W.of COURCELLES Special attention will be given to this valley, and the valley just E. of MOYBLAIN TRENCH, and hostile works and approaches.

During the pauses between the bursts immediate advantage must be taken of opportunities seen from the air or by ground observers. Unless engaging an important target all guns and howitzers will return to S.O.S.Lines after each burst.

(d) <u>Gas Bombardment.</u> If weather conditions are suitable a Gas Bombardment will be opened 2 hours before sunrise by all 4.5" and 6" Hows., and 60-prs. on the Valley N.W.of COURCELLES.
    Expenditure :- 4.5" Howitzers 350 rounds per battery
                    6"   ,,   300   ,,   ,,
                    60-prs. Any gas shell still available.

2ND DIVISION DEFENCE SCHEME - APPENDIX "A" (Continued)   Page 3

From plus 15 onwards :- *Field Arty in Back positions*

6 bursts of Intense Fire per hour; duration 3 minutes each searching up to 1,200 yards beyond our Outpost line.

Forward Field Guns and Heavies.

6 bursts of Intense Fire per hour, duration 3 minutes each searching from 1,200 yards beyond our Outpost line up to extreme range of guns, paying special attention to selected valleys.

At plus 1½ hours, and every ¾ of an hour after, gas bombardment of the valley N.W. of COURCELLES for 15 minutes.

All guns return to their S.O.S. lines after each burst.

Searching fire will be carried out by Batteries independent.

Gas bombardment will be synchronised by O.C.Heavy Arty. Group

6. O. Ps.

A sufficient number of O.Ps. will be manned by each Group by day and night to ensure the whole front being kept under continual observation.

All O.Ps. will be provided with a pointer and dial and Map board.

All O.Ps. manned by night will be provided with a rifle and a supply of rifle-grenade S.O.S. rockets, which will be used to pass on messages or signals from the front line. Each Battery position will have a "Home" O.P. near it with telephone wire laid to it.

7. AMMUNITION SUPPLY.

(a) Dumps of Ammunition will be maintained as follows :-

Calibre.	Rds. per gun at occupied gun positions.			Rds. per gun at Divl. A.R.P.
	H.E.	Shrap	Gas	
18-pr.	115	335	-	200
4.5" How.	350	-	500 per Batty.	200
18-pr A.Tk.	150	150		

(b) Ammunition is brought up by railway to sidings at:-

W 29 c 7.7
W 23 c 7.8
W 12 d 6.3

The two Divisional A.R.Ps. are on the POMMIER - ST AMAND and POMMIER - LA CAUCHIE roads, and ammunition can be drawn from these at any time by horse transport.

(c) The daily allotment of ammunition to be expended is:-

18-prs....24 rounds per gun per diem - Shrapnel.
16 rounds per gun per diem - H.E.
4.5" Hows 40 rounds per How per diem.
50% of the above should be fired by night as harassing fire

To Page 4.

Page 4.

2ND DIVISION DEFENCE SCHEME   APPENDIX "A" (Continued)

8. HARASSING FIRE ZONES.

    (a) Southern Boundary - F.25.a.0.6 - F.23.b.0.0. A.21.a.0.0.
    (b) Between Right & Centre Groups   F.11.d.4.5.- A.9.c.0.0.
    (c) Between Centre & Left Groups   F.6.a.3.4. - A.10.a.0.0.
    (d) Northern Boundary S.27.a.1.0. A.3.a.0.7 A.5.c.0.0.

9. ORDERS FOR BATTERY IN MOBILE RESERVE.

    Orders for movement and employment of Anti-Tank Battery will come from 2nd Divisional Artillery Headquarters.

    Positions and O.Ps. to cover the whole Divisional Front will be reconnoitred, together with routes to them, and these should be known to all Officers and N.C.Os. The Battery will not be brought into action East of a line passing through W 23 d centra. - E 17 c central, and against Tanks should be employed by disperse sections.

    The Battery will be prepared to turn out at the shortest notice, and during periods of special readiness will stand to one hour before sunrise daily until it is clear that no attack is impending.

    When a hostile attack begins or is indicated by a heavy bombardment, the Battery will at once harness up and hook in, and an officer will be sent to report to Right Group H.Q. The Battery will rendezvous near Track "A" about square W 28 c.

10. DEFENCE OF REAR LINES.

    Artillery positions and O.Ps. have been chosen to cover every defensive system back to G.H.Q. line (inclusive).

    In the event of a sudden hostile attack driving us back to the Second (PURPLE) system, it will be impossible to withdraw the forward guns and sections which can give great moral and material support to our infantry at this time. When all ammunition has been fired, these guns will, if possible, be destroyed, sight and breech fittings removed, and detachments withdrawn.

    The majority of the guns and howitzers at present in action can cover the Second (PURPLE) system from their present positions but will be withdrawn in succession under Group arrangements to their PURPLE positions as soon as possible after it is known for certain that we have been driven out of our first system.

    Zones should be allotted beforehand for S.O.S.Lines to cover the PURPLE Line, and these should be arranged if possible with a view to leaving no important points uncovered during the withdrawal to PURPLE positions.

    PURPLE and RED line positions and O.Ps. should be reconnoitred beforehand by as many officers and N.C.Os. as possible.

    Orders re ammunition supply for those positions will be issued later.

To Page 5.

Page 6.

2ND DIVISION DEFENCE SCHEME.   APPENDIX "A" (Continued)   LOCATIONS ETC., ETC.

UNIT	NUMBER OF GUNS.	LOCATION	ARC OF FIRE.	O. Ps.	S.O.S. LINES	WAGON LINES	REMARKS.
H.Q.R.A.	-	V 27 a 5.1	-	-	-	V 27 a 5.7	
RIGHT GROUP	Lieutenant-Colonel A.A.GOSCHEN, D.S.O., R.F.A., Commanding.						
36th Brigade R.F.A.	H.Q.	E 4 c 25.30	-	X 27 d 00.75 TOM TIT	-	ST AMAND.	
15th Battery	4 (S) 2	E 6 a 51.62 F 1 d 28.35	30°–160° 50°–115°	X 27 d 70.45 APPLE	F 23 a 7.8–F 17 c 8.5	D 15 b 7.5 W 29 d 2½25	Rear Adv.
48th Battery	5 (S) 1 Anti-Tank	E 5 d 25.55 F 2 d 40.50 F 9 c 86.42	73°–133° 74°–134°	X 27 d 70.45 APPLE	F 17 c 8.5–F 17 d 1.5 F 17 b 4.0	D 15 b 7½.70 E 4 b 3½.35	Rear Adv.
71st Battery	4 (S) 2 1 Anti-Tank	E 18 a 15.60 F 2 c 6 . 2 F 14 b 0.5	71°–111° 1,950°–138° 1,67°–134°	F 10 c 05.55 DORIS	F 23 a 7.8–F 17 c 2.5	ST AMAND W 28 c	Rear Adv.
D/36th Battery Howitzers.	4 2	E 11 c 59.00 F 9 a 10.88	500–1250 930–1830	*F 9 b 9.1 DOORPOST	F 23 e 7.8–F 17 c 8.5 F 17 d 3.0	ST AMAND	
"T" Batty.R.H.A	5 1	X 25 b 28.56 F 4 a 7.0	840–1640 115–1550	∅ F 17 c 1.5 STYLO	F 17 d 1.5–F17 b 3.0– F 17 b 1.7	W 16 a central	

* Used when necessary   ∅ Used by F.O.O. when required.

P.T.O.

Page 6

2ND DIVISION   DEFENCE SCHEME   APPENDIX "A" (Continued)   LOCATIONS ETC. ETC.

UNIT.	NUMBER OF GUNS.	LOCATION	ARC OF FIRE	O. Ps.	S.O.S. LINES	WAGON LINES	REMARKS
CENTRE GROUP - Lieutenant-Colonel P. BAXTON, D.S.O., R.F.A., Commanding.							
41st Brigade R.F.A. H.Q.		E 5 c 85.75	-	X 27 c 75.50			
9th Battery	4 (S)	X 25 d 50.80	95°-160°	X 27 c 75.50	F 11 d 3.0-F 11 d 7.5	D 9 c 30.20	Rear
	2	X 23 c 40.20	143°-196°	F 1 a 40.25		E 2 c 30.60	Adv.
				X 29 a 7.6		D 10 c 80.20	Rear
				F 5 b 80.15		W 21 b 20.20	
16th Battery	4 (S)	X 25 c 03.57	95°-135°	X 27 c 75.50	F 11 d 7.5 - F 12 c 2.8	E 2 c 30.40	
	2	F 2 d 3.2	80°-150°	F 17 c 1.4 SEXLO			
17th Battery	5 (S)	X 20 b 11.95	95°-187°	X 27 c 75.50	F 6 c 45.00-F 8 c 4.3	W 25 b 2.2	Rear
	1	X 28 a 85.30	95°-170°	X 20 b 70.35		W 18 a 70.30	Adv.
37th Battery (Howitzers)	6	X 25 b 90.00	90°-145°	X 27 c 75.50	4, F 12 c 2.3-F 12 a 4.1	D 15 a 00.30	Rear
					2, F 12 c 4.9-F 12 c 5.8	W 29 a 5.8	Adv.

Page 7

2ND DIVISION DEFENCE SCHEME. (Continued) LOCATIONS ETC. ETC.

UNIT	NUMBER OF GUNS.	LOCATION	ARC OF FIRE.	O. Ps.	S.O.S. LINES	WAGON LINES	REMARKS
LEFT GROUP. - Lieutenant-Colonel, C. F. PARRY, D.S.O., R.F.A., Commanding.							
34th(A) Bde.H.Q. R.F.A.		W 18 a 50.00		≠ A 1 b 20.80 PAINT.	—	W 18 a 50.00	
70th Battery	4 (S) 2	X 27 a 25.35 X 23 d 40.75	87°-112° 98°-163°	A 1 b 20.80 PAINT.	S 27 c 0.2 - 85.90	GAUDIEMPRE W 17 d 20.30	Rear
56th Battery (Howitzers)	/ 1.7 4 (S) 2	X 29 a 48.30 X 15 d 80.30 X 23 c 71.20	94°-172° 105°-176°	A 1 b 20.80 PAINT	S 27 c 35.50-S 27 c 85.90	GAUDIEMPRE X 18 c 20.30	Rear Adv.
14th(A) Bde.H.Q. R.H.A.		W 24 b 25.63				W 24 a 2.7	
"L" Battery	4 (S) 2 1 A-Tank	X 25 b 50.72 X 20 a 15.00 X 28 c 20.75	87°-158° 79°-148°	* X 21 a 38.55 PIG & WHISTLE * X 21 a 80.80	A 1 d 50.95 - A 2 a 70.10	D 9 c 6090	
400th Batty.	4 (S) 2	X 26 a 11.79 X 20 a 15.00	91°-153° 79°-148°		A 2 a 70.10 - A 2 b 40.40	D 9 d 30.40	
401st Batty. (Howitzers)	4 2	X 19 d 68.73 X 28 a 70.50	100°-150° 95°-184°	ø X 27 c 30.50 SUNSHINE ø X 28 c 2080 LORD NELSON	A 3 a 00.50 - A 3 c 50.80 S 27 c 35.30 -S 27 c 50.50	D 10 a 40.30 W 23 d 20.50	Rear Adv.

* Left Group O.Ps.   1 ≠ 34th Bde. O.P.   ø 14th Bde. O.Ps.

Page 7a.

2ND DIVISION DEFENCE SCHEME, APPENDIX "A" (Continued) LOCATIONS ETC.

UNIT	LOCATION	WAGON LINES	REMARKS.
78th (A) Brigade R.F.A. (Headquarters) LA CAUCHIE (V 17 b 9.0)		W 13 b 9.9	Mobile
"A" Battery	W 13 b 6.6	W 13 b 6.6	Reserve.
"B" Battery	W 13 d 3.8	W 13 d 3.8	
"C" Battery (Mob. Anti Tank)	W 13 c 6.9	W 13 c 6.9	
"D" Battery	W 19 a 4.6	W 19 a 4.6	
D.A.C.& 3 Sections	GAUDIEMPRE	GAUDIEMPRE	
14th (A) Bde.Am.Col	GAUDIEMPRE	GAUDIEMPRE	
.. Adv.Section	W 28 a 8.8	W 28 a 8.8	
34th (A) Bde.Am.Col.	GAUDIEMPRE	GAUDIEMPRE	
76th (A) Bde.Am.Col.	GAUDIEMPRE	GAUDIEMPRE	
"B A N G" Dump.	LA CAUCHIE ROAD (V 24 d 9.7)		
"W H I Z Z" Dump	POMMIER ST AMAND ROAD (D 6 b 5.8)		

2ND DIVISION DEFENCE SCHEME —— APPENDIX "A" —— MUTUAL SUPPORT.

SECTOR ATTACKED	CODE CALL	ACTION TAKEN BY	NATURE OF SUPPORT
Left of IV Corps	Help IV Corps	RIGHT GROUP	3, 18-pr Btties.Fire on S.O.S.Lines F 23 a 7.8 - F 17 b 40 F 17 o 95.95 1, 4.5" How.Bty. F 23 d 5.0 - F 23 d 5.9
Right of VI Corps	Help QUESNOY	Left Div.Arty. IV Corps.	3, 18-pr Btties.Fire on S.O.S.Lines F 23 b 0.0-F17 c 9.1 1, 4.5" How.Bty.Fire on Sunken Road in F 17 d 1.0-F 17 d 1.5
RIGHT GROUP	Help QUESNOY	Centre Group.	3, 18-pr Btties.Fire on Line F 17 b 4.0-F 11 d 5.0 1, 4.5"How.Bty.Fire on Line F 17 b 7.0-F 11 d 8.0
		Right Group	3, 18-pr Btties.Fire. F 17 b 5.0 — F 17 b 4.9 1, 18-pr Btty. F 17 b 3.0 — F 17 b 1.7 1, 4.5" How.Bty. F 11 d 5.0 — F 12 c 0.7
CENTRE GROUP	Help AYETTE.	Left Group	2, 18-pr.Btties. F 12 a 4.4 — F 6 a 5.0
LEFT GROUP	Help OSTRICH	Centre Group.	3, 18-pr Btties. F 6 c 40.46 — A 2 a 46.43 1, 4.5" How.Bty A 1 d 0.6 — A 1 d 9.8.
LEFT GROUP	Help LINCOLN	Centre Div.Arty.VI Corps	3, 18-pr Btties.Fire on Front A 2 a 0.0-S 27 d 0.0 1, 4.5" How.Bty. ", Line 100 yards beyond above.
Right of CENTRE DIVISION.	Help DOVER	Left Group.	2, 18-pr Btties.Enfilade from S 27 d 0.0 - S 28 c 0.0 1, 4.5"How.Bty. Bombard N.E. end of MOYENNEVILLE. 8.29.c.6.6 1, 4.5"How.Bty. Bombard S.W. end of MOYENNEVILLE.

2ND DIVISION DEFENCE SCHEME - TRENCH MORTARS - APPENDIX "A" (Continued)

UNIT	NUMBER OF GUNS.	LOCATION	ZERO LINES	O. Ps.	S.O.S. LINES	REMARKS	WAGON LINES
D.T.M.O.	-	V 27 a 5.1					POMMIER
X/2 T.M. Battery.	H.Q.	F 2 d 30.25	135°Grid	Front Line Posts, according to target	F 6 c 40.30-F 6 c 60.35		
	1.	F 5 a 95.80	143°Grid		F 6 c 40.30-F 6 c 60.35		
	1.	F 5 a 95.80	128°Grid		A 2 d 20.20		
	1.	S 26 c 10.20	96°Grid		A 3 b 80.40		
	1.	S 26 c 10.20	178°Grid				
	* 1.	S 26 c 10.20	104°Grid			* Spare Bed.	
	** 1.	F 11 b 05.85	164°Grid				
	1.	X 27 b 30.55	102°Grid			For defence of PURPLE LINE.	
	1.	X 27 b 30.55					
Y/2 T.M. Battery.	H.Q.	F 2 d 30.25	139°Grid	Front line Posts according to Target.	1 & 4 - { F 17 c 80.35 to F 17 d 10.50		POMMIER
	1.	F 16 b 40.75	92°Grid				
	1.	F 16 b 40.75	92°Grid				
	1.	F 18 b 40.75	139°Grid				
	1.	F 11 c 10.70	89°Grid		2 & 3 -F 11 d 40.25 to F 17 b 30.85	*Spare Bed.	
	* 1.	F 11 c 10.70	126°Grid			For defence of PURPLE LINE.	
	1.	F 2 d 30.25	76° Grid				
	1.	F 2 d 30.25					

Proposed and under Construction (7th Aug.1918).

X/2 T.M.B.	H.Q.	F 3 d 65.40	To replace H.Q. as above.	Under construction.
	4 Beds.	X 27 a 5.3	Approximate only. For defence of PURPLE Line.	Proposed.
	2 Beds.	S 25 b 20.30	For defence of AERODROME Switch	Under construction.
Y/2 T.M.B.	H.Q.	F 3 d 65.40	To replace H.Q. as above.	
	2 Beds.	F 13 b 70.10	For defence of PURPLE Line.	Under construction.
	2 Beds.	F 2 d 10.20	For defence of PURPLE Line.	Under construction.

Page 10.

2ND DIVISION SCHEME   APPENDIX "A" Continued.

POSITIONS FOR DEFENCE OF PURPLE LINE.

GROUP	No. of Position	Map Square	O. Ps.
RIGHT GROUP	PA.1	E 10 d 31.80	) Bde. O.P. F 13 c 35.00
	PA.2	E 10 c 89.83	)
	PA.3	E 10 b 61.15	) In Trench about
	PA.4	E 10 c 79.09	) E 18 d 8.4
	PB.1	E 5 c 24.63	) Bde. O.P. F 13 c 0.0
	PB.2	E 4 d 09.98	)
	PB.3	E 4 d 60.62	) Front Line F 14 a.
	PB.4	E 5 c 37.56	)
CENTRE GROUP	PE.1	W 23 b 78.48	F 1 c 2.1
	PE.2	W 23 b 91.60	F 8 b 3.7
	PE.3	W 24 a 30.01	E 6 central.
	PE.4	W 23 a 68.89	E 11 b 0.6
	PC.1	W 23 c 06.27	)
	PC.2	W 23 c 20.40	) About E 13 a 5.5
	PC.3	W 23 c 31.65	) and E 12 c 5.5
	PC.4	W 22 d 70.43	)
LEFT GROUP	PD.1	W 24 b 16.01	) Bde O.P. X 15 c 0.9
	PD.2	W 29 b 44.80	)
	PD.3	W 23 d 70.20	) About X 22 c 1.4
	PD.4	X 19 c 28.84	)
	PF.1	W 27 b 09.73	)
	PF.2	W 28 a 23.81	) About F 7 d 65.90
	PF.3	W 28 a 77.83	) and X 16 d 1.8.
	PF.4	W 22 d 46.29	)

Page 11.

2ND DIVISION DEFENCE SCHEME   APPENDIX "A" Continued.

POSITIONS FOR DEFENCE OF RED LINE.

GROUP.	No. of Position.	Map Square	O. P.
RIGHT GROUP	Z.1 Z.2 Z.3 Z.4 Y.1 Y.2 Y.3 Y.4	D 9 b 12.20 D 16 a 38.65 D 9 c 47.88 D 15 a 74.78 D 10 c 92.23 D 3 d 70.00 D 10 d 69.66 D 10 c 40.75	))) VIPER E 7 central) VIXEN E 9 c 1.6) PEAR E 9 c 3.7) PUMA E 7 1 3.4) PLUM E 3 d 5.7)
Centre	W.1 W.2 W.3 W.4	D 5 a 35.63 D 5 b 08.77 D 6 c 58.75 D 5 c 50.53	)) PLUM E 3 d 5.7) SKUNK E 3 d 3.5)
LEFT GROUP	X.1 X.2 X.3 X.4	D 11 a 20.22 D 10 b 40.01 D 4 c 53.58 D 10 b 87.27	)) DAMSON E 2 b 7.4) BUFFALO W 25 b 7.8)

All positions have been resected.

2ND DIVISION DEFENCE SCHEME ----- APPENDIX "A" HEAVY ARTILLERY.

UNIT	MAP REFERENCE	CALIBRE	No. of Guns	ARCS OF FIRE	MAXIMUM RANGE, YARDS.	O. PS.	LANE	S.O.S. POINTS.	REMARKS.
SHERER'S GROUP	LA CAUCHIE.								
276 Siege Btty.	X 14 a 12.35 E 4 b 75.35	6" How. ,,	4 2	1, 110-159 Grid 1, 84-148 Grid 2, 101-148 Grid 1, 80-150 ,, 1, 80,180 ,,	9,600 9,600 9,600 8,900 8,600	DOVE X 21 a 5.6	17	A 3 5.0- 5.9 A 5 a 5.0- 5.5	Day
336 Siege Btty.	2, W 22 d 55.30 4, X 13 d 4.6	6" How.	2 4	1, 85-155 ,, 1, 85-155 ,, 4, 97-150 ,,	9,400 8,950 8,400	PIGEON X 21 a 00.45 Day.	16	2, A 2 c 5.0-5.5 4, A 2 d 5.0-5.9	
342 Siege Btty.	X 19 b 00.05	6" How.	4	4, 90-150 ,,	9,300 9,600 9,200 9,530	QUAIL. F 13 c 95.90 Day.	15	4, A 8 c 0.0-0.9	
183 Siege Btty.	W 30 a 80.75	6" How.	4	2, 80-140 ,, 2, 80-140 ,,	9,500 9,400	GOOSE X 21 a 45.80 Day & Night.	14	4, A 7 d 5.0-5.9	
305 Siege Btty.	W 29 d 75.20	6" How.	4	1, 75-155 ,, 1, 94-180 ,, 1, 78-153 ,, 1, 87-155 ,,	9,600 8,500 9,800 9,600	PLOVER F 10 a 0.5 Day.	13	4, A 13 c 0.0-0.9	
136 Siege Btty.	E 5 b 20.90 E 8 b 95.30	9.2"How.	2 4	1, 79-139 ,, 1, 81-141 ,, 1, 76-136 ,, 1, 76-136 ,, 1, 74-134 ,, 1, 78-136 ,,	10,150 10,150 9,450 10,150 9,550 9,835	TOM TIT X 27 d 65.78 Day and Night	12 & 11	F c F 6,A 18 & 5.9- A 24 aa 5.0.	

Page 12

2ND DIVISION DEFENCE SCHEME ------ APPENDIX "A" HEAVY ARTILLERY (Continued)

PAGE 15.

UNIT	MAP REFERENCE	CALIBRE	No. of Guns.	ARCS OF FIRE	MAXIMUM RANGE.	O. Ps.	LANE	S.O.S. POINTS.	REMARKS.
34th Siege Battery.	X 7 b 70.20	9.2 How.	2	112-172 Grid	12,800		17	A 4 e 5.0-5.9	
24 Heavy Battery.	X 7 c 82.16	60-pdr.	4	85-145 "	See Remarks.	ALBATROSS X 15 d 16.13 Day & Night.	16	2, A 3 c 0.0-0.9	2 crh S.9500
	E 8 c 95.95	"	2	80-140 "	"		15	2, A 8 b 5.0-5.9	2 crh HE 11100
							14	2, A 8 d 0.0-0.9	6 crh S.12000
									8 crh HE 12500
152 Heavy Battery.	X 13 c 58.37	"	4	90-150 "	"	KITE X 20 b 95.40 Day & Night.	13	2, A 14 a 5.0-5.9	As above.
							12	2, A 14 c 0.0-0.9	2 crh S 9,200
	E 4 d 50.85	"	2	0-380 "	"		11	2, A 19 c 5.0-5.9	2 crh HE 11400
									8 crh S 9,800
									8 crh HE 12800
77 Siege Battery.	W 30 a 25.25	8" How.	4	75-145 "	11,700	COCKATOO X 15 d 41.12 Day.	14	2, A 9 d 5.0-5.9	2 crh S 9,100
	E.5 a 6.5	"	2	75-145 "	11,700		13	2, A 15 a 5.0-5.9	2 crh HE 11100
	M 27 c 67.80						12	2, A 14 d 5.0-5.9	8 crh S 9,600
									8 H.E 12,200

Southern boundary of Lane 11 is the E. and W Grid running through A 20 central, each lane is 500 yards broad.

2ND DIVISION DEFENCE SCHEME - AEROPLANE CALLS.

AEROPLANE CALL	MEANING	ANSWERED AS UNDER		
		Under Normal conditions of Trench Warfare.	During Annihilating fire	During Barrage Fire.
N.F.	Hostile Battery now firing	10 rds. per gun RAPID, to be fired by all active 4.5" Howitzers.	10 rds. per gun RAPID to be fired by at least half the guns per position covering Group Zone.	Not answered.
G.F.	Fleeting target not of sufficient importance to warrant a heavy concentration of fire.	5 rds. per gun RAPID from all active guns and 4.5" Hows. that fire on that Zone.	5 rds. per gun RAPID to be fired by at least half the guns per position covering Group Zone.	One gun per position or one section per Battery.
L.L.	A really important fleeting target, such as, a Battery limbered up and halted, an Inf.Battn. or a Cavalry regiment.	5 rds. per gun RAPID, from all active guns and 4.5" Hows. that can reach.	5 rds. per guns RAPID from all guns and 4.5" Howitzers that can reach.	One gun per position or one section per Battery.

1. In all cases, when necessary, the call will be repeated from the air, and the procedure repeated by the guns.
2. In no cases are guns or howitzers to be taken off vulnerable and important targets on which they are obtaining visibly good effect, in order to engage another target reported by the R.A.F. or any other source of information.

2nd Division Defence Scheme   Appendix B

ARRANGEMENTS FOR MANNING THE PURPLE LINE.

1. The troops specially detailed for the defence of the Purple Line are

   Right Brigade - 1 Battn.
   Left   "   - 1 Battn.
   Centre   "   - 2 Coys. which are not to be moved
                    forward unless replaced from Bn.
                    in Div. Reserve vide 2nd Div.
                    Defence Scheme para.5.

   In addition, the troops which have been fighting in the outpost line will be available.

2. The most probable operations which the Battn. of the Centre Brigade in Divisional Reserve may be called upon to carry out are -

   (a) To reinforce troops holding the Purple Line.

   (b) To hold the Purple Reserve Line if required in 99th and 6th Bde. areas.

   (c) To counter-attack in Right Bde. area in order to restore the situation if part of QUESNOY Hill is lost.

   In case of heavy bombardment this Battn. will assemble about Old German front and reserve lines about E.11.b & d - E.12.a & c.
   Battns. of the Centre Brigade on coming into Div. Reserve will carry out the necessary reconnaissances of assembly positions and of lines of advance to the Purple Reserve Line and beyond. It would depend on circumstances whether the forming up place for the counter-attack was Purple Reserve Line, ADINFER WOOD SWITCH or QUESNOY FARM TRENCH.
   In battle the O.O. will either be at 6th Brigade Battle H.Q. or arrange for a liaison officer to be there so that messages can reach him at short notice from Div. H.Q.

3. In the event of the action outlined in para.2 being required, it is probable that the Battn. in Div. Reserve would either revert to G.O.C. 6th Brigade or come under orders of G.O.C. 99th Brigade.

4. In the event of the Purple Line being held as a front line, certain M.Gs. now about the Front Purple Line would eventually be replaced by Lewis Guns, in which case Reserve positions selected by O.C. M.G.Battn. would be occupied by the guns thus set free.

5. The position of H.Q. would be as follows:-

   Right Brigade - E.7.b.7.8.
                    Front line Bn. - E.18.c.8.1.
                    Two Battns.   - E.12.c.1.4.

   Centre Brigade - W.26.b.3.6.
                    Front line Bn. - F.1.c.1.2.
                    Two Battns   - E.5.d.2.3 & E.4.c.2.5.

   Left Brigade   - W.23.c.2.8.
                    Battn. H.Q. - W.19.d.2.2.
                                  W.19.c.4.1.
                                  W.24.a.2.0.

                                                    P.T.O.

5.   A proportion of the Artillery covering the Divisional front covers the Purple Line without change of position, viz -

   Right Group 21 guns 8" Hows.
   Centre   "   18   "   6"   "
   Left   "   18   "   8"   "

   These guns would, however, be moved at the first opportunity to more suitable positions in rear.
   The remainder of the artillery covering the Infantry of the Division cannot cover the Purple Line in the present position and would be withdrawn as early as possible to suitable positions.

6.   Inf. Brigades will include in their Defence Schemes definite plans for manning the Purple Line, showing parts of the line to be occupied, Lewis Gun emplacements, positions of Coy. and Battn. H.Q.

2nd Division Defence Scheme.　　　　　　　Appendix 'C'

ACTION OF TANKS.

1. A Company No.4 Battn. (Mark V) Tanks is located in the Divisional Area, about BIENVILLERS.

2. Mark V Tank is an improvement on Mark IV, being faster and more easily handled.

3. In case of the enemy breaking through the PURPLE LINE, the functions of the Tanks will be to break up his attack, independently of any Infantry action, and to prevent him from reaching the RED LINE.

4. On a heavy bombardment breaking out, or when a hostile attack seems likely, the Tank Coy. H.Q. moves to 99th Bde. H.Q., and a Liaison Officer proceeds to Advanced Div. H.Q.

   Communication between Advanced Div. H.Q. and Tank Coy. H.Q. is being arranged by 2nd Division Signal Coy.

5. If an enemy attack develops, Tanks may be ordered to "Man Battle Position" i.e. three Sections take up a line from about E.10.d to E.11.a. The fourth Section is in Reserve.

6. The order to "Man Battle Positions" is given by the Tank Coy. Commander, who will keep in touch with Advanced Div. H.Q. through his Liaison officer.
   The shortest time in which the Tanks can reach Battle positions from BIENVILLERS is one hour. From the Battle Position the Tanks move forward when ordered to meet the enemy.

7. The Tank Coy. Commander issues his orders to his Tanks independently. He is guided by the information obtained from Div. H.Q. as to whether to use his Tanks in the direction of the COJEUL VALLEY or of QUESNOY FARM. Reports received as to how the Tanks are being used will be communicated to Brigades.
   The guiding principle in the use of this Coy. of Tanks is that action must be taken without delay, before the enemy has time to bring up Artillery.
   It is therefore impossible to employ them for a deliberate counter-attack, but Infantry will seize any opportunity that is offered by the advance of the Tanks, to regain ground.

8. Tanks required to co-operate in a deliberate counter attack will be furnished from Reserve Tank Companies.

2nd Division Defence Scheme.   Appendix D

DEMOLITIONS.

1. In each Brigade Section, certain wells, bridges etc have been prepared for demolition.
   Lists are in the possession of the C.R.E.

2. At least one officer and a sufficient party of R.E. from the Coy. working in each Brigade Section are permanently told off as a demolition party.
   These parties are in charge of the maintenance and preparations of all demolitions in their areas.

3. Orders for demolitions to be carried out will be issued by Divisional H.Q., through the C.R.E. to Field Coys.
   The Field Coy. Commanders will keep Brigadiers informed of orders received regarding demolitions. It must, however, be recognized that it may be impossible to issue orders for demolitions during a battle, and action will usually have to be taken by the Commander on the spot.

4. The Division is responsible for preparation of demolitions East of and exclusive of the villages of ST AMAND - POMMIER - BERLES AU BOIS.

5. The C.R.E. will keep Brigadiers informed through Field Coy. Commanders of all demolitions prepared in their areas.

2nd Division Defence Scheme.

APPENDIX E.

ACTION IN CASE OF ENEMY SHELLING WITH YELLOW CROSS GAS.

1. In the event of shelling by Yellow Cross Gas, the following precautions will be at once taken :-

2. (a) All troops who are not actually required as part of a garrison will be moved to a flank out of the infected area into an area not likely to be infected.

   (b) The exact area into which troops will be moved must depend on the conditions at the time, but Commanding Officers will prepare schemes shewing areas into which troops under their Command may be moved. These schemes will be approved by Brigadiers and handed over on relief.

   (c) Alternative localities should be chosen to suit different directions of the wind. Woods, villages, and valleys will be avoided.

   (d) Where it is necessary to leave a garrison, this garrison should be relieved after five hours.

3. The Officer Commanding the troops in the infected area is responsible that sentries are posted on all approaches leading into the area, and that all traffic is diverted to windward.
   Sentries will have orders -

   (a) To warn all troops and transport entering the infected area: to divert them if possible.

   (b) To see that anyone entering the infected area puts on his gas mask.

   Brigade Gas Officers should be used to define the infected area.

   Sentries will be kept on until the area is declared clear (see para. 4).

   In the event of a relief, the sentry posts will be taken over by the relieving unit.

4. The Divisional Gas Officer will decide when sentries may be taken off an infected area.

5. The organisation of gas sentries in certain areas of the alert zone will be as follows :-

   (i) ADINFER WOOD. If ADINFER WOOD is shelled, sentries will be posted by the Reserve Battalion, Left Brigade on the N.W. side of the Wood and by Companies holding the PURPLE LINE on the S.E. side.

   (ii) MONCHY VILLAGE. If MONCHY village is shelled by Yellow Cross Gas, the responsibility for posting sentries is as follows :-

   (a) MONCHY - BERLES AU BOIS Roads - 5th Inf. Bde. H.Q.

   (b) MONCHY - RANSART 3 Roads) Troops of 6th Inf.
       MONCHY - ADINFER Road   ) Bde. in or near
       MONCHY - QUESNOY Fm. Road) MONCHY.

   (c) MONCHY - ESSARTS Road and
       MONCHY - HAMMESCAMPS Road - Reserve Batt. 6th Bde.

- (2) -

    (d) MONCHY - BIENVILLERS Road - H.Q. 6th Inf. Bde.

(iii) DOUCHY. Sentries to be found by a unit detailed by G.O.C. 6th Inf. Brigade.

(iv) COJEUL VALLEY. 6th Inf. Brigade (Squares E.12, F.7, 8, 3, and 9). To be found by a unit detailed by G.O.C. 6th Inf. Brigade.

(v) COJEUL VALLEY. 5th Inf. Brigade (Squares X.29, F.7, and 5, to be found by a unit detailed by G.O.C. 5th Inf. Brigade.

(vi) QUESNOY FARM. To be found by a unit detailed by 99th Inf. Brigade.

(vii) Valley South of ADINFER VILLAGE. To be found by a unit detailed by G.O.C. 5th Inf. Brigade.

(viii) O.G.L. South of MONCHY. To be found by a unit detailed by G.O.C. 99th Inf. Brigade.

2nd Division Defence Scheme.   Appendix F
------------------------------   ----------

DEFENCE AGAINST CLOUD GAS ATTACKS.

1. Standing Orders for Defence Against Gas are contained in "S.S.193" which will be adhered to.

2. Maps shewing the GAS ZONE boundaries in the VI Corps area were issued to all concerned on 21st April, 1918, under 2nd Division No. G.S.647/14.

3. METHOD OF SPREADING THE CLOUD GAS ALARM.

    In the case of an attack by Cloud Gas, the alarm is spread by all means available; by Strombos Horns, rattles, telephones, and, if necessary, by orderly.

    A system to warn sleeping men and detached parties is arranged by all formations, and sentries are posted over dug-outs.

    Warning of cloud gas attack will be sent by telephone by sending the letters "GAS" followed by the name of the trench, or stating locality, opposite which gas is being liberated. (Full instructions are given in "S.S.193" para.5 - also published as Appendix IV "S.S.534").

    The responsibility for sending telephone messages is as under:-

    Companies :- to Coys. on flanks including Coys. of other Divns., Battn, H.Q., and when possible, direct to the Artillery.

    Battalions :- to Battns. on flanks and all Coys., Bde. H.Q., and if possible, direct to Artillery.

    Brigades   :- to Brigades on flanks, all units in Bde. area, Div. H.Q., direct to Artillery, and any outside unit which is directly connected to the Bde. Signal Exchange.

    The Division will warn:-   VI Corps.
                               Div. Artillery.
                               H.A.Group.
                               Divisions on flanks.
                               A.P.M. (who will instruct police to warn traffic).
                               Town Major, BIENVILLERS.
                                    "   POMMIER.
                                    "   ST AMAND.
                                    "   GAUDIEMPRE.

4. Strombos horns are located as follows and they will not be moved without authority from Div. H.Q.:-

Right Brigade.

        Brigade H.Q. - E.4.b.0.5.   F.15.c.2.1.
                       F.16.b.9.6.   F.14.a.3.3.
                       F.16.d.7.9.   F.13.d.1.7.
                       F.22.b.9.9.   F.12.d.9.6.
                       F.10.d.2.5.   E.18.a.1.7.
                       F.16.c.9.2.
                       F.9.d.2.8.

                                                            P.T.O.

Centre Brigade.

Brigade H.Q. -   E.4.a.8.2.   F.10.b.4.8.
                 F.11.c.8.5.   F.9.a.7.4.
                 F.11.b.5.4.   F.2.d.9.7.
                 F.5.d.7.1.   F.1.d.3.4.
                 F.5.b.8.3.   E.5.d.4.4.
                 F.11.b.3.7.
                 F.11.c.6.9.

Left Brigade.

Brigade H.Q. -   W.23.c.1.9.   X.28.b.5.6.
                 S.26.d.7.5.   X.27.b.8.4.
                 S.26.a.7.4.   X.26.a.1.9.
                 X.30.c.7.2.   X.19.d.1.6.
                 X.30.a.8.0.   X.19.c.5.2.
                 X.24.c.2.0.   W.24.c.9.2.
                 X.29.d.2.3.   E.5.b.4.6.
                 X.29.a.7.5.

Back area.   E.2.c.8.8.   D.10.c.1.1.
                 W.25.c.3.9.   V.29.c.3.9.

5.   Twelve "Sound and Light" rockets are kept by the Area Commandant GAUDIEMPRE. These rockets will be used for the alarm both by day and night in addition to the telephone. On receipt of the gas alarm by whatever means, the rockets will be fired at half-minute intervals under arrangements to be made by the officer in charge of the station.

APPENDIX G

RIGHT DIVISION DEFENCE SCHEME.

COMMUNICATIONS.

Telephonic Communication

1. An Advanced Division Exchange is established at W.20.c.2.9 and an advanced R.A.Exchange is established at W.22.d.7.5.

2. Division H.Q. Exchange at V.27.c.7.9 is connected to Advanced Division exchange by 2 lines and Advanced Div.Exchange is connected to Advanced Div.R.A.Exchange by 2 lines.
    From Division H.Q. there is a direct line to each Brigade and each Brigade has a direct line to Advanced Div.Exchange.

3. Each Infantry Brigade and R.A.Group is connected direct to Brigade and Group on Left and Right and Division H.Q. is connected direct to Division on Left and Right.

4. Exchanges are established at HUMBERCAMP and POMMIER and connect all local units in those areas. These exchanges are connected to Division H.Q. by 2 lines and Advanced Div.exchange by 1 line. They are also connected to each other. (For details see Diagram A).

Buried Cables. *See Diagram "D".*

Buried cables 8 feet deep have been put down as follows:-

W.19.c.2.6	to	W.22.d.7.5	50 pairs.
W.22.d.7.5	to	F.1.a.9.1	50 pairs.
W.22.d.7.5	to	E.10.a.9.5	50 pairs.
W.22.d.7.5	to	X.21.b.9.6	50 pairs.

for part of the distance

By means of these, buried lines exist between:-

(1) Advanced Div., all Brigades and R.A.Groups.
(2) R.A.Groups and Batteries.
(3) Brigades and Battalions (for short distances)

In order to provide a buried cable route between Batteries and O.Ps it is proposed to bury between a point X.21.a.2.8 and the N. corner of ADINFER Wood.

German buries exist as follows:-

Left Brigade Area.
    X.21.b.6.2 - X.27.b.8.6   4 pairs.
    X.21.d.8.2 - X.23.a.1.1   2 pairs.
    X.23.a.1.1 - X.24.c.1.8   1 pair.
    X.21.d.8.2 - F.5.a.0.5   2 pairs (not yet finished)
    X.27.b.7.3 - X.28.b.7.3   16 pairs (not yet completely through)

Centre and Right Brigade Area.
    E.6.a.5.0 - F.7.a.5.4   1 pair.
    F.7.a.5.4 - F.7.b.8.7   2 pairs.
    F.7.b.8.7 - F.9.b.7.2   3 pairs.

There is also one line........

COMMUNICATIONS (Contd)

There is also one line which is made up out of various old German buries running from E.18.a.5.1 to F.14.d.5.2.

These buries are in use between Brigades and Battalions and Artillery and O.Ps.

Visual Communication.

Excellent visual communication is obtainable throughout the Divisional area. Brigade H.Q. are in touch with all Battalions by this means.

Division H.Q. is in touch with all Brigades and M.G. Battalion. 2 transmitting stations are in action, No.1 at farm D.6 central and No.2 at W.28.b.6.1. From this point all Brigades are obtained. This means can also be used by Artillery to their Group H.Qrs. (For details see Diagram B).

Wireless and Power Buzzer Communication.

Wireless stations are situated as follows:-

1. Division H.Q.   V.27.a.8.1
2. Left Brigade H.Q.   W.23.c.1.8
3. Right and Centre Bde H.Q.   E.4.a.6.4
4. Battn. H.Q. Left Bde.   X.27.b.8.5

Power Buzzers and Amplifiers - see attached Diagram C.

Pigeons.

8 pigeons are supplied to each Brigade daily and fly back to lofts at SOMBRIN, COUTURELLE and GOMBREMETZ.

Contact Aeroplane

Divisional Dropping Station is situated at V.27.c.9.5.

Diagram of Communications - Right Division

DIAGRAM "A" JUNE 24TH 1915
2ND SIGNAL COMPANY. R.E.

L.B.
LEFT BRIGADE.
W.22.d.8.6.

M.L.
W.28.b.5.1.

R.B.
CENTRE & RIGHT
BRIGADES.
E.4.c.8.3.

H.V.
M.G. BATT̠N
W.26.d.7.1.

P.M.
D.6. central.

B.Z. DIV̠N. H̠Q
V.27.c.8.9.

DIAGRAM "B" JUNE 26TH 1918.
2ND SIGNAL COMPANY. R.E.

DIAGRAM OF VISUAL COMMUNICATIONS - RIGHT DIVISION

- SECRET -

LEFT BATTALION OF LEFT BRIGADE AT X.24.c.2.5.

COMPANY OF LEFT BATT'N OF LEFT BRIGADE AT S.26.d.8.6.

RIGHT BATTALION OF LEFT BRIGADE AT X.27.b.9.6.

FRONT BATTALION OF CENTRE BRIGADE AT F.9.a.8.4.

LEFT BATTALION OF RIGHT BRIGADE 500 YDS AWAY AT F.9.b.6.1.

RIGHT BATTALION OF RIGHT BRIGADE AT F.20.b.6.8.

SUPPORT BATTALION OF CENTRE BRIGADE AT F.1.c.0.0.

(DIVISIONAL DIRECTING STATION) LEFT BRIGADE AT W.23.c.1.5.

CENTRE BRIGADE AT V.30.b.8.4.

RIGHT BRIGADE 500 YDS AWAY AT E.4.c.2.4.

DIVISIONAL HQ AT V.27.c.7.7.

REFERENCE

△ WIRELESS STATION.   △ P.B. & AMPLIFIER STATION.
⊕ POWER BUZZER STATION.
〜〜〜 WIRELESS COMMUNICATION.
—〜—〜— P.B. & AMPLIFIER COMMUNICATION.

Note All Map References are taken from BUCQUOY (Comb: 1st Sheet) Scale - 1/40,000.

DIAGRAM OF WIRELESS & POWER BUZZER & AMPLIFIER COMMUNICATIONS - RIGHT DIVISION

DIAGRAM 'C' JULY 3RD 1918
2ND SIGNAL COMPANY, R.E.

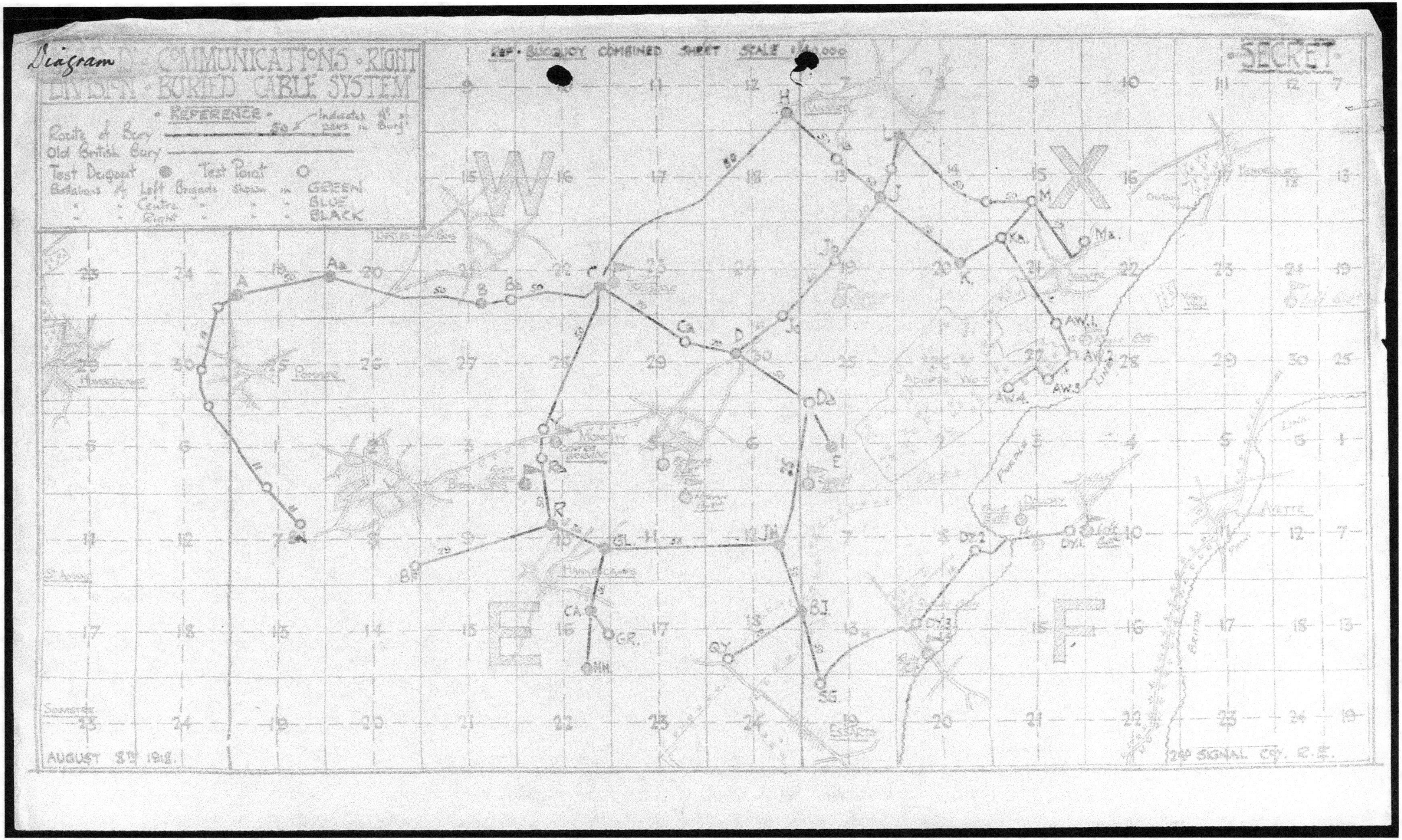
Diagram
COMMUNICATIONS · RIGHT DIVISION · BURIED CABLE SYSTEM
REF · BUCQUOY COMBINED SHEET SCALE 1/40,000
SECRET
REFERENCE
Route of Bury
50 Indicates No. of pairs in Bury
Old British Bury
Test Dugout
Test Point
Battalions of Left Brigade shown in GREEN
Centre BLUE
Right BLACK
W
X
E
F
Monchy
Hannescamps
Essarts
Ayette
Douchy
Pommier
Humbercamp
St Amand
Souastre
Adinfer Wood
Adinfer
British
Purple
Line
AUGUST 8th 1918.
2nd SIGNAL COY. R.E.

APPENDIX "H".
****

ADMINISTRATIVE ARRANGEMENTS.

(1). **MEDICAL.**

	Left.	Right.
(i). Field Ambulance Bearer Relay Posts.	X.28.b.7.5.	F.8.d.3.5. F.7.a.6.2.

	Left.	Right.
(ii). Motor Ambulance Car Stands.	X.15.a.9.5. and ADINFER (X.21.d.3.8)	MONCHY. W.29.d.8.3.

	Left.	Right.
(iii). Advanced Dressing Stations.	RANSART Brewery X.7.d.9.9.	MONCHY W.29.d.8.3.
" " " PURPLE LINE.	X.1.d.8.5.	BERLES AU BOIS W.15.c.3.0.

(iv). **Walking Wounded Collecting Post.**   BERLES AU BOIS, W.15.c.3.0.

(v). **Main Dressing Station.**   VI Corps Main Dressing Station, BAC DU SUD.

(vi). **Divisional Rest Station.**   WARLINCOURT.

(vii). **Evacuation of Sick and Wounded.**

    (a). Left and Centre Brigades. From R.A.P's by hand, carriage or wheeled stretcher to car stand at ADINFER or X.15.c.9.3., thence by car to A.D.S., RANSART or X.1.d.8.5.

    (b). Right Brigade. From R.A.P's by hand carriage or wheeled stretcher to A.D.S. at MONCHY or BERLES AU BOIS, thence by car to M.D.S.

    (c). From A.D.S's. Wounded to VI Corps M.D.S. Sick to Divl. Rest Station. By car or horse ambulances.

(2). **AMMUNITION SUPPLY.**

  (i). **Railheads** – FOSSEUX. SAULTY.

  (ii). **Corps Ammunition Dumps.** BAC DU SUD, CHAPEL SAULTY, LA BELLEVUE, L'ESPERANCE.

  (iii). **Divisional Ammunition Refilling Points (Artillery).**
POMMIER – LA CAUCHIE road (V.24.d.9.7.) (Emergency Dump only).
POMMIER – ST AMAND road (D.6.b.5.8.)
Ammunition is delivered to A.R.P's from Corps dumps by lorry, or in the case of the A.R.P. at D.6.b.5.8. by light railway, on application being made to F. Corps M.T. Column.
From A.R.P. at D.6.b.5.0., issues are made to batteries by light railway or by horsed transport.

  (iv). **S.A.A. Section.** – GAUDIEMPRE, D.1.d.9.8.

  (v). **S.A.A., Grenades, etc.** Main Divisional Dump in orchard on POMMIER – LA CAUCHIE road, W.25.a.1.7.
Issues are made on application to Officer i/c of dump, except in case of S.O.S. Signals, V.P.A. and Ground Flares for the issue of which authority of 2nd Divn. "Q" must be obtained.

(3). **R.E. DUMPS.**
  (i). **Corps R.E. Dump.**
    WARLINCOURT HALTE.
  (ii). **Divisional R.E. Dump.**
    MONCHY – L.4.a.8.4.

P.T.O......

(2).

(4). SUPPLIES.

(i). Railhead - SAULTY.
(ii). (a) Refilling Points -
    Light Railway Junction near POMMIER (D.6.a.8.2.)
    "   "   "   "   " HUMBERCAMP (V.29.c.2.5.)

Supplies are sent from Railhead to Refilling Points by Light Railway.

(b) In case of occupation of the Purple Line Refilling Point would be at (Sheet 51C) W.25.b.5.1. (LE GROSTISON FARM).

Supplies would be delivered to Wagon and Transport Lines by Train Transport.

(5). PRISONERS OF WAR CAGE.

Advanced. Near MONCHY - BIENVILLERS Road E.3.d.8.5.
Main.   On HUMBERCAMP - LA CAUCHIE Road V.29.b.1.8.

The Guard and Escort of 3 N.C.Os. and 30 Men is provided by the Divl. Salvage Company.

(6). STRAGGLERS POSTS. In the event of operations, Stragglers Posts will be established at -
(a) No. 8. W.27.d.1.9.
    No. 9. E.4.a.8.3.
    No.10. E.9.b.4.4.
    No.11. D.18.b.2.1.

The Left Straggler Post of the Corps on the Right is situated at D.22.b.8.4.

The Personnel for Straggler Posts of 4 N.C.Os. and 12 Men is provided by the Divl. Salvage Company.

(b) In case of occupation of the Purple Line Posts would established at -

No. 19. W.26.a.2.6.
No. 20. D.3.a.9.2.
No. 21. D.15.b.7.8.

The Left Straggler Post of the Corps on the Right would be situated at D.13.d.1.6.

(7). CEMETERIES.

AYETTE   - - - F.5.d.2.4.
QUESNOY FARM - - F.13.b.7.9.
BIENVILLERS   - - E.7.b.4.2.
St. AMAND   - - D.10.c.4.7.

Only the two last named cemeteries will be used, except in cases of necessity.

5th Inf. Bde.	1	10/D.C.L.I.	6
6th Inf. Bde.	2	2/N.G. Battn.	7
99th Inf. Bde.	3	Sherer's Group.	8
C.R.A.	4	A.D.M.S.	9
C.R.E.	5		

2nd Division No.
G.S. 5/96.

SECRET

Herewith copy No. X of 2nd Division Provisional Defence Scheme.

2. Infantry Brigades will forward their Defence Schemes to Divisional H.Q. in due course.

3. Appendices regarding –
   Artillery.
   Machine Gun Dispositions.
   Signalling Communication.
   Administrative Arrangements.
   Occupation of Purple Line, etc.

and maps, will be forwarded later.

4. Acknowledge.

E R Clayton
Lieut. Colonel,
General Staff, 2nd Division.

25/6/18.

July 1918
Defence Scheme

10	to	37 Division
11	to	VI Corps
12	to	2nd Signal Co
13	to	Q 2nd Division
14	to	32nd Division
15	to	Guards Division
16	to	4th Tank Bde.

LIST OF CONTENTS.

Paragraph 1. Boundaries.
2. Organisation of Defences.
3. Probable forms of attack.
4. Method of holding the line.
5. Distribution of troops.
6. Action in case of a threatened attack.
7. Anti-Tank defence.
8. Sector Guides.
9. Action of working parties.
10. Anti-Aircraft defence.
11. S.O.S. Signals.

LIST OF APPENDICES.

Appendix A. Artillery.
B. Occupation of Purple Line.
C. Action of tanks in event of enemy attack.
D. Arrangements for Demolitions.
E. Action in case of enemy shelling with Yellow Cross Gas.
F. Defence against Cloud Gas attack.
G. Communications.
H. Administrative arrangements.

M A P S.

Map A. General Map.
B. Disposition of troops
C. Disposition of Machine Guns.
D. Track Map.

DEFENCE SCHEME   **SECRET.**

RIGHT DIVISION VI CORPS.   Copy No........

1. The front held by the Division is from F.23.a.0.6 to S.27.a.1.0.

   Right Boundary - F.23.a.0.6 - F.20.a.1.5 - E.24.b.05.65 - E.24.a.3.7 - E.16.d.30.15.

   Left Boundary - S.27.a.1.0 - S.27.a.0.1 - X.22.c.6.0 - X.20.c.4.2 - W.21.c.9.3.

   Boundary between Right and Centre Brigades:- Front line at F.11.d.10.45 - F.10.d.6.5 - trench junction F.10.d.5.8 - thence along North of AYETTE AVENUE (inclusive to Right Brigade) to trench and road crossing at F.9.b.9.3 - F.9.c.7.6 thence an East and West line to E.11.c.7.6.

   Between Centre and Left Brigades:- Front line at F.6.a.3.4 - trench and road crossing F.5.b.7.5 - South of MEAL TRENCH (inclusive to Left Brigade) to F.5.a.0.2 - ~~thence due West.~~ F.3.a.6.2 (LILY LANE inclusive to Centre Brigade) F.2.b.8.5 - F.1.b.2.2 thence due West.

   These boundaries are shown on the attached map 'A'.

2. **ORGANIZATION OF DEFENCES.**

   The defences in the Divisional area are organized as follows:-

   (a) <u>Front or Outpost Line</u> - consisting of

       (i) Front line with, in places, an observation line pushed out in front.

       (ii) Support and Reserve Lines.

   (b) <u>The Second or Purple System</u> - consisting of

       (i) Purple Front line, continuously dug and wired.

       (ii) Purple Support.

       (iii) QUESNOY FARM trenches.

       (iv) The Purple Reserve.

   (c) The <u>AYETTE SWITCH</u> running from the defences about F.10.d.5.7. to the Purple System at F.9.c.5.4.

   (d) The <u>WINDMILL SWITCH.</u> From the front system in F.5.b to the Purple System South of HENDECOURT.

   (e) <u>MONCHY SWITCH.</u> OLD BRITISH and OLD GERMAN FRONT LINES.

   (f) Third or Red System.

   The Division is responsible for construction and maintenance of all defences in or East of the Purple Reserve. Trenches in the Purple System now being constructed under the C.E., VI Corps will be handed over to the Division when completed.
   The Division is not responsible for defences in rear of the Purple System.

DEFENCE SCHEME.   S E C R E T.

RIGHT DIVISION VI CORPS.   Copy No..........

1.   The front held by the Division is from F.23.a.0.6 to
S.27.a.1.0.

       Right Boundary - F.23.a.0.6 - F.20.a.1.5 - E.24.b.05.65 -
                        E.24.a.3.7 - E.16.d.30.15.

       Left Boundary - S.27.a.1.0 - S.27.a.0.1 - X.22.c.6.0 -
                        X.20.c.4.2 - W.21.c.9.3.

       Boundary between Right and Centre Brigades:- Front line at
F.11.d.10.45 - F.10.d.6.5 - trench junction F.10.d.5.8 - thence
along North of AYETTE AVENUE (inclusive to Right Brigade) to
trench and road crossing at F.9.b.9.3 - F.9.c.7.6 thence an East
and West line to E.11.c.7.6.

       Between Centre and Left Brigades:- Front line at F.6.a.3.4 -
trench and road crossing F.5.b.7.5 - South of MEAL TRENCH
(inclusive to Left Brigade) to F.5.a.0.2 - ~~thence due West.~~ F.3.a.6.2
(LILY LANE inclusive to Centre Brigade) F.2.b.8.5 - F.2.b.2.2 thence due West.
       These boundaries are shown on the attached map 'A'.

2. ORGANIZATION OF DEFENCES. *

       The defences in the Divisional area are organized as follows:-

   (a) Front or Outpost Line - consisting of

       (i) Front line with, in places, an observation line pushed
            out in front.

       (ii) Support and Reserve Lines.

   (b) The Second or Purple System - consisting of

       (i)   Purple Front line, continuously dug and wired.

       (ii) Purple Support.

       (iii) QUESNOY FARM trenches.

       (iv) The Purple Reserve.
              A
   (c) The AYETTE SWITCH running from the defences about F.10.d.5.7.
       to the Purple System at F.9.c.5.4.

   (d) The WINDMILL SWITCH. From the front system in F.5.b to
       the Purple System South of HENDECOURT.

   (e) MONCHY SWITCH. OLD BRITISH and OLD GERMAN FRONT LINES.

   (f) Third or Red System.

           * A Secret letter on this subject will be issued to
             Brigades, C.R.A. and M.G.Battalion.
                                                         P.T.O.

- 2 -

3. **PROBABLE FORMS OF ATTACK.**

It seems probable from recent experience that the enemy will avoid ADINFER WOOD in the case of an attack in strength.
The most probable forms of attack are -

(a) An attack with QUESNOY FARM Ridge as the objective, which would take place after the outpost troops of the Division on our right on HENLEY HILL had been driven in, and which would probably be combined with a large operation against ESSARTS.

(b) An attack against the high ground N. of AYETTE held by the Left Brigade.
The above might be combined with a movement up the COJEUL Valley between QUESNOY FARM Ridge and ADINFER WOOD, in order to penetrate the Purple Line and to threaten the QUESNOY FARM Ridge from the rear.

Indications of the enemy's intentions may be obtained from his gas shelling.
Special arrangements will be made by the Centre and Left Brigades to watch for and to report Yellow Cross gas shelling on ADINFER WOOD and the COJEUL Valley if an attack seems probable.

4. **METHOD OF HOLDING THE LINE.**

The front line is to be held as a fighting line from which there is to be no voluntary retirement.
In the event of an attack on the front line by -

    (a) A raid.
    (b) A local attack against some Tactical Feature,

the enemy is to be immediately counter-attacked by the supporting troops, and our line restored. Such counter-attack being made immediately, from the flanks, and from the support trenches if possible. Should the immediate counter-attack fail, a deliberate counter-attack will be organised from the troops in Divisional Reserve.

In the event of an attack with great weight bringing about a break through on a large scale, troops in supporting and reserve positions must hold their ground, and break up the enemy's attack by fire. It will be useless to fritter away supporting platoons by local counter-attacks.

Our attitude is not to become one of passive defence. Identifications must be frequently obtained by patrols. Schemes for raids must be prepared. The enemy must be harassed and caused loss by every possible means.

5. **DISTRIBUTION OF TROOPS.**

    Divisional Headquarters - V.27.c.7.7, LA BAZEQUE.
    Adv. Divisional H.Q. - old dugouts W.20.c.1.9 (Cars to W.19.c.9.3 - thence on foot along buried cable track).

Right Bde......

- 3 -

Right Brigade.   Headquarters - E.4.c.2.4.
                      2 Battns. forward system.
F.20.b.6.9 Right Battn. H.Q. ~~F.15.c.2.1~~.   Left Battn. H.Q. F.9.b.6.1.
              1 Battn. Brigade Reserve, H.Q. E.5.d.4.3.

Centre Brigade.   Headquarters E.4.a.6.3.
                       Battle H.Q. - E.5.d.3.3.
                       2 Battns. forward system.
              (1 Battn. E. of DOUCHY. 1 Battn. in Support).
         Front Battn. H.Q. F.9.a.8.4. Support Bn. H.Q. F.1.c.0.0.
         1 Bn. in Divl. Reserve about MONCHY, H.Q., E.5.d.2.3.

Left Brigade.   Headquarters W.23.c.1.9.
                       2 Battns. forward system.
         Right Battn. H.Q., X.27.b.9.5. Left Battn. H.Q. X.24.c.2.0.
              1 Battn. in Brigade Reserve H.Q., X.19.c.8.2.

The dispositions of Battns. are shewn on attached map 'B'.

In the Right and Left Brigade areas, 2 Battalions are allotted for the defence of the Front System. These Battalions are organised in depth. The Third Battalion in the Right and Left Brigade areas is definitely allotted for the defence of the Purple Line and will not be moved forward of the Purple Front Line without sanction from Divisional H.Q.

In the Left Brigade area, the Reserve Coy. from each of the front Line Battalions is located in or about the Purple Line. If moved forward of the Purple Line owing to the tactical situation, these Coys. will be at once replaced from the Battn. in Brigade Reserve.

In the Centre Brigade area, one Battn. situated in the trenches S. of MONCHY is in Divisional Reserve. Two Companies of the Support Battalion will be definitely considered as the garrison of the Purple System and will not be moved forward of the Purple Front Line without sanction from Divisional H.Q.

The 2nd M.G. Battalion is disposed in depth, in groups which approximately correspond with the Brigade areas.

As soon as certain reorganisation is completed, the fire from about 30 guns will be available to put down a barrage, either direct or indirect, for the defence of the Front Line. This barrage is designed to fill gaps in the Field Artillery barrage.

The Field Artillery is organised in 3 Groups -

Right Group, Headquarters E.5.d.25.30
Centre   "   "   W.24.b.25.65
Left   "   "   W.18.b.50.00

The Battle H.Q. of the Groups is with the Infantry Brigade which they cover.
The Batteries of each Group cover approximately the front of an Infantry Brigade.

Heavy T.Ms. There are no Heavy T.Ms. in the area.

6" Newtons. 6" Newton Mortars are located as follows:-

(a) In the front system - 2 in F.16.b., 2 in F.11.c.
                          and 4 at X.29.d.0.0.

(b) In the second system - 4 in F.13.c., F.14.a., and F.8.a.

6.   Action in case .....

6. ACTION IN CASE OF A THREATENED ATTACK.

Right Brigade. The Reserve Coy. of the Left Battn. will occupy the AYETTE SWITCH from about the Purple Front Line to about the DOUCHY - ~~AYETTE~~ BUCQUOY Road.

Left Brigade will move forward the Reserve Coy. of the Left front Battn. to WINDMILL SWITCH in X.29, getting touch with the Divn. on the left about X.23.c.4.0. This Coy. will be replaced, vide para.5.

The Battn. in Divisional Reserve will be prepared to move at short notice.

10/D.C.L.I. (Pioneers) will concentrate about MONCHY MILL SOUTH at their present billets, and will be prepared to move at short notice.

The Field Coys. R.E. will assemble as follows -

    Namely 226th Field Coy. near 5 Bde. Headquarters.
               5th and 483rd Field Coys. South of MONCHY.
under the orders of the C.R.E., and will be prepared to move at short notice.

Artillery.

If, owing to hostile artillery fire, or for any other reason, an enemy attack seems probable, the Artillery, both Heavy and Field, will open annihilating fire on the order of -
    Divisional Headquarters
    Divisional Artillery Headquarters.
    Artillery Group Headquarters *in conjunction with Inf. Brigadier*,
and, in exceptional circumstances, Inf. Brigade Headquarters.

In order to deal with a surprise hostile attack, for the first 15 minutes annihilating fire will consist of fire on approx. S.O.S. lines at a slow rate, after which if no attack develops, guns will lift on to various targets, viz. Field Arty., occupied trenches and shell holes and places likely to be occupied or made use of in case of attack. Heavy Arty. (not engaged in counter-battery work) on likely points of concentration.

The Heavy Artillery S.O.S. lines on the Divisional front are arranged to fire on the valleys -

    (a) Between A.13.d and A.2.d.
    (b) Between A.19.d and A.9.d.

In the event of a heavy bombardment opening about 3 or 4 hours before dawn, gas shell will be put down in the above valleys which are likely places of assembly for the enemy, in order to delay and disorganize his troops while forming up.. This bombardment will be timed for about 3 hours before sunrise.

7. ANTI-TANK DEFENCE.

Anti-Tank guns are in position at:-

    F.9.c.8.4.
    F.14.b.0.5.
    F.4.a.4.5.
    X.23.a.1.1.

Anti-Tank trenches.....

- 5 -

Anti-Tank trenches have been dug across the roads at:-

> F.11.c.8.7.
> F.11.b.5.4.
> F.5.d.5.1.

8. **Sector Guides.**
Brigades and 10/D.C.L.I. each provide 8 guides. These guides are intended to guide up reinforcing troops from the Red System to any part of the Divisional Sector in the case of guides from the 10/D.C.L.I. and in their own Brigade areas, in the case of guides provided by Brigades.
~~Capt. R.G. FINLAY~~, Divisional Headquarters, is the Sector Guide Commandant.
Brigades and 10/D.C.L.I. are ready to furnish guides as above at short notice.

9. **Action of Working Parties.**
In the event of an enemy attack, Infantry working parties will place themselves under the orders of the nearest Company or Battn. Commander, who will be responsible that as soon as the situation permits the parties are sent back to their own units.
Men of the 174th Tunnelling Coy. will be sent to rejoin their unit.

10. **Anti-Aircraft Defence.**

(a) The Anti-Aircraft Sections are responsible for defence against enemy aircraft at a height exceeding 3000 feet.

(b) Below 3000 feet, Commanders OF UNITS are responsible for their own defence. For this purpose Vickers or Lewis Guns should be placed in pairs, each pair when possible being about 1000 yds. apart.

(c) Should the enemy use low flying aeroplanes with which to engage the attention of trench garrisons so as to cover an attack, all ranks must understand that the garrisons of the front trenches will engage the hostile infantry while the troops in support and reserve deal with the hostile aeroplanes.

(d) Enemy aircraft will not be engaged with Rifle or Machine Gun fire unless the markings are recognisable, and the struts of the aeroplane are visible to the naked eye.
At night only when -
  (i) The aeroplane can be seen against the sky, or
  (ii) The struts can be seen when the aeroplane is in the beam of a searchlight.

(e) Certain 18-pdr. guns are detailed to engage low flying aeroplanes with a false angle of sight on S.O.S. lines. The call for this will be "Aeroplane attack".

11. **S.O.S. Signals.**
(a) The S.O.S. Signal from July 4th is a Rifle Grenade bursting into GREEN over GREEN over GREEN.
The S.O.S. Signal for the Division on our Right (IV Corps) is a Rifle Grenade bursting into RED over GREEN over RED.

(b) The S.O.S. Signal fired from a reconnoitring aeroplane is a red parachute light meaning -
"The enemy is advancing to the assault".

E.R. Clayton
Lieut-Colonel,
General Staff, 2nd Division.

July 4" 1918.

Appendix A   71st Mtg 4 (3).

for 'F.18.a.15.60' read
'E.18.a.15.60'

R.A. 2nd Div. B.M. 19/22.

AMENDMENTS TO 2ND DIVISION DEFENCE SCHEME. APPENDIX "A"

PAGE 4., Paragraph 8.

Harassing Fire Zones are amended to read :-
(a) Southern Boundary - F 23 a 0.6 - F 23 b 0.0 - A 21 a 0.0
(b) Between Right & Centre Groups - F 11 d 10.45 - A 9 c 0.0
(c) Between Centre & Left Groups - F 6 a 3.4 - A 10 a 0.0
(d) Northern Boundary - S 27 a 1.0 - A 3 a 0.7 - A 5 c 0.0.

To all recipients of Defence Scheme.

On Page 5, 71st Bty for F 18 a 15.60 READ E 18 a 15.60.

14th August, 1918.

Lieut-Colonel
General Staff 2nd Division.

R.A. 2nd Div. B.M. 19/22.

AMENDMENT TO 2ND DIVISIONAL ARTILLERY DEFENCE SCHEME.

APPENDIX "F"

Paragraph 2, Harassing Fire Zones, are amended to read as under:-
(a) Southern Boundary - F 23 a 0.6 - F 23 b 0.0 - A 21 a 0.0.
(b) Between Right & Centre Groups, F 11 d 10.45 - A 9 c 0.0.
(c) Between Centre & Left Groups, F 6 a 3.4 - A 10 a 0.0
(d) Northern Boundary, S 27 a 1.0 - A 3 a 0.7 - A 5 c 0.0.

14th August, 1918.

Major R.A.
Brigade Major R.A. 2nd Div.

2ND DIVISION DEFENCE SCHEME.   Page 1.

APPENDIX "A"   ARTILLERY

1. ARTILLERY POLICY.

Main positions will be kept well to the rear, and one or two guns per battery forward. Every possible effort will be made not to disclose Main positions, and all sniping and harassing fire etc. will be done from the forward positions – the guns being moved about if found by the enemy.

Each Main Battery position will have a "Home" O.P. near it, with telephone wire laid to it, and arrangements should be made for the siting of Battery Lewis guns and rifles for close defence.

Each Battery will also have an alternative position reconnoitred, and as far as possible prepared for occupation.

2. ANTI-TANK DEFENCE.

The defensive arrangements in this area consist of :-
(a) ~~4~~ Single 18-pdr. guns in the forward area. 300 rounds per gun are ~~will be~~ maintained at each ~~18-pr~~ position, ~~and great care should be taken to see that the~~ parts of the gun and all ammunition ~~etc. are kept in good order.~~

(b) Guns run out from Battery positions (arrangements to be made beforehand) to engage tanks that have broken through the first defences.

(c) One 18-pr. Battery ~~in Mobile Reserve at POMMIER.~~ of the Bde in Mobile Reserve

3. LIAISON ARRANGEMENTS.

The Divisional Front is held by three Infantry Brigades, each supported by a Field Artillery Group. Group Commanders are responsible for keeping the closest touch with their Infantry Brigades. In cases where the Group Headquarters and Infantry Brigade Headquarters are not at present sited together, the Battle Headquarters of the Artillery Group H.Q. will be the same as that of the Infantry Brigade H.Q. with which they are affiliated. The occupation of this H.Q., testing Communications etc. etc., should be practised.

A Liaison Officer will be provided with each battalion H.Q. under Group arrangements.

A Heavy Artillery Group (consisting of ~~two~~ one mixed Brigade~~s~~) is affiliated to this Division, and in addition, Field Artillery Groups have direct wires to certain Heavy Batteries who fire on their front.

Two Batteries of 6-inch Newton Trench Mortars are in action on the Divisional Front.

4. S.O.S.

The S.O.S. signal or message will only be sent when the enemy is actually advancing to attack our trenches. It will be sent through every available means of communication in addition to the rocket; the latter signal being continued till answered by the guns.

To Page 2.

2ND DIVISION DEFENCE SCHEME APPENDIX "A" (Continued). Page 2.

S.O.S. (continued)

It will be passed on in the following order by Stations receiving it :-

(1) Batteries.
 (a) To Batteries on their flanks.
 (b) To Brigade Headquarters.

(2) Groups.
 (a) To their Batteries.
 (b) To Groups on both flanks.
 (c) To Divisional Artillery Headquarters.

(3) *Divisional Artillery*
 (a) To Groups.
 (b) To Heavy Artillery Group affiliated to Division.
 (c) To Divisional Artilleries on flanks.
 (d) To Division "G"
 (e) To Corps R.A.

On receipt of the Signal or message all guns and Trench Mortars covering the front attacked will at once open fire on their S.O.S. lines at rates as follows:-

	18-prs.	4.5"Hows.
First 5 minutes	INTENSE	RAPID
Next 5 minutes	NORMAL	RAPID
Next 20 minutes	SLOW	NORMAL

Then Stop unless signal is repeated.

Ammunition....18-prs......75% Shrapnel, 25% H.E.
 4.5" Hows....106 Fuze.

The Divisional front is divided into 3 S.O.S. sections, reading from Right to Left, each S.O.S. section corresponding to a Brigade front.

S.O.S. Code words will be as under :-

99th Infantry Brigade front.........QUESNOY.
8th Infantry Brigade front.........AYETTE.
5th Infantry Brigade front.........OSTRICH.

The terms "Right" "Centre" and "Left" will only be used to refer to the three Divisions in the Corps. Thus "S.O.S. RIGHT" means an attack on the whole 2nd Divisional front; and "S.O.S. QUESNOY" means an attack on the 99th Infantry Brigade front.

5. ANNIHILATING FIRE.

Annihilating fire will be carried out by both Field and Heavy Artillery should there be indications that the enemy is about to attack. It will consist of bursts of Normal or Rapid fire (for not more than 10 minutes continuously) searching all hidden approaches and likely places of assembly to a depth of 2,000 yards from our line. All batteries will return periodically to their S.O.S. lines.

For the first 15 minutes this fire will be directed on or near S.O.S. lines.

The following procedure will be adopted on the opening of an intense Hostile Bombardment :-

All guns and howitzers open on S.O.S. lines at rapid rate for 15 minutes. Heavy Artillery howitzers S.O.S. lines to be continuous just beyond Field Artillery S.O.S. lines.

From plus 15....

To page 3.

2nd DIVISION DEFENCE SCHEME.(Appendix "A")   PAGE 2 A

5. COUNTER PREPARATION AND ANNIHILATING FIRE.

(a) As soon as there are indications that the enemy is preparing for an offensive, counter measures begin, and orders will be issued for increased C.B. work and harassing fire, and concentrations on T.M.positions etc. etc.

(b) <u>Counter-Mortar Bombardment.</u> Should the date of the enemy's attack be learned beforehand, a bombardment of likely T.M.positions will be ordered to take place on the previous night probably before midnight. This bombardment will consist of 2 periods of 20 minutes each at Normal rates, with an interval of 30 minutes in between the periods. Zero hour for beginning of first period will be notified by Divisional Headquarters.

<u>Ammunition.</u>   All Howitzers:-   50% 106   18-pounders 75% H.E.
                                      25% Delay   25% Shrap.
                                      25% Non-delay.

Mustard Gas shell will be used for the first period if available and weather conditions are suitable.

Field Artillery will search the whole area within 600 yards of our front line, and the Heavy Artillery the area from 600 yards to 1200 yards from our front line.

(c) <u>Annihilating Fire.</u> The primary object of annihilating fire is to crush the enemy's infantry while they are assembling or after they have assembled before their assault. It may be put down by order of the Corps, Div.H.Q., Div.Arty.H.Q., or R.F.A.Group H.Q. in conjunction with the Infantry Brigadier. The time to open fire will be judged by the intensity of the enemy's bombardment or from information received of an impending attack.

The area from our front line of outposts to a depth of 1500 yards (extended in the centre of the area to include the Valley N.W. of COURCELLES) will be thoroughly searched by Field and Heavy Artillery according to the belts shown on S.O.S.Map, attached.

The following procedure will be adopted when Annihilating Fire is ordered :- All guns and howitzers will open on their S.O.S.Lines for ten minutes at Normal rate searching back to the boundary of their annihilating fire belt. After the first ten minutes, the Field Arty. will continue to search their belt by a series of creeping barrages each of ten minutes duration at a Normal rate, paying special attention to any likely assembly places.

The series of barrages should cover the whole Group sector, each barrage being concentrated on selected areas by the Group Commander. Ammunition expenditure to average 40 rounds per gun (50% A; 50% AX)and 30 rounds per 4.5" How. (75% 106 and 25% Non-delay) per hour.

<u>Heavy Artillery.</u> The Heavy Artillery will search their belt by a series of creeping barrages each of from 15 to 20 mins. duration at Normal rate, omitting the area more than 1500 yards from our outpost line as far as the beginning of the valley N.W.of COURCELLES. Special attention will be given to this valley, and the valley just E. of MOYBLAIN TRENCH, and hostile works and approaches.

During the pauses between the bursts immediate advantage must be taken of opportunities seen from the air or by ground observers.Unless engaging an important target all guns and howitzers will return to S.O.S.Lines after each burst.

(d) <u>Gas Bombardment.</u> If weather conditions are suitable a Gas Bombardment will be opened 2 hours before sunrise by all 4.5" and 6" Hows., and 60-prs. on the Valley N.W.of COURCELLES.
Expenditure :- 4.5" Howitzers 350 rounds per battery
                  6"   ,,   300   ,,
                  60-prs. Any gas shell still available.

2ND DIVISION DEFENCE SCHEME - APPENDIX "A" (Continued)   Page 3

From plus 15 onwards :- *Field Arty in Back positions*

6 bursts of Intense Fire per hour; duration 3 minutes each searching up to 1,200 yards beyond our Outpost line.

Forward Field Guns and Heavies.

6 bursts of Intense Fire per hour, duration 3 minutes each searching from 1,200 yards beyond our Outpost line up to extreme range of guns, paying special attention to selected valleys.

At plus 1½ hours, and every ¾ of an hour after, gas bombardment of the valley N.W. of COURCELLES for 15 minutes.

All guns return to their S.O.S. lines after each burst.

Searching fire will be carried out by Batteries independently.

Gas bombardment will be synchronised by O.C. Heavy Arty. Group

6. O. Ps.

A sufficient number of O.Ps. will be manned by each Group by day and night to ensure the whole front being kept under continual observation.

All O.Ps. will be provided with a pointer and dial and Map board.

All O.Ps. manned by night will be provided with a rifle and a supply of rifle-grenade S.O.S. rockets, which will be used to pass on messages or signals from the front line. Each Battery position will have a "Home" O.P. near it with telephone wire laid to it.

7. AMMUNITION SUPPLY.

(a) Dumps of Ammunition will be maintained as follows :-

Calibre.	Rds. per gun at occupied gun positions.			Rds. per gun at Divl. A. R. P.
	H.E.	Shrap	Gas	
18-pr.	115	335	-	200
4.5" Hows	550	-	500 per Batty.	200
18-pr A.Tk.	~~200~~ 150	150		

(b) Ammunition is brought up by railway to sidings at :-

W 29 c 7.7
W 23 c 7.6
W 12 d 6.3

The two Divisional A.R.Ps. are on the POMMIER - ST AMAND and POMMIER - LA CAUCHIE roads, and ammunition can be drawn from these at any time by horse transport.

(c) The daily allotment of ammunition to be expended is :-

18-prs....24 rounds per gun per diem - Shrapnel.
16 rounds per gun per diem - H.E.
4.5" Hows 40 rounds per How per diem.
50% of the above should be fired by night as harassing fire

To Page 4.

Page 4.

2ND DIVISION DEFENCE SCHEME   APPENDIX "A" (Continued)

8. HARASSING FIRE ZONES.

    (a) Southern Boundary... F.23.a.0.6 - F.23.b.0.0 - A.2½.a.0.0
    (b) Between Rt. & Centre F.11.d.10.45 - A.9.c.0.0
    (c) Between Centre & Lt. F.6.a.3.4 - A.10.a.0.0
    (d) Northern Boundary -   S.27.a.1.0 - A.3.a.0.7 - A.5.c.0.0

9. ORDERS FOR BATTERY IN MOBILE RESERVE.

    Orders for the movement and employment of the Anti-Tank Battery will come from 2nd Divn Artillery H.Q.

    Positions and O.Ps. to cover the whole Divisional Front will be reconnoitred, together with routes to them, and those should be known to all Officers and N.C.Os. The Battery will not be brought into action East of a line passing through W 25 d central - E 17 c central, and against Tanks should be employed by dispersed sections.

    The Battery will be prepared to turn out at the shortest notice, and during periods of special readiness will stand to one hour before sunrise daily until it is clear that no attack is impending.

    When a hostile attack begins or is indicated by a heavy bombardment, the Battery will at once harness up and hook in, and an officer will be sent to report to Right Group H.Q. The Battery will rendezvous near Track "A" about square W 28 c.

10. DEFENCE OF REAR LINES.

    Artillery positions and O.Ps. have been chosen to cover every defensive system back to G.H.Q. line (inclusive).

    In the event of a sudden hostile attack driving us back to the Second (PURPLE) system, it will be impossible to withdraw the forward guns and sections which can give great moral and material support to our infantry at this time. When all ammunition has been fired, these guns will, if possible, be destroyed, sights and breech fittings removed, and detachments withdrawn.

    The majority of the guns and howitzers at present in action can cover the Second (PURPLE) system from their present positions but will be withdrawn in succession under Group arrangements to their PURPLE positions as soon as possible after it is known for certain that we have been driven out of our first system.

    Zones should be allotted beforehand for S.O.S.Lines to cover the PURPLE Line, and these should be arranged if possible with a view to leaving no important points uncovered during the withdrawal to PURPLE positions.

    PURPLE and RED line positions and O.Ps. should be reconnoitred beforehand by as many officers and N.C.Os. as possible.

    Orders re ammunition supply for those positions will be issued later.

To Page 5.

Page 5

2ND DIVISION DEFENCE SCHEME.   APPENDIX "A" (Continued)   LOCATIONS ETC., ETC.

UNIT	NUMBER OF GUNS.	LOCATION	ARC OF FIRE.	O. Ps.	S.O.S. LINES	WAGON LINES	REMARKS.
H.Q.R.A.	-	V 27 a 5.1	-	-	-	V 27 a 5.7	
RIGHT GROUP	-	Lieutenant-Colonel A.A.GOSCHEN, D.S.O., R.F.A., Commanding.					
36th Brigade R.F.A.	H.Q.	E 4 c 25.30	-	X 27 d 65.75 TOM TIT	-	ST AMAND	
15th Battery	4 (S) 2	E 6 a 51.62 F 1 d 28.35	30°– 160° 50°– 115°	X 27 d 70.45 APPLE	F 23 a 7.8–F 17 c 8.5	D 15 b 7.5 W 29 d 2.25	Rear Adv.
48th Battery	5 (S) 1 1 Anti-Tank	E 5 d 25.35 F 2 d 40.50 F 9 c 86.42	73°– 133° 74°– 134°	X 27 d 70.45 APPLE	F 17 c 8.5–F 17 d 1.5 F 17 b 4.0	D 15 b 79.70 E 4 b 31.35	Rear Adv.
71st Battery	4 (S) 2 1 Anti-Tank	E 18 a 15.60 F 2 c 6.2 F 14 b 0.5	71°– 111° 1,930°–1380° 1,877°–134°	F 10 c 05.55 DORIS	F 23 a 7.8–F 17 c 8.5	ST AMAND W 28 c	Rear Adv.
D/36th Battery Howitzers.	4 2	E 11 c 59.00 F 9 a 10.88	500°–1250° 930°–1830°	*F 9 b 9.1 DOORPOST	F 23 a 7.8–F 17 c 8.5– F 17 d 3.8	ST AMAND	
"T" Batty.R.H.A.	5 1	X 25 b 28.56 F 4 a 7.0	840°–1640° 115°–155°	∮ F 17 c 1.5 STYLO	F 17 d 1.5–F17 b 3.0– F 17 b 1.7	W 16 a central	

* Used when necessary   ∮ Used by F.O.O. when required.

P.T.O.

Page 6.

2ND DIVISION   DEFENCE SCHEME   APPENDIX "A" (Continued)   LOCATIONS ETC. ETC.

UNIT.	NUMBER OF GUNS.	LOCATION	ARC OF FIRE	O. Ps.	S.O.S. LINES	WAGON LINES	REMARKS
CENTRE GROUP - Lieutenant-Colonel P. BARTON, D.S.O., R.F.A., Commanding.							
41st Brigade R.F.A. H.Q.		E 5 c 85.75	-	X 27 c 75.50	-		
9th Battery	4 (S) 2	X 25 d 50.80 X 25 c 40.20	95°-180° 145°-196°	X 27 c 75.50 F 1 a 40.25 X 29 a 7.6 F 5 b 80.15	F 11 d 5.0-F 11 d 7.5	D 9 c 80.20 E 2 c 50.30	Rear Adv.
16th Battery	4 (S) 2	X 25 c 03.57 F 2 d 3.2	95°-135° 60°-150°	X 27 c 75.50 F 17 c 1.4 STYLO	F 11 d 7.5 - F 12 c 2.8	D 10 c 80.20 W 21 b 20.20	Rear
17th Battery	5 (S) 1	X 20 b 11.95 X 28 a 85.90	95°-167° 95°-170°	X 27 c 75.50 X 20 b 70.35	F 6 c 45.00-F 6 c 4.3	E 2 c 50.40	Rear Adv.
47th Battery (Howitzers)	6	X 25 b 90.00	90°-145°	X 27 c 75.50	4, F 12 c 2.3-F 12 a 4.1 2, F 12 c 4.9-F 12 c 5.8	W 25 b 6.3 W 18 a 70.30	Rear Adv.
						D 15 a 00.30 W 29 a 5.8	Rear Adv.

Page 4

2ND DIVISION DEFENCE SCHEME. (Continued) LOCATIONS ETC. ETC.

UNIT	NUMBER OF GUNS.	LOCATION	ARC OF FIRE.	O. Ps.	S.O.S. LINES	WAGON LINES	REMARKS
LEFT GROUP. - Lieutenant-Colonel, C. F. PARRY, D.S.O., R.F.A., Commanding.							
34th(A) Bde.H.Q. R.F.A.		W 18 a 50.00		≠ A 1 b 20.80 PAINT.	-	W 18 a 50.00	
70th Battery	4 (S) 2	X 27 a 25.35 X 23 d 4975	87°-112° 98°-163°	A 1 b 20.80 PAINT.	S 27 c 0.2 - 85.90	GAUDIEMPRE W 17 d 20.30	Rear
56th Battery (Howitzers)	1 A.T. 4 (S) 2	X 29 d 40.38 X 15 d 80.40 X 23 c 71.20	94°-172° 105°-176°	A 1 b 20.80 PAINT	S 27 c 35.30 - S 27 c 85.90	GAUDIEMPRE X 18 c 20.30	Rear Adv.
14th(A) Bde.H.Q. R.H.A.		W 24 b 25.63				W 24 a 2.7	
"P" Battery	4 (S) 2 1 A-Tank	X 25 b 50.72 X 20 a 15.00 X 28 c 20.75	81°-158° 79°-148°	* X 21 a 38.55 PIG & WHISTLE * X 21 a 80.80	A 1 d 50.95 - A 2 a 70.10	D 9 c 6090	
400th Batty.	4 (S) 2	X 26 a 11.79 X 20 a 15.00	91°-153° 79°-148°		A 2 a 70.10 - A 2 b 40.40	D 9 d 30.40	
401st Batty. (Howitzers)	4	X 19 d 68.73	100°-150°	∅ X 27 c 30.50 SUNSHINE	A 3 a 00.50 - A 3 b 50.80	D 10 a 40.50	Rear
	2	X 28 a 70.50	93°-164°	∅ X 28 c 2080 LORD NELSON	S 27 c 35.30 - S 27 c 50.50	W 23 c 20.50	Adv.

* Left Group O.Ps.   1 ≠ 34th Bde. O.P.   ∅ 14th Bde. O.Ps.

F.I.C.

2ND DIVISION DEFENCE SCHEME, APPENDIX "A" (Continued) LOCATIONS ETC.

UNIT	LOCATION	WAGON LINES	REMARKS.
76th (A) Brigade R.F.A. (Headquarters) LA CAUCHIE (V 17 b 9.0)		W 13 b 9.9	Mobile Reserve.
"A" Battery	W 13 b 6.8	W 13 b 6.6	
"B" Battery	W 13 d 3.8	W 13 d 3.8	
"C" Battery (Mob. Anti Tank)	W 13 c 6.9	W 13 c 6.9	
"D" Battery	W 19 a 4.6	W 19 a 4.6	
D.A.C. & 3 Sections	GAUDIEMPRE	GAUDIEMPRE	
14th (A) Bdo.Am.Col	GAUDIEMPRE	GAUDIEMPRE	
.. Adv. Section	W 28 a 8.8	W 28 a 8.8	
34th (A) Bdo.Am.Col.	GAUDIEMPRE	GAUDIEMPRE	
76th (A) Bdo.Am.Col.	GAUDIEMPRE	GAUDIEMPRE	
"B A N G" Dump.	LA CAUCHIE ROAD (V 24 d 9.7)		
"W H I Z Z" Dump	POMMIER ST AMAND ROAD (D e b 5.8)		

2ND DIVISION DEFENCE SCHEME ----- APPENDIX "A" ----- MUTUAL SUPPORT.

SECTOR ATTACKED	CODE CALL	ACTION TAKEN BY	NATURE OF SUPPORT
Left of IV Corps	Help IV Corps	RIGHT GROUP	3, 18-pr Btties. Fire on S.O.S. Lines F 23 a 7.8 - F 17 b 4.0 1, 4.5" How.Bty. F 23 d 5.0 - F 23 d 5.9 F 17 c 95.95
Right of VI Corps	Help QUESNOY	Left Div.Arty. IV Corps.	3, 18-pr Btties. Fire on S.O.S. Lines F 23 b 0.0 - F17 c 9.1 1, 4.5" How.Bty. Fire on Sunken Road in F 17 d 1.0 - F 17 d 1.5
RIGHT GROUP	Help QUESNOY	Centre Group.	3, 18-pr Btties. Fire on Line F 17 b 4.0 - F 11 d 5.0 1, 4.5"How.Bty. Fire on Line F 17 b 7.0 - F 11 d 8.0
		Right Group	3, 18-pr Btties. F 17 b 5.0 - F 17 b 4.9 1, 18-pr Btty. F 17 b 3.0 - F 17 b 1.7 1, 4.5" How.Bty. F 11 d 5.0 - F 12 b 0.7
CENTRE GROUP.	Help AYETTE.	Left Group	2, 18-pr.Btties. F 12 a 4.4 - F 6 a 5.0
LEFT GROUP	Help OSTRICH	Centre Group.	3, 18-pr Btties. F 6 c 40.45 - A 2 a 46.45 1, 4.5" How.Bty A 1 d 0.6 - A 1 d 9.8.
LEFT GROUP	Help LINCOLN	Centre Div.Arty. VI Corps	3, 18-pr Btties. Fire on Front A 2 a 0.0 - S 27 d 0.0 1, 4.5" How.Bty. ,, Line 100 yards beyond above.
Right of CENTRE DIVISION.	Help DOVER	Left Group.	3, 18-pr Btties. Enfilade from S 27 d 0.0 - S 28 d 0.0 1, 4.5"How.Bty. Bombard N.E. end of MOYENNEVILLE. S 29 c 0.0 1, 4.5"How.Bty. Bombard S.W. end of MOYENNEVILLE.

2ND DIVISION DEFENCE SCHEME - TRENCH MORTARS - APPENDIX "A" (Continued)

UNIT	NUMBER OF GUNS.	LOCATION	ZERO LINES	O. Ps.	S.O.S. LINES	REMARKS	WAGON LINES
D.T.M.O.	-	V 27 a 5.1					POMMIER
X/2 T.M. Battery.	H.Q.	F 2 d 30.25					
	1.	F 5 a 95.80	135°Grid	Front Line Posts, according to target	F 6 c 40.30-F 6 c 60.35		
	1.	F 5 a 95.80	143°Grid		F 6 c 40.50-F 6 c 60.35		
	1.	S 26 c 10.20	128°Grid		A 2 d 20.20		
	1.	S 28 c 10.20	96°Grid		A 3 a 60.40		
	* 1.	S 26 c 10.20	178°Grid			* Spare Bed.	
	* 1.	F 11 b 05.85	104°Grid			For defence of PURPLE LINE.	
	1.	X 27 b 30.55	164°Grid				
	1.	X 27 b 30.55	102°Grid				
Y/2 T.M. Battery.	H.Q.	F 2 d 30.25					POMMIER
	1.	F 16 b 40.75	130°Grid	Front line Posts according to Target.	(F 17 c 80.35 to F 17 d 10.50		
	1.	F 16 b 40.75	92°Grid		1 & 4 - (		
	1.	F 18 b 40.75	92°Grid		(		
	1.	F 11 c 10.70	139°Grid				
	1.	F 11 c 10.70	89°Grid		2 & 3 -F 11 d 40.25 to F 17 b 30.85	*Spare Bed. For defence of PURPLE LINE.	
	* 1.	F 2 d 30.25	126°Grid				
	1.	F 2 d 30.25	76°Grid				

Proposed and under Construction (7th Aug.1918).

X/2 T.M.B.	H.Q.	F 3 d 65.40	To replace H.Q. as above.				
	4 Beds.	X 27 a 3.3	Approximate only. For defence of PURPLE Line.			Under construction.	
	2 Beds.	S 25 b 20.30	For defence of AERODROME Switch			Proposed.	
Y/2 T.M.B.	H.Q.	F 3 d 65.40	To replace H.Q. as above.			Under construction.	
	2 Beds.	F 13 b 70.10	For defence of PURPLE Line.			Under construction.	
	2 Beds.	F 2 d 10.20	For defence of PURPLE Line.			Under construction.	

2ND DIVISION SCHEME   APPENDIX "A" Continued.

POSITIONS FOR DEFENCE OF PURPLE LINE.

GROUP	No. of Position	Map Square	O. Ps.
RIGHT GROUP	PA.1	E 10 d 31.80	) Bdo. O.P. F 13 c 35.00
	PA.2	E 10 c 89.83	)
	PA.3	E 10 b 61.15	) In Trench about
	PA.4	E 10 c 79.09	) E 18 d 8.4
	PB.1	E 5 c 24.63	) Bdo.O.P. F 13 c 0.0
	PB.2	E 4 d 99.98	)
	PB.3	E 4 d 60.62	) Front Line F 14 a.
	PB.4	E 5 c 37.56	)
CENTRE GROUP	PE.1	W 23 b 78.48	F 1 c 2.1
	PE.2	W 23 b 91.60	F 8 b 3.7
	PE.3	W 24 a 30.91	E 6 central.
	PE.4	W 23 a 88.89	E 11 b 0.6
	PC.1	W 23 c 06.27	)
	PC.2	W 23 c 20.40	) About E 18 a 5.5
	PC.3	W 23 c 31.65	) and E 12 c 5.5
	PC.4	W 22 d 70.43	)
LEFT GROUP	PD.1	W 24 b 16.01	) Bdo O.P. X 15 c 0.9
	PD.2	W 29 b 44.80	)
	PD.3	W 23 d 70.29	) About X 22 c 1.4
	PD.4	X 19 c 28.84	)
	PF.1	W 27 b 09.73	)
	PF.2	W 28 a 23.81	) About F 7 d 65.90
	PF.3	W 28 a 77.83	) and X 16 d 1.8.
	PF.4	W 22 d 46.29	)

2ND DIVISION DEFENCE SCHEME — APPENDIX "A" Continued.

POSITIONS FOR DEFENCE OF RED LINE.

GROUP.	No. of Position.	Map Square	O. P.
RIGHT GROUP	Z.1 Z.2 Z.3 Z.4 Y.1 Y.2 Y.3 Y.4	D 9 b 12.20 D 16 a 38.65 D 9 c 47.88 D 15 a 74.78 D 10 c 92.23 D 3 d 70.00 D 10 d 69.66 D 10 c 40.75	VIPER E 7 central VIXEN E 9 c 1.6 PEAR E 9 c 3.7 PUMA E 7 d 3.4 PLUM E 3 d 5.7
Centre	W.1 W.2 W.3 W.4	D 5 a 35.63 D 5 b 08.77 D 6 c 38.75 D 5 c 50.53	PLUM E 3 d 5.7 SKUNK E 3 d 3.5
LEFT GROUP	X.1 X.2 X.3 X.4	D 11 a 20.22 D 10 b 40.01 D 4 c 53.58 D 10 b 87.27	DAMSON E 2 b 7.4 BUFFALO W 25 b 7.8

All positions have been resected.

2ND DIVISION DEFENCE SCHEME ---- APPENDIX "A" HEAVY ARTILLERY.

UNIT	MAP REFERENCE	CALIBRE of Guns	No. of Guns	ARCS OF FIRE	MAXIMUM RANGE, YARDS.	O. PS.	LANE	S.O.S. POINTS.	REMARKS.
SHERER'S GROUP	**LA CAUCHIE.**								
276 Siege Bty.	X 14 a 12.35	6" How.	4	1, 110-159 Grid	9,600	DOVE X21 a 3.64	17	A 3 5.0- 5.9	*Day
	E 4 b 75.35	"	2	1, 84-148 Grid	9,600			A 5 a 5.0- 5.5	
				2, 101-148 Grid	9,600				
				1, 80-160 "	8,900				
				1, 80,180 "	8,800				
358 Siege Bty.	2, W 22 d 55.30	6" How.	2	1, 85-155 "	9,400	PIGEON	16	2, A 2 c 5.0-5.5	
	4, X 13 d 4.8		4	1, 86-155 "	8,950	X 21 a 00.45		4, A 2 d 5.0-5.9	
				4, 97-150 "	8,400	Day.			
342 Siege Bty.	X 19 b 00.05	6" How.	4	4, 90-150 "	9,300	QUAIL.	15	4, A 8 c 0.0-0.9	
					9,600	F 13 c 95.90			
					8,200	Day.			
					9,500				
183 Siege Bty.	W 30 a 80.75	6" How.	4	2, 80-140 "	9,500	GOOSE	14	4, A 7 d 5.0-5.9	
				2, 80-140 "	9,400	X 21 a 45.30 Day & Night.			
305 Siege Bty.	M 29 d 75.20	6" How.	4	1, 75-155 "	9,600	PLOVER	13	4, A 13 c 0.0-0.9	
				1, 94-180 "	9,500	F 10 a 0.5			
				1, 76-153 "	9,600	Day.			
				1, 87-155 "	9,600				
136 Siege Bty.	E 5 b 20.90	9.2"How.	2	1, 79-139 "	10,150	TOM TIT	12	6, F 18 & 5.9-	E 24
	E 8 b 95.30		4	1, 81-141 "	10,150	X 27 d 65.78 Day and Night	& 11	a 5.0.	
				1, 76-136 "	9,450				
				1, 76-136 "	10,150				
				1, 74-134 "	9,550				
				1, 76-136 "	9,835				

Page 12

2ND DIVISION DEFENCE SCHEME -------- APPENDIX "A" HEAVY ARTILLERY (Continued) PAGE 13.

UNIT	MAP REFERENCE	CALIBRE	No. of Guns.	ARCS OF FIRE	MAXIMUM RANGE.	O. Ps.	LANE	S.O.S. POINTS.	REMARKS.
54th Siege Battery.	X 7 b 70.20	9.2 How.	2	112-172 Grid.	12,800		17	A 4 a 5.0-5.9	
24 Heavy Battery.	X 7 c 82.16	60-pdr.	4	85-145 "	See Remarks	ALBATROSS X 15 d 16.13 Day & Night.	16	2, A 3 c 0.0-0.9	2 orh S.9500
		"					15	2, A 8 b 5.0-5.9	2 orh HE 11100
	E 8 c 95.95	"	2	80-140 "	"		14	2, A 8 d 0.0-0.9	6 crh S.12000
									8 crh HE 12500
152 Heavy Battery.	X 13 c 58.37	"	4	90-150 "	"	KITE X 20 b 95.40 Day & Night.	13	2, A 14 a 5.0-5.9	As above.
		"					12	2, A 14 c 0.0-0.9	2 orh S 9,200
	E 4 d 50.85	"	2	0-360 "	"		11	2, A 19 d 5.0-5.9	2 crh HE 11400
									8 orh B 9,800
									8 crh HE 12800
77 Siege Battery.	W 30 a 25.25	8" How.	4	75-145 "	11,700	COCKATOO X 15 d 41.12 D a y.	14	2, A 9 d 5.0-5.9	2 orh S 9,100
	E 5 a 6.5		2	75-145 "	11,700		13	2, A 15 a 5.0-5.9	2 crh HE 11100
							12	2, A 14 d 5.0-5.0	8 orh S 9,600
									8 H.E 12,200

Southern boundary of Lane 11 is the E. and W Grid running through A 20 central, each lane is 500 yards broad.

Page 14.

2ND DIVISION DEFENCE SCHEME — AEROPLANE CALLS.

AEROPLANE CALL	MEANING	ANSWERED AS UNDER		
		Under Normal conditions of Trench Warfare.	During Annihilating fire	During Barrage Fire.
N. F.	Hostile Battery now firing	10 rds. per gun RAPID, to be fired by all active guns and 4.5" Howitzers.	10 rds. per gun RAPID to be fired by at least half the guns per position covering Group Zone.	Not answered.
G. F.	Fleeting target not of sufficient importance to warrant a heavy concentration of fire.	5 rds. per gun RAPID from all active guns and 4.5" Hows. that fire on that Zone.	5 rds. per gun RAPID to be fired by at least half the guns per position covering Group Zone.	One gun per position or one section per Battery.
L. L.	A really important fleeting target, such as, a Battery limbered up and halted, an Inf. Battn. or a Cavalry regiment.	5 rds. per gun RAPID, from all active guns and 4.5" Hows. that can reach.	5 rds. per guns RAPID from all guns and 4.5" Howitzers that can reach.	One gun per position or one section per Battery.

1. In all cases, when necessary, the call will be repeated from the air, and the procedure repeated by the guns.
2. In no cases are guns or howitzers to be taken off vulnerable and important targets on which they are obtaining visibly good effect, in order to engage another target reported by the R.A.F. or any other source of information.

2nd Division Defence Scheme   Appendix B

ARRANGEMENTS FOR MANNING THE PURPLE LINE.

1. The troops specially detailed for the defence of the Purple Line are
   - Right Brigade - 1 Battn.
   - Left   "   - 1 Battn.
   - Centre   "   - 2 Coys. which are not to be moved forward unless replaced from Bn. in Div. Reserve vide 2nd Div. Defence Scheme para.5.

   In addition, the troops which have been fighting in the outpost line will be available.

2. The most probable operations which the Battn. of the Centre Brigade in Divisional Reserve may be called upon to carry out are -

   (a) To reinforce troops holding the Purple Line.

   (b) To hold the Purple Reserve Line if required in 99th and 6th Bde. areas.

   (c) To counter-attack in Right Bde. area in order to restore the situation if part of QUESNOY Hill is lost.

   In case of heavy bombardment this Battn. will assemble about Old German front and reserve lines about E.11.b & d - E.12.a & c.
   Battns. of the Centre Brigade on coming into Div. Reserve will carry out the necessary reconnaissances of assembly positions and of lines of advance to the Purple Reserve Line and beyond. It would depend on circumstances whether the forming up place for the counter-attack was Purple Reserve Line, ADINFER WOOD SWITCH or QUESNOY FARM TRENCH.
   In battle the O.C. will either be at 6th Brigade Battle H.Q. or arrange for a liaison officer to be there so that messages can reach him at short notice from Div. H.Q.

3. In the event of the action outlined in para.2 being required, it is probable that the Battn. in Div. Reserve would either revert to G.O.C. 6th Brigade or come under orders of G.O.C. 99th Brigade.

4. In the event of the Purple Line being held as a front line, certain M.Gs. now about the Front Purple Line would eventually be replaced by Lewis Guns, in which case Reserve positions selected by O.C. M.G.Battn. would be occupied by the guns thus set free.

5. The position of H.Q. would be as follows:-

   Right Brigade - E.7.b.7.8.
                    Front line Bn. - E.18.c.8.1.
                    Two Battns.   - E.12.c.1.4.

   Centre Brigade - W.26.b.3.6.
                    Front line Bn. - F.1.c.1.2.
                    Two Battns   - E.5.d.2.3 & E.4.c.2.5.

   Left Brigade   - W.23.c.2.8.
                    Battn. H.Q. - W.19.d.2.2.
                                  W.19.c.4.1.
                                  W.24.a.2.0.

P.T.O.

5.   A proportion of the Artillery covering the Divisional front covers the Purple Line without change of position, viz -

    Right Group 21 guns 8" Hows.
    Centre   " 18   "   6"   "
    Left   " 18   "   8"   "

   These guns would, however, be moved at the first opportunity to more suitable positions in rear.
   The remainder of the artillery covering the Infantry of the Division cannot cover the Purple Line in the present position and would be withdrawn as early as possible to suitable positions.

6.   Inf. Brigades will include in their Defence Schemes definite plans for manning the Purple Line, showing parts of the line to be occupied, Lewis Gun emplacements, positions of Coy. and Battn. H.Q.

2nd Division Defence Scheme.   Appendix 'C'
-------------------------------   ------------

ACTION OF TANKS.

1. A Company No.4 Battn. (Mark V) Tanks is located in the Divisional Area, about BIENVILLERS.

2. Mark V Tank is an improvement on Mark IV, being faster and more easily handled.

3. In case of the enemy breaking through the PURPLE LINE, the functions of the Tanks will be to break up his attack, independently of any Infantry action, and to prevent him from reaching the RED LINE.

4. On a heavy bombardment breaking out, or when a hostile attack seems likely, the Tank Coy. H.Q. moves to 99th Bde. H.Q., and a Liaison Officer proceeds to Advanced Div. H.Q.

    Communication between Advanced Div. H.Q. and Tank Coy. H.Q. is being arranged by 2nd Division Signal Coy.

5. If an enemy attack develops, Tanks may be ordered to "Man Battle Position" i.e. three Sections take up a line from about E.10.d to E.11.a. The fourth Section is in Reserve.

6. The order to "Man Battle Positions" is given by the Tank Coy. Commander, who will keep in touch with Advanced Div. H.Q. through his Liaison officer.
    The shortest time in which the Tanks can reach Battle positions from BIENVILLERS is one hour. From the Battle Position the Tanks move forward when ordered to meet the enemy.

7. The Tank Coy. Commander issues his orders to his Tanks independently. He is guided by the information obtained from Div. H.Q. as to whether to use his Tanks in the direction of the COJEUL VALLEY or of QUESNOY FARM. Reports received as to how the Tanks are being used will be communicated to Brigades.
    The guiding principle in the use of this Coy. of Tanks is that action must be taken without delay, before the enemy has time to bring up Artillery.
    It is therefore impossible to employ them for a deliberate counter-attack, but Infantry will seize any opportunity that is offered by the advance of the Tanks, to regain ground.

8. Tanks required to co-operate in a deliberate counter attack will be furnished from Reserve Tank Companies.

2nd Division Defence Scheme.   Appendix D

DEMOLITIONS.

1. In each Brigade Section, certain wells, bridges etc have been prepared for demolition.
   Lists are in the possession of the C.R.E.

2. At least one officer and a sufficient party of R.E. from the Coy. working in each Brigade Section are permanently told off as a demolition party.
   These parties are in charge of the maintenance and preparations of all demolitions in their areas.

3. Orders for demolitions to be carried out will be issued by Divisional H.Q., through the C.R.E. to Field Coys.
   The Field Coy. Commanders will keep Brigadiers informed of orders received regarding demolitions. It must, however, be recognized that it may be impossible to issue orders for demolitions during a battle, and action will usually have to be taken by the Commander on the spot.

4. The Division is responsible for preparation of demolitions East of and exclusive of the villages of ST AMAND - POMMIER - BERLES AU BOIS.

5. The C.R.E. will keep Brigadiers informed through Field Coy. Commanders of all demolitions prepared in their areas.

2nd Division Defence Scheme.

APPENDIX E.

ACTION IN CASE OF ENEMY SHELLING WITH YELLOW CROSS GAS.

1. In the event of shelling by Yellow Cross Gas, the following precautions will be at once taken :-

2. (a) All troops who are not actually required as part of a garrison will be moved to a flank out of the infected area into an area not likely to be infected.

   (b) The exact area into which troops will be moved must depend on the conditions at the time, but Commanding Officers will prepare schemes shewing areas into which troops under their Command may be moved. These schemes will be approved by Brigadiers and handed over on relief.

   (c) Alternative localities should be chosen to suit different directions of the wind. Woods, villages, and valleys will be avoided.

   (d) Where it is necessary to leave a garrison, this garrison should be relieved after five hours.

3. The Officer Commanding the troops in the infected area is responsible that sentries are posted on all approaches leading into the area, and that all traffic is diverted to windward.
   Sentries will have orders -

   (a) To warn all troops and transport entering the infected area: to divert them if possible.

   (b) To see that anyone entering the infected area puts on his gas mask.

   Brigade Gas Officers should be used to define the infected area.

   Sentries will be kept on until the area is declared clear (see para. 4).

   In the event of a relief, the sentry posts will be taken over by the relieving unit.

4. The Divisional Gas Officer will decide when sentries may be taken off an infected area.

5. The organisation of gas sentries in certain areas of the alert zone will be as follows :-

   (i) ADINFER WOOD. If ADINFER WOOD is shelled, sentries will be posted by the Reserve Battalion, Left Brigade on the N.W. side of the Wood and by Companies holding the PURPLE LINE on the S.E. side.

   (ii) MONCHY VILLAGE. If MONCHY village is shelled by Yellow Cross Gas, the responsibility for posting sentries is as follows :-

      (a) MONCHY - BERLES AU BOIS Roads - 5th Inf. Bde. H.Q.

      (b) MONCHY - RANSART 3 Roads) Troops of 6th Inf.
          MONCHY - ADINFER Road   ) Bde. in or near
          MONCHY - QUESNOY Fm. Road) MONCHY.

      (c) MONCHY - ESSARTS Road and
          MONCHY - HAMMESCAMPS Road - Reserve Batt. 6th Bde.

- (2) -

      (d) MONCHY - BIENVILLERS Road - H.Q. 6th Inf. Bde.

(iii)   DOUCHY. Sentries to be found by a unit detailed by G.O.C. 6th Inf. Brigade.

(iv)   COJEUL VALLEY. 6th Inf. Brigade (Squares E.12, F.7, 8, 3, and 9). To be found by a unit detailed by G.O.C. 6th Inf. Brigade.

(v)   COJEUL VALLEY. 5th Inf. Brigade (Squares X.29, F.7, and 5) to be found by a unit detailed by G.O.C. 5th Inf. Brigade.

(vi)   QUESNOY FARM. To be found by a unit detailed by 99th Inf. Brigade.

(vii)   Valley South of ADINFER VILLAGE. To be found by a unit detailed by G.O.C. 5th Inf. Brigade.

(viii)   O.G.L. South of MONCHY. To be found by a unit detailed by G.O.C. 99th Inf. Brigade.

2nd Division Defence Scheme.   Appendix F

DEFENCE AGAINST CLOUD GAS ATTACKS.

1. Standing Orders for Defence Against Gas are contained in "S.S.193" which will be adhered to.

2. Maps shewing the GAS ZONE boundaries in the VI Corps area were issued to all concerned on 21st April, 1918, under 2nd Division No. G.S.647/14.

3. METHOD OF SPREADING THE CLOUD GAS ALARM.

In the case of an attack by Cloud Gas, the alarm is spread by all means available; by Strombos Horns, rattles, telephones, and, if necessary, by orderly.

A system to warn sleeping men and detached parties is arranged by all formations, and sentries are posted over dug-outs.

Warning of cloud gas attack will be sent by telephone by sending the letters "GAS" followed by the name of the trench, or stating locality, opposite which gas is being liberated. (Full instructions are given in "S.S.193" para.5 - also published as Appendix IV "S.S.534").

The responsibility for sending telephone messages is as under:-

<u>Companies</u> :- to Coys. on flanks including Coys. of other Divns., Battn, H.Q., and when possible, direct to the Artillery.

<u>Battalions</u> :- to Battns. on flanks and all Coys., Bde. H.Q., and if possible, direct to Artillery.

<u>Brigades</u> :- to Brigades on flanks, all units in Bde. area, Div. H.Q., direct to Artillery, and any outside unit which is directly connected to the Bde. Signal Exchange.

<u>The Division will warn</u>:- VI Corps.
Div. Artillery.
H.A.Group.
Divisions on flanks.
A.P.M. (who will instruct police to warn traffic).
Town Major, BIENVILLERS.
" POMMIER.
" ST AMAND.
" GAUDIEMPRE.

4. Strombos horns are located as follows and they will not be moved without authority from Div. H.Q.:-

<u>Right Brigade.</u>

Brigade H.Q. - E.4.b.0.5.   F.15.c.2.1.
F.16.b.9.6.   F.14.a.3.3.
F.16.d.7.9.   F.13.d.1.7.
F.22.b.9.9.   F.12.d.9.6.
F.10.d.2.5.   E.18.a.1.7.
F.16.c.9.2.
F.9.d.2.8.

P.T.O.

Centre Brigade.

Brigade H.Q. - E.4.a.8.2.   F.10.b.4.8.
               F.11.c.8.5.   F.9.a.7.4.
               F.11.b.5.4.   F.2.d.9.7.
               F.5.d.7.1.   F.1.d.3.4.
               F.5.b.8.3.   E.5.d.4.4.
               F.11.b.3.7.
               F.11.c.6.9.

Left Brigade.

Brigade H.Q. - W.23.c.1.9.   X.28.b.5.6.
               S.26.d.7.5.   X.27.b.8.4.
               S.26.a.7.4.   X.26.a.1.9.
               X.30.c.7.2.   X.19.d.1.6.
               X.30.a.8.0.   X.19.c.5.2.
               X.24.c.2.0.   W.24.c.9.2.
               X.29.d.2.3.   E.5.b.4.6.
               X.29.a.7.5.

Back area.   E.2.c.8.8.   D.10.c.1.1.
               W.25.c.3.9.   V.29.c.3.9.

5.   Twelve "Sound and Light" rockets are kept by the Area Commandant GAUDIEMPRE. These rockets will be used for the alarm both by day and night in addition to the telephone. On receipt of the gas alarm by whatever means, the rockets will be fired at half-minute intervals under arrangements to be made by the officer in charge of the station.

APPENDIX G

RIGHT DIVISION DEFENCE SCHEME.

COMMUNICATIONS.

Telephonic Communication

1. An Advanced Division Exchange is established at W.20.c.2.9 and an advanced R.A.Exchange is established at W.22.d.7.5.

2. Division H.Q. Exchange at V.27.c.7.9 is connected to Advanced Division exchange by 2 lines and Advanced Div.Exchange is connected to Advanced Div.R.A.Exchange by 2 lines.
   From Division H.Q. there is a direct line to each Brigade and each Brigade has a direct line to Advanced Div.Exchange.

3. Each Infantry Brigade and R.A.Group is connected direct to Brigade and Group on Left and Right and Division H.Q. is connected direct to Division on Left and Right.

4. Exchanges are established at HUMBERCAMP and POMMIER and connect all local units in those areas. These exchanges are connected to Division H.Q. by 2 lines and Advanced Div.exchange by 1 line. They are also connected to each other. (For details see Diagram A).

Buried Cables.

Buried cables 8 feet deep have been put down as follows:-

W.19.c.2.6	to	W.22.d.7.5	50 pairs.
W.22.d.7.5	to	F.1.a.9.1	50 pairs.
W.22.d.7.5	to	E.10.a.9.5	50 pairs.
W.22.d.7.5	to	X.21.b.9.6	50 pairs.

By means of these, buried lines exist between:-

(1) Advanced Div., all Brigades and R.A.Groups.
(2) R.A.Groups and Batteries.
(3) Brigades and Battalions (for short distances)

In order to provide a buried cable route between Batteries and O.Ps it is proposed to bury between a point X.21.a.2.8 and the N. corner of ADINFER Wood.

German buries exist as follows:-

Left Brigade Area.
X.21.b.6.2	-	X.27.b.8.6	4 pairs.
X.21.d.8.2	-	X.23.a.1.1	2 pairs.
X.23.a.1.1	-	X.24.c.1.8	1 pair.
X.21.d.8.2	-	F.5.a.0.5	2 pairs (not yet finished)
X.27.b.7.3	-	X.28.b.7.5	16 pairs (not yet completely through)

Centre and Right Brigade Area.
E.6.a.5.0	-	F.7.a.5.4	1 pair.
F.7.a.5.4	-	F.7.b.8.7	2 pairs.
F.7.b.8.7	-	F.9.b.7.2	3 pairs.

There is also one line........

COMMUNICATIONS (Contd)

There is also one line which is made up out of various old German buries running from E.18.a.5.1 to F.14.d.5.2.

These buries are in use between Brigades and Battalions and Artillery and O.Ps.

Visual Communication.

Excellent visual communication is obtainable throughout the Divisional area. Brigade H.Q. are in touch with all Battalions by this means.

Division H.Q. is in touch with all Brigades and M.G.Battalion. 2 transmitting stations are in action. No.1 at farm D.6 central and No.2 at W.28.b.8.1. From this point all Brigades are obtained. This means can also be used by Artillery to their Group H.Qrs. (For details see Diagram B).

Wireless and Power Buzzer Communication.

Wireless stations are situated as follows:-

1. Division H.Q.   V.27.a.8.1
2. Left Brigade H.Q.   W.23.c.1.8
3. Right and Centre Bde H.Q.   E.4.a.6.4
4. Battn.H.Q. Left Bde.   X.27.b.8.5

Power Buzzers and Amplifiers - see attached Diagram C.

Pigeons.

8 pigeons are supplied to each Brigade daily and fly back to lofts at SOMBRIN, COUTURELLE and GOMBREMETZ.

Contact Aeroplane

Divisional Dropping Station is situated at V.27.C.9.5.

DIAGRAM OF COMMUNICATIONS - RIGHT DIVISION

Diagram "A" June 24th 1915
2nd Signal Company. R.E.

L.B.
LEFT BRIGADE.
W.22.d.8.6.

M.L.
W.28.b.5.1.

R.B.
CENTRE & RIGHT
BRIGADES.
E.4.c.8.3.

H.V.
M.G. BATT'N
W.26.d.7.1.

P.M. central
D.6.

B.Z. DIV'N H'Q
V.27.c.8.9.

DIAGRAM "B" JUNE 26TH 1918.
2ND SIGNAL COMPANY. R.E.

DIAGRAM OF VISUAL COMMUNICATIONS · RIGHT DIVISION

— SECRET —

Left Battalion of Left Brigade at X.24.a.2.5.

Company of Left Batt'n. of Left Brigade at S.26.d.8.6.

Right Battalion of Left Brigade at X.27.b.9.5.

F &.a. 1st Battalion of Centre Brigade at F.9.a.8.4.

Left Battalion of Right Brigade 500 yds away at F.9.b.6.1.

Right Battalion of Right Brigade at F.20.b.6.8.

(Divisional Directing Station) Left Brigade at W.23.c.1.8.

Support Battalion of Centre Brigade at F.1.c.0.0.

Centre Brigade at V.30.b.8.4.

Right Brigade 500 yds away at E.4.c.2.4.

Divisional HQ at V.27.c.7.7.

Reference
- ———— Wireless Station.
- △ P.B. & Amplifier Station.
- ⊕ Power Buzzer Station.
- ∿∿∿ Wireless Communication.
- – – – P.B. & Amplifier Communication.

Note: All Map References are taken from Bucquoy (Combined Sheet) Scale 1/40,000.

DIAGRAM OF WIRELESS & POWER BUZZER & AMPLIFIER COMMUNICATIONS – RIGHT DIVISION

Diagram "C" July 3rd 1918.
2nd Signal Company R.E.

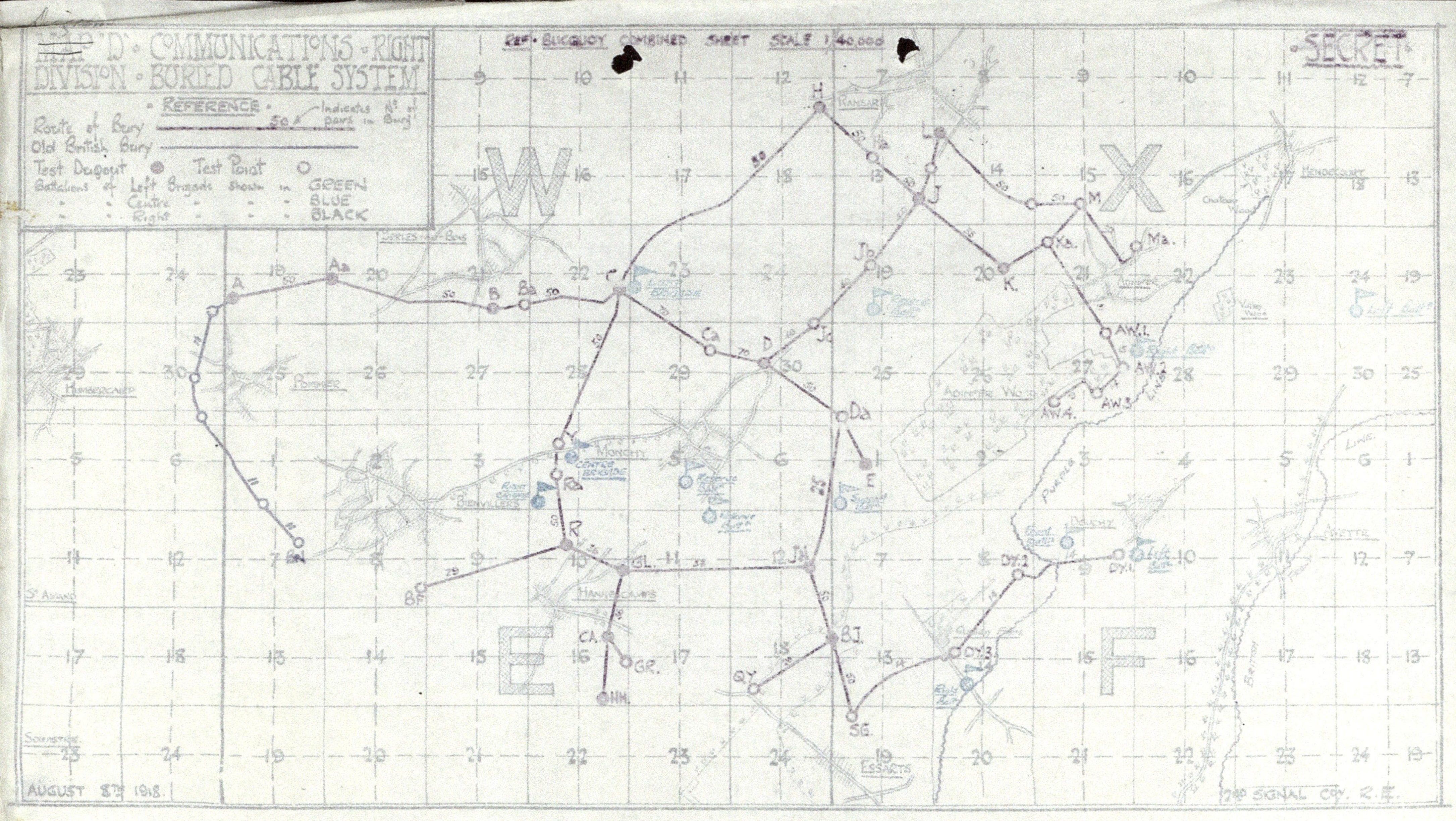

MAP "D" COMMUNICATIONS · RIGHT DIVISION · BURIED CABLE SYSTEM
REF · BUCQUOY COMBINED SHEET SCALE 1/40,000
SECRET
REFERENCE
Route of Bury
Old British Bury
Indicates No. of pairs in Bury
Test Dugout
Test Point
Battalions of Left Brigade shown in GREEN
Centre BLUE
Right BLACK
W
X
E
F
RANSART
MONCHY
BIENVILLERS
HANNESCAMPS
ESSARTS
ADINFER WOOD
AYETTE
HENDECOURT
POMMIER
HUMBERCAMP
ST AMAND
SOUASTRE
BERLES-AU-BOIS
DOUCHY
AUGUST 8TH 1918.
2ND SIGNAL COY. R.E.

APPENDIX "H".
****

ADMINISTRATIVE ARRANGEMENTS.

(1). MEDICAL.

	Left.	Right.
(i). Field Ambulance Bearer Relay Posts.	X.28.b.7.5.	F.8.d.3.5. F.7.a.6.2.
(ii). Motor Ambulance Car Stands.	X.15.a.9.3., and ADINFER (X.21.d.3.8)	MONCHY. W.29.d.8.3.
(iii). Advanced Dressing Stations.	RANSART Brewery X.7.d.9.9.	MONCHY W.29.d.8.3.
" " " PURPLE LINE.	X.1.d.8.5.	BERLES AU BOIS W.15.c.3.0.

(iv). Walking Wounded Collecting Post.   BERLES AU BOIS, W.15.c.3.0.

(v). Main Dressing Station.   VI Corps Main Dressing Station, BAC DU SUD.

(vi). Divisional Rest Station.   WARLINCOURT.

(vii). Evacuation of Sick and Wounded.

    (a). **Left and Centre Brigades.** From R.A.P's by hand, carriage or wheeled stretcher to car stand at ADINFER or X.15.c.9.3., thence by car to A.D.S., RANSART or X.1.d.8.5.

    (b). **Right Brigade.** From R.A.P's by hand carriage or wheeled stretcher to A.D.S. at MONCHY or BERLES AU BOIS, thence by car to M.D.S.

    (c). From A.D.S's. Wounded to VI Corps M.D.S. Sick to Divl. Rest Station. By car or horse ambulances.

(2). AMMUNITION SUPPLY.

    (i). Railheads - FOSSEUX. SAULTY.

    (ii). Corps Ammunition Dumps. BAC DU SUD, CHAPEL SAULTY, LA BELLEVUE, L'ESPERANCE.

    (iii). Divisional Ammunition Refilling Points (Artillery).
POMMIER - LA CAUCHIE road (V.24.d.9.7.) (Emergency Dump only).
POMMIER - ST AMAND road (D.6.b.5.8.)
Ammunition is delivered to A.R.P's from Corps dumps by lorry, or in the case of the A.R.P. at D.6.b.5.8. by light railway, on application being made to F. Corps M.T. Column.
From A.R.P. at D.6.b.5.0., issues are made to batteries by light railway or by horsed transport.

    (iv). S.A.A. Section. - GAUDIEMPRE, D.1.d.9.8.

    (v). S.A.A., Grenades, etc. Main Divisional Dump in orchard on POMMIER - LA CAUCHIE road, W.25.a.1.7.
Issues are made on application to Officer i/c of dump, except in case of S.O.S. Signals, V.P.A. and Ground Flares for the issue of which authority of 2nd Divn. "Q" must be obtained.

(3). R.E. DUMPS.
    (i). Corps R.E. Dump.
        WARLINCOURT HALTE.
    (ii). Divisional R.E. Dump.
        MONCHY - E.4.a.8.4.

P.T.O......

(2).

(4). SUPPLIES.

(i). Railhead - SAULTY.
(ii). (a) Refilling Points -
Light Railway Junction near POMMIER (D.6.a.8.2.)
"   "   "   "   HUMBERCAMP (V.29.c.2.5.)

Supplies are sent from Railhead to Refilling Points by Light Railway.

(b) In case of occupation of the Purple Line Refilling Point would be at (Sheet 51C) W.25.b.5.1. (LE GROSTISON FARM).

Supplies would be delivered to Wagon and Transport Lines by Train Transport.

(5). PRISONERS OF WAR CAGE.

Advanced.   Near MONCHY - BIENVILLERS Road E.3.d.8.5.
Main.   On HUMBERCAMP - LA CAUCHIE Road V.29.b.1.8.

The Guard and Escort of 3 N.C.Os. and 30 Men is provided by the Divl. Salvage Company.

(6). STRAGGLERS POSTS.

In the event of operations, Stragglers Posts will be established at -

(a) No. 8. W.27.d.1.9.
    No. 9. E.4.a.8.3.
    No.10. E.9.b.4.4.
    No.11. D.18.b.2.1.

The Left Straggler Post of the Corps on the Right is situated at D.22.b.8.4.

The Personnel for Straggler Posts of 4 N.C.Os. and 12 Men is provided by the Divl. Salvage Company.

(b) In case of occupation of the Purple Line Posts would be established at -

No. 19. W.26.a.2.6.
No. 20. D.6.a.9.2.
No. 21. D.15.b.7.8.

The Left Straggler Post of the Corps on the Right would be situated at D.13.d.1.6.

(7). CEMETERIES.

AYETTE   - - - F.5.d.2.4.
QUESNOY FARM - - - F.13.b.7.9.
BIENVILLERS   - - - E.7.b.4.2.
St. AMAND   - - - D.10.c.4.7.

Only the two last named cemeteries will be used, except in cases of necessity.

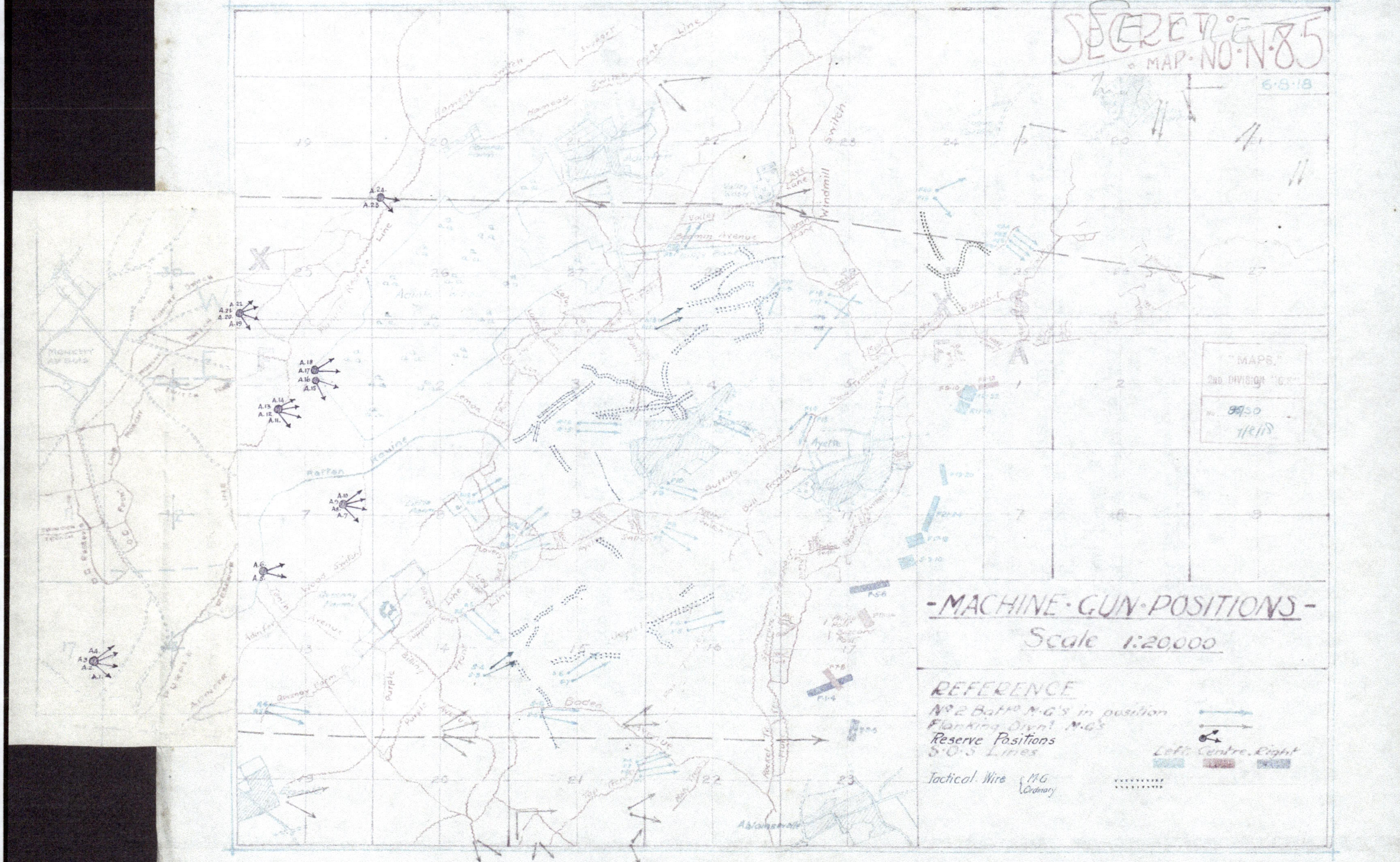

MAP "C" Office

SECRET
MAP. No. N.85
6.6.18

"MAP"
2nd AN/Bgr "C"
96.0
1618

— MACHINE·GUN·POSITIONS —
Scale 1:20000

REFERENCE
N°2 Batto M.G's in position
Flanking Dism¹ M.G.S
Reserve Positions
S·O·S lines
Tactical Wire   M.G
                    (Sidney)

Left Centre Right

SECRET

MAP D
No 5/13

TRACK MAP

Issued with XVII Corps Defence Scheme

MAP D

"MAPS."
2ND. DIVISION "G.S."
No. N/35/13.
OFFICE

2nd Division Trench Strength. 10th Sept. 1918.

Unit		Officers	O.R.	
5th Bde.	2nd Ox. & Bucks L.I.	17	439	
	2nd H.L.I.	16	357	
	24th Royal Fusiliers	17	499	
		Total Bde.	50 officers. 1,295. O.R.	
6th Bde.	1st Kings Regt.	21	583	
	2nd S. Staffs.	19	580	
	17th Royal Fusiliers	23	390	
		Total Bde.	63 officers. 1,553. O.R.	
99th Bde.	1st R. Berks. Regt.	19	409	
	1st K.R.R.C.	21	462	
	23rd Royal Fusiliers	22	466	
		Total Bde.	62 officers 1,337. O.R.	
		Total Division	175 officers 4,185 O.R.	

SECRET

MAP· N° N/91/3
"B" 9·8·18

MAP SHEWING DISPOSITIONS OF TROOPS

To accompany Right Division Defence Scheme.

REFERENCE
Companies shown thus ◯
Platoons " "
Coy. H.Q
Bn. "

Scale 1:20000

Map "B"

S E C R E T.   5th Inf. Bde. No. G.S. 740/97.

2nd DIVISION GENERAL STAFF
No. G.S. 5/145
Date 17-7-18

COPY NO.
1   24TH R.F.
2   52ND L.I.
3   2ND H.L.I.
4   5TH L.T.M. BTY.
5   6TH INF. BDE.
6   2ND GUARDS BDE.
7   99TH INF. BDE.
8   2ND DIVISION.   8a "Q"
9   NO. 2 M.G. BATTN.
10 "A" COY., 2ND M.G. BN.
11 LEFT GROUP R.F.A.
12 10TH D.C.L.I.
13 226TH FIELD COY. R.E.
14 A.D.M.S.
15 5TH BDE. SIGNAL OFFICER.
16 5TH BDE. TRANSPORT OFFICER.
17 STAFF CAPTAIN.
18 WAR DIARY.
19 FILE

1. Herewith COPY NO. 10 of 5TH INFANTRY BRIGADE DEFENCE SCHEME. This cancels Defence Scheme issued under this Office No. G.S. 740/51 dated 28/6/18.

2. Tracing marked 'C' referred to in para. 5 sub. para.(i) is forwarded herewith to 6TH and 2ND GUARDS Brigades. Copies have already been sent to Battalions under this Office No. G.S. D/Maps/11 dated 27/6/18.

3. Appendices and Maps as under are attached :-

   Appendix "A"   - S.O.S.
   "   "B"   - Orders in the event of shelling by Yellow Cross Gas.
   "   "C"   - Administrative Instructions and Track Map.
   "   "D"   - Signal Communications.
   "   "D II"- Circuit Diagram.
   "   "D III"-Diagram of Visual Communication.
   "   "E"   - Lewis Gun Positions - PURPLE FRONT LINE.

   Map "A"   - Dispositions.
   "   "B"   - Machine Gun Positions.

4. ACKNOWLEDGE.

16th July, 1918.

John C. Boys.
Major,
Brigade Major, 5th Infantry Brigade.

SECRET.   COPY NO ...8..

DEFENCE SCHEME

LEFT BRIGADE, RIGHT DIVISION, VI CORPS.

REFERENCE :- 'AYETTE' SPECIAL SHEET 1/20,000.

1. FRONTAGE AND BOUNDARIES

(a). The 2ND DIVISION holds the Right Sector of the VI Corps Front with three Infantry Brigades in the Line.

(b). The 5TH INFANTRY BRIGADE is on the Left of the 2nd Division front with the 6TH INFANTRY BRIGADE on the Right (H.Q. E.4.a.8.2.), and the 2ND GUARDS BRIGADE on the Left (H.Q. X.13.d.5.5.).

(c). The front held by the Brigade is from F.6.a.3.4. to S.27.a.1.0.

RIGHT BOUNDARY

Front Line F.6.a.3.4. to trench and road crossing F.5.b.7.5. - South of MEAL LANE (inclusive to Brigade) to F.5.a.0.2. - F.3.a.8.2. (LILY LANE inclusive to Brigade on the Right) - F.2.b.8.5. - F.1.b.2.2. - thence due West.

LEFT BOUNDARY

S.27.a.1.0. - X.22.c.6.0. - X.20.c.4.2. - W.21.c.9.3.

INTER-BATTALION BOUNDARY

A.1.b.90.55. - S.25.d.8.2. - S.25.d.57.62. - X.30.c.1.9. - X.29.central - Grid Line X.28. central - Grid Line X.25.central.

2. ORGANIZATION OF DEFENCES

The defences of the Brigade are organized as follows :-

An Outpost Zone.
A Second System.

(a). THE OUTPOST ZONE consists of :-

(i) FRONT OR OBSERVATION LINE
A line of Posts varying from 30 yards to 150 yards South of the Old German Trench which runs through F.6.a., S.25.d., S.26.c. and d. supported by a line of Posts from 100 to 150 yards N. of the Old German Trench above mentioned.

(ii) SUPPORT LINE
Lengths of trench in depth between the front line and the COJEUL RIVER.

(iii) RESERVE LINE
Lengths of Trench from the COJEUL RIVER to the PURPLE FRONT LINE.

/ (b) ....

- 2 -

(b). SECOND OR PURPLE SYSTEM

    (1). PURPLE FRONT LINE.
    (2). PURPLE SUPPORT.
    (3). PURPLE RESERVE.

(c). THE WINDMILL SWITCH
    From the Front System in F.5.b. to the PURPLE SYSTEM at F.9.c.5.4.

3. DISTRIBUTION OF TROOPS

The Front System is held by two Battalions.

RIGHT BATTALION - H.Q. at X.27.b.9.3.

  2 Companies in the Front Line (finding their own Supports)
  1 Company   in the Support Line in Lengths of Trench in F.5.a., X.29.d. and X.30.a.

  1 Company in Reserve with 2 Platoons in PURPLE FRONT LINE
          and 2 Platoons in Western end of BILLY'S BANK.

LEFT BATTALION - H.Q. at X.24.c.2.0.

  2 Companies in the Front Line (finding their own Supports).
  1 Company   in the Support Line -
      2 Platoons AERODROME SWITCH.
      2 Platoons on BOIRY - AYETTE Road.

  1 Company in Reserve with 2 Platoons in WINDMILL SWITCH (E)
       between CORN LANE and BRAN LANE.
      2 Platoons in the Eastern end of BILLY'S BANK.

RESERVE BATTALION - H.Q. at X.19.c.6.2.

  1 Company in trenches near Battalion H.Q.
  1 Company in Banks at X.19.b.0.2.
  1 Company in Bank at W.24.d.4.7.
  1 Company in Old German Trench W.24.a.6.1.

5TH L.T.M. BATTERY - H.Q. at X.20.b.3.2.

  2 guns at X.30.d.9.6.
  2 guns at S.26.c.8.5.
  2 Reserve Gun emplacements at X.27.d.7.8.

S.O.S. Lines

2 guns (A.1.d.42.90 to A.1.b.85.16.
      (A.1.d.95.20 to A.2.a.25.55.

2 guns   S.27.c.10.00 to S.27.c.27.88.

BRIGADE HEADQUARTERS - W.23.c.1.9.
  Advanced Brigade Headquarters X.27.b.20.53.

The Right and Left Battalions will be responsible for the defence of the Front System.

The Reserve Company from each of the Front System Battalions, if moved forward of the PURPLE LINE owing to the tactical situation, will be at once replaced from the Brigade Reserve Battalion.

/ Should ....

Should the enemy establish himself in any part of the OUTPOST ZONE, and local Reserves be unable to eject him, Battalions can use their Reserve Companies for counter-attack.

Battalions will inform Brigade H.Q. at once when they move these Companies forward, so that Companies of the Reserve Battalion can be ordered up to take their place.

4. Dispositions are shown on the attached Map 'A'.

4. MACHINE GUNS

"A" Company of the 2ND M.G. BATTALION is allotted for the defence of the Brigade Sector.

The positions of the Machine Guns are shown on the attached Map 'B'.

5. ARTILLERY

(i) The Brigade front is covered by the Left Group consisting of :-
   (1). 34th Army Brigade R.F.A. (less 1 Battery).
   (2). 14th Brigade R.F.A. (less 1 Battery).

S.O.S. Lines are shown on attached tracing marked 'C'.

(ii) Two 6" NEWTONS are situated at X.29.d.0.0.
   " 6" "   "   "   " S.26.c.1.4.

S.O.S. Lines :-
   2 guns on AYETTE-MOYENNEVILLE Road at F.6.b.45.33.
   1 gun at A.2.d.15.15.
   1 gun at A.3.a.58.48.

6. METHOD OF HOLDING THE LINE

The Front Line is to be held as a fighting line, from which there is to be no voluntary retirement.

In the event of an attack on the Front Line by :-

(a). A raid.
(b). A local attack against some Tactical Feature.

The enemy is to be immediately counter-attacked by the Supporting Troops and our line restored. Such counter-attack being made immediately from the flanks, and from the Support Trenches if possible. Should the immediate counter-attack fail, a deliberate counter-attack will be organized from troops in Divisional Reserve.

In the event of an attack with great weight bringing about a break through on a large scale, troops in Reserve and Supporting Positions must hold their ground, and break up the enemy's attack by fire. It will be useless to fritter away supporting platoons by local counter-attacks.

Our attitude is not to become one of passive defence. Identifications must frequently be obtained by patrols. The enemy must be harassed and caused loss by every possible means.

/ 7 ....

7. PROBABLE FORM OF ATTACK

It seems probable from recent experience that the enemy will avoid ADINFER WOOD in the case of an attack in strength. The most probable forms of attack are :-

(a). An attack with QUESNOY FARM RIDGE as the objective, which would probably be combined with a large operation against ESSARTS.

(b). An attack against the high ground N. of AYETTE.
This might be combined with a movement up the COJEUL VALLEY between QUESNOY FARM RIDGE and ADINFER WOOD in order to penetrate the PURPLE LINE and to threaten QUESNOY FARM RIDGE from the rear.
Indications of the enemy's intentions may be obtained from his gas shelling.
Special arrangements will be made to watch for and report Yellow Cross Gas shelling on ADINFER WOOD and the COJEUL VALLEY, if an attack seems probable.

8. ACTION IN CASE OF A THREATENED ATTACK.

(i) Reserve Company, Right Battalion will hold the PURPLE LINE SYSTEM in depth from X.27.d.2.0. (LOTUS LANE) to X.28.a.15.10., with one platoon moved down to F.3.a. to get touch with the troops of the 6TH INFANTRY BRIGADE in the PURPLE LINE till relieved by a Company of the RESERVE BATTALION. This platoon will then rejoin its Company.

(ii) The 2 Platoons of Reserve Company of the Left Battalion accommodated in BILLY'S BANK will move forward to WINDMILL SWITCH getting touch with the Division on the Left about X.23.c.4.0.
If the situation makes it necessary the short lengths of trench S. of BILLY'S BANK in X.28.a. and b. will be garrisoned by the RESERVE Battalion.

(iii) The RESERVE Battalion will be responsible for the defence of the PURPLE LINE and will move as follows :-

1 COMPANY - will move up and hold the PURPLE SYSTEM in depth from F.3.a.59.19 to X.27.d.2.0. relieving the Platoon of Reserve Company of Right Battalion mentioned in above sub. para. (i).

1 COMPANY - will move up and hold the PURPLE SYSTEM in depth from X.28.a.15.10. to Divisional Boundary at X.22.c.6.0.

1 COMPANY - will move up to the PURPLE RESERVE LINE with two platoons in the Front Line and two Platoons in the Support Line from ADINFER - MONCHY-AU-BOIS Road (inclusive) to X.20.c.4.2.

1 COMPANY - will be moved to Battalion Headquarters at X.19.c.6.2. to await orders.

The Reserve Battalion will not be used to restore the situation in front of the PURPLE LINE without orders from BRIGADE H.Q.

Lewis Gun positions for PURPLE FRONT LINE - see APPENDIX 'E'.

- 5 -

In the event of the PURPLE LINE being held as a front Line, certain M.G's now about the Front Purple Line would be replaced eventually by Lewis Guns.

The position of H.Q. would be as follows :-

    BRIGADE H.Q. ... ... W.23.c.3.8.
    RIGHT BATTALION ... ... W.19.d.2.2.
    LEFT BATTALION ... ... W.19.c.4.1.
    RESERVE BATTALION ... W.24.a.2.0.

9. SECTOR GUIDES

The Brigade will provide 8 guides, 2 from each Battalion, one from Brigade headquarters and one from 5th T.M. Battery.

These guides are intended to guide up reinforcing troops from the RED SYSTEM to any part of the Brigade Area.

Captain R.G. FINLAY, Divisional Headquarters, is the Sector Guide Commandant.

A record of the list of the names of these guides is kept at Brigade H.Q., who will be notified immediately of any change.

Maps showing Overland Tracks have been issued to Battalions.

10. ACTION OF WORKING PARTIES

In the event of an enemy attack, Infantry working parties will place themselves under the orders of the nearest Company or Battalion Commander, who will be responsible that as soon as the situation permits, they are sent back to their own Units.

11. ANTI-AIRCRAFT DEFENCE

(a). Os.C. Units are responsible for their own Anti-Aircraft Defence below 3,000 feet. For this purpose Lewis Guns should be placed in pairs, each pair when possible, being about 1,000 yards apart.

(b). Should the enemy use low flying aeroplanes with which to engage the attention of trench garrisons so as to cover an attack, all ranks must understand that the garrison of the front trenches will engage the hostile Infantry, while the troops in Support and Reserve deal with hostile aeroplanes.

(c). Enemy aircraft will not be engaged with Rifle or Lewis Gun fire unless the markings are recognisable and the struts of the aeroplanes are visible to the naked eye.
    At night only when :-
  (i) The aeroplane can be seen against the sky, or
  (ii) The struts can be seen when the aeroplane is in the beam of a searchlight.

(d). Certain 18 pdr. guns are detailed to engage low flying aeroplanes. The call for this will be -
    " AEROPLANE ATTACK"

12. S.O.S. SIGNALS.

(a). The S.O.S. Signal from July 4th is a Rifle Grenade bursting into :-

GREEN over GREEN over GREEN

/ The ......

- 6 -

The S.O.S. for the Division on our Right (IV Corps) is a Rifle Grenade bursting into RED over GREEN over RED.

(b). The S.O.S. Signal fired from a reconnoitring aeroplane is a RED parachute light meaning :-

" The enemy is advancing to the assault".

Orders for S.O.S. are laid down in APPENDIX 'A'.

13. TANKS

A Company of No. 4 Battalion Tanks is located in the Divisional Area about BIENVILLERS.

In the event of the enemy breaking through the PURPLE LINE, this Company is ordered to break up his attack.

The Tank Company will not be employed for a deliberate counter-attack, but Infantry will seize any opportunity that is offered by the advance of the Tanks, to regain ground.

14. GAS

(a) Action in case of enemy shelling with Yellow Cross Gas is laid down in Appendix 'B'.

(b). CLOUD GAS

Standing Orders for Defence against Gas are contained in "S.S.193" which will be adhered to. Maps showing the Gas Zone Boundaries in the VI Corps Area were issued to all concerned under 6th Inf. Bde. No. G.S. 577/188/1 dated 21/4/18.

In case of an attack by Cloud Gas, the alarm is spread by all means available; by Strombos Horms, rattles, telephones, and if necessary by Orderly.

Warning of Cloud Gas attack will be sent by telephone by sending the letters "GAS" followed by the name of the trench, or stating the locality opposite which gas is being liberated.

The responsibility for sending telephone messages is as under :-

COMPANIES - to Companies on Flanks including Companies of other Divisions, Battalion H.Q., and when possible direct to the Artillery.

BATTALIONS - to Battalions on Flanks and all Companies, Brigade H.Q., and if possible direct to Artillery.

BRIGADE - will warn - Brigades on Flanks, All Units in Brigade Area, Divisional H.Q., direct to Artillery and any outside Unit which is directly connected to the Brigade Signal Exchange.

(c). As the Areas of ADINFER WOOD and the COJEUL VALLEY, X.29.c. and d. are unoccupied, it is possible that Gas shelling on these areas might not be noticed.

/ It ....

It is necessary for the Platoon Sentries of the Battalion nearest these areas to have definite orders to watch for and report without delay all gas shelling for information of Brigade Headquarters.

15. Administrative Arrangements - see APPENDIX 'C'

16. Signal Communication - see APPENDIX 'D'.

16th July, 1918.

(signed) Major,
Brigade Major, 5th Infantry Brigade.

APPENDIX 'A'

"S.O.S."

1. For S.O.S. purposes the Divisional Front will be designated by the Code Word "RIGHT".

2. The Divisional Front will be sub-divided into three S.O.S. Sections, reading from Right to Left, each S.O.S. Section corresponding to a Brigade Front.

3. S.O.S. Code words will be as under :-

   99TH INFANTRY BRIGADE   -   QUESNOY
   6TH INFANTRY BRIGADE   -   AYETTE
   5TH INFANTRY BRIGADE   -   OSTRICH

4. Thus in case of an attack on the whole Divisional Front, the S.O.S. Message will be :-

   " S.O.S. RIGHT"

   In case of an attack on the 5TH BRIGADE FRONT the S.O.S. message will be :-

   " S.O.S. OSTRICH" etc.

5. Gas and Test S.O.S. Messages will be sent in exactly the same manner as the 'S.O.S.' substituting "GAS" or "TEST" for "S.O.S.".

6. The above orders will come into force at once.

7. Attention is drawn to 2nd Division Trench Standing Orders, Section 28.

APPENDIX 'B'

ORDERS IN THE EVENT OF SHELLING BY YELLOW CROSS GAS

1. (a). In the event of shelling by Yellow Cross Gas, troops who are not required as part of a garrison will be moved back to a flank out of the infected area into an area not likely to be infected. The exact area into which troops will be moved must depend on the conditions at the time.

   (b). Alternative areas will be chosen to suit different directions of the wind. Woods, Villages and Valleys will be avoided.

   (c). Where it is necessary to leave a garrison, this garrison will be relieved after 5 hours.

2. Os.C. Battalions in infected areas will be responsible that sentries are posted so as to ensure approaches leading into these areas are guarded, and that all traffic is diverted to windward.

3. The responsibility for posting Gas Sentries in certain areas of the 'ALERT' Zone will be as follows :-

RIGHT BATTALION :-
   ADINFER WOOD
      S.E. side - Reserve Company.
      Approaches -
         C.T. and Road in F.2.d.
         LILY LANE
         LAUREL LANE
         DOUCHY - ADINFER WOOD Road.
         LOTUS LANE
         DOUCHY AVENUE
         PURPLE SUPPORT LINE
         DOUCHY - ADINFER Road.
         LILAC LANE
         BILLY'S BANK.

   COJEUL VALLEY - (Squares X.29. and F.5) - Support Coy.
      Approaches -
         SUGAR FACTORY - DOUCHY Road.
         WINDMILL SWITCH (E)
         WINDMILL SUPPORT (W)
         Pathway in X.29.c.
         HENDECOURT - AYETTE Road.

LEFT BATTALION :-
   VALLEY South of ADINFER VILLAGE. - Reserve Company.
      Approaches -
         Pathway from BILLY'S BANK through X.28.c. a. and X.22.c.
         PURPLE FRONT LINE.
         Pathway from BILLY'S BANK through X.28.a., X.27.c.
         Trench West of PURPLE FRONT LINE.
         DOUCHY - ADINFER Road.

/ RESERVE BATTALION.

RESERVE BATTALION :-
    N.W. of ADINFER WOOD.
      Approaches -

        MONCHY - ADINFER Road.
        RABBIT WOOD - ADINFER WOOD Road.
        Pathway from RABBIT WOOD to X.20.c.9.1.
        Trenches and Road from HAMEAU FARM.

5TH INFANTRY BRIGADE H.Q.

    MONCHY - BERLES-AU-BOIS Roads -
      One Sentry at W.22.c.8.2.
      One Sentry at W.22.d.6.3.

4.   SENTRIES will have orders :-

  (a). To warn all troops and Transport entering the infected area; to divert them if possible.

  (b). To see that anyone entering the infected area puts on his Gas Mask.

5.   The Brigade Gas Officer will proceed at once to the area shelled and report to Headquarters concerned the area defined as infected.
    Sentries will remain on duty on approaches to the infected area until the area is declared clear. In the event of a relief, the sentry posts will be taken over by the relieving Unit.

6.   The Divisional Gas Officer will decide when sentries may be taken off an infected area.

APPENDIX "C".

ADMINISTRATIVE INSTRUCTIONS ISSUED IN CONNECTION WITH
5TH INFANTRY BRIGADE DEFENCE SCHEME DATED 16TH JULY, 1918.
※=

1. Ammunition Dumps are as under:-

LOCATION.	CONTENTS.
Coy.H.Q. of Front Battalions.	Minimum of 30 Boxes S.A.A. 120 Grenades and 150 Rounds V.P.A.
Front Line Battalion H.Q.	Minimum of 100 Boxes S.A.A. 480 Grenades and 600 Rounds V.P.A.
WINDMILL SWITCH. X.29.d.18.95., X.29.a.00.70.	Each 50 Boxes S.A.A.
PURPLE LINE. X.28.a.3.4., X.27.b.9.9. X.27.c.8.3., X.27.c.4.1.	Each 25 Boxes S.A.A. 120 Grenades. 150 Rounds V.P.A.
Reserve Battalion Area. X.19.c.4.2., W.24.d.0.3.	Each Dump - 50 Boxes S.A.A., 240 Grenades. 450 Rounds V.P.A.
Near Brigade Headquarters - W.23.b.1.1.	75 Boxes S.A.A., 750 Rounds V.P.A., 480 Grenades.

Brigade Headquarters and Battalion Mobile Reserves and the Divisional S.A.A. and Grenade Dump are at POMMIER.

2. R.E. Material is supplied from MONCHY R.E. (Divisional) Dump and the Corps Dumps at WARLINCOURT and WANQUETIN.

3. TOOLS. Approximately there are 650 Shovels and 250 Picks in the Front Battalions' Areas, and 200 Shovels and 150 Picks in the Reserve Battalion Area.
    Owing to the scarcity of tools these stocks should, in the event of Operations, be moved with Battalions.
    Brigade Headquarters and Battalion Mobile Reserves of Tools are kept at POMMIER and are only to be sent up on orders from G.O.C., Brigade.

4. No Reserve Dumps of Rations exist in the Area.
    Battalions have one spare days rations in hand at Transport Lines at POMMIER.

5. WATER is supplied to Front Line Battalions' in Petrol Tins under Regimental arrangements.
    Reserve Battalion is supplied from a Motor Water Tank lorry attached to Brigade Headquarters.
    There is a Well (for washing water only) in COJEUL VALLEY at X.29.c.8.5.
    Water Carts are principally filled at HUMBERCAMP.

6. MEDICAL ARRANGEMENTS.
    Bearer Relay Post.................... X.28.b.7.5.
    Ambulance Car Stands................. X.15.c.9.3. and ADINFER
                                          (X.21.d.3.8.)
    Advanced Dressing Station............ (RANSART) X.7.d.9.9. and
                                          (MONCHY) W.29.d.8.3.
    Walking Wounded Collecting Post..... BERLES-au-BOIS, W.15.c.3.0.
    Main Dressing Station............... BAC-du-SUD.

7. First Line Transport is at POMMIER (W.25.a.)
    There is no forward echelon of Transport at present - one would probably be formed at Brigade Headquarters in event of Operations.

/ para. 8..........

TRACK MAP. Scale: 1:40,000. 3rd INFANTRY BRIGADE.

APPENDIX "D"
5TH BRIGADE DEFENCE SCHEME.

SIGNAL COMMUNICATIONS
LEFT BRIGADE

TELEPHONE :-
Communication by telephone from BRIGADE H.Q. at W.23.c.1.9. to the LEFT and RIGHT Battalions at X.24.c.3.0. and X.27.b.9.3. respectively is worked through a Brigade Forward Station at X.23.a.1.5.
This Station is connected to Brigade Headquarters by 5 lines in an 8'-0" buried cable route and to Front Battalions by alternative routes all of which are either stapled in trenches throughout their length or buried in old German cable routes.
Overland and Trenched cable is maintained to the Forward Station for use in the event of temporary destruction of the bury.
The RESERVE Battalion H.Q. at X.19.c.6.2. and the T.M.BATTERY H.Q. at X.20.b.3.2. are in direct communication with Brigade H.Q. and the Forward Station.
Each Front Battalion has lateral communication with its flank Battalions and direct communication with the Artillery that covers its front.
"A" COMPANY, 2nd M.G.Battalion H.Q. at X.28.a.7.3. and the BRIGADE O.P. at X.27.b.9.1. are connected to the Right Battalion exchange.
BRIGADE HEADQUARTERS is also in direct communication with :-
  DIVISION.
  Advanced Divisional Exchange (Y.B.R.)
  Flank Brigades.
  Left Group Artillery.
  226th Field Coy. R.E.
Circuit Diagram is forwarded as Appendix "DII" to 5th Brigade Defence Scheme.

VISUAL.
See Appendix "DIII" to 5th Brigade Defence Scheme.
Test messages are sent 4 times daily from front to rear.

PIGEONS
4 birds are sent daily to the Left and Right Battalions. The lofts are at SAULTY and practice pigeon messages are transmitted from Battalion to Brigade H.Q. in approximately 20 minutes.

POWER BUZZER AND AMPLIFIER :-
A Power Buzzer at the Front Company H.Q. of the LEFT Battalion works to a combined Amplifier and P.B. Station at the Left Battalion H.Q. This station is in touch with a combined Power Buzzer, Amplifier and W/T Station at the RIGHT Battalion H.Q.
There is lateral P.B. and A communication between Right Battalion LEFT Brigade and Front Battalion, CENTRE Brigade.

WIRELESS
W/T Set at Right Battalion H.Q. works to the Divisional directing station at LEFT Brigade H.Q. W.23.c.1.8.
W/T Set at Left Brigade H.Q. works to Divisional H.Q.

RUNNERS :-
There are two runner Relay Posts between Brigade H.Q. and the Front Battalions.
NO. 1 Relay Post (6 runners) is at "R.S." W.24.d.8.1.
NO. 2 Relay Post (6 runners) is at HAMEAU FARM X.20.b.55.25.
Runners leave Brigade H.Q. with Battalion Posts 4 times daily at 8.30 a.m., 12.30 p.m., 5.30 p.m. and 8.30 p.m.

DESPATCH RIDERS :-
D.R's leave Division 3 times daily at 7.30 a.m., 1 p.m. and 7.30 p.m. for LEFT Brigade H.Q. Brigade posts to Division leave on the D.R's return journey.
One D.R. is stationed at Brigade H.Q. and is in readiness for special runs.

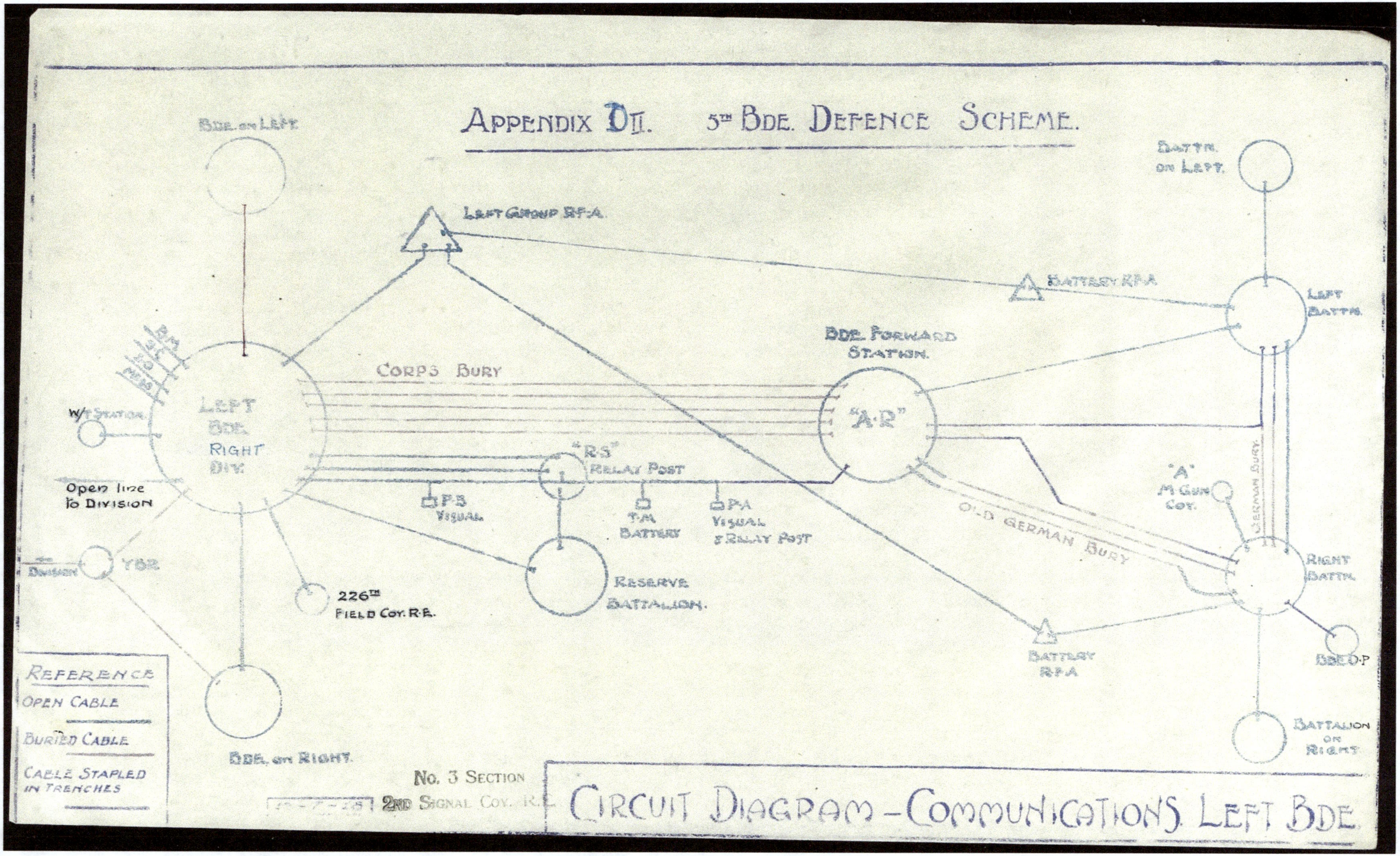
APPENDIX DII. 5TH BDE. DEFENCE SCHEME.
BDE. ON LEFT
LEFT GROUP R.F.A.
BATTERY R.F.A.
BATTN. ON LEFT
LEFT BATTN.
BDE. FORWARD STATION.
CORPS BURY
LEFT BDE. RIGHT DIV.
W/T STATION
"A·R"
"R·S" RELAY POST
P.B. VISUAL
T.M. BATTERY
P.A. VISUAL & RELAY POST
Open line to Division
DIVISION
YBR
226TH FIELD COY. R.E.
RESERVE BATTALION.
OLD GERMAN BURY
GERMAN BURY
"A" M. GUN COY.
RIGHT BATTN.
BATTERY R.F.A.
BDE. O.P.
BATTALION ON RIGHT
BDE. ON RIGHT
REFERENCE
OPEN CABLE
BURIED CABLE
CABLE STAPLED IN TRENCHES
No. 3 SECTION
2ND SIGNAL COY. R.E.
CIRCUIT DIAGRAM - COMMUNICATIONS LEFT BDE.

Appendix DIII. 5th Bde. Defence Scheme.

Left Brigade HQ "L.B"

"P.B" (W.24.a.3.2)

"P.A" (X.20.b.3)

Left Battn. H.Q.

"R.P" (Front Line Coy HQ)

Right Battn. H.Q.

"M.L" (W.28.b.3.)

Telephonic Communication

Visual to Centre Bde.

Visual to Division

Diagram of Visual Communications
Left Bde — Right Division
12-7-16

No. 3 Section
2nd Signal Coy. R.E.

APPENDIX "E"
LEWIS GUN POSITIONS - PURPLE FRONT LINE.

POSITION.		FIRING ON
F.3.a.58.12.	Alternative	N. of E. and W. of S.
F.3.a.88.45.	Alternative	N. of E. and W. of S.
F.3.b.20.80.	Alternative	S. of E. and S.
X.27.d.54.02.	Single	South.
X.27.d.93.10.	Alternative	E. and S.W.
X.28.c.05.26.	(Present M.G. Positions)	S.E.
X.28.c.25.50.	Alternative	N.E. and S.
X.28.a.21.10.	Single	N.E.
X.28.a.22.47.	Single	N.E.
X.28.a.41.77.	Single	S.E.
X.22.c.61.10.	Two	S.E. and S.

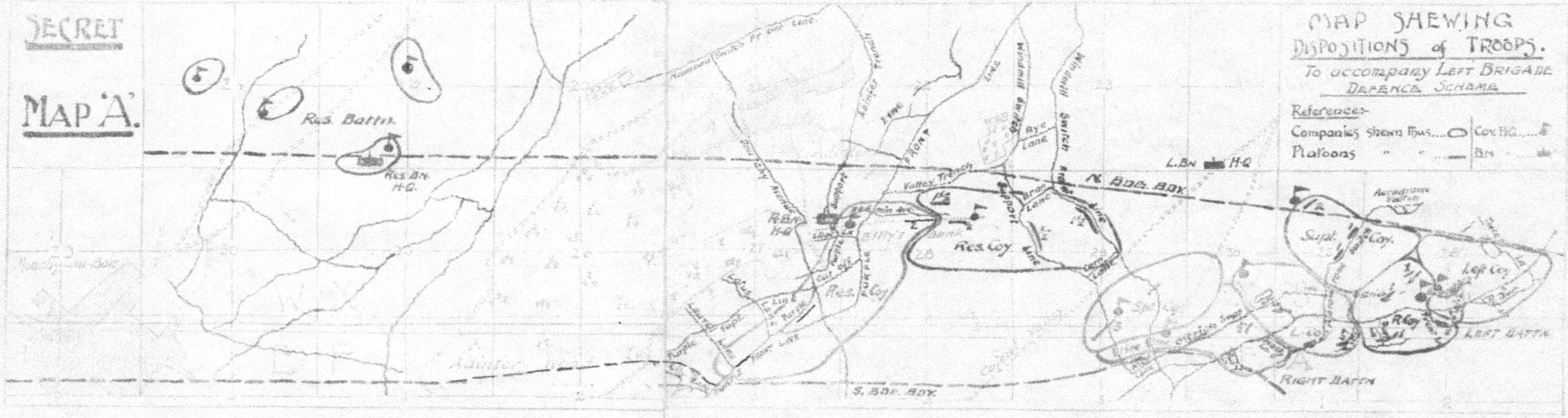
SECRET
MAP 'A'.
MAP SHEWING
DISPOSITIONS of TROOPS.
To accompany LEFT BRIGADE
DEFENCE SCHEME
Reference:-
Companies shewn thus
Platoons
Coy. H.Q.
Bn.
Res. Battn.
Res. Bn. H.Q.
L. Bn H.Q.
N. Bde. Box
S. Bde. Box
Windmill Switch
Rye Lane
Support Line
Valley Trench
Front Line
Support
R. Bn. H.Q.
Billy's Bank
Res. Coy
Purple
Cut Off
Lotus
Laurel
Supt. Coy.
Left Coy.
R. Coy
Aerodrome
Left Battn.
Right Battn.

MAP 'B'

SECRET.

MACHINE GUN POSITIONS.

Scale: 1:20000

FLANKING D.D.E. M.G's shewn......

B.E.F. FRANCE & FLANDERS.

2 DIVISION.

H.Q. GENERAL STAFF.

1918 JULY.

B.E.F. FRANCE & FLANDERS

2 DIVISION.

H.Q. GENERAL STAFF.

1918 JULY.

1300